# MUSLIM LEGAL THOUGHT IN MODERN INDONESIA

Indonesia has been home to some of the most vibrant and complex developments in modern Islamic thought anywhere in the world. Nevertheless little is known or understood about these developments outside Southeast Asia. By considering the work of the leading Indonesian thinkers of the twentieth century, R. Michael Feener, an intellectual authority in the area, offers a cogent critique of this diverse and extensive literature and sheds light on the contemporary debates and the dynamics of Islamic reform. The book highlights the openness to, and creative manipulation of, diverse strands of international thought that have come to define Islamic intellectualism in modern Indonesia. This is an accessible and interpretive overview of the religious and social thought of the world's largest Muslim majority nation. As such it will be read by scholars of Islamic law and society, Southeast Asian Studies and comparative law and jurisprudence.

R. MICHAEL FEENER is Associate Professor of History at the National University of Singapore. His recent publications include, as editor, *Islam in World Cultures: Comparative Perspectives* (2003) and *Islamic Law in Contemporary Indonesia: Ideas and Institutions* (forthcoming).

# MUSLIM LEGAL THOUGHT IN MODERN INDONESIA

R. MICHAEL FEENER
*National University of Singapore*

CAMBRIDGE
UNIVERSITY PRESS

CAMBRIDGE UNIVERSITY PRESS
Cambridge, New York, Melbourne, Madrid, Cape Town,
Singapore, São Paulo, Delhi, Tokyo, Mexico City

Cambridge University Press
The Edinburgh Building, Cambridge CB2 8RU, UK

Published in the United States of America by Cambridge University Press, New York

www.cambridge.org
Information on this title: www.cambridge.org/9780521188050



First published 2007
First paperback edition 2011

*A catalogue record for this publication is available from the British Library*

ISBN 978-0-521-87775-6 Hardback
ISBN 978-0-521-18805-0 Paperback

*For Nana, and Little Nana, with much love and many thanks*

As there were many Reformers, so likewise many Reformations; every Countrey proceeding in a peculiar Method, according as their national interest together with their constitution and clime inclined them, some angrily and with extremitie, others calmely, and with mediocrity, not rending, but easily dividing the community, and leaving an honest possibility of a reconciliation . . .

Sir Thomas Browne, *Religio Medici*

# *Contents*

# *Acknowledgments*

For all the solitude of early morning and late night scribbling sessions, writing a book is never an individual affair. Every work represents not only the fruit of intellectual conversations with colleagues both living and long dead, but also less ethereal relationships with all those who help the writer along the way. The list of those to whom I have become indebted over the years spent in preparation of this volume is too long to be presented in full here. I am grateful to all of them, first and foremost to my family. My mother and father have supported me in so many ways since the beginning of my studies, and they deserve so much more than I could ever possibly repay. My maternal grandmother and those who gathered at her kitchen in Salem have been sources of great encouragement as well as inspiration, and she is very much missed. My wife, Mayuko, and our children John and Irene now provide me with much of both and so much more.

Like family, one's teachers give much that can never be adequately acknowledged, let alone repaid. I have been blessed with a number of truly great teachers over the years, foremost among them Merlin Swartz. Well beyond the specifics of anything he taught me about medieval Ḥanbalism and the parsing of classical Arabic texts, he continues to serve as a model for me of what one can become as a scholar and a human being. This work has also benefited from the influence of other mentors who have exerted extraordinary amounts of time and energy in teaching me and supporting my research. H. Moh. Koesnoe taught me much about Java, Islam, and perseverance, as well as almost everything I know about the fields of *adat* law and Dutch academic jurisprudence. I consider myself extremely fortunate to have had as my first teacher of Islamic Studies Fred Denny, who introduced me to Pak Koesnoe, as well as to a wider world of conversations that I have continued to explore ever since leaving his classroom in Boulder. Over the years many of these teachers have also come to accept me as a colleague, and I am particularly grateful for having my work benefit from discussions with Herbert Mason, David Eckel, Ray Hart,

Frank Korom, David Reisman, Brannon Wheeler, David Buchman, Tim Carmichael, Rob Rozenhal, Vincent Cornell, Ebrahim Moosa, Abdulkader Tayob, Dirk Vandewalle, Hasan Hanafi, Rifyal Ka'bah, Busthanul Arifin, Peri Bearman, David Powers, Clark Lombardi, Marion Katz, Anna Gade, Azyumardi Azra, Michael Foster, June O'Connor, Andrew Abalahin, Bill Roff, Michael Laffan, Nico Kaptein, Kees van Dijk, Wim Stokhof, Dan Lev, Michael Foat, Ken Brashier, Steve Wasserstrom, Arthur McCalla, Laura Hendrickson, Michael Irmscher, David Sacks, Ray Kierstead, Salah Khan, Hal Nevis, Una Kim, Bob Hefner, and Mark Cammack as well as my colleagues in the UCR SEATRiP Program and the faculty and students of Reed College. Special mention should also be made of the dozens of language teachers who have helped me enter into the various conversations that inform this book, with particular thanks to Farouk Mustafa and John Wolff. The complete manuscript was read by Merle Ricklefs, Wael Hallaq, Merlin Swartz, and Henk Maier, who attempted to save me from many errors. Angela Predisik and Saira Hickey helped tremendously with formatting the text, notes, and bibliography. The shortcomings that remain after such scrutiny should fall squarely upon my own shoulders.

A number of universities and other institutions have also supported my research on this project, and I would like to thank Boston University, Reed College, and the University of California at Riverside for both providing me with facilities on campus, and allowing me time away for archive work, interviews, and writing. On these travels abroad I have been generously hosted by the Fulbright Scholars' Program and its office in Jakarta (AMINEF), the Indonesian National Islamic University (UIN), IAIN Wali Songo at Semarang, the American Research Center in Egypt, the American Institute for Yemeni Studies, and the International Institute for Asian Studies. Beyond such institutional homes, however, I have also been extremely fortunate in having had a number of individuals and families make me feel welcome and facilitate my work around the world. Here special thanks are due to Nelly Paliama, Dewi Zamira, Jen Chun, Josine Stremmelaar, Daniele Lambrechts, Peter and Françoise Fetchko, Tom Seitz, Robin Bush, Harsoyo, H. Asnawi Parampasi, A. Salam Z. A., Singgih Riphat, Darmawaty Yioda, Bobby Lee and Doreen Lee, as well as to the Tagawa and Yokota families of Hiroshima. *Obaachan, gogo no ocha no hitotoki o arigatou.*

To all of them, and the many I cannot mention here by name, Thank you.

# *A note on transliteration*

Rendering the technical terminology of Indonesian Islamic scholarship into English poses some unique challenges to Islamicists because of the preponderance of Arabic loan words – sometimes via Persian, Tamil, or other intermediary usages – into Bahasa Indonesia and other languages of the region. While the origin of these terms is Arabic, many have become commonplace in contemporary Indonesian and in the process have taken on distinct local meanings. In ways analogous, for example, to that through which the Greek *πανδοκειον* was transmitted in the Arabic form *funduq* to become in Italian *fondaco* (foreign merchants' hostel), this same Arabic term was rendered into Malay and Javanese as *pondok*, which eventually came to refer to a rural residential school for the teaching of *fiqh* and other Islamic religious sciences. Thus when used in scholarly treatments of modern religious discourses in the Indonesian language – or other Muslim vernaculars for that matter – hyper-Arabization of technical terminologies can be considerably misleading and obscure important aspects of specific local usages.

When dealing with the uses of these terms in their Indonesian context, then, one is forced to decide whether to present them in a format recognized in English-language scholarship for the transliteration of the Arabic terms from which they are ultimately derived, or to simply give them in their contemporary Indonesian form. Those who adopt the first not only over-technicalize their presentations, but also risk assuming that the terms they are dealing with necessarily imply all the same fields of meaning in Indonesian as they do in the original Arabic. Those who opt for the second method, on the other hand, are in danger of making their work appear, cosmetically at least, less acceptable to other scholars who work on various aspects of Muslim societies outside of Southeast Asia and, more consequentially, to miss opportunities to connect local discussions of particular issues to broader discourses elsewhere in the Muslim world.

In this book I have opted for something of a middle course between these two poles. It is inevitable that, in attempting this, occasions arise that simply demand apparently arbitrary judgment calls. Nevertheless I have attempted to maintain consistency throughout by means of the following system: When dealing with the contents of specific Indonesian texts in which Indonesianized Arabic terms are being used in distinct ways, they are reproduced here in the form that they were presented in the text immediately under discussion. In more general discussions, however, as well as in dealing with Indonesian-language examples in which certain Islamic technical terms are being used in direct dialogue with Arabic sources and debates carried out in that language, they will be given full diacriticals following the Arabic transliteration system used by the Middle East Studies Association (MESA). The same system of diacritics has been used to render the names of authors writing in Arabic and the titles of their works, as well as in reference to texts in Southeast Asian languages published in the modified forms of the Arabic script known as *jawi* (Malay) or *pegon* (Javanese), with the additional conventions of:

P = ڤ, G = گ, C = چ, Ng = ڠ, and Ny = ڽ.

For a catalog of Arabic and Persian loan-words adopted and adapted into the more general Malay-Indonesian vocabulary beyond those technical terms used in religious scholarship, see Russell Jones, *Arabic Loan-words in Indonesian: A Checklist of Words of Arabic and Persian Origin in Bahasa Indonesia and Traditional Malay, in the Reformed Spelling* (London: School of Oriental and African Studies, 1978).

For an overview of transliteration of more technical Arabic terms into Bahasa Indonesia and their equivalents in various standard systems employed in international scholarship, see Johannes den Heijer, and Ab Massier, *Pedoman Transliterasi Bahasa Arab* (Jakarta: INIS, 1992). While the title of this work is in Indonesian, the introductory texts explaining its methodology and the organization of the charts of transliterated words contained in it are all printed here both in Indonesian and English. The Roman-script Indonesian employed there reflects the most recent standardization developed during the New Order period.

# *Abbreviations*

| | |
|---|---|
| Ar. | Arabic |
| *BKI* | *Bijdragen tot de Taal-, Land- en Volkenkunde* |
| *BSOAS* | *Bulletin of the School of Oriental and African Studies* |
| *DB* | *Dictionnaire Biographique des Savants et Grandes Figures du Monde Musulman Peripherique, du XIXe siècle a nos jours* |
| DDII | Dewan Dakwah Islamiyah Indonesia |
| DPR | Dewan Perwakilan Rakyat |
| DPRD | Dewan Perwakilan Rakyat Daerah |
| Dt. | Dutch |
| *EI2* | *The New Encyclopaedia of Islam* |
| HMI | Himpunan Mahasiswa Islam |
| HTI | Hizbut Tahrir Indonesia |
| IAIN | Institut Agama Islam Negeri |
| ICMI | Ikatan Cendekiawan Musilm se-Indonesia |
| IIAS | International Institute for Asian Studies |
| *IJMES* | *International Journal of Middle East Studies* |
| *ILS* | *Islamic Law and Society* |
| Ind. | Bahasa Indonesia |
| INIS | Indonesia–Netherlands Islamic Studies |
| ISIM | Institute for the Study of Islam in the Modern World |
| ISTAC | International Institute of Islamic Thought and Civilization |
| IRCICA | Research Centre for Islamic History, Art & Culture |
| ITB | Institut Teknologi Bandung |
| JIL | Jaringan Islam Liberal |
| JIMM | Jaringan Intelektual Muhammadiyah Muda |
| Jp. | Japanese |
| *JMBRAS* | *Journal of the Malay Branch of the Royal Asiatic Society* |
| *JRAS* | *Journal of the Royal Asiatic Society* |
| *JSBRAS* | *Journal of the Straits Branch of the Royal Asiatic Society* |
| Jv. | Javanese |

| | |
|---|---|
| KITLV | Koninklijk Instituut voor Taal-, Land- en Volkenkunde |
| *KHI* | *Kompilasi Hukum Islam* |
| KISDI | Komite Indonesia untuk Solidaritas Dunia Islam |
| LIPIA | Lembaga Ilmu Pengetahuan Islam dan Arab |
| LKiS | Lembaga Kajian Islam dan Sosial |
| LP3ES | Lembaga Penelitian, Pendidikan dan Penerangan Ekonomi dan Sosial |
| Mal. | Malay |
| *MIDEO* | *Mélanges de l'Institut Dominicain d'Études Orientales* |
| NU | Nahdlatul Ulama |
| P3M | Perhimpunan Pengembangan Pesantren dan Masyarakat |
| PKI | Partai Komunis Indonesia |
| PERSIS | Persatuan Islam |
| *RMM* | *Revue du Monde Musulman* |
| *SI* | *Studia Islamika* |
| *TA* | *Tashwirul Afkar: Jurnal Refleksi Pemikiran Keagamaan dan Kebudayaan* |
| UIN | Universitas Islam Negara |
| UU | Undang-Undang |
| *WI* | *Die Welt des Islams* |
| YKF | Yayasan Kesejahteraan Fatayat |

# *Preface: Toward an intellectual history of modern Indonesian Islam*

Over the past century, Muslim thinkers in the Indonesian archipelago have cultivated remarkable capacities for innovative work by integrating diverse strands of modern Muslim thought from around the world into communication with ideas developed in Europe, North America, and elsewhere by non-Muslim thinkers. In bookstalls surrounding the campus of the National Islamic University (Universitas Islam Negeri/ UIN) at Ciputat in South Jakarta, one can find not only classical Arabic *fiqh* texts and works by modern Middle Eastern authors, but also vernacular translations of Freud, Gramsci, and Foucault alongside hundreds of original Indonesian works that creatively engage with various combinations of these materials. Nowhere else in the Muslim world that I know of presents this kind of cosmopolitanism to such an extent. It is impossible, for example, to find Arabic translations of the Indonesian works of Hazairin on bilateral inheritance or Sahal Mahfudh' on "Social *Fiqh*" in Cairo. On the other hand, it is relatively easy to obtain Indonesian translations and discussions of the work of Muslim scholars from the Middle East and beyond, such as Ḥasan Ḥanafī (Egypt), Mohamed Arkoun (France), Muḥammad ʻĀbid Jābirī (Morocco), AbdolKarim Shoroush (Iran), Khaled Abou El Fadl (US), Farid Esack (South Africa), and Nasr Abu-Zayd (the Netherlands), not to mention dozens of publications by non-Muslim scholars of Islamic Studies, and thinkers in other fields ranging from cultural anthropology to critical studies – all in an afternoon's browsing through bookshops in Jakarta or Yogya.

This book aims to introduce major trends in Indonesian Muslim thought on issues of law and society over the past century to non-Indonesian readers, through the construction of a preliminary road map to some key trajectories through an immense body of heretofore understudied sources. Its scope is ambitious, admittedly perhaps overly so. Nevertheless such a risk is, I believe, worth taking at this point in attempting to remedy the relative neglect of this important material in a number of potentially relevant fields:

History, Anthropology, and Islamic and Southeast Asian Studies. For well over a decade now international observers have written – for the most part in rather vague terms – of purportedly important developments in modern Indonesian Islamic thought. However, more nuanced understandings of the situation continue to be impeded by the dearth of works able to provide an overview of the vast and diverse corpus of Islamic religious texts published in the country over the full course of the twentieth and early twenty-first centuries. The relative inattention to the religious and social thought of the world's largest Muslim majority nation is of course a problem for obvious demographic reasons. It is, however, all the more regrettable given the fact that Indonesia presents a particularly vibrant and dynamic case through which to examine innovative interpretations of Islam in relation to transforming conceptions of education, epistemology, texts, and traditional authority that are relevant to modern developments in Muslim societies around the world.[1]

Given the impossibility of producing a comprehensive survey of the immense amount of material produced by Indonesian Muslims on religious and social issues over the past century, any scholar approaching this area of study is unavoidably faced with considerable challenges of selection. In the pages that follow I have had to make innumerable choices as to which scholars to mention, and which of their respective works to discuss. Some Indonesia specialist readers will inevitably have cause to question specific instances of inclusion or omission. I heartily welcome scholarly disagreement with my choices, since one of my goals in researching and writing this book has been to energize further conversations on the development of Islamic thought in modern Indonesia. For the present work I have sought to strike a balance between works that continue to be popular today (as evidenced by a track record of reprints and citation in contemporary debates) and those whose popularity may have been eclipsed, but which my research shows to have been significant in earlier periods.

Throughout, my first and primary criterion for selection has been that of a work's relevance to the expansion of conversations in one particular field of Muslim discourse in Indonesia – namely, that of Islamic law. Unfortunately, however, this leaves beyond consideration in this book the work

[1] I have discussed some of the broader theoretical problems and possibilities of such work in "Cross-Cultural Contexts of Modern Muslim Intellectualism: Reflections on a History of Islamic Legal Thought in Indonesia," Paper prepared for the Modern Muslim Intellectual History conference held at Utrecht, September 2005. A synopsis of the issues raised in that presentation has been published as "Contemporary Islam and Intellectual History," *Institute for the Study of Islam in the Modern World Review* 17 (Spring 2006), 24–5.

of a number of prolific Indonesian Muslim intellectuals whose publications are in areas outside of Islamic legal thought – for example, the work of scholars coming from a social science background including: Kuntowijoyo, Ahmad Syafi'i Ma'arif, Komaruddin Hidayat, Fachry Ali, Bahtiar Effendy, Masjkuri Abdillah, Abdul Munir Mulkhan, and others. Furthermore, attention is directed primarily to published written works and the ideas developed therein, rather than to the political careers and public personae of various figures discussed in the following chapters. Much has already been written about this in international scholarship, and rather than retracing those paths this study seeks to complement them by adding another dimension to the discussions.

The focus of this book is on tracking the dynamics of Indonesian conversations on Islamic legal thought, an important aspect of intellectual and broader public discussions in many Muslim societies. Taking legal thought as the central topic of this study is, however, not only a reflection of the long-established centrality of jurisprudence to the history of Islamic learning, but also of my own position in the field of Islamic studies, in which my work has been shaped by recent advances in the field of "Islamic law and society." Over the past two decades a remarkable body of work has been produced in this area combining technical expertise and innovative analytical approaches to a wide range of developments across the classical and modern periods.[2] Despite the extraordinary quantity of this recent work on the history of Islamic legal theory and practice, however, very little of it has dealt with Indonesia or other areas of Southeast Asia.[3] Studies of Islamic law in that part of the world have for the most part been produced either locally in the Indonesian language or by foreign Indonesia specialists.[4] Generally speaking, however, these studies have tended to concentrate more on the development of legal institutions and positive legislation than on the intellectual and jurisprudential discourses of Islamic law in the country.[5] The relationship between legal theory and practice is, of course, by

[2] Full citations to works of this type that have been influential in the formation of my own understandings of the historical development of Islamic law are included in the bibliography.

[3] One very recent significant exception to this can be found in a theme issue of the journal *Islamic Law and Society* 12.1 (2005) ed. Nico J. G. Kaptein and Michael F. Laffan on the subject of "*Fatwās* in Indonesia".

[4] A collection of recent work of this type can be found in R. Michael Feener and Mark E. Cammack, eds., *Islamic Law in Contemporary Indonesia: Ideas and Institutions* (Cambridge, MA: Harvard University Press, 2007).

[5] One notable exception to this tendency has been the award-winning recent work of John Bowen, which combines ethnographic and textual studies in a theoretically informed discussion of Indonesian legal pluralism. John R. Bowen, *Islam, Law and Equality in Indonesia: An Anthropology of Public Reasoning* (New York: Cambridge University Press, 2003). In the section of his book dealing with the

no means a determining one in Islam, any more than in any other tradition.[6] Nevertheless the ongoing conversations about jurisprudence and its contemporary permutations remain important as a medium through which legal, religious, and social change is processed and re-integrated into evolving understandings of the tradition. The relevance of this material can, accordingly, be seen as much if not more in relation to broader understandings of Islam and local conceptions of the Muslim community than with law in its formal, institutional sense.

The chapters that follow comprise detailed examinations of the ways in which Indonesian Muslim scholars and activists have formulated new conceptions and interpretations of Islamic law through creative readings and syntheses of diverse materials including Islamic scriptural sources, texts of classical Muslim jurisprudence, and modern Middle Eastern and "Western" academic writings read in light of rapidly evolving social, economic, and political contexts. Thus, while its particular focus is on developments of legal theory, this book can also be read as an introduction to modern Indonesian Islam more generally, since its coverage of major currents in intellectual and public discourses among Muslims over the past century reflects a range of broader dynamics in the community's changing understandings of religion and its role in contemporary society.

development of specifically Islamic legal discourses, Bowen refers to the general outline of that history that I presented in my 1999 Boston University dissertation. The present study further develops and considerably expands upon that earlier work.

6 This point has been made in connection with material from the medieval and modern periods in the work of Sherman Jackson in "Fiction and Formalism: Toward a Functional Analysis of *Uṣūl al-fiqh*," *Studies in Islamic Legal Theory*, ed. Bernard G. Weiss (Leiden: E. J. Brill, 2002), 177–201.

CHAPTER I

# *Technology, training, and cultural transformation*

> When a change in a society's self-awareness has become at all widely disseminated, that society's styles of thinking and acting have been irreversibly altered.
>
> – J. G. A. Pocock, "Time, Institutions and Action"

The late nineteenth and early twentieth centuries witnessed a number of remarkable developments in Muslim institutional and intellectual history, as a result of which the very categories and structures of traditional religious authority were subjected to fundamental challenges. This had a significant impact not only upon social and cultural institutions, but also on the form and content of Islamic religious and legal debates in the modern period. This being said, however, some qualifying remarks must be made with regard to the apparent novelty of the modern situation. For among these relatively recent developments are also distinctly traceable and historically significant threads of continuity that have run through centuries of Islamic history.

## MODERNIZATION AND TRADITIONS OF REFORM

Internal reform is part of a well-established dynamic visible throughout the histories of various societies in the Muslim world. During the first half of the twentieth century, Henri Laoust remarked insightfully on the importance of the legacy of the medieval Ḥanbalī scholar Ibn Taymiyya (d. 1328) to the modern Salafiyya movement,[1] and later historians have since ventured more general reflections on the role of Ḥanbalism, Sufism, and other established modes of Islamic religious understanding in the dynamics of reform movements throughout Muslim history. These developments established

[1] Henri Laoust, *Essai sur les doctrines sociales et politiques de Takī-d-dīn Ahmad b. Taimīya, canoniste Hanbalite né à Harrān en 661/1262, mort à Damas en 728/1328* (Cairo: Imprimerie de l'Institut Français d'Archéologie Orientale, 1939), 541–63.

legacies that became accessible in new ways to successive generations of Muslim reformers who worked in increasingly complex contexts not only of internal Islamic religious debates, but also of the increasing encroachment of European imperial interests and cultural challenges in the late nineteenth and early twentieth centuries.

Aspects of all of these factors contributed to complex dynamics of "modernization" among Muslim communities of Southeast Asia and elsewhere in the late nineteenth and early twentieth centuries. In particular the introduction of steam-powered transportation and the print revolution in communications technology facilitated by European expansion into various Muslim societies during the second half of the nineteenth century fostered the formation of new constellations of people and ideas that made for creative re-imaginings of the world, and set new historical processes in place. The various elements in this social transformation thus worked together to radically alter not only the physical and economic landscapes of the region, but its intellectual and cultural vistas as well.

In his unfinished magnum opus *The Venture of Islam*, Marshall Hodgson discussed this phenomenon in general terms as the "Great Western Transmutation" – a systematizing revolution of bureaucratization, rationalization, and "technicalization" of Muslim societies, and much of the rest of the world during the late nineteenth and early twentieth centuries.[2] However, while many of the technological and organizational aspects of these transformations were originally introduced to Muslim societies from Europe – most often in the context of projects of imperialist expansion and colonial control – the diverse ways in which they interacted with local established practices and newly felt local needs show that Muslims in these rapidly modernizing societies were not merely passive objects in these processes initiated by the West. In fact, these various new technologies and institutions were not only important because of the ways in which they facilitated European expansion into Muslim societies in the nineteenth century, but also for the ways in which they created new opportunities for connections and the exchange of ideas between Muslims from different regions.[3] These interactions, in turn, contributed to the development of new ways of thinking about religion, law, and society all across the Middle East, Africa, and Asia.

2 Marshall G. S. Hodgson, *The Venture of Islam: Conscience and History in a World Civilization* (Chicago: University of Chicago Press, 1974), III, 176–222.

3 I have discussed these developments in relation to the Indonesian Archipelago, the Arabian Peninsula, and the broader Indian Ocean world in R. Michael Feener, "Islam, Technology and Modernity in the Nineteenth and Early Twentieth Centuries," in *The New Cambridge History of Islam*, vol. VI (Cambridge: Cambridge University Press, forthcoming).

In Muslim Southeast Asia during the last decades of the nineteenth century a number of exterior influences, although previously in evidence both from the West and various areas of the wider Muslim world itself, were becoming increasingly pronounced as they interacted with a complex array of local institutions to produce new expressions of Malay-Muslim culture. While these changes were many, some general pattern of their effects can be seen in the appearance of three new, or newly reformulated, institutions in Muslim Southeast Asia: voluntary associations, educational reform, and the print media. These three facets of modernization comprised the primary foci for William Roff's pioneering study of Malay nationalism. Together they form a constellation of categories that can prove useful in other studies, including the present one, aimed at tracing the relationship of technological and institutional developments to intellectual history.[4] While indebted to Roff's model for establishing the contexts out of which modern Indonesian Muslim thought emerged, this book is not simply a reworking of his study with comparable data from the neighboring archipelago. His now classic work was more directly concerned with understanding the growth of a new national elite in the Malay peninsula, whereas the work in hand attempts to trace a considerably different trajectory that highlights both the content and contours of twentieth-century Indonesian Islamic religious and intellectual debates.

The space for these discussions was established in the interstices of new schools, new readings, and new communities fostered by educational reform, print, and voluntary associations. In an attempt to highlight their extensive inter-connections, the material discussed in this chapter will be arranged topically, rather than strictly chronologically, with overlapping discussions of the respective aspects of these three developments. Of these changes proliferating across Muslim societies during the latter half of the nineteenth century, print was paramount, as it was largely through this medium that other new institutions were first imagined and increasingly incorporated into local practice.

## TEXTS AND TEACHERS OF THE *PESANTREN* TRADITION

By the time that these transformations were taking place, local traditions of Islamic religious scholarship in Arabic as well as in Malay, Javanese, and

[4] William Roff, *The Origins of Malay Nationalism*, 2nd edn (Kuala Lumpur: Oxford University Press, 1994, originally published by Yale University Press, 1967).

other languages of the archipelago were already well established.[5] Scholars bearing the name (*nisba*) al-Jāwī appear in Arabic sources as far back as the thirteenth century,[6] and a recently revised death date for the author of some of the oldest surviving works of Sufi literature in Malay now places the oft-cited Ḥamza Fanṣūrī in the middle of the sixteenth.[7] The surviving textual record expands considerably after that with works not only of *taṣawwuf*, but also in the Islamic religious sciences of *tafsīr*, *uṣūl al-dīn*, and *fiqh*, well represented in texts produced in Muslim Southeast Asia during the seventeenth and eighteenth centuries.[8]

We have increasing numbers of texts surviving from an even wider range of local centers in the region over the course of the nineteenth century, ranging from Bima in the east of the Archipelago to the Malay areas of what is today southern Thailand in the west. In the later nineteenth century, it was a scholar hailing from this region, Aḥmad b. Muḥammad Zayn b. Muṣṭafā al-Faṭānī, who was placed in charge of printing Malay language materials at the Ottoman government press at Mecca.[9] Nevertheless in print, as well as in manuscript, the writings of many nineteenth-century Southeast Asian scholars in the field of Islamic jurisprudence still tended to follow in well-established traditions of the Shāfiʿī *madhhab*.[10] It was texts of this type that formed the heart of the curricula at *pesantren* and analogous institutions of Muslim learning across the Archipelago, and it is to such constellations of Shāfiʿī *fiqh* scholarship, *pesantren* education, and its associated complexes of religious and cultural praxis that I refer in this study as "traditionalism."

*Pesantren* is the Javanese designation for a traditional Muslim educational institution of a type similar to that referred to in other parts of the region by various other names including *pondok*, *surau*, and *dayah*.

[5] For an overview of these developments, see R. Michael Feener, "Southeast Asian Localisations of Islam and Participation within a Global *Umma*, c. 1500–1800," in *The New Cambridge History of Islam*, III (Cambridge: Cambridge University Press, forthcoming).

[6] R. Michael Feener and Michael F. Laffan, "Sufi Scents across the Indian Ocean: Yemeni Hagiography and the Earliest History of Southeast Asian Islam," *Archipel* 70 (2005): 185–208.

[7] Claude Guillot and Ludvik Kalus, "La stèle funéraire de Hamzah Fansuri," *L'Horizon nousantarien: Mélanges en hommage à Denys Lombard* IV, *Archipel* 60 (2000): 3–24.

[8] For introductions to major works and authors of this period, as well as an extensive bibliography of extant published texts and secondary scholarship, see Peter Riddell, *Islam and the Malay-Indonesian World: Transmission and Responses* (Honolulu: University of Hawai'i Press, 2001).

[9] C. Snouck Hurgronje, *Mekka in the Latter Part of the Nineteenth Century* (Leiden: E. J. Brill, 1931), 286–87.

[10] In fact, Martin van Bruinessen has noted that the list of works in this tradition commonly studied in Southeast Asia very closely resembles the standard works of *fiqh* traditionally taught in Shāfiʿī areas of Kurdistan. *Kitab Kuning, Pesantren dan Tarekat: Tradisi-tradisi Islam di Indonesia* (Bandung: Mizan, 1995), 112–30.

Although some such schools were earlier associated with local sultanates in seaports or other urban areas, over the course of the nineteenth century *pesantren* increasingly became a phenomenon of rural areas. Linking these schools scattered through the countryside were elaborate webs of intermarriage between many of the leading families of religious scholars. Beyond this, there was great emphasis placed on the highly valued bond between students and their teachers, and these ties also linked rural scholars with colleagues living in disparate areas.[11] Students and teachers associated with these schools were thus linked in scholarly networks that extended from local circles to the broader community of scholars in Mecca, Medina, and the maritime Muslim cities ringing the Indian Ocean littoral. Prior to the mid-nineteenth-century expansion of steamship routes across the archipelago and connecting beyond to Arabia, however, participation in such networks was the privilege of only a relatively small circle of scholars. Only with the diffusion of more efficient means of communication and transportation was travel between the Middle East and Southeast Asia a possibility for greater numbers of Muslims in the region.

Study in *pesantren* and similar institutions of Islamic education in nineteenth-century Southeast Asia was an intensely interpersonal affair under the close direction of one's teacher (Jv. *kyai*). Students (Jv. *santri*) began their studies with memorization of the Qur'ān and Arabic grammar, and then centered on the study of *fiqh*.[12] The texts of Islamic religious sciences studied in this milieu have come to be referred to as *kitab kuning*, a body of texts composed not only in Arabic, but also in Arabic-script forms of various Southeast Asian languages. Studies of Islamic law in such a curriculum were limited almost exclusively to the study of *furū*ʿ (particular rulings) with very little surviving evidence of systematic education in the more theoretical discourses of jurisprudential methodology (*uṣūl*). In the early twentieth century, however, a new awareness of alternative approaches to interpreting the sources of, and actively reformulating Islamic law developed as increasing numbers of Southeast Asian Muslims came into contact with reformist colleagues in the Middle East. Upon their return to the

[11] For a brief introduction to the *pesantren* milieu, see Martin van Bruinessen, "Pesantren and Kitab Kuning: Continuity and Change in a Tradition of Religious Learning," in *Texts from the Islands: Oral and Written Traditions of Indonesia and the Malay World*, ed. Wolfgang Marschall (Berne: University of Berne Institute of Ethnology, 1994), 121–46.

[12] L. W. C. van den Berg, "Het Mohammedaansche Godsdienstonderwijs op Java en Madoera en de daarbij gebruikte Arabische boeken," *Tijdschrift voor Indische Taal-, Land- en Volkenkunde* 31 (1886): 518–55. A century later another Dutch scholar conducted an even more extensive survey of literature used in *pesantren* curricula, which showed considerable continuities among the changes since the later nineteenth century, Martin van Bruinessen, "Kitab Kuning: Books in Arabic Script Used in the Pesantren Milieu," *BKI* 146 (1990): 226–69.

Archipelago, they engaged their coreligionists, and not just those technically trained in the Islamic religious sciences, to expand local conversations on Islamic law and society.

With the spread of modern Islamic reformist sensibilities in the region over the course of the early twentieth century, *pesantren* came to be viewed by increasing numbers of Southeast Asian Muslims as places of deferential submission to the authority of barely comprehended Arabic texts which were uninspiringly glossed by *kyai* who attracted students as much by the potential of gaining blessings, as for any educational benefit. The *santri* were (so it was charged) rarely encouraged to ask critical questions relating to the interpretations of the texts being studied. Thus what had earlier been perceived as a culturally valued system of transmitting authoritative readings of religious texts was now viewed by reformists as uncritical submission to fallible human tradition that had come to block clear understandings of the meaning of revelation. What the reformers proposed, in short, was the circumvention of traditional learning through an idealized conception of the unmediated encounter between individual readers and the pure text of scripture.

In recent years a number of scholars have remarked upon such changes in the patterns of Muslim religious and cultural discourse in terms of the emergence of more heterogeneous voices who have come to challenge the position of the established *'ulamā'* as authoritative interpreters of Islamic tradition.[13] The context in which this has occurred has recently been described as one of "increasingly open contests over the authoritative use of the symbolic language of Islam."[14] The developments have had epistemological as well as social and political implications, as Eickelman and Piscatori have noted. They observe that since the texts produced by these new Muslim intellectuals:

> often refer to published sources and provide arguments that invoke recognizable authorities, the implication is that the audience is familiar with the texts and the principles of citation. Not all in the audience can follow such arguments in detail, but they recognize the forms of authority. This form of argument may even be more important for religious leaders not primarily identified with traditional learning . . .[15]

[13] For a concise overview of these developments, see Dale F. Eickelman, "The Coming Transformation in the Muslim World," 1999 Templeton Lecture on Religion and World Affairs delivered at the Foreign Policy Research Institute in Philadelphia on June 9, 1999. This text is available online at: www.drsoroush.com/PDF/E-CMO-20000100-Eickelman.pdf

[14] Dale F. Eickelman and Jon W. Anderson, "Redefining Muslim Publics," in *New Media in the Muslim World: The Emerging Public Sphere* (Bloomington: Indiana University Press, 1999), 1.

[15] Dale F. Eickelman and James Piscatori, *Muslim Politics* (Princeton: Princeton University Press, 1996), 39.

Such changes were facilitated by the revolutions in communications technology that made possible unprecedented increases in the amount of interaction between previously unconnected or voiceless parties, and reconfigured conceptualizations of scholarly and religious authority. Print also served to bring texts to new audiences such as that of an expanding newspaper readership. In this way, for example, published *fatwās* could now be addressed to broader segments of society well beyond the small circles of classically trained Muslim religious scholars, including the largely secular-educated elite that formed the constituencies of Salafi reformists in the early twentieth-century Middle East.[16] Within the Indonesian Archipelago too, the spread of literacy and print culture – particularly in roman-script forms of vernacular languages – expanded the number of people who could directly engage with the interpretation of Islamic religious texts.

## THE PRINTED WORD IN A CALLIGRAPHIC ARCHIPELAGO

Printing had been known in the archipelago since the seventeenth century through the work of Dutch-controlled presses at Batavia. The first productions appear to have been public legal texts in the form of broadsides (Dt. *plakkaten*), followed by religious works in Latin and Portuguese, as well as Dutch. Texts were also produced there in Malay – at first in transliteration and later in the Arabic script (*jawi*), one surviving early example of which is a compendium of Muslim inheritance law published together with a Dutch translation in parallel columns in 1760.[17] However there was a lag of nearly two centuries between the establishment of the first presses in Batavia, and the wide-scale adoption of print among Muslim populations of the Archipelago. By the early nineteenth century, printing and the distribution of printed texts had spread across the region through the activity of Christian missionary societies in cities ranging from Malacca and Bengkulu to Kupang and Ambon.[18] The earliest evidence of Muslim printing in Southeast Asia dates from the 1840s, and as Ian Proudfoot has noted, until the turn of the twentieth century Muslim religious texts there were produced almost exclusively through lithograph technology

[16] Jakob Skovgaard-Petersen, *Defining Islam for the Egyptian State: Mufis and Fatwas of the Dār al-Iftā* (Leiden: E. J. Brill, 1997), 78–79.

[17] Katherine Smith Diehl, *Printers and Printing in the East Indies to 1850 – vol. 1, Batavia* (New Rochelle: Aristide D. Caratzas, 1990), 3–56.

[18] A. T. Gallop, "Early Malay Printing: an Introduction to the British Library Collections," *JMBRAS* 63.1 (1990): 85–124.

that could replicate many of the conventions of established chirographic cultures.[19]

Islamic religious texts (referred to in Malay as *kitāb*) were an important part of a wide range of works produced by Malay presses during the second half of the nineteenth century. However, a surviving Singapore catalog from *c.* 1893 lists only more popular literary texts in indigenous poetry (*syair*) and prose (*hikayat*) genres. Such evidence has led one historian to posit that over the latter decades of the nineteenth century Islamic values and identity were transmitted through such popular forms of Islamic literature to "the general book-buying public."[20] While this may be true on one level, these very same decades correspond to the careers of a number of prominent and prolific Southeast Asian *'ulamā'* writing in the *kitāb* genre, including Aḥmad al-Faṭānī (d. 1906) and Muḥammad 'Umar Nawawī al-Jāwī (a.k.a. Nawawi Banten, d. 1897). Thus what we may actually be seeing here is more a reflection of marketing strategies than of moving inventories, for *kitāb* authors wrote technical works for quite specialized, scholarly readerships. What is certain is that there was a phenomenal increase in the number of printed works of all kinds in the Malay world between 1886 and 1920. During this period, however, the relative importance of *jawi* script Malay books in the Straits Settlements, for example, began to experience a relative decline in relation to Chinese, English, roman-script Malay, and periodical publications.[21] Thus over the late nineteenth and early twentieth centuries, new kinds of texts for new kinds of readers suddenly seemed to explode onto the scene, setting a stage for a substantive transformation of the traditional epistemologies that had heretofore been framed by constraints on the accessibility of texts in what Ian Proudfoot has described as "the manuscript economy." As he describes these developments, "Reading material, once costly, scarce, and sequestered had become cheap, plentiful, and accessible. This change could not occur without affecting the way reading materials were thought about, and located in society."[22]

The proliferation of print culture in the later nineteenth century in short contributed to the spread of new reading habits and the creation of new

[19] Ian Proudfoot, "Mass Producing Houri's Moles, or Aesthetics and Choice of Technology in Early Muslim Book Printing," in *Islam: Essays on Scripture, Thought, and Society – A Festschrift in Honour of Anthony H. Johns*, ed. Peter G. Riddell and Tony Street (Leiden: E. J. Brill, 1997), 161–84.

[20] Ian Proudfoot, "A Nineteenth-Century Malay Bookseller's Catalogue," *Kekal Abadi* 6.4 (Dec. 1987): 6; Proudfoot, *The Print Threshold in Malaysia* (Clayton: Monash University Center of Southeast Asian Studies, 1994), 26.

[21] Ian Proudfoot, "A Formative Period in Malay Book Publishing," *JMBRAS* 59 (1986): 101–32.

[22] Ian Proudfoot, "From Recital to Sight-Reading: The Silencing of Texts in Malaysia," *Indonesia and the Malay World* 30.87 (2002): 119.

cultural conversations in Southeast Asia as in many other Muslim societies at the time. Rather than the reading out loud of Islamic religious texts in formal educational settings such as those of the *pesantren* milieu, new practices of silent reading developed among new literate sectors of society. Over the course of the twentieth century, print came to serve as the medium for the publication of texts in other new genres, including novels, short stories, and modern forms of bureaucratic manuals. The rise of new, modern genres of printed texts was, however, just one of a number of ways in which rapid technological changes of the period were to have pronounced impact upon the very nature of language and textual authority in various Muslim societies. In his pioneering study of modernizing transformations of Islamic legal documents in Ottoman Yemen, Brinkley Messick has demonstrated that the shift from spiral to straight-ruled texts involved more than just matters of graphic stylistics. For, as he argues, the adoption of the layout conventions of modern printing technology signaled "changes in the basic epistemological structure of the document, with the principles underpinning the document's construction and its authority."[23] Such social transformations accompanying the technological innovations of modern text production were to have an immense influence on understandings of Islam in Southeast Asia and elsewhere during the late nineteenth and early twentieth centuries.

Aside from the creation of new texts for new readers, the spread of print technology also had significant impacts within traditional literate sectors of Muslim Southeast Asia such as those of the *'ulamā'* and the courts of the region's myriad local sultanates. For example, the late nineteenth-century ruler of Riau, East Sumatra, Muḥammad Yūsuf, had devoted considerable energies during his forty-two-year reign to the establishment of a library of over 500 religious books collected from Mecca, Medina, India, and Cairo.[24] These works were kept in the Penyengat Mosque, and most of them seem to have been print editions, rather than manuscripts.[25] During that period, Pulau Penyegat and other regional centers such as Langkat developed their own facilities for the publication of printed texts in Arabic as well as

[23] Brinkley Messick, *The Calligraphic State: Textual Domination and History in a Muslim Society* (Berkeley: University of California Press, 1993), 234–36.

[24] Before this time, the majority of Arabic-script books available in the region were imported from the Middle East: Mecca, Istanbul, and especially Cairo. Yves Gonzalez-Quijano, "Le livre arabe dans les pays du subcontinent sud et sud-est asiatique," *Archipel* 40 (1990): 45.

[25] Virginia Matheson, "Pulau Penyengat: Nineteenth Century Islamic Centre of Riau," *Archipel* 37 (1989): 162.

Arabic-script forms of Malay and other regional languages.[26] The titles produced at such places were a diverse lot, but among the various novelties produced by these presses at the turn of the twentieth century were works in the traditional Islamic religious sciences. However, even in texts of this type, print had the effect of making more widely available a range of titles and authors that were not typically included in established *pesantren* curriculum.

In the field of *fiqh* in particular, an important aspect of these changes was the increased availability of works outside of the Shāfiʿī *madhhab* that had been historically dominant in Muslim Southeast Asia. While we do have some manuscript evidence of earlier works discussing the variant rulings of different schools (*ikhtilāf*),[27] the comparative study of different *madhhab*s was considerably facilitated by the appearance in print of works such as Shams al-Dīn Langkatī's *Ikhtilāf al-madhhab yang empat,* of which there are extant copies of 1904 and 1905 editions.[28] Encounters with such texts contributed to the relativization of the authority of the traditional school of *fiqh* in the region in relation to other established sets of rulings and jurisprudential methodologies. However, beyond this, traditional Shāfiʿī dominance on local interpretations of Islamic law were also confronted with other, more dramatic challenges during this period in the form of modern reformist agendas that called for the outright rejection of the models of *fiqh* connected to established *madhhabs.* This became a central plank in the platform of a new, "young" generation of reformers known as the *kaum muda.*

## *IJTIHĀD* JOURNALISM

When, at the turn of the twentieth century, Haji Abdullah Ahmad (d. 1933) returned home to the Minangkabau region of West Sumatra after a four-year period of study in Mecca he began attacking what he perceived as *bidʿa* (blameworthy innovation) in its local manifestations through various means. His primary venue for these campaigns, however, was through print

[26] U. U. Hamidy, *Riau Sebagai Pusat Bahasa dan Kebudayaan Melayu* (Pekanbaru: Bumi Pustaka, 1983), 67–70; Jan van der Putten, "Printing in Riau: Two Steps Toward Modernity," *BKI* 153.4 (1997): 717–36. H. A. Fuad Said, *Syekh Abdul Wahab, Tuan Guru Babussalam* (Medan: Pustaka Babussalam, 1983).

[27] For example, the *Khilāf al-Shāfiʿī wa Abī Hanīfa* (Cod.Or. 1253), and *Kitāb ikhtilāf al-madhāhib* (Cod.Or.1986). E. P. Wieringa, *Catalogue* of *Malay and Minangkabau Manuscripts in the Library of Leiden University and other Collections in the Netherlands* (Leiden: Legatum Warnerianum, 1998), 15–16, 209.

[28] Ian Proudfoot, *Early Malay Printed Books A Provisional Account of Materials Published in the Singapore-Malaysia Area up to 1920, Noting Holdings in Major Public Collections* (Kuala Lumpur: Academy of Malay Studies, 1993), 264.

as he became a local agent for the distribution of periodicals published in Cairo and Singapore. Prominent among the journals then being read by Muslim reformers in Southeast Asia was *al-Imām* which was published in Singapore from 1906 to 1908 under the editorship of another Mingangkabau Muslim reformer, Taher Djalaluddin (b. Ampek Angkek, Bukittinggi, 1869).[29] Many of its articles were drawn from the pages of *al-Manār* and echoed the reform agendas of its editors, Muḥammad Abduh (d. 1905) and Rashīd Riḍā (d. 1935).[30] After the end of *al-Imām's* run, Abdullah Ahmad started his own monthly magazine at Padang entitled *al-Munīr*, which was published from 1910 to 1915.[31]

The pages of these periodical publications presented a variety of new, and newly reformulated textual presentations of issues relating to Islamic law. These included news of developments in different Muslim countries that served to inform comparative reflections on law, politics, and social order as well as exhortatory articles calling for the abandonment of traditional jurisprudence in favor of direct reference to the primary sources of Islam in addressing contemporary questions – a "return to the Qur'ān and *Sunna*" in the oft-repeated phrase of the modern reformists.[32] The operative term in all this rhetoric was *ijtihād,* and the readerships of the reformist periodicals were not only urged to accept the need for re-interpretations of Islamic law, but also to try to understand the scriptural sources of the tradition so that they could see and understand the clear implications of scriptural texts for themselves.

Aside from the news and essay articles on diverse social and political topics these new periodicals also published pieces reflecting a more traditional Muslim legal genre, albeit in ways updated to meet the needs and desires of a modern mass readership in their regular *fatwā* columns. To them readers would address questions pertaining not only to matters of practice, but also to matters of doctrine, and proper belief. A subsequent issue might then reprint (a paraphrase of) the original question and a response from

[29] Abu Bakar Hamzah, *Al-Imam: Its Role in Malay Society, 1905–1908* (Kuala Lumpur: Pustaka Antara, 1991).

[30] The impact of *al-Manār* on Islamic reformism in Southeast Asia has been discussed in J. Bluhm, "A Preliminary Statement on the Dialogue Established Between the Reform Magazine *al-Manar* and the Malayo-Indonesian World," *Indonesia Circle* (1983): 35–42; and Jajat Burhanudin, "Aspiring for Islamic Reform: Southeast Asian Requests for *Fatwās* from *al-Manār*," *ILS* 12.1 (2005): 9–26.

[31] *al-Munīr* was published by Hadji Abdullah Ahmad, with the assistance of Haji Abdul Karim Amrullah (Haji Rasul), among others, at Padang Panjang from 1910 to 1915. Rusjdi, "Sedjarah Penerbitan Madjalah al-Munir: Pelopor Pers Islam dengan Aliran Moderen jang dibawanja," *Gema Islam* 1.1 (1962): 22–25.

[32] This slogan – *Kembali kepada al-Qur'an dan al-Sunna* – was also the title of the widely influential book by Moenawar Chalil that will be discussed in chapter 2.

the experts of the publications' editorial board. In some cases these were jurists with substantial training in the Islamic religious sciences, but in this new medium other types of individuals also took up the pen of the mufti, responding based on a combination of scripturalism and the modern rationalism that the reform spirit of these periodicals so highly valued. The producers and readership of these periodicals were actively opposed to such established (and in their view outmoded) institutions as organized Sufi orders (Ar. *ṭuruq*/ Mal. *tarekat*) and the established systems of religious learning in *pesantren*-type schools, as well as classical models of jurisprudence (*fiqh*). In the place of these traditions the reformists advocated the creation of a new arena for public discussions of issues previously restricted to the ranks of traditionally trained *'ulamā'*.

An increasing number of Muslim reformist organizations at the turn of the century came to capitalize on print as a primary means for communicating their broader programs for the modernization and mobilization of Islam. The amount of published material available in the Archipelago increased dramatically between 1890 and 1910, especially after changes to censorship laws passed by the Netherlands Indies government in 1906. From that time on an increasing number of new periodicals emerged as organs for various Muslim reformist, as well as other cultural, religious, and political, groups. For example, Haji Muhammad Misbach began publishing the monthly paper *Medan Moeslimin* at the central Javanese city of Surakarta in 1915, and later expanded his operations to publish another periodical entitled *Islam Bergerak*. He used these publications as part of a complex of modern institutions that also included an Islamic bookstore, a hotel for traveling activists, and a new style school – all directed to novel agendas of the social and political mobilization of Islam in the first decades of the twentieth century.[33]

Analogous complexes of publishing, educational, and other institutions in the Archipelago during the early twentieth century arose in relation to the proliferation of other periodicals published not only in Malay and other local languages, but in Chinese and Arabic as well.[34] The Arab "Awakening" (*nahḍa*) in particular was a significant factor for the development of new understandings of Islam and Islamic law in the modern period, as many of the central issues debated in Arabic among diaspora communities intersected with arguments being developed in the Malay periodical

[33] Takashi Shiraishi, *An Age in Motion: Popular Radicalism in Java, 1912–1926* (Ithaca: Cornell University Press, 1990), 32.

[34] Hendrik Kraemer, "La presse arabe aux Indes néerlandaises," *RMM* 46 (1921): 214–19; Nico Kaptien, "An Arab Printer in Surabaya in 1853," *BKI* 149.4 (1993): 356–52.

press.[35] Local Hadrami populations in the early twentieth century produced a spate of new publications that contributed to increasingly sharp debates on the very nature of the Arab and Muslim communities during this period.[36] The various Arab and broader Muslim organizations in the Netherlands Indies differed among themselves on particular ideological agendas, but together they established an array of new institutional and intellectual frameworks for the reform of Islam and, in turn, Islamic legal thought in the Archipelago.

On the pages of their new periodicals, as well as in the region's schools and in the din of an emerging modern public sphere, discussions of issues central to Islamic law and jurisprudence were liberated from the closed circles of traditionalist religious scholars and made available and accessible to a much wider public. Such shifts in the demographics of potential participants in discussions about Islamic law and society were reflected in changes in the way that texts were presented – from technical treatises and scholarly compendia to the essays and *fatwā* columns of *ijtihād* journalism. Ultimately these adjustments of form and organization impacted upon the epistemological structuring of the religious knowledge transmitted by Islamic religious texts. As this occurred, possibilities arose for new interpretations of the textual sources of Muslim jurisprudential discourse, and visions of the ways in which they might be taught.

## EDUCATION REFORM

Although there were long-standing traditions of Islamic education in many areas of the archipelago, the turn of the twentieth century there witnessed the introduction of several major structural, curricular, and institutional innovations. The Netherlands East Indies government had introduced new school systems to the Archipelago during the late nineteenth century. Under the so-called Ethical Policy (Dt. *ethische politiek*)[37] administrations of the

[35] See, for example, the memoirs of the Irshād movement recently edited by Aḥmad Ibrahīm Abū Shūk, *Ta'rīkh ḥarakat al-iṣlāḥ wā'l-irshād wa-shaykh al-irshādiyyin Aḥmad Muḥammad al-Sūrkatī fī Indūnīsiyā* (Kuala Lumpur: Dār al-Fajr Mālayziyā, 2000).

[36] Natalie Mobini-Kesheh, "The Arab Periodicals of the Netherlands East Indies, 1914–1942," *BKI* 152.2 (1996): 236–56.

[37] The "Ethical Policy" had its roots in strains of humanitarianism and economic liberalism of growing prominence among Dutch administrators in the Indies during the late nineteenth century. Working under a notion that the Netherlands owed the colonies a "debt of honor" (*Eereschuld*) from their long years of exploitation, educational and development projects were proposed to foster prosperity among the colonized. This was not pure altruism, however, as much of it was seen by its designers as ultimately leading to the creation of a stronger market for Dutch products in their dependencies. See J. S. Furnivall, *Netherlands India: A Study of Plural Economy* (Cambridge: Cambridge University

early twentieth century the number of native schools were significantly expanded and by 1915 there were more than 1,200 established across Java and Madura.[38] The model of modern education that they embodied was soon recognized as a valuable commodity for those seeking to establish themselves within the colonial economic and social hierarchies. Thus they were quickly imitated by local populations as a means for independent social advancement, with the most influential of them being those of the Taman Siswa network of nationalist private schools founded by Ki Hadjar Dewantara.[39] At the same time, it also inspired Muslim reformists during this period to re-imagine both the form and content of religious education. By the early years of the twentieth century, an increasing number of Muslim reformists were devoting extensive energies to the development of their own, Islamic alternative forms of "modern" schools.[40]

In 1905 Sunan Pakubuwana X of Surakarta ordered the establishment of one of the first modern style *madrasa* in Java, the Madrasa Manba' al-'Ulūm, and around the same time recent returnees from Mecca such as Hadji Abdul Karim Amrullah (a.k.a. Hadji Rasoel, d. 1949) were active in the formation of new Islamic schools in West Sumatra.[41] Over the years that followed, such institutions proliferated across the region from Kelantan and Singapore to the eastern islands of the Archipelago. Accompanying the programs of several reformist movements of this type and sometimes in competition with or in opposition to colonial schools, a new energy was exerted in reforming (sometimes in the most literal sense of the word) the institutions of Muslim education in order to better serve the needs of the community. Many of these new schools were integrally linked with wider developments in some of the other major innovations of the day, including voluntary associations and print culture. Over the course of the twentieth century such

Press, 1967), 225–37; and Gé Prince, "Dutch Economic Policy in Indonesia," in *Economic Growth in Indonesia, 1820–1940*, ed. Angns Maddison and Gè Prince (Dordrecht: Foris Publications, 1989), 203–26.

[38] Shiraishi, *An Age in Motion*, 28–29.

[39] For an overview of the Taman Siswa movement, see Kenji Tuschiya, *Democracy and Leadership: The Rise of the Taman Siswa Movement in Indonesia*, trans. Peter Hawkes (Honolulu: University of Hawaii Press, 1987).

[40] For an overview of such developments in another region of Indonesia, see Taufik Abdullah, *Schools and Polititcs: The Kaum Muda Movement in West Sumatra 1927–1933* (Ithaca: Cornell University Southeast Asia Program, 1971).

[41] For a short history of the Manba' al-'Ulūm, see Muhamad Hisyam, *Caught Between Three Fires: The Javanese Penghulul under the Dutch Colonial Administration, 1882–1942* (Jakarta: INIS, 2001), 140–46. In Southeast Asia the term *madrasa* was not widely used before the earlier twentieth century for local institutions of Islamic learning. By the time that use of the term was introduced from the Middle East during this period it took on local valences implying a distinctly "modern" form of Muslim schooling.

innovations were influential far beyond the sphere of specifically reformist schools, with some of these new methods of instruction eventually being imitated even by traditionalist institutions such as the *pesantren*.[42]

At many of these new Islamic schools renewed emphasis was placed on developing the skills necessary for forming individual interpretations of text, rather than on memorizing established rulings of past authoritative teachers or mastering the methodology of *fiqh* as practiced within the Shāfiʿī *madhhab*. Indonesian Muslim reformists of the early twentieth century increasingly advocated the utilitarian conception of Arabic linguistic knowledge as a tool (*ilmu alat*) that would enable students to engage in their own, direct interpretation of scriptures, rather than having to base their understandings of Islam upon what they referred to as "blind imitation" (*taklid buta*).[43] Such a renewed emphasis on the importance of the Arabic language for religious education was an important plank in *Salafi* reformist agendas in the Middle East as well at that time, as can be seen from an *al-Manār fatwā* addressed to a Sumatran correspondent in 1910.[44]

As has already been mentioned, interactions between Muslim scholars in the Middle East and the Indonesian archipelago were greatly increased and accelerated following the expansion of steamship travel between these two regions in the late nineteenth and early twentieth centuries. The impacts of this increased interaction in the field of Islamic education were pronounced and wide-ranging. For one, it facilitated the increasing numbers of Arab economic migrants from the southern Arabian area of Hadramawt that fueled the local Arab "awakening" in the Archipelago, and donors from this prosperous diaspora in Southeast Asia then funded new kinds of schools back home like the *ribāṭ* at Tarīm – an institution that was economically supported by remittances from Singapore.[45] At the same time, the increasing dominance of steamship transport in the Indian Ocean also exponentially

[42] As will be discussed in chapters 6 and 7, such changes within the *pesantren* milieu came to produce some dramatic effects that have impacted in significant ways on the development of Indonesian Islam in the late twentieth and early twenty-first centuries.

[43] For a study of one important Indonesian activist working in this area of reformed Arabic-language education, see Syafruddin Didin, "Maḥmūd Yūnus wa ittijāhātuhu fī tajdīd taʿlīm al-lugha al-ʿarabiyya bi indūnīsiyā," *SI* 2.3 (1995): 173–98.

[44] *al-Manār* 12: 904/ cited in Henri Laoust, "Le réformisme orthodoxe des 'Salafiya' et les caractères généraux de son orientation actuelle," *Revue des Études Islamiques* (1934): 205. More recently, the extensive interactions of Salafism and Arabism in the Middle East during this period have been explored in Itzchak Weismann, *Taste of Modernity: Sufism, Salafiyya, and Arabism in Late Ottoman Damascus* (Leiden: E. J. Brill, 2001).

[45] Anne K. Bang, *Sufis and Scholars of the Sea: Family Networks in East Africa, 1860–1925* (London: Routledge, 2003), 63.

expanded the number of travelers from the Archipelago bound for Arabia, and for Mecca in particular. The vast majority of those passengers were pilgrims intending only short stays in the Holy City. Among them, however, were a small but influential number of Southeast Asian Muslims who stayed in Mecca for extended periods of study – years or even decades.

During the late nineteenth century, a significant permanent community of these "Jawi" scholars was well established at Mecca, as documented by Snouck Hurgronje during his time there in 1885. A number of the new Islamic reformist schools mentioned above were founded by such figures upon their return to the archipelago. However, amid the turbulent transition between Ottoman and Wahhābī rule in the Hijaz during the early twentieth century, increasing numbers of Southeast Asian Muslim students began flocking to other Middle Eastern destinations, and particularly to Egypt. By the 1920s Cairo had become not only home to a large community of Southeast Asian Muslim students, but also a flourishing center of publishing for Islamic religious texts and even periodicals printed in Arabic-script Malay.[46] Michael Laffan has discussed the importance of study in Mecca and Cairo, as well as of the publications produced there in the development of modern conceptions of national identity among the "Jawa."[47] Aside from the political dimensions, these developments also had a significant impact upon conceptualizations of Islam as a religion, and the interpretation of Islamic law.

For example, in Egypt, al-Azhar underwent wide-ranging programs of reform in the early twentieth century under the direction of Muḥammad Abduh, and later Maḥmūd Shaltūt.[48] These changes involved not only reconstructions of the traditional curricula of Islamic religious and legal studies, but also the transformation of its administration along rational, scientific and comparative lines. The reconceptualizations of "modern" Islamic education that were envisioned by these reformers were then communicated to Southeast Asia by returning students, as well as through the periodical press, and thus came to act as a significant influence on the new Muslim schools being founded in the Archipelago at that time.

In the early twentieth century Arab inspirations for Islamic educational reform could also be found locally within the Netherlands Indies. For

[46] William R. Roff, "Indonesian and Malay Students in Cairo in the 1920s," *Indonesia* 9 (1970): 73–87.

[47] Michael Laffan, *Islamic Nationhood and Colonial Indonesia: The Umma below the Winds* (London: Routledge, 2003).

[48] Bernard Botiveau, "Note sur les étudiants indonésians présents à l'Université Al-Azhar du Caire," *Archipel* 40 (1990): 41; Mona Abaza, *Indonesian Students in Cairo: Islamic Education, Perceptions and Exchanges* (Paris: Cahier d'Archipel, 1994).

example, the Jam'iyyat Khair (discussed further below) set up an Arab school on modern lines in Batavia in 1911, attracting activists and instructors from various parts of the Arab world, including Aḥmad Sūrkatī from the Sudan, Muḥammad 'Abd al-Ḥamīd of Mecca, and Muḥammad Thaib of Morocco.[49] However, the example of this school also demonstrates the potential for considerable doctrinal diversity within these new-style Islamic schools for, soon after arriving in the Indies, Aḥmad Sūrkatī became involved in sharp debates with the Hadrami Sayyid sponsors of the Jami'iyyat Khair school on touchstone reformist issues in Islamic legal debates, such as that of hierarchical equivalence in Muslim marriage (*kafā'a*). By 1915 Sūrkatī had split from the organization and established his own school, the Jam'iyyat al-Islam wal-Irshad, which soon spread into a network of schools advocating a modern Islamic reformist agenda opposed to what it viewed as the "feudalism" of the Sayyids associated with the Jam'iyyat Khair.[50]

The spread of such schools, however, did not progress unimpeded for long, and in 1925 the "Guru Ordinance" was passed by the Dutch colonial government of the Netherlands Indies in an attempt to tighten administrative control over Islamic education hitherto governed by the more lenient 1905 rulings.[51] These strictures were imposed upon settled *pesantren* teachers as well as traveling preachers (*muballigh*) and the rapidly expanding class of highly mobile Muslim reformists, reflecting the colonial administration's growing concern over the potential social and political impact of their activities. Despite such measures, however, the number of new-style Islamic schools continued to expand through and after this period. Increasingly, they proliferated under the direction of Muslim voluntary associations such as the Islamic modernist organization Muhammadiyah (founded 1912), whose schools spread well beyond Java and eventually covered levels ranging from primary to university.[52] From the 1920s onward, networks of new-style schools were also established by the traditionalist Nahdlatul Ulama (NU), as well as by a number of other, smaller organizations, including al-Washliyyah, Perserikatan Ulama, and the Nahdlatul

[49] Sumit Mandal, "Forging a Modern Arab Identity in Java in the Early Twentieth Century," in *Transcending Borders*, ed. de Jonge and Nico Kaptein (Leiden KITLV Press, 2002), 163–84.

[50] Ahmed Ibrahim Abu Shouk, "An Arabic Manuscript on the Life and Career of Aḥmad Muḥammad Sūrkatī and his Irshādī Disciples in Java," in *Transcending Borders*, ed. de Jonge and Kaptein, 203–18.

[51] Harry J. Benda, *The Crescent and the Rising Sun: Indonesian Islam under the Japanese Occupation 1942–1945* (The Hague: W. van Hoeve Ltd., 1958), 74.

[52] Amir Hamzah, *Pendidikan dan Pengajaran Muhammadiyah dalam Masa Pembaharuan Semesta* (Malang: Ken Mutia, 1965).

Wathan.[53] By the 1930s, such schools for both men and women were being set up across the archipelago, and in such institutions students were coming into relationships with Islam and Islamic law in ways that differed significantly from those cultivated in the traditional *pesantren* milieu.[54] In Chapter 2, we will follow more closely the developments of another small but influential Muslim voluntary association that established its own network of schools, the Persatuan Islam (PERSIS).

## THE RISE OF VOLUNTARY ASSOCIATIONS

As a direct response to the bureaucratized institutions of colonialism, as well as a reflection of similar developments in other areas of the Muslim world, new kinds of voluntary associations began appearing throughout the Archipelago during the early decades of the twentieth century. The histories of these various organizations are inextricably connected with other aspects of modernization in this period, including both the dissemination of print culture and the introduction of new kinds of schools to the colonial populations of the Netherlands Indies. For example, many of the most prominent nationalist organizations of the early twentieth century were first developed among students at the Dutch colonial medical school (School tot Opleiding van Inlandse Artsen/ STOVIA) in Batavia, including the Boedi Oetomo (1908), Tri Koro Dharmo/ Jong Java (1915), de Jong Sumatranen Bond (1917), de Studerende Vereniging Minahasa (1918), and Jong Ambon (1918).[55]

Over this same period myriad other associations of different types formed across the Archipelago. They included a broad spectrum of social and ideological interests, ranging from literary and scientific clubs to labor and trade organizations, to community co-operative ventures, educational collectives, and religious movements. Over time some were even transformed into political parties, as was the case with the Sarekat Islam in 1915 and the Boedi Oetomo after 1918.[56] These various institutions variously contributed to the creation of a new social space for personal action in the

[53] Nu'man Abd al-Hayy, and Shahafari Ash'ari, *Organisasi Nahdlatul Wathan dan Perjuangan* (Pancor Lombok: Penerbit NW, 1989), 116–22.

[54] Hasbullah, *Sejarah Pendidikan Islam di Indonesia* (Jakarta: PT Raja Grafindo Persada, 1995), 94–105.

[55] Hans van Miert, "Een Koel Hoofd en een Warm Hart: Nationalisme, Javanisme, en Jeugdbeweging in Nederlands-Indië, 1918–1930" (Leiden University Dissertation, 1995), 41. The later histories of these various organizations developed along diverse trajectories with, for example, Jong Java and the Jong Sumatraten Bond becoming considerably more vocal in their demands in the 1920s.

[56] Robert van Niel, *The Emergence of the Modern Indonesian State* (The Hague: W. van Hoeve, 1970), 171–74.

public sphere, and often served the purpose of establishing new arenas for action outside of traditional religious and social institutions, thus allowing considerably greater freedom for individual action reinforced by a new source of communal support. In the case of some of the larger of these new organizations, new systems of supra-local communication and mobility were created which could then work together or compete with the more established networks such as that of the traditional *ʿulamāʾ*.[57]

Increasingly after the first decade of the twentieth century, Muslims in various parts of the archipelago began organizing themselves along the lines of modern voluntary associations, although not always based upon a modernist or reformist ideological platform. Diaspora communities in the archipelago such as that of the Hadrami Arabs, founded organizations with various combinations of religious and other interests such as the above-mentioned Jamiʿyyat Khair 1905, which combined concerns for the preservation of Arabic language and ethnic identity with certain forms of traditionalist forms of Islam.[58] Indigenous associations later formed in response to such diaspora organizations. One early example of such an organization was the West Javanese Hajatul Qulub, which was founded by Haji Abdulhamid in 1911 as an educational and economic association. The Hajatul Qulub organized lectures on Islamic religious topics for the benefit of its constituents, and worked to establish a local weaving enterprise that would be able to compete in the market with Chinese traders. Because of its repeated clashes with the Chinese community, however, the Hajatul Qulub was banned by the Dutch administration in 1915.[59]

Other local movements were more successful – temporarily, at least – in evading colonial censure and expanding beyond their local points of origin. A prime example of this is the Sarekat Dagang Islamiyah (Islamic Commercial Union) founded by Tirtoadisurjo at Batavia in 1909.[60] Within

[57] However, this is not to say that these more established networks entirely passed away. In fact, in some ways they too were influenced by the emerging social patterns of modernity and integrated themselves within its structures. This can, for example, be seen in the development of the Nahdatul Ulama as a modern institutionalization of the already present networks of traditionalist *kyai*. Zamakhsyari Dhofier, *Tradisi Pesantren: Studi tentang Pandangan Hidup Kyai* (Jakarta: LP3ES, 1982), 100–34.

[58] For more on the history of this organization, see Natalie Mobini-Kesheh, *The Hadrami Awakening: Community and Identity in the Netherlands Indies, 1900–1942* (Ithaca: Cornell University Southeast Asian Studies Program, 1999).

[59] After 1916 the *Hajatul Qulub* continued its educational endeavors under the new name of *Persyarikatan Ulama*. Deliar Noer, *The Modernist Muslim Movement in Indonesia: 1900–1942* (New York: Oxford University Press, 1973), 70–71.

[60] For accounts of the development of *Sarekat Islam* and its role in the emerging Indonesian nationalist movement, see George McTurnan Kahin, *Nationalism and Revolution in Indonesia* (Ithaca: Cornell University Press, 1952), 65–70; and Benda, *Crescent and Rising Sun*, 41–45.

a year the organization's first extension branch opened at Bogor, and thence expanded rapidly. In 1911 Tirtoadisurjo encouraged Haji Samanhudi to found a Sarekat Dagang Islamiyah branch for batik traders in Surakarta, and thence the organization evolved into what was to become the nation-wide political party Sarekat Islam after the name of its branch in Surabaya was simplified by H. O. S. Tjokroaminoto the following year.[61] The ideological orientation of Sarekat Islam underwent a significant shift in 1915 when Haji Agus Salim joined the organization and helped to foster internal movements for the establishment of modern reformist and Pan-Islamist ideas as the guiding agendas for the movement.[62]

In the years that followed, other organizations began appearing in Java that advanced rather different visions for the relative role of Islam in society. Not all of these organizations were centered on programs of Islamic religious reform, and in fact many of them were founded in direct opposition to such movements. For instance, the Comité voor het Javaansch Nationalisme was formed in 1917 as a counterweight against the increasing prominence of Islamic reformist associations, which it viewed as foreign to "authentic" Javanese culture.[63] The activities of this organization interacted with developments in the legal sphere through its support of agendas aimed at increasing the role of customary or *adat* law in society, as opposed to visions of a legal system that would devote more significant attention to Islam and Muslim jurisprudence as sources for a system of Indonesian national law.[64]

The rise of such organizations active in the cultural, economic, and political spheres was paralleled in the area of more specifically religious concerns in 1912 with the founding of Muhammadiyah at Yogyakarta by K. H. Ahmad Dahlan.[65] By the mid-1920s, Muhammadiyah branches were established well beyond Java to Bengkulu and the Minangkabau region of

[61] Van Niel, *Emergence*, 101–49.

[62] An early sketch of the organization which makes particular reference to its activities in the areas of printing and publishing can be found in A. Cabaton, "La "Sarékat Islam"," *RMM* 21 (1912): 348–56. For the text of the basic religious platform for this organization, see "Reglement Umum Bagi Ummat Islam (jang didirikan atas usaha Partij S. I. Indonesia)," Appendix in Amelz, *H. O. S. Tjokroaminoto, Hidup dan Perdjuangannja* (Jakarta: Bulan Bintang, n.d.), II, 87–142.

[63] Van Miert, *Een Koel Hoofd*, 92–128.

[64] In 1927, the Dutch colonial government recognized the prominence of *adat* over Islamic law as formal legal policy in the Basic Law of the East Indian colonies. Nur Ahmad Fadhil Lubis, "Institutionalization and the Unification of Islamic Courts under the New Order," *SI* 2.1 (1995): 38.

[65] Solichin Salam, *K. H. Ahmad Dahlan, Reformer Islam Indonesia* (Jakarta, 1963). See also James L. Peacock, "Dahlan and Rasul: Indonesian Muslim Reformers," in *The Imagination of Reality: Essays in Southeast Asian Coherence Systems*, ed. A. L. Becker and Aram A. Yengoyan (Norwood, NJ: ABLEX Publishing, 1979), 245–68. Five years later, K. H. Ahmad Dahlan also founded a women's

Sumatra, as well as at Banjarmasin and Amuntai in Kalimantan.[66] This organization generally refrained from formal participation in party politics, preferring to focus its energies on educational and charity work from an Islamic reformist perspective that drew inspiration from the writings of Muḥammad Abduh, and more particularly Rashīd Riḍā, as well as its interactions with Sūrkatī's al-Irshād movement.[67] In the decades following its establishment the Muhammadiyah increasingly embodied a *Salafi* vision of modernism in which a modernist emphasis on the rationality of Islam was significantly tempered by a scripturalist orientation to Islamic law that was a dominant concern informing Muhammadiyah's understanding and practice of *ijtihād*.

The reformist vision of Muhammadiyah often resonated with those of local movements based in the different areas of the archipelago to which it spread. This was particularly the case in the Minangkabau region of West Sumatra which, as noted above, had been increasingly engaged with Islamic reformist currents originating out of the Middle East since the nineteenth century. In the early years of the twentieth century, various voluntary associations had been established in connection with the spread of new-style schools and reformist periodicals in that region, including the Soap Cooperative for students of the *Surau Djembatan Besi* and the Sumatera Thawalib that supported the establishment of the Diniyah School in 1915. This was the first Islamic school in the area to introduce a class system, and a standard curriculum including various subjects of general knowledge, drawing upon models that its founder, Zainuddin Labai al-Junusi, had encountered while a student in Egypt. One of the first students at this school was his sister Rahmah al-Yunusiyah, who later went on to pursue an activist career of her own, founding a women's clinic and yet another new-style Islamic school (Perguruan Putri Padang Panjang) in West Sumatra.[68]

In response to this proliferation of reformist and other organizations, more traditionally oriented *'ulamā'* began to organize themselves as well. In 1926 an association of *kyai* known as the Nahdatul Ulama (NU) was founded by K. H. Hasjim Asjari, the leader of a *pesantren* in Jombang, East

division of the organization named Aisyiyah, see Baroroh Baried, "Une mouvement de femmes musulumanes: Aisyiyah," *Archipel* 13 (1977): 129–36.

66 Noer, *The Modernist Muslim Movement,* 78.

67 J. Bluhm-Warn, "Al-Manar and Ahmad Soorkattie," in Riddell and Street, eds., *Islam*, 295–308.

68 Aminuddin Rasyad, "Rahṃa al-Yūnusiyya: Mu'assisa al-ma'had al-dīnī li'l-banāt Padang Panjang, Sūmaṭra al-gharbiyya," *SI* 4.2 (1997): 109–55.

Java.[69] While the membership of this association consisted for the most part of traditionalist scholars sharing an adherence to established local traditions of the Shāfiʿī *madhhab* and various Sufi orders, they also nonetheless saw the practical benefits of modern organizational models and attempted to adapt them to suit their own purposes. Such flexibility has marked aspects of this organization since its inception as various configurations of *fiqh* scholarship, social pragmatism, organizational experimentation, and engagement with Indonesian national politics have shifted over the course of the NU's complex history.[70] In the process it has grown to become what today is often said to be the largest Islamic organization in Indonesia, if not the entire world.

Although the ideological agendas and practical programs implemented by these numerous voluntary associations varied to a considerable extent, most of them involved themselves in a common range of activities that included charity work as well as educational programs and the publication and dissemination of their own texts. These developments have had broad and significant impacts on nearly all aspects of Muslim religious, social, cultural, and intellectual history in modern Indonesia. In the particular area of Islamic jurisprudence many of these organizations also created special internal bodies concerned with the production of their own interpretations of Islamic law. For example, in January 1928, the congress of Sarekat Islam established the Majlis Ulama, and later that same year also saw the establishment of the Majlis Tarjih as an institution for the exercise of 'collective *ijtihād*' (*ijtihād jamāʿī*) in relation to matters of *ʿibādāt* (ritual observances).[71] The NU also formed their own committees for the discussion of questions pertaining to Islam.[72] However, while the NU's decisions

[69] Atjeh Aboebakar, *Sedjarah Hidup K. H. Wahid Hasjim dan Karangan Tersiar* (Jakarta: Panitia Buku Peringatan Alm. K. H. A. Wahid Hasjim, 1957), 109. For a collection of articles related to the history of this organization, see Greg Barton and Greg Fealy, eds., *Nahdatul Ulama, Traditional Islam and Modernity in Indonesia* (Clayton: Monash Asia Institute, 1996).

[70] Thus while the NU's appeal to the tradition of Muslim scholarship has been a mainstay of the organization from its very inception, in more recent years the organization has developed in some very non-traditional ways. This is due in part to its "modernized" bureaucratic structure and the more recent influence of well-funded non-governmental organizations, many of which have provided considerable financial support for projects involving the NU. As we shall see, however, it has thus opened itself up in new ways allowing for some of its members to experiment with ideas on the cutting edge of Muslim legal and jurisprudential thought in Indonesia. These developments will be discussed in chapters 6 and 7.

[71] M. Fathurrahman Jamil, "The Muhammadiyah and the Theory of Maqasid al-Shariʿah," *SI* 2.1 (1995): 59.

[72] For a short note on the methodology employed by this body, see Madaniy Malik, "Cara Pengambilan Hukum Islam dalam Bachtsul Masail Nahdlatul Ulama (Sebuah Alternatif Pengembangan)," *Aula: Majalah Nahdlatul Ulama* (December 1991): 53–63.

were often distinct in their reliance on traditional *fiqh* materials, their *fatwās* were disseminated through the association's publications and networks of schools in ways quite analogous to the mechanisms characteristic of more reformist organizations.

The development of voluntary associations, print culture, and educational reform has thus been so integrally linked in these contexts that it is difficult to speak of any one of these phenomena in isolation from the others. Together they may be viewed as the legs of a triangle, each of which intersects with and supports the other two; some new publications served to broadcast the particular programs of certain organizations to a general public, and still others were designed with the specific intention of being used as curricula for their own schools. These schools drew on the financial and structural resources of a number of voluntary associations and in turn facilitated the development of a population more familiar with the pedagogy and epistemological structures of print culture than with those of the more traditional *pesantren* milieu and its associated manuscript culture. Together these complex changes contributed to wide-scale transformations of the religious, intellectual, and legal cultures of Muslim communities of the Indonesian archipelago.

The next chapter will present a more in-depth discussion of the ways in which an extensive array of new kinds of schools, public preaching, and especially *ijtihād* journalism was aggressively deployed in the service of the agenda of Islamic religious and social reform advanced by the voluntary association known as PERSIS. This organization's most prominent representative launched his first calls for *ijtihād* in drastic terms, striking at the very epistemological bases of traditional Muslim jurisprudence. As we shall see, however, these first radical critiques helped to pave the way for reform and a reorientation to traditional Muslim jurisprudence that was to be continued by later writers and thinkers, including those of considerably more moderate orientations.

CHAPTER 2

# *The open gate of* ijtihād

> Aḥmad b. Ḥanbal once said: "A man must be severely limited in his knowledge if he chooses to imitate another person in matters of belief." Indeed it is not permissible that we should follow others uncritically, not even men of the caliber of Abū Bakr, ʿAlī, Aḥmad, or Shāfiʿī.
>
> Ibn al-Jawzī (d. 1201), *Kitāb Akhbār al-Ṣifāt*

Critical studies of the history of Islamic law and jurisprudence by European scholars had for most of the twentieth century been preoccupied with the question as to when, if ever, the "gate of *ijtihād*" was closed. While the fine points of an imagined chronology of this event were disputed among Orientalists, there seemed to be until relatively recently something of a consensus that this closure did indeed occur and that its result was a prolonged period of "ankylose" that was shaken into activity once again only in the modern period.[1] A powerful challenge to this view was proffered by Wael Hallaq in a landmark 1984 article that demonstrated the continuing practice of various forms of *ijtihād* throughout Islamic history as well as its significance in the development of both theoretical jurisprudence and positive law over the centuries.[2] Since then a number of studies have been devoted to the subject that have served to further our understanding of *ijtihād*/ *taqlīd* discourses in Islamic history. One general point that comes through this body of work is the importance of distinguishing between diverse definitions and understandings of both *ijtihād* and *taqlīd* as used by different authors in various periods and contexts.

[1] A classic statement of this position can be found in J. Shacht, "Classicisme, traditionalisme et ankylose dans le loi religieuse de l'Islam," in *Classicisme et déclin culturel dans l'histoire de l'Islam* (Paris: G.-P. Maisonneuve, 1957), 141–66.

[2] Wael B. Hallaq, "Was the Gate of *Ijtihād* Closed?" *IJMES* 16 (1984): 3–41. As radical as such an argument seemed to many Western-trained Islamicists at the time, the continuous practice of *ijtihād* in Muslim history is something that was clearly expressed in the work of Muslims through at least the early nineteenth century, such as in the introduction to al-Shawkānī's biographical dictionary of *mujtahids, Badr al-Ṭāliʿ* (Beirut: Dār al-maʿrifa, n.d.), 2–4.

In the chapters that follow, reference will be made to a number of modern Indonesian Muslim thinkers, all of whom spoke and wrote about *ijtihād*, although not necessarily in the same way. In general it could be said that most agreed that the practice of *ijtihād* involved a measure of individual effort in arriving at legal decisions for cases in which no clear textual ruling was evident. Just how such efforts were to be undertaken, however, was the subject of considerable debate, ranging from advocacy of a direct return to the primary sources of the Qur'ān and *Sunna* to a more regulated application of the jurisprudential methods of one or more of the established "schools of *fiqh*" (*madhhabs*).

For most of its documented history, Muslim education in Southeast Asia was largely focused upon the study of jurisprudence (*fiqh*).[3] In the traditional milieu of the *pesantren* and similar institutions in Southeast Asia this study remained confined almost completely to branch rulings on particular questions (*furū'*) rather than on the sources of law and methodological principles of jurisprudence (*uṣūl*). In such a setting most scholars and jurists tended to restrict themselves to rulings within the framework of the locally established Shāfi'ī *madhhab*. Nevertheless there is some evidence of Southeast Asian *'ulamā'* exploring the study of *uṣūl* and exercising various forms of *ijtihād* for themselves. For instance, the Javanese scholar Mahfuz al-Termasi (d. 1919) wrote a three-volume work on *uṣūl* to complement his prolific publications on the subject of *ḥadīth* studies.[4] For all this, however, al-Termasi was not a modernist reformer, but rather remained very much part of the cultural and intellectual complex of what contemporary scholars have come to refer to as traditionalism, that is one in which technical discussions of jurisprudence and other Islamic religious sciences were the special preserve of scholars trained and acculturated into the *pesantren* milieu.

During the early years of the twentieth century, however, a new, more broad-based interest in the study of *uṣūl* and the pursuit of *ijtihād* emerged in the spaces created by the modernization processes described in chapter 1.[5] Muslim reformers of the period aggressively critiqued traditionalist

[3] The primacy of *fiqh* in pre-modern Muslim education has been emphasized repeatedly by George Makdisi. See, for example, "Muslim Institutions of Learning in Eleventh-Century Baghdad," *BSOAS* 24 (1961): 1–56; and "Law and Traditionalism in the Institutions of Learning of Medieval Islam," in *Theology and Law in Islam*, ed. G. E. von Grunebaum (Wiesbaden: Otto Harrassowitz, 1971), 75–88.

[4] For an extensive discussion of al-Termasi and a bibliography of his works see Abd. Rahman, "The Pesantren Architects and their Socio-Religious Teachings, 1850–1950" (University of California, Los Angeles dissertation, 1997), 141–65.

[5] Van Bruinessen notes that works on *uṣūl* first began to attract wider attention by the *kaum muda* reformists in the 1920s. For instance, the reformist magazine *al-Ittifāq wa'l-iftirāq* contained

understandings of Islam and the institutionalized practices that established the authority of the *'ulamā'*, such as the certification (*ijāza*) that was such a central part of traditional Muslim education.[6] In doing so, journalists, activists, and teachers in modern schools established new models of Islamic religious authority that had a formative impact upon subsequent developments in Indonesian discourses on Islamic law and jurisprudence. In order to see how this came to be in the earlier decades of this century, we will examine the life and works of two major authors, both of whom were associated with an organization known as the Persatuan Islam (PERSIS): Ahmad Hassan (d. 1958) and Moenawar Chalil (d. 1961). These discussions will highlight some of the particular ways in which voluntary associations, educational reform, and print culture served to create new spaces for the radical reconstruction of Islamic religious and jurisprudential epistemology.

## PERSIS POLEMICS AND RELIGIOUS REFORM

The Persatuan Islam (PERSIS) was founded at Bandung in September 1923 as an organization to promote Islamic study and other activities, hosting discussions of reformist and modernist ideas that were spreading throughout the region at that time, as disseminated through publications such as *al-Manār* and *al-Imām*, and the viewpoints brought to these debates were considerably diverse.[7] The original leaders of PERSIS were Haji Zamzam and Haji Muhammad Junus, both members of Bandung's merchant class with serious interest in, and commitment to, Islamic education.[8] Less than a year after its founding, however, a Singapore-born Muslim named A. Hassan joined the organization and his dominating presence initiated a fundamental change in the character of PERSIS.

Under Hassan's influence, the orignally open and ideologically mixed character of the organization was transformed into a more unified one with an uncompromising insistence on a scripturalist orientation to Islamic

numerous writings on *uṣūl* which excerpted from such works as Shāfi'ī's *Risāla*, and Ibn Rushd's *Bidāyat al-Mujtahid*. Martin van Bruinessen, "Kitab Kuning: Books in Arabic Script Used in the Pesantren Milieu," *BKI* 146 (1990), 250.

6 Hassan, *Soal-Jawab*, 1179.

7 On the initial internal diversity of PERSIS: Howard M. Federspiel, *Islam and Ideology in the Emerging Indonesian State: The Persatuan Islam (PERSIS), 1923–1957* (Leiden: E. J. Brill, 2001), 84–6.

8 Haji Zamzam had spent over three years studying at the *Dār al-'ulūm* at Mecca, and H. Muhammad Junus was known as a collector who owned a library of books on Islamic subjects. Howard M. Federspiel, *Persatuan Islam: Islamic Reform in Twentieth-century Indonesia* (Ithaca: Cornell University Press, 1970), 12.

reform. Thence PERSIS came to be known as an association that advocated strict, literal allegiance to the text of the *Qur'ān* and what it considered to be reliable *ḥadīth*, and sharply criticized those Muslims who accepted any other standards of religious authority apart from these. Following this orientation PERSIS launched a series of virulent public polemics against traditionalist Muslims who upheld a belief in the necessity of adherence to one of the four established *madhhabs* and the foundational authority of their respective imams.

The targets of PERSIS polemics were not limited to traditionalist Muslims alone, however, for the organization also attacked new Islamic sects emerging at the time in the Netherlands East Indies, especially the Aḥmadiyya Qadyan.[9] PERSIS actively engaged in polemics with all whom they viewed as opponents of their interpretation of "true" Islam, including Communists and Christians. These polemics were carried out in a number of fora, including well-publicized and well-attended public debates between Hassan and representatives of opposing groups.[10] Often the extracts from these debates were published alongside other articles designed to respond to perceived attacks on Islam in a journal published by PERSIS for precisely this reason, entitled *Pembela Islam* (Defender of Islam).

The PERSIS press produced a considerable number of books and booklets in both Latin- and Arabic-script Malay/Indonesian as well as Sudanese and even a small number of English titles. Many of these texts were written by Hassan himself. The works of PERSIS authors, especially those of Hassan and his colleague Moenawar Chalil were often oriented toward technical matters of ritual practice (*'ibādāt*). In this sense PERSIS was at the forefront in introducing aspects of the technicalities of jurisprudential debate into the public forum and away from the monopolistic control formerly wielded by the formally trained *'ulamā'*. This relative emphasis has continued to characterize PERSIS' activities to this day.[11] PERSIS as an organization

9 For a short study of the early history of the Aḥmadiyya in Indonesia and its conflicts with PERSIS and other Muslim groups, see G. F. Pijper, "De Ahmadijah in Indonesia," in *Bingkisan Budi: Een bundel opstellen aan Dr. Phillipus Samuel van Ronkel door vrienden en leeringen aangeboden op zijn tachtigste verjaardag 1 Augustus 1950* (Leiden: A. W. Sijtoff, 1950), 247–54.

10 Such debates were popular forums with reformist Muslim groups outside of Indonesia as well. Decades earlier they had already been employed by members of the Deoband School in British India. Barbara D. Metcalf, *Islamic Revival in British India: Deoband, 1860–1900* (Princeton: Princeton University Press, 1982), 215ff.

11 This has recently been noted, for example, in a study of PERSIS' women's organization, Peristri. See Lies M. Marcoes-Natsir, "Profil Organisasi Wanita Islam Indonesia: Studi Kasus Peristri," in *Wantia Islam Indonesia dalam Kajian Tekstual dan Kontekstual*, eds Lies M. Marcoes-Natsir and Johan Hendrik Meuleman (Jakarta: INIS, 1993),106. One can also see echoes of this in the later career of former Masjumi activist M. Natsir, particularly in his founding of the Dewan Da'wah Islamiyah Indonesia (DDII).

is no longer a major player on the national scene, with its activities largely restricted to West and East Java, North Sumatra, and a handful of other local areas. However Hassan's (and to a lesser extent Chalil's) works continue to be reprinted and read in contemporary Indonesia. The lasting impact of PERSIS publications is also reflected in more diffuse trends within contemporary Indonesian Islam, such as in the continuing popularity of published defenses of Islam from perceived attacks – something which was a defining characteristic of the organization's flagship journal, *Pembela Islam*.

*Pembela Islam* enjoyed a wide circulation across the archipelago, as well as in the Malay Peninsula in the early decades of the twentieth century. Through this publication and its associated activities, PERSIS found a distinctive niche for itself in relation to other Muslim voluntary associations as the pre-eminent "Defender" (*Pembela*) of Islam against various perceived affronts. At the second Al-Islam Congress held at Solo, Central Java from May 2–7, 1939 it was announced that the Congress had appointed a commission headed by PERSIS to make continuous investigation into insults against Islam in general and to prepare any defense against them.[12] *Pembela Islam* was in print from 1929 until 1933, and was later replaced by another title, *Al-Lisaan*, in 1935.[13] In his study of the early history of PERSIS, Howard Federspiel has referred to both these titles as "ideological magazines" that served to bring together otherwise unconnected local "committees" dedicated to the defense of Islam against perceived attacks.[14] As will be discussed further in chapter 4, this type of ideological motivation has remained a powerful force among some sectors of the Indonesian Muslim community to this day.

PERSIS was a major producer of *ijtihād* journalism for Muslim Southeast Asia, publishing a number of magazines in addition to *Pembela Islam* such as *al-Fatwā*. This periodical was printed in *jawi*-script Malay from 1931 and had subscribers in Sumatra, Kalimantan, and the Malay peninsula, as well as in Java.[15] A considerable portion of the content of this and other PERSIS periodicals dealt with legal and jurisprudential issues

[12] Noer, *The Modernist Muslim Movement*, 246.
[13] Syafiq A. Mughni, *Hassan Bandung: Pemikir Islam Radikal* (Surabaya: Bina Ilmu, 1980), 77.
[14] Federspiel, *Islam and Ideology*, 91–100. Federspiel sees the ideologization of Islam under PERSIS as a further development of the ideas of earlier Indonesian Muslim political leaders including Tjokroaminoto and Hadji Agoes Salim. More on the legacy of these trends toward ideologization and defensive posturing in Indonesian Islam will be discussed in chapter 4 examining the later career of the early PERSIS activist M. Natsir.
[15] Noer, *The Modernist Muslim Movement*, 91.

and followed a precedent set for 'magazine *fatwās*'[16] established by earlier reformist periodicals such as *Al-Manār*, edited by Muḥammad Abduh and Rashīd Riḍā. These two reformers are often cited as formative influences on the development of modern movements for Islamic reform in Southeast Asia and elsewhere. Unfortunately, however, such references have taken on the aspect of something of a mantra with little thought going into what such a statement might mean, and without acknowledging the significant differences in the individual reform agendas of these two figures.[17]

Abduh had argued that the reason for the sorry state of the Muslims in his day was that they had lost the pristine simplicity of their faith under a mass of outdated and unreasonable tradition that had shackled Muslim societies to a static or backward orientation; thus making them easily susceptible to conquest and exploitation by the modernized West. In order to move forward and revive the glory of the early days of Islam, Abduh believed that Muslims had first to go back to the simple foundations of their faith, stripping away layer after layer of the popular practices and medieval scholasticism that had accrued upon the message of the Prophet and the practice of his companions. Thence new interpretations could be formulated through the use of modern, rational, approaches to the texts of Qur'ān and *ḥadīth*. Such an agenda has characterized what has come to be referred to as Islamic modernism.

Riḍā's approach, however, differed from the modernism of Abduh in its relative restriction of the range of human reason in such interpretive processes. Thus Riḍā is more accurately identified with the *Salafi* strand of modern Islamic reformism favoring more explicitly scripturalist views of Islam with an emphasis on determining regulations for ritual behavior that would be 'true' to the example set by the Prophet and free of the 'innovations' imposed by the interpretations of medieval Muslim scholasticism.[18] One of the defining characteristics of the modern *Salafiyya* was its

[16] On the place of such writings in the larger history of *fatwās*, see Muhammad Khalid Masud, Brinkley Messick, and David S. Powers, "Muftis, *Fatwas*, and Islamic Legal Interpretation," in *Islamic Legal Interpretation: Muftis and their Fatwas* (Cambridge, MA: Harvard University Press, 1996).

[17] Some of Abduh's particular *fatwās* can, however, be traced as clear inspiration for a few specific reformist positions in Southeast Asian Islam. An example of this is the famous Transvaal *Fatwā* that was solicited by a Muslim of South Africa on the permissibility of, among other things, eating meat slaughtered in the name of God by the "People of the Book." See Charles C. Adams, "Muhammad Abduh and the Transvaal *Fatwa*," in *The MacDonald Presentation Volume*, ed. William G. Shellabear *et al.* (Princeton: Princeton University Press, 1933), 11–30. Hassan, for example, seems to have ruled according to this decision in one of his own *fatwās* on the subject, see A. Hassan *et al.*, *Soal-Jawab, tentang berbagai Masalah Agama* (Bandung: Diponegoro, 1985), 386.

[18] For a general introduction to *Salafiyya*, Henri Laoust, "Le Réformisme orthodoxe des 'Salafiya' et les caractères généraux de son orientation actuelle," *Revue des Études Islamiques* (1934): 175–224.

insistence that, once the essential body of Islamic practice was clearly and unambiguously defined, this could then serve to dictate a uniform model of Islamic practice acceptable to all Muslims and suitable to life in any time or place. Modern *Salafis* believed that only when this was accomplished would Muslims see the end of internal disputes that characterized the divisions between existing schools of law, and all would constrain themselves to follow the clear and basic models of universal Muslim practice. One of the most influential early exponents of this approach in Muslim Southeast Asia was Ahmad Hassan.

## Ahmad Hassan

A. Hassan was born at Singapore in 1887 where his father was a reporter, writer, and publisher of Tamil books and newspapers. His mother, Hajjah Muznah, was originally from India, but had met her husband in Surabaya.[19] As a young boy Hassan was educated in the Qur'ān and religious studies by his father, and later attended Malay and English schools in Singapore, although he never formally completed elementary school or any other more advanced level of formal education. In his youth Hassan devoted considerable energies to the study of languages, eventually gaining competence in Arabic, English, and Malay as well as his parents' native Tamil. After the fourth grade, however, he shifted his interest primarily to religious studies, which he pursued in a loosely structured way with a number of prominent local teachers until around 1910.

From his father, Hassan also learned the trade of letters, apprenticing informally in the printing/publishing business and writing for various newspapers and magazines in Singapore and Indonesia. By 1909 he was active for the journal *Utusan Melayu*, where his first polemical publication was a strident critique of the local *Tuan Kadli* (Muslim judge) who used to conduct investigations in a place where men and women were seated together.

[19] Some biographers, however, claim that his mother was in fact a Javanese. Such points of detail vary from time to time in the sources available. The earliest attempt at a biography is probably that of Roebaie Widjaya, who published a short article during Hassan's lifetime. "Biografia – A. Hassan: Pengarang, Kritikus dan Debat Islam," *Hudjdjatul Islam* 1.1 (Aug. 1956): 35–41. From then on such short studies proliferated in various journals and one was even attached to a later edition of the collection of "Questions and Answers" issued by PERSIS under the title *Soal-Jawab* (Hassan *et al.*, *Soal-Jawab*, 1266ff.). Around the same time, short monographs also began to appear which included some summarized accounts of the general points of Hassan's religious and legal thought, including: Mughni, *Hassan Bandung*; Anshari, H. Endang Saifuddin, and Syafiq A. Mughni, *A. Hassan: Wajah dan Wijah Seorang Mujtahid* (Bandung: Firma al-Muslimun, 1985). These drew to a certain extent on the earlier articles as synthesized by Federspiel in his McGill University dissertation, later published by Cornell. Federspiel, *Persatuan Islam*.

Such social mixing of the sexes continued to be viewed with abhorrence by Hassan throughout his life.[20] This first foray into the public forum of debate resulted in his being temporarily prohibited from giving public lectures in his native Singapore.

In 1921, Hassan moved to Surabaya where he employed himself in attempts at various occupations ranging from petty trader to tire vulcanizer. While he appears never to have achieved marked success in any of these businesses, he did profit from new contacts made there with several members of Sarekat Islam, including H. O. S. Tjokroaminoto.[21] From Surabaya, Hassan moved to Kediri, and then on to Bandung in 1925, where he met Haji Zamzam and others from the PERSIS study circle. Upon joining the organization, he quickly rose to prominence as one of the association's most prominent figures. There he also turned to writing once again, and became PERSIS' most prolific author and eventually the key spokesman of the entire organization.

Hassan wrote prodigiously to fill the pages of PERSIS periodicals such as *Pembela Islam*, and at the same time produced a considerable number of monographs, large and small.[22] Most of these works were published on the organization's own press, where Hassan involved himself in every technical aspect of the writing, editing, printing, and binding processes. This deep immersion in the technical side of print culture appears to have had a tremendous effect on Hassan, for at times he even used its imagery to explain points of religious law. For example, in the preface to one of his books, he writes: "Just as in the printing of a book, one needs certain equipment such as block letters, a press, a trained printer, and so on, however the printer, the press, and the block letters do not become part of the book . . . [Thus] the ink and paper could be called *rukun* (principles) and other elements such as the printer, his press, and the block letters could be seen as *syarath* (rules)."[23]

In 1940 Hassan moved, along with his printing press, from Bandung, West Java to Bangil, East Java.[24] There he remained actively involved with the educational and publishing activities for PERSIS until his death on

[20] This particular aspect of Hassan's character seems to have led him to certain inconsistencies in the application of his scripturalist jurisprudential and interpretive methodology to certain issues concerning women. Examples of this include his definition of those parts of a women's body that must remain covered, his prohibition of the presence of women at communal prayer, and his attempt to justify the apocryphal Islamic story of Eve's creation from a rib (*Soal-Jawab*, 1069, 87, 446, 1526).

[21] See Amelz, *H. O. S. Tjokroaminoto: Hidup dan Perdjuangannja* (Jakarta: Bulan Bintang, n.d).

[22] For bibliographies of Hassan's works, see Federspiel, *Persatuan Islam*, 222–24; Mughni, *Hassan Bandung*, 129–31; and Akh. Minhaji, "Ahmad Hassan and Islamic Legal Reform in Indonesia, 1887–1958" (Montreal: McGill University dissertation, 1997), 379–86.

[23] *al-Boerhan*, xxxv–xxxvi. [24] Federspiel, *Islam and Ideology*, 117.

10 November 1958. In addition to authoring his own monographs, polemical pamphlets, instructional booklets, innumerable magazine articles, and a prodigious amount of *fatwā*, Hassan translated older works and composed new ones in fields ranging from ritual behavior to *ḥadīth* studies. At Bangil he also established the new Pesantren PERSIS school, whose administration was later taken over by his son, A. Qadir Hassan.[25] Despite its use of the *pesantren* designation, however, this was an institution structured in the manner of a modern school and emphasizing scripturalist approaches to Islam, rather than the traditional studies in the Shāfiʿī *madhhab* characteristic of earlier *pesantren*. The Bangil *pesantren* has since its founding remained a small but disproportionately influential force in the shaping of Indonesian Islamism, and laying the groundwork for the Saudi-sponsored Institute for the Islamic and Arabic Sciences (LIPIA) in Jakarta.[26]

## SCRIPTURALISM AND *IJTIHĀD*

The "young generation" (*kaum muda*) of reformers described in chapter 1 often critiqued established practices and understandings of Islam as unjustified innovations (*bidʿa*) that had come to be followed with "blind" imitation (*taqlīd*) by the traditionalists of the "old school" (*kaum tua*). For many of them, as well as for Hassan, the way to avoid both *taqlīd* and *bidʿa* was through *ijtihād*, or the exercise of individual effort in deriving legal rulings directly from the texts of revelation.[27] What they seemed glibly oblivious to, however, was the fact that their modern, mass-based scripturalist appeals to *ijtihād* themselves comprised one of the most dramatic innovations in Islamic history.

Hassan emphasized his own adherence to the Qurʾān and *Sunna* in order to distinguish his work from the ways in which he perceived some of his contemporaries to have confused *ijtihād* with the simple expression of personal opinion.[28] In attempting to police the pool of participants in his type of *ijtihād*, Hassan thus had to compromise somewhat on his

[25] His son also published a short monograph on *uṣūl al-fiqh*, Abdul Qadir Hassan, *Ushul Fiqih* (Bangil: Yayasan al-Muslimun, 1992) (4th printing). This work is largely a restatement of his father's principles and is printed as an inexpensive paperback still widely available, especially through the distribution channels of *Media Dakwah*.

[26] Rémy Madinier, "Du temps des chameaux à celui du béton radioactive 'les nouveaux usages islamistes du passé'," *Archipel* 64 (2002): 151–52.

[27] As we shall see below, Hassan restricted the practice of *ijtihād* strictly to questions on worldly matters (*muʿāmalāt*). On questions of religious and ritual practice (*ʿibādāt*) he allowed only a careful adherence to that which could clearly be established based upon the text of the Qurʾān and the *Sunna* (*Soal-Jawab*, 91).

[28] *al-Boerhan*, xxxvii; *Soal-Jawab*, 22.

populist rhetoric.[29] Acknowledging that not all Muslims would be able to exercise *ijtihād* on their own, Hassan nevertheless refused to allow those who could not simply to follow *taqlīd.* Rather, he insisted that they more actively participate through what he referred to as *ittibāʿ* (lit. "following [of 'proper' precedent]"). Hassan maintained that *ittibāʿ* differed from *taqlīd* in that it implied "critical" rather than "blind" acceptance of the opinions of those who were more familiar with the scriptural sources of Islamic law. According to Hassan's understanding of *ittibāʿ* then, one who asked for a decision on some legal question was obliged to also ask the *mujtahid* for the proof text upon which the decision was based.[30]

In establishing this, any element of *bidʿa* had to be recognized and thence eliminated by checking every practice against the touchstones of the Qurʾān and *Sunna.* For this reason Hassan devoted a substantial part of his writing to the reaffirmation of these sources as the primary foundation of all legal rulings. In determining the potential legal import of these texts, Hassan expended considerable energy writing on the classification and evaluation of *ḥadīth* reports in a way that reveals the special importance he placed on the *Sunna* as an aid to interpreting and specifying the general rules set forth in the Qurʾān.[31]

Hassan's major work of Qurʾānic exegesis, *Tafsir al-Furqān*, first appeared serially starting in 1928, and was finally published in complete form only in 1956.[32] The work may actually be seen as more of an Indonesian "translation" of the Qurʾān than work of *tafsīr* proper as what little non-literal interpretation there is comes only in the form of short footnotes. Nonetheless, it also contains a fairly lengthy preface in which the author outlines his method of interpretation by laying out a set of radical scripturalist exegetical principles differing significantly from most works produced in Southeast Asia before that time.

Over the course of Muslim intellectual history, the study of *tafsīr* had developed a number of sub-disciplines to facilitate the process of deriving

[29] This is one aspect of modern Salafism that appears to have considerable roots in the earlier tradition. As Michael Cook has described the work of one prominent Ḥanbalī scholar in the ninth century, "Ibn Qutayba was no man of the people, and his message is populism with an audibly upper-class accent." See "Ibn Qutayba and the Monkeys," *Studia Islamica* 89 (1999): 45.

[30] *Soal-Jawab*, 389. [31] *al-Boerhan*, vi–vii.

[32] A. Hassan, *Tafsir al-Furqān* (Bangil: Dewan Daʿwah Islamiyah Indonesia, 1986). The title which Hassan chose for his work is interesting in itself. In Arabic, *al-furqān* means, literally, "the criterion [between good and evil]" and has traditionally been used as a reference to the Qurʾān itself. Abduh elaborated on this term extensively in his own works of exegesis where he took it to refer to the faculty of reason; see J. J. G. Jansen, *The Interpretation of the Koran in Modern Egypt* (Leiden: E. J. Brill, 1980), 21–23. Hassan, however, uses it in the more direct sense of the absolute textual authority of the Qurʾān in the determination of right and wrong.

relevant interpretations from the sacred text. One of these sub-fields that has come to be of considerable importance for many modern reformers is that of *al-nāsikh wa'l-mansūkh*, or "that which abrogates, and that which is abrogated."[33] The principle of abrogation (*naskh*) has thus become a productive means by which apparent contradictions in the texts of revelation are reconciled by determining their relative chronological ordering. Muslim exegetes have put forward a number of justifications for this, although most rely primarily on 2 (*al-baqara*): 106: "Whatever *aya* ['sign' or 'Qur'ānic verse'] we cancel or cause to be forgotten, we reveal another, better one . . ." While there have been a wide variety of positions as to which and exactly how many verses might have been abrogated, in general one can trace a general trend in the modern period toward reducing the number of verses considered to be *mansūkh*. Along such lines we can situate the interpretation put forth by Sir Sayyid Ahmad Khan (d. 1898). He contended that over the centuries Muslim scholars have come to accept fewer and fewer verses as abrogated and thus felt justified to continue this process of reduction to zero. In advancing his argument, he criticized the reliability of the *ḥadīth* employed by the advocates of *naskh* and what he perceived as the "nonsensical arguments of the jurists."[34] While some other early-modern reformers, including Muḥammad Abduh, were not so radical as Ahmad Khan,[35] others inclined toward rejecting *in toto* the theory of abrogation as applied to individual *Qur'ānic* verses. For example, the radical Egyptian exegete Sayyid Quṭb (d. 1966) attempted to reconcile verses seen by earlier authors as an example of abrogation by arguing that they in fact each refer to different subjects.[36] Hassan also proclaimed a total rejection of *naskh* as

[33] For an early modern overview of classical developments in this sub-field of Qur'ānic studies, see Jalāl al-Dīn Suyūṭī, *al-Itqān fī 'ulūm al-Qur'ān* (Beirut: Dār ibn Kathīr, 1407H./ 1987), II: 700–23. On conceptualizations of *naskh* in the history of Islamic jurisprudence, John Burton, *The Sources of Islamic Law: Islamic Theories of Abrogation* (Edinburgh: Edinburgh University Press, 1990).

[34] "at first the number of abrogated verses was thought to be more that five hundred; then, as Shah Wali-Allah has written in *Fawz al-Kabīr*, al-Suyūṭī and others confined their number to twenty; then Shah Wali-Allah limited *naskh* (abrogation) to only five verses. When Sir Sayyid saw that the number of abrogated verses had been reduced from five hundred to five, he became convinced that nowhere in the Qur'ān did *naskh* actually occur . . ." Altaf Husayn Hali, *Hayat-i Javad* (Kanpur: 1901), 219–20, cited in Ernest Hahn, "Sir Sayyid Ahmad Khan's 'The Controversy over Abrogation (in the Qur'ān)': An Annotated Translation." *Muslim World* 44.2 (1974): 124.

[35] J. Jomier, *Le commentaire Coranique du Manar: Tendances modernes de l'exégèse Coranique en Égypte* (Paris: Éditions G.-P. Masionneuve & Cie, 1954), 196.

[36] See A. A. Nayed, "The Radical Qur'anic Hermeneutics of Sayyid Qutb,' *Islamic Studies* 31.3 (1992); and J. M. S. Baljon, *Modern Muslim Koran Interpretation, 1880–1960* (Leiden: E. J. Brill, 1968), 49. For a more richly detailed study of the Quṭb's reading of the *Qur'ān* and selection of passages from *Fī Ẓilāl al-Qur'ān* in English translation, see Olivier Carré, *Mysticism and Politics: A Critical Reading of Fī Ẓilāl al-Qur'ān by Sayyid Quṭb, 1906–1966*, translated from the French by Carol Artigues and revised by W. Sheppard (Boston: E. J. Brill, 2003).

applied to verses of the Qur'ān on the grounds that it would compromise the perfect qualities (*i'jāz*) of the text.[37]

In his *Tafsir al-Furqān* and other writings, Hassan was clear in his disavowal of the possibility of any one Qur'ānic verse abrogating another.[38] However at the same time he did not completely abandon all approaches to the Qur'ānic text concerned with the traditionally determined chronological sequence of revelation.[39] For he continued to make use of works on *asbāb al-nuzūl*, or the "occasions of revelation" in which *ḥadīth* reports were used to establish the contexts for the first revelation of particular Qur'ānic verses.[40] Hassan used this sub-discipline of Qur'ānic studies in order to determine the proper usage of individual verses as grounds for legal rulings. In an attempt to circumvent what he regarded as problematic in the traditional works of Muslim scholarship in this area, Hassan went back to the *ḥadīth* reports that he deemed reliable in order to establish the contexts of particular occasions. All this being said, Hassan maintained that such investigations were not necessary in the case of all Qur'ānic verses, as in general most could be understood simply by the clear (literal) meaning of the text.

Another area in which the disciplines of Qur'ānic exegesis and *ḥadīth* study intersect in the writings of Hassan is on the subject of *isra'iliyyāt*, traditions of narrative commentary attributed to early Jewish and Christian converts to Islam. He characterized such reports as "excessive and extraneous reports from the Jews, most of which are weak and false." In connection with these we find an example of Hassan's use of *matn* criticism, a sub-discipline of technical *ḥadīth* studies, in which he is forced to admit that although the chain of transmission (*isnād*) of these *ḥadīth* may appear sound, the meaning expressed in the text of the *ḥadīth* itself may nonetheless be suspect, and thus in need of corroboration from a Qur'ānic verse or another, sounder *ḥadīth*. This is in accordance with Hassan's dogmatic position that the Qur'ān and "sound" *ḥadīth* are never actually in conflict with each other or themselves. The two sources must be studied in a complementary fashion, recognizing always the absolute priority of the Qur'ān while at the same

37 "Those who say so [i.e. supporting the theory of *naskh*] are of shallow understanding and are too willing to diminish the dignity of the Qur'ān" (*Soal-Jawab*, 381).

38 E.g., *al-Boerhan*, xiii; *Soal-Jawab*, 379–83; and *al-Furqān*: xxxiv–xxxvi.

39 Indeed in one of these same published works Hassan also maintained that knowledge of *nāsikh-mansūkh* remains a requirement to be fulfilled by every would-be *mujtahid* (*al-Boerhan*, xxxvii).

40 This is a sub-discipline of *tafsīr* that investigates the situations and contexts in which various verses were revealed. A summary of classical Muslim positions on various individual verses in this field of Qur'ānic studies can be found in the handbook compiled by al-Suyūṭī, *Lubāb al-nuqūl fī asbāb al-nuzūl* (Tunis: al-Dār al-Tūnisiyya lil-nashr, 1402H./ 1981).

time relying upon *ḥadīth* texts to clarify and specify the general statements contained in the Qur'ān.[41]

Although Hassan discussed *ḥadīth* in many of his works, his most extensive efforts in this field may be seen in his translation and annotation of Ibn Ḥajar al-'Asqalānī's *Bulūgh al-Marām*.[42] Although selections from this work's chapter on *ṣalāt* had been adapted into Arabic-script Malay as early as 1812 by the eminent scholar of the *pesantren* tradition Da'ud b. 'Abd Allāh al-Faṭānī,[43] Hassan's work was one of very few Malay-language texts on *ḥadīth* studies available in the Indonesian Archipelago during his day. Since then it has remained one of the most popular works of its kind, going through numerous reprints.[44] Hassan's translation of this work was part of his larger project which included not only bringing alternative works from the Islamic tradition into the standard corpus of works used in Southeast Asia, but it was also a way to illustrate with concrete examples some of the classifications and interpretations of *ḥadīth* which he had put forward elsewhere, such as in *al-Boerhan*.

In his emphasis on the study of *ḥadīth* as an integral part of the jurisprudential process, Hassan was engaging in a project that had attracted the attention of reformists from throughout the Muslim world during his day. Whereas for much of Muslim history, the specialized sub-disciplines associated with *ḥadīth* study were not uniformly integrated into the more dominant general course of studying Islamic law and jurisprudence, in the modern period this seems to have undergone something of a change.[45] The renewed emphasis on the study of *ḥadīth* was linked with renewed

[41] *al-Furqān*: xix–xxi.

[42] A. Hassan, *Tarjamah Bulughul Maraam (Ibnu Hajr al 'Asqalani) Berikut Keterangan dan Penjelasannya* (Bangil: Pesantren Persatuan Islam, 1991). This text is still currently used in PERSIS study circles, including those of it's women's auxiliary, Peristri. See Marcoes-Natsir, "Profil Organisasi Wanita Islam Indonesia," 106.

[43] *Bulūgh al-Marām* (Mecca: Maṭba'a al-mīrrīya al-kā'ina, 1310 H./ 1892–3). Snouck Hurgronje mentions this work being studied by Southeast Asian Muslim scholars in a report he addressed to the Resident of Lampung at Teluk Betung in 1897. C. Snouck Hurgronje, *Ambtelijke Adviezen van C. Snouck Hurgronje: 1889–1936*, ed. E. Adriaanse ('s-Gravenhage, Martinus Nijhoff/ Rijks Geschiedkundige Publicatiën, 1957), III, 2006.

[44] More recently, a larger number of *ḥadīth* works have become widely available in Indonesia, including a translation of al-Ṣan'ānī commentary on the *Bulūgh al-Marām*, entitled *Subul al-salām sharḥ bulūgh al-marām min jama' 'adillat al-ahkām*: al-Ṣan'ānī, Muḥammad b. Isma'īl al-Khalānī, in *Subulus Salam: Hadits-hadits Hukum* (Surabaya: al-Ikhlas, n.d.). In recent years translation projects to bring out nearly all of the classically established Six Books of *ḥadīth* collections have made the knowledge of prophetic tradition in Indonesia more widespread than ever before. Now even more commentaries on these works are making a strong appearance in general bookstores, including al-Zabīdī, *Ringkasan Shahīh al-Bukhārī* (Bandung: Mizan, 1997).

[45] Daniel W. Brown, *Rethinking Tradition in Modern Islamic Thought* (Cambridge: Cambridge University Press, 1996), 111–12.

calls for the exercise of *ijtihād* referring back directly to the primary sources of Islamic law: the Qur'ān and *Sunna*. In this way reformers attempted to bypass the intermediate rulings on a given issue enshrined in the corpus of the established *madhhabs*.

The revival of interest in *ḥadīth* took various forms in different parts of the Muslim world, ranging from the radical posturing of public practice by the *Ahl-i Ḥadīth* in South Asia to the scholarly and popular press polemics of Egypt in the first decades of the twentieth century.[46] A younger contemporary of Hassans' – the Meccan-born Malay scholar Idrīs al-Marbawī (d. 1989) – was active in Cairo during the 1930s–50s composing an immense *jawi*-script Malay translation of and commentary on the *ḥadīth* collection (*Jāmi'*) of al-Tirmidhī (d. 892).[47] In his general preface to this work, Marbāwī discusses Tirmidhī's tri-partite schema to classify each *ḥadīth* according to the categories of *ḥasan* (fair), *ṣaḥīḥ* (sound), and *gharīb* (odd), and then goes on to present the ten subdivisions of the category of *ṣaḥīḥ* developed in Abū Bakr Muḥammad b. 'Abd Allāh al-Ma'āfirī b. Arabī's (d. 1148) commentary on this same collection (*'Āriḍa al-Aḥwadhī*).[48] For Hassan, however, the whole point of such *ḥadīth* scholarship was not the construction of an abstract typology, but rather in determining the value of a given text as a source for legal rulings. Thus he generally framed his discussions only in terms of the major distinction between *ḥadīth* which can be considered sound (*ṣaḥīḥ*) and those which he deemed to be weak (*ḍa'īf* ).[49]

The critical re-evaluation of *ḥadīth* used in support of established Islamic legal rulings was a common practice among *Salafi* reformists in the Middle East during the early decades of the twentieth century, under whose direction works of medieval Muslim scholarship from the Ḥanbalī school were revived, published, and widely disseminated.[50] Hassan drew on such sources, as well as other Arabic texts that were then being made available in

46 For an overview of these debates, see Metcalf, *Islamic Revival*, 265–96; and G. H. A. Juynboll, *The Authenticity of the Tradition Literature: Discussions in Modern Egypt* (Leiden: E. J. Brill, 1969).

47 Muḥammad Idrīs 'Abd al-Ra'ūf al-Marbawī, *Baḥr al-māzī* (Cairo: Muṣṭafā al-Bābī al-Ḥalabī, 1933–55), 22 vols. This work has become popular in the curricula of some schools in the Malay Peninsula and other parts of mainland Southeast Asia, and there has even been a single-volume, roman script handbook of excerpts from it published recently in Singapore. In contemporary Indonesia, however, the work is little known.

48 al-Marbawī, *Baḥr al-māzī*, I, 5–7.

49 Even when, in the introduction to his collection of *fatwās*, Hassan does actually discuss the further categorization of *Ṣaḥīḥ ḥadīth*, he maintains little difference between four out of five of them for purposes of establishing legal rulings (*Soal-Jawab*, 16).

50 A major example of this in the field of *ḥadīth* studies is Ibn al-Jawzī, *Kitāb al-mawḍū'āt* (Medina: Maktaba al-Salafiya, 1966–68). This same medieval Ḥanbalī scholar is the author quoted in the epigraph to this chapter.

the Archipelago for the first time thanks to the spread of print technology and modern distribution channels. Thus, for example, in developing his approach to *ḥadīth* studies, Hassan made use of the *Nayl al-awṭār* by the Yemeni *mujtahid* al-Shawkānī (d. 1832),[51] and further cites al-Shawkānī's work of Qur'ānic exegesis among the references for his own *Tafsir al-Furqān.*[52] He also translated a lengthy section on *ijmā'* from al-Shawkānī's major work on *uṣūl al-fiqh* into Indonesian as supporting evidence for one of his *fatwās.*[53] Shawkānī's various works had come to play an important part in Muslim reform movements in many parts of the Muslim world from the nineteenth century onwards.[54] Within the specific history of Islam in Southeast Asia, Hassan helped to introduce certain aspects of Shawkānī's œuvre into the conversations of modern reformists, and discussions of this Yemeni scholar's works have grown in popularity among diverse groups of Indonesian Muslims since the 1990s.[55]

Beside al-Shawkānī, Hassan also drew on a number of other Muslim scholars who were previously rarely, if ever, included in the canon of traditionalist Shāfi'ī scholars studied in Southeast Asia at that time.[56] For example, during his early days in Surabaya, Hassan had been exploring Ibn Rushd's (d. 1126) *Bidāyat al-Mujtahid*, a work which compares the rulings of various schools, designed to serve as a reference for individual scholars in their pursuit of *ijtihād.*[57] In one published response to

51 al-Shawkānī, Muḥammad b. 'Alī b. Muḥammad, *Nayl al-awṭār sharḥ muntaqā li-akhbār min aḥādīth sayyad al-akhyār* (8 vols.) (Beirut: Dār al-fikr, 1414 H./1994). Since Hassan's time this work has become available in a full Indonesian translation. For more on Shawkānī and his work in the field of Islamic legal theory, see Bernard Haykel, *Revival and Reform in Islam: The Legacy of Muhammad al-Shawkani* (New York: Cambridge University Press, 2003).

52 *Fatḥ al-qadīr al-jāmi' bayn fannī al-riwāyat wa al-darāyat min 'ilm al-tafsīr* (6 vols.) (Damascus: Dār ibn Kathīr, 1414H./ 1994).

53 *Soal-Jawab*, 1531–50. The original work which Hassan translated from is Muḥammad b. 'Alī al-Shawkānī, *Irshād al-fuḥūl ila taḥqīq 'ilm al-uṣūl.* In addition to the popular Beirut edition, this Arabic text has also been published at Surabaya by Aḥmad b. Sa'd b. Nu'man.

54 Including, for example, among the Alusis of Baghdad and the Damascene Salafiyya. D. Commins, *The Salafi Islamic Reform Movement in Damascus* (Oxford: Oxford University Press, 1990), 25.

55 One interesting aspect of these developments has been the selectivity of references to Shawkānī's works by Indonesian Muslims of different orientations. For example, in recent years Indonesian Salafi reformists and those associated with the modernist Muhammadiyah most often refer to Shawkānī's work of *ḥadīth* criticism (*Nayl al-awṭār*), while young thinkers associated with the traditionalist Nahdlatul Ulama more often cite his work on *uṣūl al-fiqh* (*Irshād al-fuḥūl*).

56 Akh. Minhaji, "Ahmad Hassan and Islamic Legal Reform in Indonesia, 1887–1958" (McGill University dissertation, 1997), 181–83.

57 Recently this work also has been made available in a full Indonesian translation, Ibnu Rusydi, *Bidayatul Mujtahid wa Nihayatul Muqtashid* (Jakarta: Trigenda Karya, 1997). My own Arabic copy of this work is a Singapore edition acquired in the Arab quarter near Surabaya's Sunan Ampel mosque – one of Hassan's former stomping grounds. It is an older printing and quite likely that which Hassan would have had access to during his time there. Muḥammad b. Aḥmad b. Muḥammad b. Aḥmad b. Rushd al-Qurṭubī, *Bidāyat al-Mujtahid* (Singapore: al-Ḥaramayn, n.d.).

an inquiry on books recommended for study, Hassan suggested that students with enough Arabic begin with such works as the *Tafsīr Ibn Kathīr, Nayl al-awṭār, Subūl al-salām*, and the *Kitāb bidāyat al-mujtahid.*[58] Not a single title in this list is one that would have been considered a standard reference in the *pesantren* milieu of his day. What he supplies instead is a list of works from various times and places (fourteenth-century Syria, eighteenth-century Yemen, thirteenth-century Andalusia), as well as from diverse *madhhab* orientations (Ḥanbalī, Zaydī, Shāfi'ī, and Mālikī), that had become popular among modern Muslim reformists in the Middle East in the early twentieth century. Through his selection of such works in his own references, Hassan brought new perspectives into the Malay/ Indonesian language discourse on Islamic issues and stimulated productive debates which continue in some ways to this day.

## CRITIQUING "CONSENSUS" AND OTHER INDICATORS

Beyond his particular works on various aspects of the Qur'ān and *ḥadīth*, Hassan attempted to place these two primary sources into the wider framework of a revitalized scripturalist methodology for determining Islamic legal rulings – something which he viewed as crucial for the revitalization of Islam in the lives of individual Muslims as well as Indonesian society as a whole. He wrote about such issues in many of his works, but his most concentrated formulation of general principles appeared in the lengthy preface to *al-Boerhan*, which was published in 1928 in both roman-script Malay and a Sundanese translation and remained one of the only Indonesian-language monographs on the subject until 1959.[59] It was planned as a multivolume work covering various aspects of Islamic law and arranged according to the traditional organization of *fiqh* texts, i.e. starting with the chapters on ritual purity and then working through other issues of *'ibādāt* in sequence before moving on to more worldly matters (*mu'āmalāt*).[60]

In his approach to *fiqh*, Hassan argued that through the critical study of the sources of law and the methods used to apply them, Muslims could free

[58] *Soal-Jawab*, 1497.

[59] In that year an Indonesian scholar at Cairo, A. Hanafie, published a slim Indonesian-language volume that continued some of the conversations initiated by Hassan and even attempts to establish a genealogy of innovative jurisprudential thought that extends through al-Shawkānī from al-Shāṭibī to the Indonesian author Hasbi Ash Shiddieqy, whose work will be discussed in chapter 3. Hanafie's *Usul Fiqh* (Jakarta: Widjaja, 1959) was reprinted three times before 1963.

[60] Hassan paid great attention to following this pattern, as can be seen in his apologetic footnote explaining the accidental transposition of the sections dealing with intention during rites of purification and the use of perfumes (*al-Boerhan*, 73, n. 1).

themselves from the shackles of "blind imitation" (Ind. *taklid buta*) and purify their religion from unnecessary and even dangerous human innovations (*bid'a*). Furthermore he argued that even the imams of the *madhhabs* themselves forbade their followers to imitate them "blindly," a point which, as we shall see, was echoed by a number of other prominent Indonesian Muslim thinkers in the decades that followed.[61] In his re-evaluations of their legacies, however, Hassan had also to account for the various other legal conventions that had come to be established as sources of law (*uṣūl*) in Sunni legal theory. In this he went back to scrutinize the foundations of such extra-scriptural indicators (*istidlāl*) and then reconstruct a methodology of jurisprudence which he considered to be more faithful to the Prophet's message as he understood it. In this way he attempted to find some ultimate grounding for such jurisprudential devices within the Qur'ān and *Sunna* themselves. Once this was accomplished, Hassan argued, reference to any of these indicators in and of themselves would be superfluous.[62] Conversely, any aspect of jurisprudential method that was not well established in the Qur'ān or *Sunna* (as Hassan understood them) was rejected from his scripturalist approach to Islamic law.

A prime example of this may be found in his discussions of *ijmā'* (consensus), in which Hassan distinguished between two types of *ijmā'*: (1) that of the Prophet's companions (*al-ṣaḥāba*), and (2) that of later *'ulamā'*. As for the first, he recognizes it as a valid source of law, maintaining that their consensus must have been validated by Muḥammad himself, either by direct precedent or silent approval.[63] The second type of consensus may be further classified into two types: (a) that which is based directly on the Qur'ān and *Sunna*, and (b) that which is based upon the personal considerations, opinions, and understandings of the *'ulamā'*. Hassan recognizes the first of these, but not as being a source of law in its own right – as in such cases one already had a clear basis for the ruling in scripture.[64] The second type is more problematic for him, as he repeatedly expressed the view that mere opinion can never serve as a valid source of law.[65]

Rather than simply dismissing traditional understandings of *ijma'*, he chose to investigate any possible bases for them in the primary sources of the Qur'ān and *Sunna*. Traditionally, many *'ulamā'* have justified the use of *ijmā'* as a source of law through reference to a small constellation of similarly worded *ḥadīth* texts, the basic import of which is, "My community will never agree upon an error." Hassan was uncomfortably forced to admit

[61] *Soal-Jawab*, 390. [62] E.g. in the case of his discussion of *ijmā'* (consensus), *al-Boerhan*, xxi.
[63] *al-Boerhan*, xli; and *Soal-Jawab*, 23. [64] *al-Boerhan*, xxi. [65] *Soal-Jawab*, 20.

that some variants of this *ḥadīth* are transmitted according to reliable chains of transmission (*isnād* ). Thus he turned to a re-interpretation of the text (*matn*) to make his point, arguing that the basic idea of this *ḥadīth* is that the community of the Prophet will not unanimously do any wrong, since there will always be some among them who do what is right. From this it logically follows that at times all Muslims could be right, and at others some among them may be wrong, but they will never be completely wrong down to the very last believer.[66] Understanding it in this way, he concludes that this *ḥadīth* simply cannot serve as a justification for *ijmā*ʿ as an independent source of law.

Hassan was equally uncomfortable with the ambiguity inherent in the ways in which processes of reasoning by analogy (*qiyās*) had come to be used as a means of determining Islamic legal rulings within the Shāfiʿī *madhhab* and other established schools of Muslim jurisprudence. Thus he argued against the speculative dimensions of analogical reasoning, and advanced various interpretive criteria in an effort to ensure greater fidelity to the literal texts of scripture; for example, he insisted that every new exercise of *qiyās* must make its primary reference to the text of revelation itself, and not simply to an earlier product of analogy.[67] Furthermore, as with the case of any exercise of *ijtihād*, Hassan limited such interpretive work strictly to cases concerning *muʿamalāt* ("worldly transactions") maintaining that any such analogical accretion upon the realm of *ʿibādāt* (religious worship) would be considered the most objectionable form of *bidʿa*.

## QUESTIONS AND ANSWERS

Hassan's positions on aspects of the methodology of Islamic jurisprudence were more concretely expressed and popularly circulated through the decisions published in his prodigious output of magazine column *fatwās*. Many of these texts were compiled into the four volumes of *Soal-Jawab* that have been reprinted numerous times and remain popular with Indonesian readers to this day.[68] The subject matter is loosely arranged in a way similar to that of *fiqh* books, although not with the careful attention to order that

[66] *Soal-Jawab*, 1485.

[67] *al-Boerhan*, xiv–xvii. Hassan himself distinguishes between two kinds of *qiyās*: (1) based in the source of law, and (2) based on the subject matter. For further discussion of this in English, Minhaji, "Ahmad Hassan," 126–63.

[68] The four-volume set has been continuously reprinted for over four decades and copies of it can usually be found in Indonesian bookstores as well as in the private libraries of a great number of Muslims in the country, including many who are not necessarily members of PERSIS or affiliated directly with reforms of its scripturalist stripe. In this collection, the *fatwās* are for the most part

characterized Hassan's organization of *al-Boerhan*. The decisions presented in the various *fatwās* are often rather radical in their departure from traditionalist positions, thus reflecting Hassan's own scripturalist methodology of *fiqh*.

Most editions of *Soal-Jawab* contain a lengthy preface in which Hassan elaborates the methodology employed in his *iftā'*, or the process of issuing a *fatwā*. Elsewhere he has also written on his ideals of the etiquette of *istiftā'*, or asking for a *fatwā*, emphasizing that those requesting a *fatwā* may ask only for the ruling, "according to God and His Prophet," and not according to the teachings of any particular *madhhab*. Thus petitioned, the *mufti* must respond based directly upon his own reading of the Qur'ān and *Sunna*, and in cases where a *mufti* feels uncomfortable basing his decision on an unsupported analogy, Hassan states that he must humbly admit that he does not know the correct ruling and allow the questioner to seek his answer elsewhere.[69]

The majority of the *fatwās* contained in *Soal-Jawab* concern themselves with matters of *'ibādāt*, and on such subjects Hassan maintains an adamant rejection of all religious practices for which a firm foundation cannot be found in the Qur'ān and *Sunna*. Any traditional observations lacking a clear scriptural precedent are to be regarded as *bid'a* and subsequently abandoned. One example of Hassan's reaction to such practices comes in his *fatwā* on various aspects of the traditional celebration of Muḥammad's birthday (*mawlid al-nabī*) in the Indonesian Archipelago, which often included the ritual recitation of poems in Arabic. Questions concerning the legitimacy and regulation of *Mawlid* observances have long posed a problem to Muslim jurists of a reformist orientation. Despite their efforts, they have often been unable to overcome the popular enthusiasm for these traditions in many parts of the Muslim world.[70]

Some prominent modern *'ulamā'* in Indonesia as elsewhere have resorted to issuing ambiguous responses in order to avoid provoking negative public reactions. Hassan, however, did not shy away from controversy and refused to compromise his position on the issue. Not only did he condemn the

written by Hassan, although a number of them were also contributed by his PERSIS colleagues, including Mohammad Ma'sum and H. Mahmud Aziz.

[69] Such an emphasis on the *mufti*'s humility in admitting the limitations of his own knowledge is something related about Hassan himself by several of his biographers.

[70] For an overview of the development of these observances and the scholarly opinions on them in the pre-modern Arab world and Muslim West, N. J. G. Kaptein, *Muhammad's Birthday Festival* (Leiden: E. J. Brill, 1993). Kaptein has also published the text of a collection of Meccan *fatwās* that were published with Malay translations in the late nineteenth century, some of which dealt with this same subject: *The Muhimmāt al-Nafā'is: A Bilingual Meccan Fatwa Collection for Indonesian Muslims from the End of the Nineteenth Century* (Jakarta: INIS, 1997), 50–51, 156, 58, 160, 64, 163.

practice of standing up at a certain point in the recitation of a poem in praise of the Prophet, a subject which had long been a favorite with reformist polemicists,[71] but he also issued a more general ruling which discouraged the ritual recitation of these texts altogether.[72] While at first this appears as a simple matter of the application of Hassan's scripturalist position on matters of *ʿibādāt*, it is also indicative of broader epistemological dimensions to his thought. For, later on in the text of this same *fatwā*, we read:

> Reading a book in Arabic without understanding what is written in it is offensive to Reason and prohibited by Religion [i.e. Islam], because Religion has been given to us in order to make us understand, not to make us more ignorant.[73]

Here we have a striking and concise expression of Hassan's larger worldview and especially his rejection of the traditionalist religious epistemology associated with Muslim education in the *pesantren* milieu.

In that system, the Islamic religious texts were read and memorized in Arabic, with the teachers sometimes providing partial translations, interpretations, and/or summaries in Malay or the pupils' native language. Such methods of learning by rote were the antithesis of Hassan's own, substantially auto-didactic, education which placed emphasis more on first obtaining requisite proficiency in the languages needed for further independent study. Seen in this light, Hassan's critique of one apparently irrational religious practice functions to support a much wider platform of religious reformism, including the movements for educational reform described in chapter 1. What Hassan advocates here is an ostensibly pragmatic understanding of ritual practice that could complement a more modern lifestyle.[74] It is not however, necessarily, an appeal to the more

[71] *Soal-Jawab*, 371–74. For more on the debates of this issue in the Indonesian context see N. Kaptein, "The Berdiri Mawlid Issue among Indonesian Muslims in the Period from c. 1875 to 1930," *BKI* 149 (1993): 124–53.

[72] Hassan also advised against such practices in connection with the commemoration of any revered figure from the Muslim past, arguing that if one was truly intent on remembering the life and works of a particular person that the most appropriate tribute simply would be to write a sober biographical account of them designed to be read as would any other book (*Soal-Jawab*, 1507–10). This particular observation was made in a *fatwā* concerning the ritual recitation of the *manāqib* of the Sufi 'saint' (Ar. *walī*) ʿAbd al-Qādir al-Jilānī; formerly a widespread practice in some areas of the Archipelago, see G. W. J. Drewes, and R. Ng. Poerbatjaraka, *De Mirakelen van Abdoel-Kadir Djaelani* (Bandoeng: A. C. Nix & Co., 1938). Modern Islamic reformism has had a tremendous impact on the production of Indonesian texts dealing with the lives of highly regarded Muslim personages from the Indonesian Archipelago. See R. Michael Feener, "Shaykh Yusuf and the Appreciation of Muslim 'Saints' in Modern Indonesia," *Journal for Islamic Studies* 18 (1999): 112–31.

[73] *Soal-Jawab*, 374.

[74] This trend is evident in the work of other early twentieth-century Indonesian reformers as well. For example, in the preface to an official school text on Islamic ritual obligations, Mahmud Yunus (d. 1982) let students know that his instructions for how to properly perform the Hajj were, "based

rationalized interpretations of Islam along the lines being developed by Muḥammad Abduh and some of his younger contemporaries in Egypt.[75] In fact, Hassan tended more toward the Salafism of Abduh's Syrian *protégé* Rashīd Riḍā than any form of explicit rationalism of the kind sometimes referred to as Neo-Mu'tazilism.

Aside from the *fatwās* on issues of religious practice *per se*, the *Soal-Jawab* compendia also include decisions on some of the foremost social issues of his day, particularly those that became central to the religious and political debates between the reformists and their opposition.[76] These included, for example, the sayyid controversy on the question of whether a female descendant of the Prophet was allowed to marry a non-*sayyid*. In some Muslim cultures this had been prohibited under consideration that such descent marked one off as a member of a special group of Muslims with distinct rights and privileges. The Hadrami sayyids associated with the Jami'iyyat Khair maintained the importance of such distinctions, but they were rejected by reformists such as Aḥmad Sūrkatī, who argued that such hierarchies had no sound basis in the Qur'ān and *Sunna* and violated the basic Islamic principle of the equality of all believers before God.[77] Hassan held a similar position on this issue, and issued a *fatwā* that accused those who would prohibit such intermarriage of "forbidding what God has made lawful."[78]

Hassan's radical approach to the methodological issues underlying the formation of Islamic legal decisions had a profound impact on developments in Indonesian Islam during the early part of the twentieth century. As

upon my own practice in the Holy Land, and not according the 'theories' found in the *fiqh* texts commonly studied in Islamic religious schools, because there is a great difference between theory and practice." Mahmud Yunus, *Haji ke Mekkah: Seri ibadat untuk kanak-kanak dan dewasa* (Jakarta: Hidakarya Agung, 1979, 13th reprint).

[75] For more on these modern movements espousing more rationalization of Islamic religious thought, see Robert Caspar, "Le Renouveau du Mo'tazilisme," *MIDEO* 4 (1957): 144–201; and Khalid, Deltev, "Some Aspects of Neo-Mu'tazilism," *Islamic Studies* 8 (1969): 319–47. It was considerably later that Indonesian thinkers such as Harun Nasution began to draw on such developments. See Harun Nasution, *Muhammad Abduh dan Teologi Rasional Mu'tazilah* (Jakarta: UI Press, 1987); and *Islam Rasional: Gagasan dan Pemikiran* (Bandung: Mizan, 1995). For an English-language introduction to these developments, Richard C. Martin and Mark Woodward, with Dwi S. Atmaja, *Defenders of Reason in Islam: Mu'tazilism from Medieval School to Modern Symbol* (Oxford: One World, 1997).

[76] For further discussions of some of Hassan's more important *fatwā*, see Minhaji, *Ahmad Hassan*, 200–90.

[77] For more on the *Sayyid* debate in the Netherlands Indies, Huub de Jonge, "Discord and Solidarity among the Arabs in the Netherlands East Indies," *Indonesia* 55 (1993): 73–90.

[78] *Soal-Jawab*, 581. For an outstanding overview of the trope of permission and prohibition and the history of its interpretation in Muslim societies outside Southeast Asia, see Michael Cook, *Commanding Right and Forbidding Wrong in Islamic Thought* (Cambridge: Cambridge University Press, 2001).

a pioneer of a vigorous agenda of publicizing *ijtihād* in modern Southeast Asia, he was a prominent proponent of bringing the discussion of Islamic religious and legal issues outside the walls of traditionalist *pesantren* and into the emerging Indonesian public sphere. Not all of those reading Hassan's popular columns may have agreed with his particular stances on certain issues, but many were nonetheless attracted to the more general message of reform and the empowerment of rank-and-file Muslims, such as this former tire vulcanizer from Singapore, to exercise *ijtihād* for themselves.

Some have argued that Hassan's stringent rulings on particular issues were unacceptable to the majority of Indonesian Muslims, and because of this he may have alienated more people than he attracted. It is not in connection with any particular *fatwā*, however, that Hassan's influence on the history of Islam in Indonesia was most significant. Rather what has made a much more considerable impact upon subsequent developments of Indonesian discourse on Islamic law was the attention Hassan placed on developing a "clear" model of *ijtihād* based upon an explicitly stated scripturalist line of interpretation. This aspect of his work comes through most clearly in his handbook of jurisprudential methodology entitled *al-Boerhan*, where Hassan developed critical expositions of established means of determining Islamic legal rulings to the Indonesian Muslim community at large. This important aspect of Hassan's work, however, has been largely neglected by most historians commenting on his work. For while his "blasting open of the gate of *ijtihād*" as sounded through his sometimes fiery *fatwās* was important, Hassan's contribution to the development of twentieth-century Indonesian Islamic discourse includes more than just that. For not only did he "open" the gate of *ijtihād*, but he also attempted to demonstrate that any real reform would have to be accomplished through a comprehensive approach to scripture and its interpretation, rather than simply tinkering with outdated and inconvenient legal rulings. Thus Hassan can be seen to have exercised a significant influence on Indonesian Islam that extends well beyond the limited circles of PERSIS alone.[79]

[79] Some members of PERSIS do take a particular pride in maintaining Hassan's spirit of *ijtihād*, while at the same time recognizing the limitations of his treatments of particular issues. For example, in the 1996 edition of *Pengajaran Shalat*, a notice is inserted on the last page which acknowledges that A. Hassan did not cover every aspect of the subject as a matter of course. Thus the editors of the *Majalah al-Muslimun* at Bangil openly solicit questions and suggestions to be considered in the preparation of subsequent editions: A. Hassan, *Pengajaran Shalat: Cara Shalat beserta Dalil-dalil-nya* (Bangil: Pustaka Tamaam, 1996), 326. In addition to this, a number of significant authors and public figures have worked to continue the project of Hassan in the area of scripturalist reform, including his son Abdul Qadir Hassan and the former of Dewan Da'wah Islam Indonesia (DDII), Anwar Harjono, see Robert W. Hefner, "Print Islam: Mass Media and Ideological Rivalries among Indonesian Muslims,"

## MOENAWAR CHALIL

Moenawar Chalil was born into a family of traders and religious scholars at Kendal, Central Java in 1908.[80] Like Hassan he began his religious education under his father, and then moved on to study under other prominent local religious teachers (Jv. *Kiyai*), including his uncle. However Chalil never combined this traditional style of religious education with studies in a modern style school. Instead his initiation into the world of modern institutions came when he joined the local branch of Sarekat Islam at the age of seventeen. There he became involved in some of the group's more militant activities that eventually resulted in a government order for Chalil's imprisonment. However due to his father's prominent local connections, the order was stayed in consideration that Chalil would be sent by his father to continue his religious studies in Arabia. He stayed in Mecca from 1926 to 1929, during which time Wahhābī interpretations of Islam had become dominant in the Hijaz under Saudi rule. As no extensive data is currently available on just who his teachers in Arabia were or what circles he studied in there, it is difficult to document his explicitly Wahhābī ties, although it does appear that in the Hijaz he further immersed himself in reformist thought, continuing a development that he had already begun back in Central Java with other members of Sarekat Islam.

Nevertheless it would be quite misleading to label Chalil as simply a Wahhābī *protégé*, as through his readings in Arabic he also developed a considerable appreciation of the modernist writings of Muḥammad Abduh and that scholar's considerable openness to the role of reason in the interpretation of religious texts.[81] However Chalil does not seem to have gone as far as Abduh in this, as he strove to keep any exercise of rational interpretation within the bounds of conformity to a scripturalist regard for the

*Indonesia* 64 (1997): 77–104. Hefner has also noted the role of Hassan in introducing M. Natsir to the writings of the Indian Islamist leader Abul A'la Mawdudi, thus introducing yet another stream of radicalism into the emerging Indonesian discourse on the relationship between Islam and government (*Civil Islam*, 103). The work of Natsir and Harjono will be discussed further in chapter 4.

80 Published biographies of Moenawar Chalil are considerably rarer than those available for Hassan. Most of what has been written is in the form of short, unpublished papers in Indonesia. The only systematic work done in this area to date has been by Dr. Thoha Hamim in his 1996 McGill University dissertation, "Moenawar Chalil's Reformist Thought: A Study of an Indonesian Religious Scholar (1908–1961)," 26–56.

81 Some attempt at evaluating the formulation of a fusion of the ideologies of Wahhābism and Egyptian Modernism may have been undertaken by Chalil himself in a work entitled *Dua Sedjoli Pembangun Alam Islamy: Muhammad Abdul Wahhab dan Muhammad Abduh*. Unfortunately I have only seen reference to this rare and difficult to locate work in secondary sources and have as yet been unable to examine the work itself ("H. Moenawar Chalil," *Minggu Abadi*, Feb. 25, 1960).

Qur'ānic text and reliable *ḥadīth*. It is in this sense that one might perceive a certain Wahhābī influence, although here similar ideas could also have been had from the emerging Salafism of Rashīd Riḍā and his fellow travelers.[82]

After Indonesian independence in 1945, Chalil found employment in government service, and eventually became the head of the Ministry of Religious Affairs district office in Semarang, Central Java, although when his reformist principles came into conflict with the terms of his government employment, he chose to resign. Thereafter he returned to his activities in various Islamic reformist voluntary associations, especially with the Muhammadiyah, for which he served as a teacher in its Madrasah al-Wusta and the Majlis Tabligh. Within this same organization he also became a member of the Central Majlis Tarjih, an internal body organized to respond to the growing number of requests for *fatwās* advanced by Muhammadiyah members.[83] Chalil also served in similar positions in other similar *fatwā*-producing bodies, including a term spent as the chair of the Majlis Ulama PERSIS and later of the Central Majlis Shura of Masjumi.[84] In such capacities he was able to broadcast his views on legal issues broadly through these organizations' regular publications and other public announcements.[85]

Since Chalil's return from his period of study in the Middle East he had become increasingly active in Islamic voluntary associations and continued to pursue such opportunities to spread the reformist message into new areas and venues. In 1935 he began publication of *Swara Islam*, which although not formally associated with PERSIS adopted a format quite similar to that of that organization's popular organs of *ijtihād* journalism. It contained regular columns in the question-and-answer (*soal-jawab*) format of "magazine *fatwās*," polemical articles on various aspects of ritual practice, and transcriptions of Chalil's often sharp debates with various opponents, much like those of A. Hassan printed in *Pembela Islam*. *Swara Islam*, however, was published in Javanese rather than Malay, becoming quite possibly the first (and only) journal of its kind in that language. Previously Islamic

[82] Thus, for example, in the bibliography attached to *Kembali Kepada al-Qur'an dan As-Sunnah*, Chalil lists as a source Riḍā's *al-Wahdat al-Islāmiyya*, but not a single work by Abduh.

[83] The Majlis Tarjih Muhammadiyyah was founded during the organization's conference at Yogyakarta in 1928. Abdul Rahman Asmuni, *Majlis Tarjih Muhammadiyah* (Yogyakarta: IAIN Sunan Kalijaga, 1985).

[84] This organization was first established by the Japanese wartime administration and later transformed into an Islamic political party after Indonesian independence in 1945.

[85] Chalil published frequently in the Masjumi daily *Abadi* and the journal *Hikmah*, edited by M. Natsir, as well as many informally affiliated publications such as *Panji Masjarakat* which has had strong ties to the Muhammadiyah.

reformist publications in Southeast Asia were printed in either Arab-script or Latin-script Malay, although PERSIS did take the remarkable step of publishing a considerable amount of material in Sundanese. Javanese, however, was the language with the largest number of native speakers in the Netherlands Indies, many of whom tended to identify more closely with the traditionalist leadership of rural *pesantren* than with the modernizing urban reformists. With the publication of *Swara Islam*, Chalil made a significant effort to advance the cause of Islamic reform among his fellow Javanese in ways that combined aspects of modern and *Salafi* agendas with a qualified appreciation of local traditions of Islamic learning.

## SANTRI SCRIPTURALISM

In addition to his ongoing activities in the Muhammadiyyah, PERSIS, and later Masjumi, Chalil was also involved with another organization that played a significant, although as yet largely unrecognized role, in the development of Muslim jurisprudence in twentieth-century Indonesia, the Lajnah Ahli-ahli Hadith Indonesia. This association dedicated to the reform of religious learning through a renewed emphasis on the study of *ḥadīth* was founded at Solo in June 1941 under the direction of Imam Ghozali along with other like-minded reformists such as Muhammad Ma'shum of PERSIS. The project of the revitalized *ḥadīth* study as advocated by the *Lajnah* reflects the prime importance that Chalil placed on the *Sunna* in his written works.[86]

Reflecting on the history of Islamic education in Indonesia, one can better appreciate just how revolutionary this modern and self-conscious re-emphasis of *Sunna*-oriented piety was. For up until that time, *ḥadīth* studies as such were rarely taught as part of the traditional *pesantren* curriculum except where specific traditions were incorporated into works of traditionalist *fiqh*.[87] In the *pesantren* milieu there was little primary research into the standard *ḥadīth* compilations, and almost none of the critical studies of the texts and their transmitters known in the larger world of Muslim scholarship as *al-jarḥ wa'l- ta'dīl.* Thus the newly energized attention to the texts of *ḥadīth* as a direct source of law, rather than in their "processed" form as part of scholastic tradition, reflects the shift in understandings of religious knowledge and authority effected by modern Muslim reform movements. In the Arab Middle East, for example, reformers produced new compendia of *fiqh* based on more vigorous conceptualizations of *Sunna*, one of the

[86] *Kembali kepada Al Qur'an dan As-Sunnah*, 7–9, 73–75.
[87] van Bruinessen, "Kitab Kuning," 226–69.

most popular of these being the *Fiqh al-Sunna* of Sayyid Sābiq (d. 2000).[88] Similar works, however, were also generated by Indonesian scholars themselves including the eighteen-volume *al-Fiqh al-Nabawwy: Fiqih Berdasar Atas Pimpinan Nabi s.a.w.* that Chalil co-authored with Imam Ghozali.[89]

A more concise source for understanding Chalil's emphasis on *ḥadīth* study for projects of Islamic religious reform can be found in what has come to be viewed as his signature work, *Kembali kepada al Qur'an dan As-Sunnah* ("Return to the Qur'ān and the *Sunna*"), first published in 1956.[90] In the original author's preface to this work, Chalil makes it clear that he intended it to be a sequel to his *Biografi Empat Serangkai Imam Mazhab*,[91] as well as a prologue to his larger work of *Fiqh al-Nabawwy. Kembali kepada al Qur'an dan As-Sunnah* is divided into two major sections, the first of which consists of short chapters each of which focuses on a select few Qur'ānic verses or *ḥadīth* texts which explain the position of the Qur'ān and *Sunna* as the fundamental guides for belief and human conduct.[92] In the second section, chapters are devoted to establishing the Qur'ān and *ḥadīth* as the primary sources of law and defining their relationship to such extra-scriptural legal sources as *ijmā'* and *qiyās* within the context of debates on *ijtihād, taqlīd, ittibā'* and the related issues of *bid'a* and adherence to one of the four established *madhhabs*.

Among these chapters the one in which Chalil discusses *maṣlaḥa*, or the consideration of public interest as a source of law, is of particular importance for later developments in Indonesian Islam.[93] There Chalil emphasized the

88 This work intended to provide a comprehensive handbook of normative practice and it advertised itself as closely based upon reliable prophetic traditions and the text of the Qur'ān. Such a streamlined statement of orthopraxy was seen in the service of reuniting an internally fractured Muslim community. As the author himself states in the introduction, "By blindly following the *madhhabs* and losing the guidance of the Qur'ān and *Sunna* and by closing the door to juristic reasoning, this nation lost its unity . . . which the Messenger of Allah, upon whom be peace, had warned about." An Indonesian translation of this work has since become available: Sayyid Sabiq, *Tarjamah dan Koreksi Fiqhus Sunnah*, trans. M. Thalib (Bandung: Gema Risalah Press, 1996).

89 This work was published at Solo by Al-Ma'murijah publishers (n.d.).

90 Since then it has gone through at least ten reprints. References to this work throughout the present study are to Moenawar Chalil, *Kembali kepada Al Qur'an dan As-Sunnah* (Jakarta: Bulan Bintang, 1996), 10th edn.

91 Moenawar Chalil, *Biografi Empat Serangkai Imam Mazhab* (Jakarta: Bulan Bintang, 1955). More will be said on this work below.

92 It should be noted that in this work Chalil himself explicitly emphasized that the Qur'ān remains the first source of law; thus agreeing with Hassan in the general reformist program of maintaining the prominence of the text above all else, *Kembali kepada Al Qur'an dan As-Sunnah*, 14–17, 25–48. The *Sunna* then serves to clarify and specify the rulings of the Qur'ān in an established position as the second source of law, *ibid.*: 192, 202–09.

93 For an overview of *maṣlaḥa* in Sunni legal theory, see Hallaq, *History of Islamic Legal Theories*, 112–13. For a brief overview of the role of *maṣlaḥa* in informing decisions by *fatwā* councils in modern Indonesia, see Khoiruddin Nasution, "*Maslahah* and Its Application in Indonesian *Fatwā*," *SI* 3.4 (1996): 103–36.

importance of *munāsaba* (suitability) and the five universals (*kulliāt al-khams*)[94] that must be used as a determination of what is to be regarded as the public interest in relation to the broader aims of the law (*maqāṣid al-sharī'a*). In doing so he quotes rather extensively from al-Shawkānī's *Irshād al-fuḥūl*, including that author's recapitulations of previous positions taken by al-Qarāfī (d. 1285), al-Juwayni (d. 1085), and others who recognized various considerations of *maṣlaḥa mursala* in the Sunni *madhhabs*. Chalil further supports his conceptualization of *maṣlaḥa* as a basis for legal rulings in this chapter by reference to the work of the medieval Ḥanbalī jurist Najm al-Dīn Ṭūfī (d. 1316) in building upon al-Shawkānī's argument that while *al-maṣāliḥ al-mursala* may be used as a method to guide one's investigations into a particular ruling, it may not serve as a source of law in and of itself.[95]

Chalil's chapter on considerations of public interest in the context of *fiqh* is one of the first extensive treatments of the topic in Southeast Asian Islamic literature and thus became one of the major ways in which these conversations were initiated among modern Muslim reformers in the archipelago.[96] Over the second half of the twentieth century, *maṣlaḥa* has become a central topic of public debate over the interpretation of Islamic law in Indonesia with regard to a broad range of issues. Chalil, however, introduced the concept in a more restricted sense, insisting that considerations of *maṣlaḥa* can only figure into the formation of Islamic legal rulings for issues of inter-personal affairs (*mu'āmalāt*). For Chalil maintains, as does Hassan, that any such extra-scriptural legal indicator has no bearing upon matters of ritual practice (*'ibādāt*). Any such modification to the rules explicitly established by God's revelation would amount to *bid'a* and as such was strongly condemned by both of these prominent PERSIS spokesmen.[97]

In thus delineating the spheres of *'ibādāt* and *mu'āmalāt* in relation to the issue of *maṣlāḥa mursāla*, Chalil reveals a reflection of the way in which he understands these same distinctions in the larger context of the issue of *ijtihād* and *taqlīd*. Chalil agreed with Hassan that while the gate of *ijtihād* remains always open, it is to be exercised only in cases dealing with *mu'āmalāt*.[98] In that sphere, *ijtihād* may be exercised by anyone with the requisite ability to understand and interpret the texts, and in fact the

94 That is, the protection of life, religion, property, thought, and progeny.

95 *Kembali Kepada al Qur-an dan As-Sunnah*, 257–58.

96 No other earlier discussion of *maṣlaḥa* (such as those evoked on the pages of early reformist *ijtihād* journalism) has had the good fortune of remaining in print for over five decades. Chalil's *Kembali Kepada al-Qur'an dan As-Sunnah* has enjoyed nearly constant reprintings to this day by a string of Indonesian publishers.

97 For more on Chalil's objections to *bid'a* see *Kembali Kepada al-Qur'an dan As-Sunnah*, 276–81.

98 *Kembali Kepada al-Qur'an dan As-Sunnah*, 373.

practice of such *ijtihād* is necessary if Islam is to maintain its relevance to the lives of Muslims in changing times. For those who cannot fulfill these basic requirements of a modern *mujtahid*, however, Chalil (like Hassan) prescribes *ittibā'* which he interprets as following the example of the Prophet and his companions and not that of the later jurists of any of the established schools.[99] Thus when asking for a *fatwā* a petitioner should also demand to be shown the Qur'ānic verse or *ḥadīth* texts upon which the *mufti*'s decision is based. In this spirit of "returning to the basic sources" (*Kembali Kepada al-Qur'an dan As-Sunnah*) every Muslim can be liberated from the shackles of *taqlīd* as it was understood by Chalil and the other PERSIS reformists.

## BETWEEN PERSIS AND THE *PESANTREN* LEGACY

Despite these appeals for *ijtihād*, however, Chalil never went to the extent of a complete rejection of the intellectual legacies of the Islamic religious sciences. This may be at least in part a reflection of the strong links that he had and maintained to the world of the Javanese *kyai* and his generally more appreciative attitude toward aspects of *fiqh*, the established *madhhabs*, and the *pesantren* tradition than was common among Hassan and his other PERSIS colleagues. Chalil continued to maintain a qualified respect for the authority of previous scholarship and interpretation in the field of *fiqh*. For all of his radical rhetoric of reform, Chalil remained convinced that the job of legislating in accordance with the Qur'ān and *Sunna* is best left to those with specialized training in the religious sciences who would balance the scriptural precepts contained therein with more general considerations of the particular demands of life in a modernizing world. Such a model of authority is one in which Chalil, with his background in the tradition of Javano-Muslim scholarship that entitled him to use the title of *Kyai*, could comfortably fit.[100] It is one that would not appear to be as accommodating to Chalil's contemporary Hassan, with his limited formal education and checkered career as a printer, petty trader, and tireman.[101]

Thus in Chalil we can see something of a tendency to moderate the extreme kind of scripturalist reformism represented by Hassan; one which

99 *Kembali Kepada al-Qur'an dan As-Sunnah*, 376–78.

100 For instance, in some places he tends to accept the authority of some later *'ulamā'* as authoritative without conducting an investigation of their individual rulings himself. Thus we often read such statements as, "Imam Suyūṭī delcares this *ḥadīth* sound . . ." etc. in the course of his arguments.

101 Although Federspiel has noted something of a greater relative openness to some aspects of traditionalist scholarship in the later development of the Bangil branch of PERSIS. Federspiel, *Islam and Ideology*, 267–68.

seems to have left a much more enduring, broad-based impression upon subsequent developments in Indonesian Islam. From the writings of Hassan to those of Chalil one can notice something of a shift in orientation which came to have significant consequences for emerging debates in the areas of *fiqh* and *uṣūl al-fiqh*. Like Hassan, he drew heavily upon the works of Rashīd Riḍā and *Salafi* press editions of medieval Ḥanbalī authorities such Ibn al-Qayyim al-Jawziyya (d. 1350), as well as the work of al-Shawkānī. However Chalil also looked to other sources for inspiration, including modern Egyptian writers carrying forward aspects of Abduh's rationalizing approach to Islamic religious reform, such as Muḥammad Ḥusayn Haykal and Muṣṭafā al-Manfaluṭī.[102]

Alongside such modern Muslim writers, Chalil continued to cite medieval Muslim scholars known to local curricula of *pesantren* and other traditionalist schools in the earlier history of Southeast Asian Islam, such as the Qur'ān exegetes Baghawī (d. 1122) and al-Khāzin (d. 1340). Such authorities had come to be largely abandoned by later reformers for their use of unreliable *ḥadīth* and *isra'iliyyāt*, but Chalil continues to keep them part of the conversation, albeit in a critical engagement.[103] Thus Chalil's scripturalism, unlike that of Hassan, was not necessarily that of everyman but rather one which was to be left in the hands of trained religious specialists, albeit not those of the traditionalist *'ulamā'*. He thus mapped out the territory for a new type of Muslim religious authority, one who had acquired a thorough knowledge of the established sources of Islamic law, but who was not bound by the framework of a particular *madhhab*.

Chalil's critiques of *taqlīd* then did not necessarily imply a rejection of all past scholarship in the Islamic religious sciences. Rather he advanced examples of ways in which such legacies could be constructively used in the formation of a new legal theory and a revitalization of the Sharī'a that was responsive to the changing needs of the times. His creative reorientation toward traditional Muslim scholarship is perhaps most clearly reflected in his volume of biographies of the imams of the four established Sunni *madhhabs*. In that work he emphasized in particular those attributes of the imams which reflect modern Muslim reformist concerns: their love for and defense of the Qur'ān and *Sunna*, their courage in proclaiming the truth, and their forthrightness. Thence Chalil went on to outline each of the four schools' theories on the sources (*uṣūl*) of law in order to emphasize that each of these *madhhabs* represents not a static body of rulings but rather a

102 Munawar Chalil, *Nilai Wanita* (Jakarta: Alma'arif, 1954).

103 For an overview of the decline of *isra'iliyyāt* and other narrative forms of early *tafsīr* in Southeast Asia, see Feener, "Notes toward a History of Qur'ānic Exegesis," 53–54.

methodology through which one can derive legal rulings based primarily upon the Qur'ān and *Sunna*. He thus argued that the true way of the Imams is not *taqlīd*, but rather following them in *ijtihād*.[104] In this way he strove to balance an appreciation of the great Muslim scholars of the past with the reformist ideal of transcending the reified boundaries between the various *madhhabs* in the interest of Muslim unity.[105]

Chapters 6 and 7 will explore further later Indonesian attempts to rejuvenate *madhhab* methodology in the service of reformist agendas. Before that, however, chapter 3 will take up developments in the early decades of Indonesian independence in which an upsurge of nationalist sentiment contributed to movements for the creation of a new, Indonesian national school of jurisprudence.

104 Moenawar Chalil, *Biografi Empat Serangkai Imam Mazhab* (Jakarta: Bulan Bintang, 1955), 194–95.
105 *Kembali Kepada al-Qur'an dan As-Sunnah*, 378–83.

CHAPTER 3

# *An "Indonesian* madhhab"

> Frequently in one part of the world, that is held for the law of nations, which is not so in another. Now this law of nations is proved in the same manner as the unwritten civil law, and that is by the continual experience and testimony of the Sages of the Law.
>
> Hugo Grotius, *De Jure Belli ac Pacis*

Over the first few decades following the achievement of national independence in 1945 the fledgling nation of Indonesia faced new struggles as it sought to define itself.[1] During this time, conflicts between the Nationalists, Socialists, Communists, and Islamists were most pronounced in debates over the constitutional basis for the state and the model of law promulgated by it. It was in this context that some Indonesian thinkers began a movement that was unprecedented in the history of Islamic law: the creation of a new "national" *madhhab* for the Muslim inhabitants of the Republic. These developments were significantly affected by the drastic changes in the politics and social order of the newly independent country, while at the same time deeply rooted in the legal models of the former colonial state.[2] Under the Dutch, the institutional role of Islamic law in many Muslim areas of their East Indies territories was progressively subsumed within a system of legal administration characterized by a complex congeries of courts ruling according to the Dutch colonial code and various local systems of customary law (*adatrecht*). Developments in both the colonial discourse of *adat* law and Islamist reactions against it combined in rather unexpected ways to contribute to movements for the creation of a new "national school of *fiqh*" (*madzhab nasional, madzhab Indonesia*) in

[1] The material covered in this chapter has been previously published as R. Michael Feener, "Indonesian Movements for the Creation of a 'National *Madhhab*'," *Islamic Law and Society* 9.1 (2002): 83–115.

[2] The legacy of Dutch colonial law weighed heavy on the young Indonesian Republic and to a certain extent this remains true today. A measure of the state of things through the late New Order period may be gleaned from the extensive legal materials compiled in *De Wetboeken, Wetten en Verordeningen, Benevens de Grondwet van de Republiek Indonesië* (Jakarta: P. T. Ichtiar Baru,-van Hoeve, 1992).

the early Indonesian Republic. In this chapter these developments will be approached through an examination of the two figures who wrote most extensively on the subject: Hasbi Ash Shiddieqy and Hazairin.

## THE MOBILIZATION OF ISLAM IN WARTIME INDONESIA

Along with other political and economic factors, the colonial manipulation of Islamic law in several parts of the Archipelago further contributed to the resentment against the Dutch administration felt by local *'ulamā'*. This was particularly the case in Aceh at the northern tip of Sumatra which, in the early decades of the twentieth century, had only recently come fully under direct Dutch control. Although the incursion of Dutch economic and political hegemony had long met resistance from Muslim leaders there, the opposition now assumed more modernized forms such as that of the Persatuan Ulama-Ulama Seluruh Aceh (PUSA), founded in 1939 by Mohammad Daud Beureu'eh. The frustration and resentment felt by many Indonesian Muslims seems to have facilitated also the relatively warm reception that the Japanese received from some of them upon first taking the islands from Dutch control in the name of the "Great East Asian Co-Prosperity Sphere" (Jp. *Dai-tōa kyōei-ken*).[3]

Under the Japanese occupation, Indonesian Islam underwent remarkable changes in structure and organization as modern methods were employed for the mobilization of the Muslim population.[4] As M. C. Ricklefs has pointed out, while both the Dutch and the Japanese wanted to control Indonesia for their own interests, they pursued this objective in very different ways.[5] The Dutch were accustomed to imposing an "orderly quiet" on Muslim activities in their colonies whereas the Japanese, strapped by imposing wartime demands for energy and resources, chose to administer through mass mobilization. As a result, a number of Muslim groups that

[3] The best study of developments in Indonesian Islam during the Japanese occupation remains H. J. Benda, *The Crescent and the Rising Sun: Indonesian Islam under the Japanese Occupation 1942–1945* (The Hague: W. van Hoeve, 1958). Useful information on the organizational and mobilization policies of the Japanese in Indonesia can be found in the selection of primary sources translated in Harry J. Benda, James K. Irikura, and Koichi Kishi, eds., *Japanese Military Administration in Indonesia: Selected Documents* (New Haven: Yale University Southeast Asia Studies, 1965), 133–65.

[4] However, there were also other contemporary mobilizations of the Indonesian population at this time, including that of the Indonesian Communist Party (PKI). For more on these counter-mobilizations, see Anton Lucas, *Local Opposition and Underground Resistance to the Japanese in Java, 1942–1945* (Melbourne: Monash University Centre of Southeast Asian Studies, 1986).

[5] M. C. Ricklefs, *A History of Modern Indonesia c. 1300 to the Present* (Bloomington: Indiana University Press, 1993), 201–11.

were strengthened by Japanese institutional support emerged from the war more powerful than they had ever been under the Dutch.[6] Following the surrender of the Japanese, Muslim groups which had gained a more organized power base and more sophisticated political skills played an important role in the early formation of the independent Republic of Indonesia.[7]

Even before the Japanese surrender, however, Indonesian Muslims had begun to assert their political will. In June of 1945, the nine members of Soekarno's Advisory Council came to a compromise on a draft for the Preamble to the Constitution that came to be known as the "Jakarta Charter" (*Piagam Jakarta*). This document included the controversial pronouncement that the Republic was founded on a set of principles, the first of which being "the belief in God, with the obligations for adherents of Islam to practice Islamic law."[8] The second clause in this phrase was later struck from the preamble as a concession to the Christian populations of the eastern archipelago. This move was viewed by some Muslim Indonesians as a betrayal of their aspirations for independence and an ungracious recompense for their participation in the struggles that led to it.[9]

As resentment mounted in some sectors of the Indonesian Muslim community over the wording of the final version of the Preamble to the Constitution as well as the Nationalists' stance toward organized Islamic religious and political groups more generally, the government of the new Republic realized that certain compromises would have to be made. One of the most significant of these was the establishment of an Indonesian Ministry of Religious Affairs in January 1946.[10] The organization of this ministry

[6] For more on the intricate relationship of the Japanese Occupational Administration and the religious leadership of Muslim Indonesia, see Yasuko Kobayashi, "Kyai and the Japanese Military," *SI* 4.3 (1997): 65–98.

[7] On August 14, 1945, the very day of the bombings that led to the Japanese surrender, Kartosuwirjo proclaimed the Islamic state *Negara Islam Indonesia*, and within a few months of the Japanese surrender, the Muslim umbrella organization *Masjumi* transformed itself into a political party at a meeting in Yogyakarta. See B. J. Boland, *The Struggle of Islam in Modern Indonesia* (The Hague: Martinus Nijhoff, 1982), 42; and Karl D. Jackson, *Traditional Authority, Islam, and Rebellion: A Study of Indonesian Political Behavior* (Berkeley: University of California Press, 1980), 9.

[8] "ke-Tuhanan, dengan kewadjiban mendjalankan sjari'at Islam bagi pemeluk-pemeluknja . . .", Muhammad Yamin, *Naskah Persiapan Undang-undang Dasar 1945* (Jakarta, 1959–60), I, 145. See also Boland, *The Struggle of Islam*, 26, and Appendix I. This phrase came to be referred to as the "Seven Words" in later constitutional debates.

[9] Appendices containing some relevant primary materials can be found in H. Endang Saifuddin Anshari, *Piagam Jakarta, 22 Juni 1945: Sebuah Konsensus Nasional tentang Dasar Negara Republik Indonesia, 1945–1949* (Jakarta: Gema Insani Press, 1997). A shorter version of this work in English can be found in the same author's M. A. thesis, "The Jakarta Charter of June 1945: A History of the Gentleman's Agreement between the Islamic and the Secular Nationalists in Modern Indonesia" (McGill University Institute of Islamic Studies, 1976).

[10] See Deliar Noer, *The Administration of Islam in Indonesia* (Ithaca: Cornell Modern Indonesia Project, 1978); and Boland, *The Struggle of Islam*, 105–12.

grew out of the Office for Religious Affairs established under the Japanese occupational government. The movement for its continuation and incorporation into the state structure of independent Indonesia was rejected at first by the secular Nationalists, but mounting pressure eventually convinced the government to grant a major concession to Muslim interests in the form of a full government ministry under the direction of H. M. Rasjidi.[11] Capitalizing on the one foothold that self-conscious Muslim interests were granted in the administration of the Republic, leaders of the Ministry turned it from a mere political concession into an active agent for the mobilization of Muslims and the further Islamization of society over the years that followed.[12]

Progress in this direction did not proceed unimpeded, as the Ministry of Religious Affairs faced a number of significant challenges during the two decades of Soekarno's rule. Eventually, however, it managed to consolidate its power and came to engage actively with the affairs of other government departments.[13] This can be seen, for example, in the subordination of the (Islamic) religious court systems to the Ministry of Religious Affairs rather than the Ministry of Justice. This administrative arrangement further complicated the already confusing and contradictory amalgam of legal systems operating in the country.[14] Moreover, some major developments in the area of national education were placed directly under the control of the Ministry of Religious Affairs to the exclusion of direct involvement by the Ministry of Education, the most striking example of this being the

[11] For more on Rasjidi's life and works, see Endang Basri Ananda, ed., *70 Tahun Prof. Dr. H. M. Rasjidi* (Jakarta: Harian Umum Pelita, 1985); Andrée Feillard, "Rasjidi, (Haji) Mohammad," *DB*, I, 34–36; and Azyumardi Azra, "Guarding the Faith of the Ummah: The Religio-Intellectual Journey of Mohammad Rasjidi," *SI* 1.2 (1994): 87–120.

[12] Although the Ministry of Religious Affairs was established primarily in consideration of Muslim interests, in later years its official structure came to include also separate sections addressing the needs of Indonesia's various religious communities: Muslims, Catholics, Protestant Christians, Hindus, and Buddhists. Nonetheless, perhaps even more than its demographic qualifications would dictate, to this day the Muslim section dominates all others and generally controls the Ministry itself.

[13] On the place of the Ministry of Religious Affairs in both local and national configurations of power during 1950s, see Clifford Geertz, *The Religion of Java* (Chicago: University of Chicago Press, 1960), 200–14.

[14] Daniel Lev, *Islamic Legal Courts in Indonesia* (Berkeley: University of California Press, 1972). For more on the subsequent institutional development of Islamic law in the Indonesian national court structure, see Busthanul Arifin, *Pelembagaan Hukum Islam di Indonesia: Akar Sejarah, Hambatan dan Prospeknya* (Jakarta: Gema Insani Press, 1996), as well as the essays contained in Amrullah Ahmad, ed., *Dimensi Hukum Islam dalam Sistem Hukum Nasional, Mengenan 65 Th. Prof. Dr. H. Busthanul Arifin*, SH (Jakarta: Gema Insani Press, 1996). A more sociologically oriented study of these developments can be found in Cik Hasan Bisri, *Peradilan Islam dalam Tatanan Masyarakat Indonesia* (Bandung: PT Remaja Rosdakarya, 1997).

establishment and expansion of the National Islamic Studies Institutes, or IAIN.

## THE IAIN AND INDONESIAN ISLAM

The earlier impetus for educational reform, which began at the primary and secondary levels with the formation of the new-style schools discussed in chapter 1, had by the mid-twentieth century led to movements for analogous innovations in higher education. Local developments in these directions progressed in various parts of the archipelago, often under the auspices of major voluntary associations such as the Muhammadiyah. On a national level one of the major advances in this direction came with the establishment of the IAIN system which has spread throughout the Archipelago over the second half of the twentieth century.[15]

The earliest origins of these institutions also arose during the tumult of the Japanese war-time occupation of Indonesia, when the Sekolah Tinggi Islam (STI) was founded at Jakarta, under the initiative of Muhammad Hatta, K. H. A. Kahar Muzakkir, K. H. Mas Mansjur, K. H. Fatchurrahman Kafrawi, and K. H. Faried Ma'ruf. During the revolution this school was moved to Yogyakarta and in 1950 it underwent administrative restructuring, while also being renamed as the Perguruan Tinggi Agama Islam Negeri (PTAIN).[16] This institution was founded with the mission of:

> providing higher education and becoming a center for the development and deepening of Islamic religious knowledge. In working toward this goal, it is also charged with laying down a foundation for the formation of moral and educated people who have an awareness of their responsibilities for the prosperity of Indonesian society and the world in general, all upon the basis of *Pancasila*, culture, Indonesian nationality, and reality.[17]

Over the following decade and a half, the importance of the PTAIN grew as the only significant concession granted by the national government to organized Islam during a period in which *Masjumi* and other Muslim institutions found themselves increasingly on the defensive against Soekarno's leftward march. As the PTAIN continued to develop through the early

[15] For a general history of the development of the IAIN system, see Johan Hendrik Meuleman and Henri Chambert-Loir, "Les Instituts islamiques publics indonésiens," in *Madrasa: La Transmission du Savoir dans le Monde Musulman*, ed. Nicole Grandin and Marc Gaborieau (Paris: Éditions Arguments, 1997), 199–216.

[16] *Peraturan Pemerintah* no. 34, tahun 1950.

[17] *Buku Tahunan IAIN 'Al-Djami'ah Al-Islamijah Al-Hukumijah' 1960–1962* (Jogjakarta: IAIN "Al-Djami'ah Al-Islamijah Al-Hukumijah," 1962), 12.

1960s, it underwent further institutional restructuring, and yet another name change to Institut Agama Islam Negeri (IAIN).[18] Of the many administrative decrees issued in the course of these changes, some specified political appointments to a number of the highest administrative positions. These included a number of the most prominent Muslims in the country, including Teungku Mohamed Hasbi Ash Shiddieqy, who was appointed Dean of the Sharīʿa Faculty in 1960.[19]

## HASBI ASH SHIDDIEQY

Hasbi was born on 10 March 1904 at Lhok Seumawe, Aceh, to a family that claims descent from the Prophet's close companion, the first Caliph, Abū Bakr al-Ṣiddiq (d. 634).[20] As a member of the Acehnese *ʿulamāʾ* elite, Hasbi studied the Islamic religious sciences first under his father and then under a number of prominent local shaykhs. From the start, Hasbi's father forbade him to study the Latin alphabet, which he equated with the "Dutch infidels." Later, however, Hasbi asked one of his friends to teach him the alphabet in order to escape from the disadvantages of illiteracy in this increasingly popular script for writing Malay/Bahasa Indonesia. After completing his studies in 1920, he returned home to Lhok Seumawe where he met one of the founders of the reformist journal *al-Imām* who had recently arrived in Aceh from Singapore.[21] Through this connection Hasbi became attracted to reformist ideas and eventually decided to pursue them more systematically at the *al-Irsyad* school in Surabaya (East Java).

Over the next few years, he became increasingly involved with several reformist organizations and educational institutions.[22] During the wartime

[18] *Peraturan Peresiden Republik Indonesia* no. 11 tahun, 1960; *Penetapan Menteri Agama* no. 43 tahun, 1960; *Peraturan Menteri Agama* no. 15 tahun, 1961; *Penetapan Menteri Agama* no. 35, tahun, 1960.

[19] *Penetapan Menteri Agama* no. 35, tahun 1960; *Buku Tahunan*, 21–22.

[20] Biographical materials are plentiful for Hasbi. The relevant information has been compiled into the major accounts produced by Hasbi's son, Nourouzzaman Shiddiqi, "Muhammad Hasbi Ash Shiddieqy: Pembaruan Pemikiran Islam," in *Jeram-Jeram Peradaban Muslim* (Yogyakarta: Pustaka Pelajar, 1996), 217–53; *Fiqh Indonesia: Penggagas dan Gagasannya* (Yogyakarta: Pustaka Pelajar, 1995); Yudian Wayhudi, "Hasbi's Theory of Ijtihād in the Context of Indonesian Fiqh" (Diss. McGill University, 1993), 12–23. Unless otherwise indicated the short biographical sketch that follows is drawn primarily from these sources.

[21] Moh. Salim al-Kalali was active in the establishment of the modernist organization Islam Menjadi Bersatu at Kutaradja (Banda Aceh). Roff, *Origins of Malay Nationalism*, 56, 64. He lent *Salafi* publications of the works of Ibn Taymiyya and Ibn al-Qayyim al-Jawziyya to Hasbi for further study.

[22] In 1927, Hasbi formally joined al-Kalali's Islam Menjadi Bersatu and in the following year he was appointed head of a new but short-lived al-Irsyad branch school at Lhok Seumawe. In 1929 he

Japanese occupation of Indonesia, Hasbi assumed a number of significant posts and after independence he quickly rose through the ranks of the Muslim reformist organization Masjumi and also founded a local branch of PERSIS at Lhok Seumawe.[23] While engaged in this organizational and educational work, Hasbi was also active in the mass media, regularly writing columns and articles for a number of magazines, newspapers, and journals. However, his most long-lasting contributions to Indonesian Islamic thought came about through his involvement with the Indonesian system of State Islamic Studies Institutes (IAIN), which began with his appointment as a lecturer at Yogyakarta (Central Java) in 1951.

By 1960, while dean of the Sharīʿa Faculty, he served as the general coordinator for post-graduate courses in Islamic law for its staff. In addition to his administrative work and teaching at the IAIN, Hasbi also worked more than any other single Indonesian author for the production of materials to be used in the curricula of these institutions. A significant part of this involved the translation of classical and contemporary works of Islamic scholarship from Arabic into Indonesian, thus facilitating the participation of younger scholars without traditional training in the Islamic religious sciences in the public intellectual discourses on religion and its place in society.[24] Here Hasbi made a valuable contribution by greatly expanding the canon of texts informing earlier Indonesian Muslim scholarship.

Working in the expanding national system of IAIN, Hasbi placed the creation of a new corpus of works on Islamic subjects squarely within the framework of developments in the field of education. A number of Hasbi's works that were originally intended to serve as instructional materials for the IAIN curriculum have remained in print in multiple re-editions since his death in 1975. Most recently, in 1997, the Semarang (Central Java) based publisher Pustaka Rizki Putra reissued over a dozen of his most popular works in new editions in which the language, spelling, and style have been updated to make them more accessible to contemporary Indonesian readers.

Hasbi's connections with the IAIN brought him into increased contact with intellectual currents in the wider Muslim world. Through these

became the head of the newly founded al-Huda school at Krueng Mane and in 1931 he was elected as the first leader of the local branch of the Jong Islamiten Bond. Shortly thereafter, however, he moved once again to Kutaradja (Banda Aceh) where he attained high-level positions in the Nadil Ishlahil Islami, Muhammadiyah, and other reformist organizations. While there he also taught at several local schools and eventually founded his own in 1940 under the name Darul Irfan.

23 During that period, Hasbi served on the Religious Courts (Jp. *Shūkyō-kai*), the Achehnese Regional Government Advisory Board (Jp. *Achi Shu sangikai*), the Sumatran Central Representative Body (Jp. *Sumatora Chūo sangi-in*), the Islamic Council for Support of Great East Asian Prosperity (*Majelis Agama Islam untuk Bantuan Kemakmuran Asia Timur Raya*), and other administrative departments.

24 *Tafsir Al-Bayaan*, 5.

channels, and as a reflection of Soekarno's non-aligned ideology and relationship with Gamal ʿAbd al-Nasser, institutional relationships developed between the IAIN and the then newly reorganized al-Azhar in Egypt.[25] One of the most public manifestations of this increasingly warm relationship may be seen in the exchange of prominent honorary doctorate degrees. In 1958, the popular Indonesian author and religious figure Hamka was awarded this degree from al-Azhar. In 1962 the Indonesian IAIN conferred the same honor on the rector of al-Azhar, Maḥmud Shaltūt (d. 1963).[26]

The selection of Shaltūt for this distinction reflects not only the political dimensions of contemporary Egyptian–Indonesian relations, but also an affinity of religious orientation between the Azharite Shaykh and the administration of IAIN. In the presentation speech for this honorary degree, Shaltūt was praised for being not only a *mufassir* and scholar of *fiqh*, but also a 'sociologist' who was in touch with the problems of contemporary society and knew how to address them.[27] Hasbi shared this appreciation of Shaltūt with his IAIN colleagues and drew extensively on the works of the Azharite Shaykh and his contemporary countrymen in the formulation of his new model of Indonesian *fiqh*. A careful reading of Hasbi's writings reveals the considerable influence of other contemporary Egyptian figures on his thought as well. In addition to Shaltūt, for example, Hasbi drew extensively upon the work of Muḥammad Muṣṭafā al-Marāghī (d. 1945). In fact, some of Hasbi's contemporaries charged that his *Tafsir al-Bayaan* was little more than an Indonesian translation of Marāghī's work.

## EXPANDING THE CORPUS OF ISLAMIC STUDIES IN INDONESIA

Of all the Egyptian influences upon Hasbi's work, however, it is that of Shaltūt that is most pronounced in his writings on the methodology of

[25] In fact, Egypt was the first nation to acknowledge Indonesian independence in 1945. However the ideological affinities of this relationship have much more to do with emerging conceptions of post-colonial nationalism than with Islam. Rizal Sukma, *Islam in Indonesian Foreign Policy* (London: RoutledgeCurzon, 2003), pp. 26–8. For more on the relationship between internationalist ideologies and the reformation of Muslim religious institutions in modern Egypt, see J. Skovgaard-Petersen, *Defining Islam for the Egyptian State: Muftis and Fatwas of the Dar al-Ifta* (Leiden: E. J. Brill, 1997), 189–93.

[26] Muchtar Jahja, "Pidato Promosi," 109–27. For more on the life and works of Shaltut, see Wolf-Dieter Lemke, *Mahmud Saltut (1893–1963) und die Reform der Azhar* (Frankfurt am Main, 1980); and Kate Zebiri, *Mahmud Shaltut and Islamic Modernism* (Oxford: Clarendon Press, 1993).

[27] Jahja, "Pidato Promosi," 132. It is interesting to note here that during Shaltūt's day, the *kulliyat uṣūl al-dīn* at al-Azhar began to include sociology as part of its standard curriculum. See Jacques Jomier, "Programme et orientation des études à la faculté de théologie d'Al-Azhar (*kulliyat uṣūl al-dīn*)," *Revue des Études Islamiques* 44 (1976): 253–72.

Islamic textual reasoning.[28] Shaltūt's combination of emphasis on interpreting the Qur'ān in its own terms, addressing legal questions in his *tafsīr*, and accessibility, appealed strongly to Hasbi.[29] What one observer has said of Shaltūt could also be applied to Hasbi, that is that they both worked to "demystify the Islamic disciplines of *fiqh* and *tafsīr* to make them more accessible to lay Muslims."[30] Hasbi also drew on Shaltūt's approach to *ḥadīth* as a central aspect of his own interpretive enterprise, as for example in his writings on the application of the *Sunna* where he maintained a distinction between the legally binding and merely customary elements of the *Sunna*.[31]

In doing this, Hasbi situated himself in a line of argument stretching backwards through the Egyptian reformer to the renowned eighteenth-century Indian mystic, *ḥadīth* scholar, and jurist Shāh Waliullah al-Dihlawī. This figure was one of the most prominent pre-modern proponents of a distinction between the words and deeds of Muḥammad as Prophet, and the routine behavior of his everyday life.[32] This idea was eagerly developed by Shaltūt, and it appears that it was through this later reformer that significant elements of al-Dihlawī's thought were introduced to Hasbi and his modern Indonesian audience.

Following a division between *'ibādāt* and *mu'āmalāt*,[33] Hasbi observed a basic and pervasive distinction between that which is essentially related to God and that which is concerned with human life on earth.[34] This

[28] Important ideas from Shaltūt's *al-Islām: 'Aqida wa sharī'a* were introduced to Indonesian Muslims through Hasbi's work decades before the first complete translation of this work into Indonesian as: *Islam: Aqidah dan Syari'ah*, trans. Abdurrahman Zain (Jakarta: Pustaka Amani, 1986).

[29] Shaltūt's work in this field has since become available in Indonesian translation as *Tafsir al-Quranul Karim, Pendekatan Syaltut dalam Menggali Esensi al-Quran* (Bandung: Diponegoro, 1989). For more on Shaltūt's *tafsīr*, see Zebiri, *Mahmud Shaltut*, 128–80.

[30] Before its publication as a book, this work was printed in the periodical *Risālat al-Islām*, a journal devoted to the "unifying of the denominations of Islam" (*taqrīb bayna al-madhāhib*). Zebiri, *Mahmud Shaltut*, 181; J. J. G. Jansen, *The Interpretation of the Koran in Modern Egypt* (Leiden: E. J. Brill, 1980), 14–15.

[31] Hasbi Ash Shiddieqy, *Problematika Hadits sebagai Dasar Pembinaan Hukum Islam* (Jakarta: Bulan Bintang, 1964).

[32] By Hasbi's day, some of al-Dihlawī's ideas had also been introduced to Muslim Southeast Asia via another route, i.e. by an elder generation of reformists from Singapore and the Malay peninsula such as Tok Khorasani. See William R. Roff, "An Argument about How to Argue," in *Islamic Legal Interpretation: Muftis and their Fatwas*, ed. Muhammad Khalid Masud, Brinkley Messick, and David S. Powers (Cambridge, MA: Harvard University Press, 1996), 226.

[33] In one telling discussion of this dichotomy, Hasbi refers to the second category as *adat* rather than *mu'āmalāt*, at times indiscriminately alternating his usage of these two terms (*Pengantar Ilmu Fiqh*, 20ff).

[34] Such general distinctions between the realms of what might be rendered in English the "eternal" and the "temporal," respectively, are elaborated in *Falsafah Hukum Islam* (Jakarta: Bulan Bintang, 1975), 89 ft. Hasbi grounded his discussion of this distinction in the *ḥadīth* report of Muḥammad's mistaken advice to workers cross-pollinating date-palm trees.

was in turn reflected in his conception of the humanity of Muḥammad in his role as God's prophet. Hasbi thus distinguished between *ḥadīth* that are legally binding (*tashrī'*) and those that are not (*ghayr al-tashrī'*, or *al-irshād*). Through the establishment of this distinction, he could at once do away with certain 'innovations' in religious practice, while at the same time helping to free Indonesian Muslims from imitation of what he regarded as outdated Arabic styles of dress, diet, and personal hygiene.[35] Those *ḥadīth* that Hasbi determined to be of continued, legally binding relevance were collected into a multivolume compilation entitled, *Koleksi Hadis-Hadis Hukum*.[36]

In his advocacy of a critical approach to the *ḥadīth* as the basis for legal rulings, Hasbi drew upon an impressive selection of earlier and contemporary authorities.[37] In so doing he continued his work toward further expanding the corpus of *ḥadīth* scholarship in Indonesia by PERSIS writers and activists such as Hassan and Chalil. While Hasbi dealt with the *Sunna* in nearly everything he wrote, his most concentrated exploration of the study of *ḥadīth* is presented in his *Sejarah dan Pengantar Ilmu Hadits*.[38] This book is not only an introduction to *ḥadīth* study, but also a history of its associated fields of the Islamic religious sciences. Hasbi regarded the knowledge of such history as critical for achieving a better understanding of Muslim tradition in its relationship to present circumstances and possible future development.[39] This reflects a much larger theme running throughout many of his works: a concern with presenting the historical development of Muslim scholarship in various fields.[40] In doing so he argued for the importance of viewing doctrinal and legal positions in light of the specific historical contexts that conditioned them. According to Hasbi this contextualized understanding of tradition was in turn intended to facilitate its reinterpretation in consideration of contemporary conditions.

True to the PERSIS reformist background of his youth, Hasbi saw his works on Qur'ān and *ḥadīth* studies as integral steps toward the purification of revealed law from the corruptions of human innovation. An

[35] See, for example, his *Kriteria antara Sunnah dan Bid'ah* (Jakarta: Bulan Bintang, 1967).

[36] *Koleksi Hadis-Hadis Hukum*, 6 vols. (Jakarta: Yayasan Teungku Muhammad Hasbi Ash Shiddieqy, 4th printing 1994).

[37] His sources range from Ibn al-Jawzī's *Kitāb al-mawḍū'āt* to al-Shawkānī's *Nayl al-awṭār*.

[38] Semarang: Pustaka Rizki Putra, 1997 (1st edn, 1953).

[39] *Sejarah dan Pengantar Ilmu Hadits*, 24–25.

[40] In addition to *Sejarah dan Pengantar Ilmu Hadits*, Hasbi wrote similar handbooks on the Qur'ānic sciences (*Sejarah dan Pengantar Ilmu al- Qur'an/ Tafsir*) and jurisprudence (*Pengantar Ilmu Fiqh*) as well as lengthy biographies of the *imams* of the various legal schools in the Sunnī, Shī'ī, and even the Ẓāhirī tradition as represented by the eleventh-century scholar Ibn Ḥazm (*Pokok-pokok Pegangan Imam Mazhab*).

important corollary to this was the refutation of unthinking alliance to any one of the previously established schools of law (*madhhabs*). For Hasbi, however, this critical stance was tempered by an openness to exploring what was useful in the writings of the various existing schools, as Hasbi contended that modern Muslims could benefit from a careful selection of previous rulings that are relevant to the contemporary situation.[41] The practice of comparing the rulings of several law schools on particular topics (*ikhtilāf*) and choosing the most beneficial and appropriate of them is referred to in modern Indonesian jurisprudential discourse as *talfiq*.[42] In the twentieth century this legal device was used extensively in many countries by Muslims seeking the reform of Islamic law, especially in the area of family law.[43] By Hasbi's time this orientation had already gained significant ground through the work of modern reformers like al-Marāghī and Shaltūt.[44] Marāghī called for a renewed *ijtihād*, one that would transcend the boundaries of any one of the established legal schools and thus overcome the limitations of school sectarianism (*madhhabiyya*).[45] His work was continued by Shaltūt, who reinvigorated the science of comparative Muslim legal studies with the publication of his *Muqāranāt al-madhāhib fi'l-fiqh*.[46]

[41] This might be seen as an extension of the earlier work of Moenawar Chalil in his *Biografi Empat Serangkai Imam Madzhab*. See *Pokok-pokok Pegangan Imam-imam Mazhab* (Jakarta: Bulan Bintang, 1973).

[42] The use of *talfiq* here overlaps with what is often referred to in analogous Arabic-language discussions as *takhayyur* ("eclectic expedient"). However in the present discussion I will preserve the technical terms as they are used in the Indonesian-language discourse which is the primary focus of this study. For an overview of *talfiq* tracing its developments in modern Muslim jurisprudence through Arabic sources, see Birgit Krawietz, "Cut and Paste in Legal Rules: Designing Islamic Norms with *Talfiq*," *WI* 42.1 (2002): 2–40.

[43] J. N. D. Anderson, "Recent Reforms in Family Law in the Arab World," *Zeitschrift für vergleichende Rechtswissenschaft* 65 (1963). Perhaps the most enthusiastic proponent of this eclectic approach in twentieth-century Indonesia has been Ibrahim Hosen, who proposed a radical application of *talfiq* in several of his essays, including "Taqlid dan Ijtihad: Beberapa Pengertian Dasar," in *Kontekstualisasi Doktrin Islam dalam Sejarah*, ed. Budy Munawar-Rachman (Jakarta: Yayasan Paramadina, 1994). Hosen's work will be discussed further in chapter 6.

[44] Shaltūt was praised by one of Hasbi's IAIN colleagues for not being an "*'alim mazhabi*" but rather a scholar with a wider knowledge of many schools of law who is able to make well-informed comparisons and critiques of their various positions on a given issue. Muchtar Jahja, "Pidato Promosi," 117ff.

[45] See Muṣṭafā al-Marāghī, *Al-ijtihād fi-Islām* (Cairo: al-Maktab al-fann, 1959).

[46] (Cairo: Muḥammad 'Alī Subayh, 1953). This work was compiled in collaboration with Muḥammad 'Alī Sayis, and was later translated into Indonesian as *Perbandingan Mazhab dalam Masalah Fiqih* (Jakarta: Bulan Bintang, 1973). Shaltūt's work in this area comprises a major part of his career, including not only the writing of the above-mentioned work, but also his twenty-five years of involvement in the Jamā'at al-taqrīb bayna al-madhāhib and the publication of its journal *Risālat al-Islām*, which first printed Shaltūt's *tafsīr* in a series of regular installments (Zebiri, *Mahmud Shaltut*, 24–26).

The work of Hasbi, Shaltūt, and al-Marāghī drew on a tradition of Islamic legal literature extending back through Ibn Rushd, but read in light of a modern trend away from exclusive adherence to any particular school that is often associated with the reformist agenda of *al-Manār*. As argued in chapter 2, however, references to this journal and its editors Abduh and Riḍā as a (if not *the*) source of modern Islamic reformism in Southeast Asia often reflect vague conceptions of reform, rather than any documented intellectual lineage. Muslim agendas for reform aimed at overcoming traditional *madhhab* boundaries may in fact be traced back through the early modern period. Here one might track another example of the influence of al-Dihlawī's thought, as mediated by Shaltūt,[47] and/or further influences from the work of some of al-Dihlawī's near contemporaries working in North Africa and the Arabian peninsula, such as al-Shawkānī and Aḥmad b. Idrīs.[48] Thus, here again, it should be clear that the simplistic attribution of the roots of 'reformism' in Indonesian Islam to *al-Manār* alone does not do justice to the complex developments of Muslim thought in twentieth-century Southeast Asia.[49]

## A *MADHHAB* FOR A MODERN NATION

Hasbi's work in the direction of transcending established *madhhab* boundaries, however, was but a prelude to his broader project of constructing a new system of distinctively "Indonesian *fiqh*," or *Fiqih Indonesia*. Hasbi maintained that only by reconceptualizing the approach to scripture and law in terms of the specific conditions of Indonesian society and the needs of Muslims living therein could Islam remain a vital force in the lives of believers. This required a new jurisprudence that possessed a heightened awareness of the needs and conditions facing Muslims in the newly

[47] Since Hasbi's day, al-Dihlawī's work in this area (*Al-Inṣāf fī bayān asbāb al-ikhtilāf* ) has become directly available in Indonesian translation as *Sebab-sebab Munculnya Madzhab Fiqih*, trans. Abd. Wadud Nafis and Darmanto (Jakarta: Arista Brahmatyasa, 1996).

[48] For an introduction to the thought of these authors, see al-Shawkānī's "Al-Tuhaf fī madhāhib al-salaf," and "Al-Qawl al-mufīd fī adillat al-ijtihād wa'l-taqlīd," *Al-Rasā'il al-salafiyya fī ihyā' sunnat khayr al-bariyya* (Beirut: Dār al-kitāb al-'arabī, 1994/1414H), 127–42, and 191–251, respectively, as well as Aḥmad b. Idrīs, *Risālat al-radd 'alā ahl al-ra'y*, ed. Bernd Radtke, J O'Kane, K. S. Vikør, and R. S. O'Fahey, *The Exoteric Ahmad Ibn Idris: A Sufi's Critique of the Madhahib and the Wahhabis* (Leiden: E. J. Brill, 2000), 47–130.

[49] This is not to say, however, that Abduh and Riḍā were not influential in at least some spheres of modern Indonesian Islam. For example, one may detect more distinct lines of influence upon the work of Aḥmad Sūrkatī and Moenawar Chalil. Nonetheless, even in the case of the Muhammadiyah, it is clear that the influence of Abduh's thought was only one aspect of the complex phenomenon of the transmission of modern Muslim reformism to Southeast Asia. See Arbiyah Lubis, *Pemikiran Muhammadiyah dan Muhammad Abduh: Suatu Studi Perbandingan* (Jakarta: Bulan Bintang, 1993).

independent Indonesian state, while at the same time referring to the Qur'ān and the *Sunna* as its ultimate sources. The raw materials for the creation of such a school also included considerations of local culture and practice, *'urf* and *adat*, respectively.[50] At the same time Hasbi drew upon elements of several historical *madhhabs*, including that of al-Shāfi'ī, which traditionally has been the predominant school of law in Muslim Southeast Asia.

Hasbi's movement toward the creation of an Indonesian *madhhab* marks a significant turning point in his thought, and, more generally, in the development of Indonesian Islam. For although he was earlier attracted to the scripturalist reformism characteristic of A. Hassan, he later followed more of the critical approach to classical *fiqh* scholarship evidenced in the work of Moenawar Chalil.[51] Both A. Hassan (the pre-eminent spokesman for PERSIS) and Hasbi called for a reinvigorated exercise of *ijtihād*, but they understood the term in different ways. PERSIS writers tended to understand *ijtihād* primarily as an exercise in which past (mis)interpretations of the law could be identified and eliminated within the process of a "return to the Qur'ān and *Sunna*," to borrow Chalil's phrase.[52] Hasbi recognized the relevance of this type of *ijtihād*, but only as a preliminary step toward the reformulation of Islamic law. He argued that after the 'pure' essence has been distilled from scripture, it becomes the responsibility of the *mujtahid* to make those laws and teaching more directly relevant to the lives of Muslims living in his society.

For Hasbi, the application of Islamic law needed to be approached in a way that recognized the realities of contemporary local conditions. In the

[50] Over the past decade a number of important studies have appeared that have contributed greatly to our understanding of *'urf* and its place in the workings of Islamic law. See Baber Johansen, "Coutumes locales et coutumes universelles aux sources des règles juridiques en Droit musulman hanéfite," in *Annales Islamologiques* 27 (1993): 29–35/ *Contingency in a Sacred Law* (Leiden: E. J. Brill, 1999), 163–71; Gideon Libson, "On the Development of Custom as a Source of Law in Islamic Law: *al-rujū'u al-urfi ahadu al-qawā'idi al-khamsi allatī yatabannā 'alayhā al-fiqhu*," *Islamic Law and Society* 4.2 (1997), 131–55; and Haim Gerber, *Islamic Law and Culture* (Leiden: E. J. Brill, 1999), 105–15. Hasbi's ideas on *'urf* as a source of law exposed him to criticism from certain circles, as in Indonesia and elsewhere such a position was controversial. In Egypt, for example, a minority of *qāḍīs* rejected custom outright, even in those cases where there existed no clear conflict with the Sharī'a. Ron Shaham, *Family and the Courts in Modern Egypt: A Study Based on Decisions by the Sharī'a Courts, 1900–1955* (Leiden: E. J. Brill, 1997), 230. Since Hasbi's day further work on the potential of *'urf* as a source of Islamic law in Indonesia has been promoted by Ahmad Azhar Basyir. See, for example, Basyir, *Hukum Adat bagi Umat Islam* (Yogyakarta: Nur Cahaya, 1983); and "Pokok-pokok Ijtihad dalam Hukum Islam," in *Ijtihad dalam Sorotan*, ed. Haidar Bagir and Syafiq Basri (Bandung: Penerbit Mizan, 1988), 46–64. For a short introduction to this author's legal thought, see Siti Handaroh, "Hubungan antara Adat dan Maslahat: Studi tentang Pemikiran Ahman Azhar Basyir," in *The Qur'an and Philosophical Reflections* (Yogyakarta: Titian Ilahi Press, 1998), 3–26.

[51] See, for example, his *Kriteria antara Sunnah dan Bid'ah* and *Penoetoep Mulut*, which stridently attacked *bid'a* in religious practice.

[52] As taken from his signature work *Kembali kepada Al Qur'an dan As-Sunnah*.

contexts of the newly independent nation, this led him toward a project of Indonesianizing the discourse on Islamic jurisprudence. Hasbi attempted this through an appeal for an understanding of the relationship between *adat* and Islamic law that viewed them in terms of a complementary, rather than antagonistic, relationship.[53] His discussions of this are in many ways reminiscent of those of his older Egyptian contemporary, 'Abd al-Wahhāb al-Khallāf (d. 1956).[54] This is not to say, however, that Hasbi was simply borrowing yet another brick from the edifice of Egyptian modernism. Rather he actively and selectively appropriated certain aspects of al-Khallāf's thoughts on *'urf* (custom) that Hasbi saw as potentially useful to his own work toward a new and distinctively Indonesian aim, the creation of a 'national school of law.' This use of local cultural contextualization in the interpretation and application of 'purified' scriptural precepts represents something new insofar as it was self-consciously understood as not merely another step toward the ongoing reform of Islamic law, but as a creative *national* endeavor to institute a new legal methodology on an analogous footing to that of the established ways of *fiqh*.

Hasbi envisioned the formulation and application of this new Indonesian *fiqh* as being undertaken through a reformulated process of "collective *ijtihād*." He elaborated upon this idea in connection with discussions of *ijmā'* and within the context of debates over the nature of the relationship between Islam and the Indonesian state. There Hasbi distinguished between the *ijmā'* of the early Muslim community and that of his time.[55] He maintained that older decisions based on consensus should be reviewed and that new legally binding decisions can continue to be made by a body of legislators. In this he combined his nationalist understanding of *ijtihād* with contemporary reformulations of *shūrā*, hoping thereby to establish a more well-defined place for Islamic law in the modern Indonesian nation-state. Hasbi envisioned this to be the work of an organized body of authorities (which he referred to as *ahl al-hall wa'l-'aqd*) formed from the corps of IAIN graduates that he had such an influence in molding. This, according to Hasbi, would serve as a guarantee against the fracturing of the community

[53] This is particularly clear in the way in which Hasbi addresses the issue in relation to considerations of "public interest" (*maṣlaḥa*). See his *Kriteria antara Sunnah dan Bid'ah* (Jakarta: Bulan Bintang, 1967), 68–77.

[54] However al-Khallāf, it should be noted, generally spoke in terms of *'urf* rather than *adat*. See his *Masādir al-tashrī' al-Islāmī fīmā lā nass fīhi* (Cairo: Dār al-kitāb al-'Arabī 1955); and *'Ilm uṣūl al-fiqh* (Cairo: Matba'a al-naṣr, 1956). For a discussion of some aspects of al-Khallāf's jurisprudence, see Wael B. Hallaq, *A History of Islamic Legal Theories: An Introduction to Sunni Usul al-Fiqh* (Cambridge: University Press, 1999), 220–24.

[55] *Asas Hukum Tata Negara Menurut Sjari'at Islam* (Yogyakarta: Matahari Masa, 1969), 37.

and provide for a unified legislation for the national government under the rubric of a specifically Indonesian *madhhab*.[56] Here we find an important intersection between his ideas on legal theory and his more concrete institutional aspirations for the development of Islam in Indonesian society.

Hasbi based his general arguments in favor of the creation of an Indonesian system of *fiqh* upon his reading of the history of Islamic jurisprudence and its primary development in the first centuries of Islam. He maintained that due to the context in which it developed, certain elements of Arab and Middle Eastern culture established themselves in classical theories of jurisprudence. In short he asserted that much of what traditionally has been considered as 'Islamic law' should actually be thought of as "Arab *fiqh*."[57] Hasbi recognized that the contemporary conditions in which Indonesian Muslims lived posed many new questions, and demanded new answers to old ones, thus necessitating a new and more immediately relevant approach to *fiqh*. Thus he sought to find ways in which the legal and moral precepts of the Qur'ān were relevant to contemporary conditions and issues. In this sense, one might talk of a bi-directional movement in Hasbi's approach: first turning back toward the original sources in order to determine the essential message of the law; and then turning toward the contemporary situation in order to determine the appropriate interpretation and application of scriptural precepts to particular cases and conditions. Here one detects a foreshadowing of Fazlur Rahman's approach that would subsequently enjoy an important place in Indonesian Islamic thought.[58]

Hasbi's conceptualization of Indonesian *fiqh* rested upon an historicized understanding of the Muslim intellectual tradition. The various elements upon which he drew included: a reformist-inspired call for *ijtihād* and critical evaluation of *ḥadīth*, an openness to the wider tradition of Muslim legal scholarship beyond the confines of any one particular *madhhab*, and an understanding of the importance of adapting legal principles and rulings to the actual situation of Muslims living in contemporary Indonesia. In this way he was able to build upon the initial impetus for reform in Indonesia

[56] *Falsafah Hukum Islam*, 329, 340.

[57] Awareness of this problem continues to play a role in the thought of contemporary Indonesian thinkers. See, for example, Atho' Mudzhar, "Fiqh dan Reaktualisasi Ajaran Islam," in *Kontektualisasi Doktrin Islam dalam Sejarah*, ed. Budhy Munawar-Rachman (Jakarta: Yayasan Wakaf Paramadina, 1994), 374.

[58] The influence of Rahman's thought on developments in contemporary Indonesian Islam comes both through the work of his prominent Indonesian students, such as Nurcholish Madjid, and the popularity of his works available in Indonesian translation. These developments will be discussed further in chapter 5.

by developing a more ambitious project of reconstructing Islamic tradition in a way that addressed the needs and concerns of a rapidly changing Indonesian society.

## ADAT LAW AND HAZAIRIN

While Hasbi was working on the formation of a distinctively modern and Indonesian system of *fiqh*, parallel developments in the sphere of academic legal studies were being advanced by Hazairin (d. 1975), a Bengkulu (Sumatra)-born, Dutch-trained scholar of customary, or *adat* law. This field of study had a complex history with relation to the administrative institutions of the Netherlands Indies, which should be taken into account when we examine both the context in which Hazairin worked, and the significance of his efforts to bring aspects of this tradition into discussions of Islamic law in Indonesia.

As Dutch colonial control over the Archipelago strengthened during the late nineteenth and early twentieth centuries, a number of gifted Orientalist scholars were employed to advise the government on religious and native affairs, the most prominent being C. Snouck Hurgronje.[59] Snouck combined expertise in Arabic and Islamic studies with an extensive knowledge of the languages and cultural conditions of Muslims living in various parts of the Archipelago,[60] and his unique combination of qualifications was greatly appreciated by the Dutch colonial government, which he served in various capacities. His scholarly works were so integrally linked to his position as advisor to the colonial government that a clear and total disentanglement of the two is almost impossible.[61] Consequently, Snouck's writings

[59] For those not familiar with Dutch, several studies may serve as an introduction to this scholar and his work, including G. W. J. Drewes, "Snouck Hurgronje and the study of Islam," *BKI* 113 (1957): 1–15; and J. Waardenburg, *L'Islam dans le Miroir de l'Occident* (Paris: Mouton, 1962). Snouck's involvement in colonial policy, especially during the Aceh War has attracted substantial criticism by both Indonesian and Western authors. See, for example, W. F. Wertheim, "Counter-insurgency Research at the Turn of the Century: Snouck Hurgronje and the Acheh War," *Sociologische Gids* 19 (1972): 320–28.

[60] The most popular of Snouck's works, ethnographies of Aceh and Mecca, are available in English translation, *The Achehnese* (Leiden: E. J. Brill, 1906); and *Mekka in the Latter Part of the 19th Century* (Leiden: E. J. Brill, 1931). (*n.b.* The second comprises only a partial translation from the second volume of the original work in German). Aside from these his numerous shorter pieces on a number of issues have been collected into seven volumes and published as *Verspreide Geschriften /Gesammelte Schriften* (Bonn: Kurt Schroeder Verlag, 1921–27). Important statements of Snouck's views on *adatrecht* can be found in volume IV of this collection, as well as in *The Achehnese*.

[61] Collections of his papers addressed to colonial officials have been collected and published as a kind of academic work of their own. See Adriaanse, and Gobée, *Ambtelijke Adviezen van C. Snouck Hurgronje: 1889–1936* ('s-Gravenhage: Martinus Nijhoff, 1957).

should be viewed within the context of the Dutch colonial administration, which was dominated during his day by the emergence of the "Ethical Policy."

A significant element of Snouck's approach to the administration of "Native Muslims" in the Netherlands Indies was the categorical separation of *Sharīʿa* from *adat* (custom) in the realm of law. Following Snouck, the founder of systematized "customary law" (*adatrecht*) studies in the Netherlands, Cornelius van Vollenhoven, urged that greater attention be given to *adat* as a source of law in the pluralistic legal system of the Netherlands Indies.[62] Van Vollenhoven contrasted this living law of the villages with what he characterized as "lifeless Islamic school-law,"[63] and sharply condemned the theories of scholars such as L. W. C. van den Berg (1845–1927) who maintained that Indonesians who professed to being Muslims thereby implicitly accepted all the laws of their adopted faith at the time of conversion.[64] In contrast to what he regarded as the "wholly erroneous supposition that law follows religion," van Vollenhoven argued that "indigenous law forms the bulk, and the scraps of religious law merely the incidentals, of *adat law*."[65] During the late nineteenth and early twentieth centuries the Dutch academic disputes over the relative positions of different legal systems took on an increased administrative importance in developing an often bewilderingly pluralistic legal culture of Nederlands Indië.[66] In these discussions

[62] Van Vollenhoven's system of *adatrecht* is systematically laid out in the first two volumes of his *Het Adatrecht van Nederlansch-Indië* (Leiden: E. J. Brill, 1918–31). Selections from this lengthy and difficult work have been translated into English by J. F. Holleman and published together with a helpful introduction by H. W. J. Sonius, J. F. Holleman and H. W. J. Sonius, eds., *Van Vollenhoven on Indonesian Adat Law* (The Hague: Martinus Nijhoff, 1981). Van Vollenhoven's shorter essays on various aspects of *adat* law in Indonesia have also been collected and published as *Miskenningen van het Adatrecht: Vier Voordrachten aan de Nederlandsche-Indische Bestuursacademie* (Leiden: E. J. Brill, 1909), as well as his *Opstellen over Adatrecht: 1901–31* (Leiden: E. J. Brill, 1933). The term *adatrecht* actually originated in an article written by Snouck in 1893, and van Vollenhoven acknowledged Snouck's role in the initial development of the study of *adat* law throughout his writings, perhaps most explicitly in *De Ontdekking van het Adatrecht* (Leiden: E. J. Brill, 1928), 106–10. Although van Vollenhoven repeatedly cited Snouck's work with enthusiastic approval, considerable differences between the two have been highlighted in Benda, *The Crescent and the Rising, Sun*, 66–69.

[63] van Vollenhoven, *Indonesian Adat Law*, 18.

[64] The theory came to be referred to as *receptio in complexu*. Van den Berg's argument for the recognition of Islamic and other religious laws as binding for their native adherents was put forth in a number of important articles, including "Mohammedaansch recht en adat," *Het Regt in Nederlansch-Indië* 43 (1884): 137–55; "De afwijkingen van het Mohammedaansche familie- en erfrecht op Java en Madoera," *BKI* 41 (1892): 454–512; and "Nalezing . . ." 45 (1895): 291–314. Van Vollenhoven makes references to Snouck's "devastating" critiques of van den Berg in *De Ontdekking van het Adatrecht*, 111.

[65] van Vollenhoven, *Indonesian Adat Law*, 11.

[66] The pluralism of the Netherlands Indies' legal system was formalized in 1847 with the enactment of the Algemene Bepalingen van Wetgeving, which divided the population into two groups of

van Vollenhoven was working in what he viewed to be the tradition of the seventeenth-century Dutch jurist Grotius, quoted at the head of this chapter on legal pluralism and "unwritten law."[67] These ideas continued to animate discussions of *adat* among Indonesian scholars well into the era of independence.[68]

In 1927 the Dutch colonial government, under the influence of van Vollenhoven and his prominent students, officially established the prominence of *adat* law as formal legal policy in the East Indian colonies. With this came an increased institutionalization of the study of traditional law (*adatrecht*), which was now geared toward training not only academics and advisors, but also administrators of this law in the Dutch East Indian colonies.[69] In this context van Vollenhoven's pupil, B. ter Haar, played an important role. Ter Haar also departed from what has been described as the "orthodoxy" of van Vollenhoven's Reception Theory of *adatrecht* in publicly problematizing the perceived relation between law and local custom.[70] His re-envisionings of *adat* law were disseminated not only through his scholarly publications, but perhaps even more importantly through his work of training Indonesian scholars and jurists in Batavia.[71]

Until his death in a wartime Japanese internment camp, ter Haar served as the teacher of a number of Indonesian students who later went on to play influential roles in the constitutional and legal debates in the young Indonesian republic. Among ter Haar's many Indonesian students it was Hazairin who became most actively involved in discussions of Islamic law

determinant legal status: Europeans and Natives. Subsequent amendments to this classification continued to revise this categorization to account for other groups such as Chinese, Arab, and Indian immigrants who were classified as "Foreign Orientals." C. van Vollenhoven, "Vreemde Oosterlingen," in *Verspreide Geschriften* (Haarlem: H. D. Tjeenk Willink & Zoon, 1935), III, 221–24.

67 Indeed in addition to his many publications on the subject of *adat* law, van Vollenhoven also wrote extensively on Grotius and his legacy, with over 250 pages devoted to such topics in his 'Collected Works' (*Verspreide Geschriften*).

68 For a selection of writings on the subject by one of the most systematic scholars in the later Indonesian *adat* law tradition, see Moh. Koesnoe, *Kapita Selecta Hukum Adat: Suatu Pemikiran Baru* (Jakarta: Ikatan Hakim Indonesia, 2002), especially 1–136, and 169–234.

69 A short but incisive study of this phenomenon in English can be found in Roy Ellen, "The Development of Anthropology and Colonial Policy in the Netherlands: 1800–1960," *Journal of the History of the Behavioral Sciences* 12 (1976): 303–24. A more recent and richly detailed history of the men and institutions associated with the development of this academic-administrative complex can be found in C. Fasseur, *De Indologen: Ambtenaren voor de Oost, 1825–1950* (Amsterdam: Bert Bakker, 1993).

70 For a discussion of these differences in *adat*-law thinking, see Peter J. Burns, *The Leiden Legacy: Concepts of Law in Indonesia* (Jakarta: PT Pradnya Paramita, 1999), 246–54.

71 B. ter Haar, *Het adatproces der inlanders* (Leiden: E. J. Brill, 1915); "Adaterfrecht op Java: Rechtsvorming en Rechtstoepassing," *Indisch Tijdschrift van het Recht* 148 (1938): 201–39; and *Adat Law in Indonesia*.

that would have scandalized his mentor.[72] After completing his dissertation under ter Haar at the University of Indonesia in 1936, Hazairin spent three more years there as a junior lecturer before being posted as a specialist on *adat* law and assistant to the colonial courts in South Tapanuli (Sumatra).[73] During the Japanese occupation he was employed as an advisor on *adat* law for the military administration. After independence he continued on in Tapanuli as head of the new National Court, and then returned briefly to Bengkulu before relocating to Jakarta.

In the capital Hazairin was first appointed to a post in the Ministry of Justice, but at the same time he was increasingly returning to academic pursuits, accepting a teaching position in *adat* and Islamic law at his alma mater and, later, as a member of the Curatorial Board of IAIN Syarif Hidayatullah, Jakarta. It was in this capacity that he made some of his most significant contributions to Indonesian Muslim thought as he increasingly turned toward Islamic religious issues and their relation to *adat* law. Hazairin, however, had received little or no formal religious schooling in his youth. His knowledge of Islamic religious subjects came largely from self-study rather than the tutelage of a teacher in a more traditional Muslim milieu. Despite this non-traditional background, Hazairin was respected by many Muslims as a man of considerable personal piety.[74] He was an anomaly in his time, a Dutch-trained legal scholar in the *adat* law tradition who came to be considered as an advocate for the further Islamization of law in Indonesia.[75] In this his claim to authority rested not on his credentials as an *'ālim*, but rather on his personal commitment to Islam.[76]

[72] The biographical sketch of Hazairin in this chapter draws largely upon that of Iskandar Ritonga in his 1995 thesis from IAIN Jakarta, "Pemikiran Hazairin tentang Pembaharuan Hukum Islam di Indonesia," 14–37. Other information and anecdotes can be found in the memorial essays of Bismar Siregar, Hasbullah Bakry, Potan Arif Harahap, and S. M. Amin that are included in Sajuthi Thalib, *Pembaharuan Hukum Islam di Indonesia, in memoriam Prof. Mr. Dr. Hazairin* (Jakarta: Penerbit Universitas Indonesia, 1981).

[73] There he founded an Islamic University (Perguruan Tinggi Islam Djakarta, later Universitas Islam Jakarta) in 1951. In the capital Hazairin became active in politics, becoming co-chairman of the Great Indonesia Party (PIR) and eventually Minister of Internal Affairs (1953–54). However, when his term of office was cut short due to the internal split of his supporting party, he was granted a series of high-level positions in the Ministry of Justice (1954–59), and subsequently in the Ministry of Education and Culture. See Boland, *The Struggle of Islam*, 118; Ritonga, "Pemikiran Hazairin," 20–22.

[74] See, for example, the admiring essay of Bismar Siregar, "Prof. Mr. Dr. Hazairin Seorang Mujahid Penegak Hukum Berdasar Ke-Tuhanan Yang Maha Esa," in *Renungan Hukum dan Iman* (Jakarta: Grafikatama Jaya, 1988), 87–104.

[75] Throughout his writings, Hazairin alludes to the importance of a personal commitment to his faith in the formulation of his ideas on law (e.g. *Hukum Kewarisan Bilateral*, 1).

[76] This is a phenomenon for which Dale Eickelman has noted significant parallels in the modern Middle East. See Dale F. Eickelman, "The Art of Memory: Islamic Education and Its Social Reproduction," *Comparative Studies in Society and History* 20 (1978): 485–516.

Not being a traditional Islamic scholar, Hazairin composed no works of *tafsīr* proper, or in any other of the standard genres in the Islamic religious sciences. Instead he wrote general essays and modern-style legal works that were in a palpable sense self-consciously infused with an Islamic spirit. As a non-*'ālim* who dared to enter into discussions of Islamic law, Hazairin was criticized by the *'ulamā'* (whose exclusive territory this traditionally was) for not fulfilling the technical requirements of a *mujtahid*. To such criticisms, however, Hazairin was quick to respond by commenting with sadness on the present state of the Muslim community. Well beyond this, however, Hazairin worked to forge new models of *ijtihād* that posed new and rather overwhelming challenges to the "traditionalist" scholars who dominated many of the formal institutions of Islam in Indonesia during his day.[77]

Hazairin blamed the distressing situation of the contemporary Indonesian *umma* on the way in which Indonesian Muslims had adhered slavishly to the thought of the *'ulamā'* of the past, which blocked direct access to scripture and froze its message in a setting no longer appropriate to contemporary contexts.[78] His own work attempted to address this problem directly by publishing books and essays that approached important issues of Islamic legal interpretation in new forms and formats, especially that of the Western-inspired academic idiom in which he was trained. This led him to concentrate his energies on the composition of creative works on Islamic subjects that went beyond Indonesian translations and adaptations of works and genres rooted in the classical Arabic tradition.

As a pious Muslim and a professionally trained scholar of *adatrecht*, Hazairin concerned himself with the relationship between religion and custom in the sphere of law.[79] This remained one of his primary interests throughout his career. To this issue Hazairin brought a perspective incorporating current conceptualizations of Indonesian nationalism. As he wrote in his essay "Indonesia Satu Masdjid," Hazairin hoped that his work would

> serve to stimulate further thoughts and efforts toward the realization of our goal of, as far as is possible, bringing the structure of our national system into accord with the goals of an Islamic society for the Muslim peoples of Indonesia.[80]

[77] Mark Cammack, "Indonesia's 1989 Religious Judicature Act: Islamization of Indonesia or Indonesianization of Islam?" *Indonesia* 63 (1997): 149–50.

[78] Hazairin, "Hukum Baru di Indonesia," *Tujuh Serangkai tentang Hukum* (Jakarta: Tintamas, 1974), 135–37.

[79] One of his early Indonesian language publications focused specifically on this problem, *Pergolakan Penjesuaian 'Adat kepada Hukum Islam* (Jakarta: Bulan Bintang, 1951).

[80] *Indonesia Satu Masdjid* (Jakarta: Bintang Bulan, 1952), 14.

Toward this end he worked on several fronts to promote the reform and reinterpretation of Islamic law in line with the needs and concerns of the emerging Indonesian nation in the face of modernity. This, he insisted, would require some fundamental rethinking of the way in which Islam has been traditionally understood in his society.

In November 1951, Hazairin inaugurated a new Muslim college, the Perguruan Tinggi Islam (PTI) at Jakarta, by delivering a speech entitled "Islamic Knowledge and Society."[81] In this address, Hazairin put forward a distinction between "knowing Islam" (*tahu akan Islam*, i.e. being able to pray, etc.) and "knowledge of Islam" (*pengetahuan tentang Islam*). He then insisted that 'knowledge of Islam' is what must be most actively pursued in specialized institutions such as the PTI. Hazairin envisioned the graduates of such programs as forming cadres of new *mujtahids* educated not only in traditional religious subjects but also in modern sciences, a combination that would help them to better understand their religion in terms of the living realities of their society. Such scholars, Hazairin continued, were all but absent from the ranks of traditionally trained *'ulamā'*, whom he considered generally unaware and often incapable of comprehending the complex social realities of twentieth-century Indonesia.

Hazairin saw the reform and reinvigoration of Islamic law in Indonesia not as an individual matter but rather, as it was for Hasbi, a collective endeavor to be undertaken by representatives of the community in an officially organized body having some determined relationship with the state. It was for this reason for example, that, Hazairin advocated the utilization of local mosque structures in the formation of a Dewan Fatwa (Fatwa Council) to issue decisions on questions of religious law and to serve as a parallel body to the government's Representative Assembly.[82] Like Hasbi, Hazairin's ideal was to see a new generation of scholars working within the context of a modern and distinctly Indonesian national *madhhab*. Their task would be one of creating and actively contributing to the ongoing development of an Islamic legal methodology aimed at addressing issues in ways particularly appropriate to both local cultural contexts and national concerns.

At just about the same time that Hasbi was developing his conception of an Indonesian *fiqh*, Hazairin was also calling for the formation of a new school of Indonesian Muslim jurisprudence, which he originally referred

[81] *Ilmu Pengetahuan Islam dan Masjarakat* (Jakarta: Yayasan Perguruan Tinggi/Tintamas, 1951).
[82] See *Indonesia Satu Masdjid*.

to as *Madzhab Nasional.*[83] Both Hasbi and Hazairin agreed that the rulings of the new *madhhab* should not only be in conformity with the cultural realities of Indonesia but also should refer back to the Qur'ān and the *Sunna* of the Prophet as its ultimate sources of authority. The construction of this new approach would have been impossible without the exercise of a broad kind of *ijtihād*, something that was considerably easier to advocate in Indonesia after the pioneering work of the first generation of modern Indonesian Muslim reformers. Although he was trained in the Westernized academic background of *adat* law, Hazairin shared with modern Muslim autodidacts like Hasbi and even earlier thinkers and activists associated with PERSIS a concern for the reform of Islam and its role in contemporary society.[84]

Despite such similarities of their general aims, Hasbi and Hazairin brought very different interpretive approaches to their respective conceptualizations of an Indonesian national *madhhab*. In the introductory essay to his volume on Indonesian family law, Hazairin stated that his views on the bilateral structure of Islamic inheritance law are fundamentally based upon the Qur'ān, and intended as a corrective substitution for the prevailing patrilineal model established by non-Indonesian Muslim jurists.[85] But Hazairin did not limit himself to simply stripping away layers of earlier exegesis from the text of the Qur'ān, going on to construct a new contextualized reading of the relevant texts, one that was grounded firmly in his modern academic approach to describing and analyzing the social and cultural frameworks of contemporary Indonesia.

Based upon his study of *adat* law, Hazairin demonstrated that within Indonesia various communities based their inheritance customs upon three basic models: patrilineal, matrilineal, and bilateral (or parental). He argued that the majority of Indonesian Muslim societies tended toward a bilateral organization. For this reason, such a system would best serve as the model for a new, unified system of Islamic inheritance law for the developing Indonesian nation. Noting the discrepancies between such systems and the patrilineal model of Arabian society that had been so influential in

[83] In his *Hukum Kekeluargaan Nasional*, Hazairin acknowledged Hasbi's analogous work on *Fikih Indonesia*. Eventually the two ideas converged somewhat in Indonesian popular discourses, collapsed under the rubric of "*Madzhab Indonesia.*" Hazairin's terminology of "*madzhab nasional*" however reflects a kind of nationalistic orientation toward conceptions of Islamic law that was to be further advanced among some Indonesian Islamist groups in the later twentieth century. These developments will be further discussed in chapter 4.

[84] Indeed Hazairin drew directly upon Hassan's work on inheritance law (entitled, *Al-Faraa'idl*) in elaborating his own arguments for *bilateral* inheritance. See, for example, *Hukum Kewarisan Bilateral*, 135.

[85] *Hukum Kekeluargaan Nasional*, 2.

the early formulation of Islamic inheritance law, Hazairin contended that the inclusion of certain elements of Arabian customary law should not be considered part of the revealed law, but simply an historical accident arising from the place and time in which God's last messenger lived.

Hazairin maintained that in order for the *Sharīʿa* to become the actual "living law" of Indonesian society, it must be reinterpreted according to current cultural conditions, and not according to some foreign and historically distant situation.[86] This led him to propose a reinterpretation of Islamic law based upon the clear, specific rulings and more general principles of the Qur'ān and the *Sunna*, while simultaneously keeping an eye on their application in a society that included a "parental" (or bilateral) social structure. For, as Hazairin argued throughout his work, "man-made ethics and laws that do not conflict with the general axioms of the religious law remain valid [under Islam]."[87] Along these lines he maintained a distinction between what he saw as the "eternal laws of the Qur'ān and *Sunna*" and the temporally and culturally restricted glosses on them by the authors of classical works of *fiqh*.[88] In short, what he proposed was the establishment of a new system of inheritance that interpreted and elaborated upon the scriptural precepts of the Qur'ān and *Sunna* in terms of a *bilateral*, rather than a patrilineal, model of kinship.[89]

Through his studies of cultural anthropology and *adat* law, Hazairin attempted to understand the Qur'ān in light of the particular needs and concerns of Muslims living in Indonesia. In promoting his agenda of *ijtihād*, Hazairin elaborated a critique of *taqlīd*, which he defined polemically as 'blind imitation'. He also critqued what he viewed as the popular tendency

[86] For example, in *Hukum Kekeluargaan Nasional*, 30–33, 114; and *Denokrasi Pancasila* (Jakarta: Bina Aksara, 1970).

[87] *Hukum Kewarisan Bilateral menurut Qur'an dan Hadith* (Jakarta: Tintamas, 1958, 6th printing 1982), 74.

[88] "Fungsi dan Tujuan Pembinaan Hukum Dalam Negara Republik Indonesia yang Demokratis dan Berdasarkan Hukum," in *Tujuh Serangkai tentang Hukum* (Jakarta: Tintamas, 1974), 45.

[89] Hazairin's use of the term *bilateral* has led to some misunderstanding, especially by foreign scholars of Indonesian law and society. Some assume that the concept necessarily implies equal shares of inheritance for both sons and daughters of the deceased, as opposed to the traditional Muslim system whereby daughters receive half-shares of those allocated to their brothers. However this is not the case. Hazairin maintained that such a system of *bilateral* or *parental* inheritance could be in effect only for non-Muslim Indonesian citizens (*Hukum Kekeluargaan Nasional*, 102). For Hazairin, the Qur'ānic stipulation of differential shares to one's male and female children, respectively, was based upon a clear and authoritative scriptural foundation that could not be neglected or reasoned away. See Hazairin, *Hukum Kewarisan Bilateral Menurut Qur'ān dan Hadīth* (Jakarta: Tintamas, 1958); Hazairin, *Hukum Kekeluargaan Nasional*, 55–74. What could be reinterpreted was the extra-Qur'ānic system that grew out of traditional Arabian social custom and thence came to be incorporated within the body of laws of inheritance according to the established Sunni schools. *Hukum Kewarisan Bilateral*, 28ff.

for Muslims to conflate adherence to Arabian custom with the observance of Islamic law.[90] This distinction between *agama* (religion) and *adat* (custom) is a clear reflection of Hazairin's academic training in customary law. In his own words:

> Thus it becomes clear that the law of the Qur'ān can be exercised in every corner of the Muslim world without making every individual society therein a carbon copy of Arab society, as long as Muslims are able to free themselves from the shackles of *taqlīd* binding them to the ways of the traditional *'ulamā'* and the Arab social practices of a thousand years ago and return to the practice of *ijtihād* themselves. Through this they may reinterpret the religious principles and laws contained within the Qur'ān and *Sunna*, and then go on to reconcile their own particular age and society with those lofty precepts.[91]

Herein can be noted a paradigmatic shift between Hazairin's thought and that of earlier Indonesian Muslim reformers. For even Hasbi, writing at roughly the same time as Hazairin and sharing a similar openness to considerations of local custom in establishing legal rulings, tended to view the issue in terms of the classical Islamic categories of *Sunna* and *bid'a*.[92] Hazairin recast the discussion in terms of categories that reflected his own training in the Dutch colonial education system and the field of *adat* law, and in terms that went beyond the earlier reformist rhetoric of "blameworthy innovation."

In his evaluation of the relative positions of Islam and *adat* in the field of law, Hazairin argued that religion was to be the measure of the validity of *adat* and not vice versa, as had been the case under Dutch colonial law.[93] The study of *adat* law at the time was dominated by the Reception Theory which stipulated that, in the Netherlands East Indies, Islamic law was only valid to the extent that it had been received into the customary practice of local communities. Hazairin worked intensely to discredit Dutch Reception Theory[94] in Indonesian legal culture and to remove its influence from the legislative and judicial systems of the independent Indonesian

90 *Hukum Islam dan Masjarakat*, 8.

91 "Ilmu Pengetahuan Islam dan Masyarakat," in *Tujuh Serangkai tentang Hukum* (Jakarta: Tintamas, 1974), 106–07.

92 This theme recurs throughout his writings, see especially Hasbi Ash Shiddieqy, *Kriteria antara Sunnah dan Bid'ah* (Jakarta: Bulan Bintang, 1967).

93 In fact, he insisted on the repeal of all inheritance laws drafted during the colonial period in order to clear the slate for legislation derived according to his own jurisprudential methodology. Hazairin, *Hukum Kekeluargaan Nasional*, 33–34.

94 *Hukum Kekeluargaan Nasional*, 14. That is, the acceptance of Islamic law as binding only to the extent to which elements of it have been incorporated into the local system of customary law.

republic.[95] For many of his Dutch teachers and Indonesian colleagues in the field of *adat* law, a form of cultural relativity became a primary basis for their model of a theory of legal pluralism. However, Hazairin's unique position in the *adat* law school was defined in terms of his relationship to both Islam and Indonesian nationalism.[96] The first provided him with an absolute reference for moral and legal values that served as an ultimate anchor for the relative positions of the various traditional legal cultures of the Archipelago. This still, however, leaves the problem of the multiplicity of local adaptations and interpretations of the Sharīʿa, which frustrated efforts to create a uniform administration of the country. Where most of the Dutch and Dutch-trained scholars of *adat* law divided the Archipelago up into a catalogue of discrete Culture Areas, Hazairin conceived of the entire nation as sharing a basic core of 'Indonesian' *adat*. In this way he could postulate a single, overarching system of national law whose ultimate moral grounding proceeded from what he perceived to be the eternally valid teachings of Islam, as interpreted according to the needs and conditions of Muslims living in contemporary Indonesia.

As mentioned above, Hazairin exerted his most extensive efforts toward Indonesian legal reform in the area of inheritance law,[97] discussing his ideas on this subject in a number of publications. including *Hendak Kemana Hukum Islam Hukum Kekeluargaan Nasional*, and *Perdebatan dalam Seminar Hukum Nasional tentang Fara'idh tahun 1963* and *Hukum Kewarisan*

[95] Hazairin went well beyond a purely academic critique of Reception Theory, in famously labeling it the "theory of the Devil" (*Teori Iblis*). Hazairin, *Hukum Kekeluargaan Nasional*, 8. This castigation of Dutch colonial policies of legal pluralism remains an oft-reprised trope of Indonesian Islamists to this day.

[96] Indonesian nationalism helped to distinguish a number of early Indonesian jurists from their Dutch teachers and colleagues. Very few of them, however, combined such patriotism with a more developed formal commitment to Islam.

[97] Inheritance law remains Hazairin's signature field in the history of Indonesian *fiqh*. For a survey of diverse positions on inheritance law as elaborated within the corpus of classical Islam, see Cilardo, Agostino, *Dritto Ereditario Islamico delle Scuole Giuridiche Sunnite (Hanafita, Mālikita, Šāfiʿita e Hanbalita) e delle Scuole Giuridiche Zaydita, Zāhirita e Ibādita* (Rome: Instituto per l'Oriente C. A. Nallino, 1994). For critical studies of the early development of this system, see David S. Powers, *Studies in Qur'an and Hadith: The Formation of the Islamic Law of Inheritance* (Berkeley: University of California Press, 1986); and Richard Kimber, "The Qur'anic Law of Inheritance," *Islamic Law and Society* 5.3 (1998): 291–325. Islamic inheritance law becomes even more complicated in settings such as Indonesia, where strong pre-Islamic cultural traditions of intestate inheritance radically impact upon the ways and extent to which the traditional prescriptions of *fiqh* are elaborated. For an in-depth study of the interactions between customary law, Islamic law, and colonial law in one Indonesian community, see Franz von Benda-Beckmann, *Property in Social Continuity: Continuity and Change in the Maintenance of Property Relationships through Time in Minangkabau, West Sumatra* (The Hague: Martinus Nijhoff, 1979); for an anthropological study of more recent cases from Indonesia, see John R. Bowen, "'You May Not Give it Away': How Social Norms Shape Islamic Law in Contemporary Indonesian Jurisprudence," *Islamic Law and Society* 5.3 (1998): 382–408.

*Bilateral Menurut al-Qur'an dan Hadith.*[98] He also pursued a number of other projects related to the reformulation of a national family law and the drafting of the *RUU Hukum Kekeluaragaan*. His thoughts on, and position in, the development of this legislation are recorded in a preface to his *Hukum Kekeluargaan Nasional.*[99] There Hazairin dealt extensively with the reform of marriage law, seeking increased legal protection for Indonesian women in rulings on such issues as polygamy by invoking considerations of public interest (*istiṣlāḥ*).[100] In these pages Hazairin reveals a more comprehensive view of his understanding of Islamic legal change in Indonesia, comprising a "social revolution" that would, in the spirit of the Qur'ān, overcome the feudal practices and institutions of the colonial period. Here the *national* aspects of his new *madhhab* emerge most clearly as he holds up the movement to reform Islamic jurisprudence as a testament to the greatness of the modern Indonesian *umma*.[101]

### *FIQIH INDONESIA*

In their formulations of the building blocks for an Indonesian *madhhab*, Hasbi and Hazairin differed in a number of significant ways that reflect their respective educational backgrounds. Hasbi immersed himself in the Arabic tradition of Muslim scholarship and approached the formation of an Indonesian *madhhab* in a manner that grew out of, yet transcended, the previously existing schools. He took into consideration various opinions on different legal questions from a number of different schools. This approach had a long pedigree in the established sub-disciplines of *ikhtilāf* and *muqāranat al-madhāhib*, and their reconsideration by Muslim scholars from the modern Middle East. Hazairin, on the other hand, approached the issue from the perspective of the particular cultural conditions of Indonesian life, as viewed through his formal training in the Dutch academic tradition of *adat* law.

While on a formal/institutional level movements for the creation of an Indonesian *madhhab* passed away along with Hasbi, Hazairin, and their generation, the more lasting impact of their attempts for subsequent developments of Indonesian Muslim thought should be recognized. For in

98 According to the publisher, this book combines two of Hazairin's earlier works, *Hukum Kewarisan Bilateral Menurut al- Qur'an* and *Hukum Kewarisan Bilateral Menurut Hadith*.

99 Hazairin, *Hukum Kekeluargaan Nasional, ditambah dengan Lembaran Kerja untuk Rancangan Undang-undang Hukum Kewarisan Nasional Republik Indonesia* (Jakarta: Tintamas, 1982).

100 "Kesusilaan dan Hukum," *Tujuh Serangkai tentang Hukum* (Jakarta: Tintamas, 1974), 74–92.

101 *Hukum Kekeluargaan Nasional*, 4–6.

broadcasting the notion that Islamic jurisprudence could be reformed and reformulated along particular "national" lines, these two thinkers developed a new paradigm of modern Indonesian Muslim thought that drew upon significant aspects of local historical contexts to create a new "way" (*madhhab*) of conceptualizing an ideal order for society. In developing models of contextualization that sought material for their methodologies both within the Arabic-language tradition of Islamic legal scholarship and local cultural conceptions as interpreted within an inherited Western academic tradition, these thinkers forged new paths in Islamic legal thought that have continued to inspire lively discourse in Indonesia over the past half century. The works of both men constitute important contributions toward establishing major trends in contemporary Muslim debates over religion and law in Indonesian society. Their legacies have, however, often been developed in unexpected directions, as will be discussed with regard to the work of one of Hazairin's most prominent students in chapter 4.

CHAPTER 4

# *Sharī'a Islam in a* Pancasila *nation*

> Everything found in both the eastern and western pagan State is also found in a Christian State, but this all receives a different meaning and is revived in the spirit of Truth. There is dominion in the Christian State, but dominion not in the name of its own power, rather, in the name of the common weal and according to the directions of Church authority. There is in the Christian State subordination, but not out of slavish fear, rather, voluntarily and according to conscience . . . Rights exist in a Christian State, but rights which flow not from a boundless human egoism . . . In a Christian State there is law, but not in the sense of simple legitimation of existing relationships, rather in the sense of their reform according to the ideas of supreme Truth.
>
> V. S. Soloviev, *On the Christian State and Society*

The discussion of the work of Hazairin and Hasbi Ash Shiddieqy in chapter 3 presented some of the ways in which developing notions of Indonesian nationalism had come to frame discussions of Islamic law and society in the mid twentieth century. While both Hasbi and Hazairin advocated the further Islamization of Indonesian society, neither of them really questioned the position of Soekarno's *Pancasila* ideology as the official basis for the Indonesian state. Other Indonesian Muslims, however, had more totalizing visions of the role of Islam in modern Indonesian society, advocating the formal implementation of one vision of the Sharī'a or other through a variety of strategies in their attempts to establish what they viewed as an "Islamic state." Some took up armed struggle in the regional Darul Islam movements of the 1940s–50s.[1] Others mobilized into Islamist political parties, and among the many that were founded during this period the one that has had the most lasting impact has been Masjumi, the abbreviated name for the Madjelis Sjoero Moeslimin Indonesia (Indonesian Muslim Consultative Assembly), which had its early roots as a Muslim

[1] For an overview of these movements, see C. van Dijk, *Rebellion under the Banner of Islam: The Darul Islam in Indonesia* (The Hague: Martinus Nijhoff, 1981).

administrative organization set up by the Japanese during the wartime occupation of the archipelago.

## MASJUMI

Masjumi was founded in 1943 to be an umbrella organization for various Indonesian Islamic groups serving the interests of mobilization under the Japanese occupation. Under such an organizational rather than an ideological rubric, Masjumi had originally brought together Muslims of a wide variety of orientations, ranging from traditionalists to modernists. With the defeat of the Japanese and the Indonesian declaration of independence in 1945, Masjumi transformed itself into a political party with its own paramilitary wing.[2] In the process, the leadership of the party came to be dominated by Western-educated Muslims such as the Amsterdam-trained Dr. Soekiman Wirjosandjojo.[3] However, the figure who eventually came to most prominently define and represent the Masjumi platform was M. Natsir (d. 1993), who emerged as Indonesia's most prominent voice of Islamist opposition to Soekarno's use of *Pancasila* as the nation's official ideology.

During the early years of Soekarno's presidency in the 1940s, the interests of the military, leftists, those who were more Islamically oriented in politics, and others, hung in a delicate balance. During the 1950s, however, divisions within the ranks of politicized Indonesian Muslims made the fault lines within Masjumi more apparent as reformists sympathetic to the scripturalist agendas of such groups as PERSIS and the Muhammadiyah competed fiercely with the traditionalists associated with the NU for control of the Ministry of Religious Affairs and potential influence over the official interpretation of Islam in schools, courts, and official publications that such a position could provide.[4] These tensions eventually resulted in the NU splitting from Masjumi in 1952 to form its own political party.

[2] The paramilitary wing was named "Hizboellah," and in support of its mission Masjumi's leaders argued that it is a universal obligation (*fardhoe ʿain*) for Muslims to take up armed *jihād* (*melakoekan peperangan Djihad*) in defense of the country when invaded by *koeffar*. *Anggaran Dasar dan Rentjana Perdjoeangan Masjoemi Partai Politik Indonesia* (Bukit Tinggi: Dewan Pemimpin Daerah Masjoemi Soematera Barat, Apr. 1946), 36–37.

[3] Tamar Djaja, *Dr. Soekiman Wirjosandjojo, Ketua Oemoem 'Masjoemi'* (Boekit Tinggi: Penjiaran Ilmoe, n.d), 5.

[4] Tensions over the administration and jurisdiction of the courts were further complicated by departmental contestations over the administration between the Ministry of Religious Affairs and the Ministry of Justice. See Notosusanto, *Peradilan Agama Islam di Djawa dan Madura* (Yogyakarta, 1953), 12–15. For a more comprehensive history of these developments, see Daniel S. Lev, *Islamic Courts in Indonesia*.

Rifts within Masjumi continued to be a problem even after the majority of traditionalists associated with the NU had left the party.[5] One of the primary factors in preventing further dissolution of the party during this period was the strong leadership exercised by Natsir.

## M. NATSIR

Born in 1908 in West Sumatra where he attended the Hollands-Inlandsche School and Mulo, Natsir later moved to Bandung to continue his studies at the Algemene Middelbare School, where he further developed the proficiency in European languages that was to become such an important resource for him later in his career. It was also during that time that he first met A. Hassan and began to associate with PERSIS.[6] At Bandung, Natsir became an avid student of Hassan, attracted by both his ideas on scripturalist religious reform, and his vision of Islam as a social and political system.[7]

By 1932, Natsir had become head of a PERSIS school called Pendidikan Islam, which he energetically worked to expand through establishing a teacher's training school in Bandung and by setting up branches in other cities across Java. Later he also served as a teacher in the new PERSIS Pesantren founded in 1936.[8] However as mentioned in chapter 2, the PERSIS Pesantren differed significantly from the type of traditional Javanese institution of the same name. Most significantly, under PERSIS, Pesantren was reconceptualized as a center for the propagation of Islamic reformist agendas, rather than simply a place for the teaching of *fiqh* and other traditional Islamic religious sciences.

Such reconceptualized, reformist *pesantren* proliferated across Indonesia in the second half of the twentieth century, and graduates of these

5 Such internal divisions were recognized as a problem during the 1954 Masjumi Convention (Muktamar VII) where the party leadership issued an explicit statement on its respect for the various positions of the established *madhhabs* followed by Indonesian Muslims, while also specifically stating that "the Masjumi Party should not get itself caught up in disputes over technical differences of legal opinion (Ind. *chilafiah*) that would result in shattering the unity of the *umma*," *Muktamar Masjumi ke VIII – 22–29 Des. 1956 di Bandung* (Jakarta: N. V. Pertjetakan Gunung Sahari, 1956), 50.

6 Soebadio Sastrosatomo, "Percikan Pemikiran Dr. Mohammad Natsir dalam Pergumulan Intelektual di Indonesia," in *M. Natsir: Sumbangan dan Pemikirannya untuk Indonesia*, ed. Anwar Harjono (Jakarta: Penerbit Media Dawah, 1995), 103–09. For an evocative description of PERSIS and its early activities in Bandung, see Ajip Rosidi, *M. Natsir: Sebuah Biografi I* (Jakarta: Girimukti Pasaka, 1990), 15–80.

7 Anwar Harjono *et al.*, *M. Natsir: Sumbangan dan Pemikirannya untuk Indonesia* (Jakarta: Penerbit Media Da'wah, 1995), 52.

8 Howard M. Federspiel, *Islam and Ideology in the Emerging Indonesian State: The Persatuan Islam (PERSIS), 1923–1957* (Leiden: E. J. Brill, 2001), 114–15.

institutions have come to have a significant voice in public debates over the role of Islam in Indonesian society. Natsir's own contributions to developments in this direction continued throughout his later career, as another organization that he founded the Dewan Dakwah Islamiyah Indonesia (DDII) came to play an important role in carrying forward the legacy of the Bangil *pesantren* through its involvement in the foundation of the Saudi-affiliated Institute for the Islamic and Arabic Sciences (LIPIA) at Jakarta in the late 1980s.[9]

## "ISLAM AS IDEOLOGY"

In addition to working actively in connection with PERSIS schools, Natsir was also a frequent contributor to the association's publications, editing *Pembela Islam* and writing for various other journals, sometimes under the pseudonyms A. Muchlis and I.S. His rhetorical talents and organizational energies facilitated his rapid rise through the ranks of PERSIS, and by 1937 he was on its management board.[10] Through his work in PERSIS, Natsir developed an understanding of the relationship between ritual behavior and ideological mobilization that was to have a deep impact on the work of his later career in the DDII, as will be discussed below. While working so energetically for PERSIS through the 1930s, he was also engaged with developments in other activist organizations such as the Jong Islamieten Bond and the Sarekat Islam.

It was through his association with Sarekat Islam that Natsir came into contact with another Muslim leader who was to have a formative effect on him – H. Agus Salim.[11] It was under Salim that he began to learn more about formal organization building and the workings of a political party.[12] Indeed, in an interview near the end of his life, Natsir made the point of mentioning that although at Bandung he studied more closely

[9] Rémy Madinier, "Du temps des chameaux à celui du béton radioactive 'les nouveaux usages islamistes de passé'," *Archipel* 64 (2002): 152.

[10] Peter Burns, *Revelation and Revolution: Natsir and the Panca Sila* (Townsville, Australia: Committee of South-East Asian Studies, James Cook University of North Queensland, 1981), 4. On Natsir's early involvement with PERSIS, see also Federspiel, *Islam and Ideology*, 113–20.

[11] Collected essays on Salim's life can be found in *Seratus Tahun Hadji Agoes Salim* (Jakarta: Penerbit Sinar Harapan, 1984). For an anthology of his writings in Dutch and Indonesian, see *Djedjak Langkah Hadji A. Salim: Pilihan Karangan Utjapan dan Pendapat Beliau dari Dulu sampai Sekarang* (Jakarta: Tintamas, 1954). One of his small booklets on Islamic theology is also available in English translation as H. Agus Salim. *A Philosophical Explanation of Tauhid, Taqdir, and Tawakkal*, trans. J. T. Salim (Jakarta: PT Intermasa, 1987).

[12] Anwar Harjono *et al.*, *M. Natsir: Sumbangan dan Pemikirannya untuk Indonesia* (Jakarta: Penerbit Media Da'wah, 1995), 52.

under A. Hassan, he actually felt that he benefited more in the long term from the guidance of H. Agus Salim.[13] On the level of ideas, he was influenced in particular by Salim's conception of the Islamic religious basis for Indonesian nationalism.[14] Throughout more than six decades of public life, a central preoccupation of Natsir's writings was nationalism and its relationship to Islamic religious ideals and the political aspirations of the Indonesian *umma*. In the course of formulating his views on this subject, Natsir came to understand nationalism (*kebangsaan*) as a utilitarian means to preserve Islamic religious values, rather than an ultimate end in itself.[15] In this he appears to have been less interested in formal institutions of law and government than in Islam as an abstract ideal. In fact, in their respective platforms for the 1955 elections, Masjumi, under Natsir's leadership, did not put much emphasis on legal matters, whereas the NU advanced aspirations for the creation of a council of ʿulamāʾ to settle cases in line with traditionalist understandings of *fiqh*.[16]

Natsir's Islamist idealism is reflected even in some of his early writings and speeches from the 1930s in which he speaks of nationalist aspirations for an independent state more as instrumental in the service of Islamic religious objectives than as ends in themselves.[17] The energy that he exerted in further exploring this issue increased dramatically as Natsir rose to prominence as one of the most articulate voices in the Masjumi political party during the later 1940s. By the early 1950s, his thoughts on this had come to fruition with the publication of his landmark essay *Islam as Ideology*. In this text, Natsir built his argument for envisioning Islam as an all-encompassing system of law and society by referencing the oft-quoted line from the British Orientalist H. A. R. Gibb, "Islam is indeed much more than a system of theology; it is a complete civilization."[18] Natsir, however, developed

[13] M. Natsir, *Pendidikan, Pengorbanan, Kepemimpinan, Primordialisme, dan Nostalgia* (Jakarta: Media Daʿwah, 1987), 14.

[14] Harjono *et al.*, *M. Natsir: Sumbangan dan Pemikirannya*, 11. Michael Laffan has described in detail Salim's role in developing Islamic conceptions of Indonesian nationalism, see *Islamic Nationhood and Colonial Indonesia: The Umma Below the Winds* (London: RoutledgeCurzon, 2003), 181–89.

[15] Asna Husin, "*Philosophical and Sociological Aspects of Daʿwah: A Study of Dewan Dakwah Islamiyah Indonesia*" (Columbia University dissertation, 1998), 80.

[16] Rémy Madinier and Andrée Feillard, "At the Sources of Indonesian Political Islam's Failure: The Split between the Nahdlatul Ulama and the Masyumi in Retrospect," *SI* 6.2 (1999): 1–38.

[17] Burns, *Revelation and Revolution*, 12. Here one can see one of the significant ways in which the political platform of Masjumi reflected positions earlier developed among PERSIS activists. The connections between these two organizations have been described in terms of a "special relationship" by Federspiel, *Islam and Ideology*, 259–64.

[18] Natsir, *Islam Sebagai Ideologie* (Jakarta: Penjiaran Ilmu, 1950), 7. There, as well as in his essay "Agama dan Politik," *Capita Selecta* II, 157 (written February, 1950), Natsir presents the English of Gibb's statement somewhat differently, using "religious system" for Gibb's "system of theology."

this totalizing model toward the idea of a systematized world- or life-view, arguing that Muslims have "a life-view (Dt. *levensbeschouwing*) and ideology of their own, just as Christians have, and just as Fascists or Communists have their own respective worldviews and ideologies."[19]

Elsewhere, Natsir equates the ideology of Islam with a philosophy of life (*falsafah hidup*) in which considerations of the world beyond (*akhīra*) can never be separated from the affairs of this world (*dunya*).[20] Reading through his statements on ideology as a totalizing worldview reflecting "deeply held commitments"[21] one would not be surprised to come across a formal definition of Islam as a complex for carrying ideals and inspirations echoing the "long-lasting moods and motivations" of a Geertzian "cultural system". Indeed, what is particularly striking in this discourse is the way in which Natsir argues for an understanding of the essence of Islam that is completely framed by categories developed in modern European thought – just as elsewhere he draws on Emile Durkheim and William James for his definition of "religion" more generally (Ind. *agama*), and derives his vision of Islam in history from Lothrop Stoddard's *New World of Islam*.[22]

In relying so heavily on modern Western authorities for his understanding of Islam, Natsir is clearly in line with a pervasive – though little recognized – trend of Islamism in Indonesia and elsewhere over the past half century.[23] Beyond that, however, Natsir's specific conception of Islam as a complete ideology and cultural system was put forward to counter

B. J. Boland originally pointed to this discrepancy in *The Struggle of Islam in Modern Indonesia* (The Hague: Martinus Nijhoff, 1982), 79. For the English original of Gibb's remarks, see *Whither Islam? A Survey of Modern Movements in the Muslim World* (London: Victor Gollancz Ltd., 1932), 12.

19 Natsir, *Islam Sebagai Ideologie*, 10. 20 Natsir, *Islam Sebagai Dasar Negara*, 3.

21 Natsir, *Pendidikan, Pengorbanan*, 77–78.

22 E.g. in Natsir, *Islam Sebagai Dasar Negara*, 79, 20. The latter seems ironic in light of his calls earlier in this same pamphlet to reject the *gedachte-traditie* of European Orientalism. Such an ambivalent relationship with Orientalist scholarship became a common pattern in the works of later *da'wa*-minded Indonesian Muslims. For example, in the speech delivered on the award of his honorary doctorate by Hazairin at the Universitas Islam Djakarta, Aboebakar Atjeh both warned of the "poisons" slipped into Western writings on Islam while at the same time urging students to study the great achievements of Islamic learning in the works of Brockelmann, Nicholson, and Gibb. A. Atjeh, *Islam – Sumber Djihad* (Jakarta: Universitas Islam Djakarta, 1967), 54–55, 31.

23 For example, in enumerating the major influences on his intellectual development Natsir's younger contemporary, H. M. Rasjidi, pointed to the work of Snouck Hurgronje, Louis Massignon, and W. C. Smith alongside that of 'Abd al-Rāziq and Aḥmad Sūrkatī. H. M. Rasjidi, *Islam dan Indonesia di Zaman Modern: Pidato mengkukuhkan jand diutjapkan pada tgl. 20 April 1968 di Aula Univesitas Indonesia, penagkatan Guru Besar Hukum Islam dan Lembaga Islam* (Jakarta: Bulan Bintang, 1968). In Natsir's own writings he clearly indicates that the source for his knowledge of the classical Islamic tradition comes not from Arabic texts, but rather from the writings of European Orientalists. See, for example, his essays on the work of medieval Muslim philosophers in *Capita Selecta*, I (Bandung: N. V. Penerbitan W. van Hoeve).

what he perceived to be tendencies within contemporary Indonesia to limit discussions of Islam strictly to religious and ritual matters, rather than to more fully integrate Islam's implications into discussions of public life. Such efforts to foster broader social and political visions of Islam reflect clearly some of the ways in which the influence of Agus Salim served to redirect some of the reformist energies of Natsir toward ends different from those of Hassan and his PERSIS colleagues.

Natsir's development of a politicized agenda of reformist Islam in Indonesia developed a line of argument that increasingly emphasized a conflict between Islamic and secular conceptions of Indonesian nationalism.[24] Toward this end, a considerable section of Natsir's *Islam sebagai Ideologie* is taken up critiquing the work of the Egyptian scholar ʿAlī ʿAbd al-Rāziq (d. 1966) and the use that Soekarno made of his ideas on the separation of religion from government in early Islamic history.[25] Soekarno was inspired by ʿAbd al-Rāziq's arguments to the effect that, as Muḥammad had ordained no particular system of government before the time of his death, Muslims could adopt whatever political system they saw as best serving their contemporary needs. Natsir, however, was unwilling to cede arguments on Islam and politics to his secular nationalist opponents' appeal to this modern Egyptian authority.

While opposing Soekarno's vision of a largely secular *Pancasila* vision of Indonesian nationalism, however, Natsir also maintained that his political ideologization of Islam was not tantamount to a 'theocracy.' What he meant by this, however, was rather specific; that is, he strove to distinguish his ideal of a state in which Islam was the basis of the state (*dasar negara*) and the Sharīʿa was the law of the land, from one that would be governed by a regime of clerics. The ultimate goal, repeatedly emphasized, was to establish a state that could facilitate the creation of a society in which Muslims would be empowered to develop their own projects of piety as well as "Islamic" agendas of social, economic, and political justice.

[24] In response to Soekarno's calls to "rejuvenate" (*me-'moeda'-kan pengertian Islam*), Natsir argued that what was needed was not a 'rejuvenation' (*memudakan*) of Islam, but rather a 'simplification' (*memudahkan*) of understandings of Islam that would facilitate the implementation of its ideals in modern Indonesia. For Natsir maintained that Islam was a perfect, self-sufficient system and therefore it is not in need of any outside influences, accretions, or reinterpretations. Thus he reacted sharply to Soekarno's calls for a 'cure' to the ailments currently suffered by Islam by insisting that "Islam is not sick, and it is not in need of any 'Doktor'." Mohd. Natsir, *Islam dan Akal Merdeka* (Tasikmalaja: Persatoean Islam, 1947, originally appeared in *Panji Islam* (Medan, 1941), 34–38).

[25] His controversial work on this subject is *al-Islām wa uṣūl al-ḥukm* (Cairo, 1925). A short biographical sketch and excerpts from his writings in English translation can be found in Louis Awad, *The Literature of Ideas in Egypt, Part I* (Atlanta: Scholars Press, 1986), 154–65.

### NATSIR, *PANCASILA*, AND MASJUMI

Natsir was general head of Masjumi from 1949 to 1958. Toward the end of this period the party developed into a vocal oppositionist faction expressing the growing antipathy between its leader and the increasingly left-leaning government of Soekarno. Earlier on, however, Natsir was appointed to various ministerial positions in the Soekarno government in the late 1940s and early 1950s,[26] and through the early 1950s Natsir continued to speak and write of what he saw as the complementary relationship between the social visions of Islam and *Pancasila*. Until 1954, Natsir was still publicly defending *Pancasila* and its principle of "the One-ness of God" (*Ke-Tuhanan Yang Maha Esa*), expressing such views in a number of oft-reprinted speeches, including "*Apakah Pantjasila Bertentangan dengan Adjaran Al-Quran*?" (Is Pancasila in conflict with the teachings of the Qur'ān?).[27]

As the Indonesian Communist Party (Partai Komunis Indonesia/PKI) grew in influence under the leftward march of Soekarno's government in the later 1950s, Natsir abandoned his earlier attempts at reconciling *Pancasila* and Islam.[28] Through this period, Natsir reacted increasingly sharply to the ways in which he saw *Pancasila* being more aggressively reasserted as a symbol of resistance to the idea of an Islamic state in Indonesia.[29] Later in life, Natsir reflected on his speeches in the earlier 1950s that sought to reconcile Islam and *Pancasila* as a reflection of changing social and political contexts – arguing that up to that time both Islam and *Pancasila* were working partners in early Indonesian attempts to address pressing issues of state and society. He is careful, however, to add that for him even in these early discussions the ultimate supremacy of Islam in relation to *Pancasila* was never in question.[30] What is clear is that Natsir's evolving understandings of Islam as an ideology, as well as his conception of the Islamic state, were resolutely nationalist. In this respect Natsir stood clearly within what James Piscatori has referred to as the "modern intellectual consensus on the

[26] Serving as minister of information under three different cabinets (1946, 1947, 1948–49), and as prime minister, 1950–51. Burns, *Revelation and Revolution*, 5–6.

[27] *Capita Selecta* II, 144–50. Originally delivered in May 1954.

[28] The increasingly sharp Masjumi reactions against the threat that Communism posed in taking over the *Pancasila* state at the time are evidenced in such polemic pamphlets as *Kami Memanggil* (Jakarta: Dewan Pemimpin Partai Masjumi Bahagian Penerangan, 1955).

[29] Indeed, one of the leading Communist representatives in the Konstitutante, Sakirman, made the argument that *Pancasila* was an "instrument of struggle." Margaret Bocquet-Siek and Robert Cribb, *Islam and the Panca Sila* (Townsville, Australia: Committee of South-East Asian Studies, James Cook University of North Queensland, 1991), iii, 78.

[30] Natsir, *Pendidikan, Pengorbanan*, 34–36.

nation-state" among Muslim thinkers that gained ground in the Middle East during the twilight of the Ottoman Empire.[31]

In forming his conceptions of Islamic ideology as the foundation of the Indonesian state, Natsir was, moreover, not impressed by arguments for non-confessional approaches defining the Indonesian state that called attention to the demographic realities of Indonesian religious diversity. Instead, he consistently upheld the primacy of ideology over empirical evidence.[32] Responding to disparities between his vision of a "pure" Islamic Indonesia and the actual condition of the country's population, he argued, "should we not change the facts in the direction of the ideology? It should not be the other way round."[33] Over the decades that followed, Natsir pursued this goal of social transformation by various means including preaching, propaganda, and the polls.

The potential instrumental role of elections toward the establishment of an Islamic state in Indonesia was particularly highly regarded by Natsir, at least before the 1955 general election. He appears, however, to have understood democracy in terms of pure majoritarianism, with little emphasis placed on guarantees of the rights of minorities in a representative system. Majority vote was thus sufficient to confer legitimacy as well as to confirm the agenda – and the legal order – of the statistically largest sector of society:

> those who reject Islamic laws out of consideration of not harming the feelings of non-Muslims harm the Muslims whose number is twenty times greater than those of other groups. For this would mean an encroachment upon the rights of the majority.[34]

In his view, the sheer fact that a demographic majority of Indonesians identify themselves as Muslims implies that all those who acknowledge Islam as their religion should also then necessarily accept a particular understanding of the Qur'ān that was self-evident to modern Muslim reformists like himself; that is, an unchanging "Qur'ānic law" valid for all times and places.[35] Following such an essentialized understanding of the Qur'ān as a source of law, Natsir came to view the Sharī'a as the only possible means

[31] James P. Piscatori, *Islam in a World of Nation-States* (Cambridge: Cambridge University Press, 1986), 76–100.

[32] The utopian nature of Natsir's vision here echoes a common theme of Islamist visions of social order in other modern Muslim societies as well.

[33] Burns, *Revelation and Revolution*, 47 – quoting an article by Natsir in an August 1940 issue of *Pandji Islam* that was later reprinted in *Capita Selecta* II, 483.

[34] Burns, *Revelation and Revolution*, 28 – quoting *Capita Selecta* I, 486.

[35] M. Natsir, *Tindjauan Hidup* (Jakarta: Penerbit Widjaya, 1957), 60.

through which to ensure the political justice necessary for social stability. Implementing the law of Islam in modern Indonesia, he argued, would reflect the cultural values and "living law" of the country's Muslim majority, and establish distinct delimitations of rights and obligations between rulers and the general population.[36]

Masjumi's political struggles to advance this agenda in Indonesia, however, experienced several significant setbacks in the 1940s–50s, particularly in the 1955 general election. All through this period Natsir, then general head and primary public spokesman for the party, had worked strenuously among Masjumi constituents and the Indonesian Muslim community at large to convince voters of the importance of this election.[37] While occasionally reminding his listeners that electoral success should not be regarded as an ultimate goal, he argued that it was nonetheless a very important step toward the greater goal of "fully Islamizing" Indonesian society, and he considered participation in the party's campaign to be a religious obligation (*Fardhu ain dalam agama*).[38] Despite such efforts, however, Masjumi's electoral performance in 1955 was disappointing, taking a slim majority (53 percent) in only one province (Central Sumatra), and earning returns of only between 10 percent–45 percent in most other areas.[39]

Worrying that the disappointment over election returns would lead some Masjumi supporters to "give up their principles or change their opinion," the party leadership spun the results as an "eye opener" to the challenges facing the Indonesian *umma*. In particular, they emphasized the fact that although "90 percent" of the Indonesian population is identified as Muslim, only a small minority of them could be said "to know and be aware of Islam" (*tahu dan sadar akan Islam*).[40] Thus chastened by their failure in the sphere of electoral politics, some Masjumi leaders began to search for other ways through which to pursue the further Islamization of Indonesian society. By the time of the eighth Masjumi conference in December, 1956, the party was already formulating new strategies in a forum then recently established

[36] M. Natsir, *Demokrasi di bawah Hukum* (Jakarta: Penerbit Media Da'wah, 2002 – based upon lectures given in 1966), 8–15.

[37] See, for example, *Anggaran Dasar dan Roemah Tangga – Program Perdjoeangan dan Program Oesaha-Tjepat* 'Masjoemi' *Partai Politik Islam* (Bogor: Penerbit Masjoemi, 1946), 37–38.

[38] Natsir, *Tindjauan Hidup*, 37. This book was compiled from speeches given before Masjumi audiences between 1954 and 1956.

[39] Robert Cribb, *Historical Atlas of Indonesia* (University of Hawaii Press, 2000), 163–64.

[40] *Muktamar Masjumi ke VIII – 22–29 Des. 1956 di Bandung* (Jakarta: N. V. Pertjetakan Gunung Sahari, 1956), 58–59.

for debates over the formal basis of the Indonesian state, known as the Constituent Assembly (*Konstituante*).[41]

Over the first decade of independence leading up the 1955 elections, Indonesia had experienced a rapid run through the successive promulgation of a number of provisional constitutions in 1945, 1949, and 1950. In 1956 the Constituent Assembly was charged with the task of developing a permanent constitution for the country.[42] It was in session from November 10, 1956 to June 2, 1959. Some of the most formally articulated statements of the ideological platforms of the various factions were put forward in November–December 1957, when the three major blocks of Constituent Assembly delegates – those advocating *Pancasila*, Islam, and Marxist ideologies, respectively – debated fiercely over the basis for the state (*dasar negara*).[43] The antagonistic debates that characterized their meetings have been described by Adnan Buyung Nasution as "ideological, absolutist, and antagonistic, so that the parties did not come closer to each other but on the contrary were driven farther apart."[44] Natsir's 1957 speech before the Constituent Assembly highlighted aspects of modern Indonesian agendas for the establishment of Islam as the foundation for the nation's legal system which, although yet unrealized, continue to inspire more recent generations of Islamists in the country.

## *ḤUDŪD* AND "NATURAL LAW"

In that historic speech, Natsir voiced a strong rejection of *Pancasila* as an empty abstraction of "colorless neutrality" and argued for the establishment of Islam as the ideological foundation of the Indonesian state. Only Islam, he argued, could serve to ground the constitution in what he believed to be "the true feelings and beliefs of the people." The evocation of various understandings of the Sharīʿa as the "living law" of Indonesian society was also common among Natsir's contemporaries such as Hazairin, and has ever

[41] An overview of Masjumi Muktamar decisions from 1946 to 1954 can be found in *Muktamar Masjumi ke VIII*, 28–50.

[42] For a discussion of the interactions between various Islamic political parties including Masjumi and the NU within the framework of the Constituent Assembly, see Daniel S. Lev, *The Transition to Guided Democrary: Indonesian Politics, 1957–1959* (Ithaca: Cornell University Modern Indonesia Project, 1966), 123–32.

[43] The texts of the major speeches of these sessions are available in English translation, in addition to having been published in Indonesian, Bocquet-Siek and Cribb. *Islam and the Panca Sila*; *Tentang Dasar Negara Republik Indonesia dalam Konstituante* (Jakarta: Kementerian Penerangan, 1954–58).

[44] Adnan Buyung Nasution, *The Aspiration for Colonial Government in Indonesia: A Socio-legal Study of the Indonesian Konstituante, 1956–1959* (Jakarta: Pustaka Sinar Harapan, 1992), 41.

since become a common trope in the rhetorical appeals of contemporary Indonesian Islamists for the formal implementation of Islamic law.

This same speech also contains one of the clearest statements of one of Natsir's trademark innovations in Indonesian Muslim thought, which he referred to as "Theistic Democracy" – a system in which the sovereignty of the people was to be exercised within certain limits that had been determined by God. The language Natsir used there is reminiscent of a phrase used throughout his writings on Islamic law when discussing divinely imposed limitations placed on the exercise of human reason in the practice of *ijtihād*. The word he used to refer to these 'limits' in both senses was *ḥudūd*, a term which in Islamic legal discourses and Islamist political rhetoric is usually used to refer to canonically established corporeal punishments for certain stipulated offenses. Natsir, however, spoke of *ḥudūd* in a rather unconventional way, describing these "limits" (set by God) as "universal moral principles" in a way reminiscent of some Western discourses on natural law.[45]

The body of ideas referred to as Natural Law in European traditions of philosophy and jurisprudence is both broad and internally diverse.[46] Among them, however, some scholars perceive certain shared characteristics, including an assumption that there are objective values embodied by law that can be accessed through human reason, as well as the general sense that civil law not only governs individuals in society, but that it is also itself governed by certain external constraints.[47] Natsir's conception of Islamic law could be described by these broad parameters as well. Citing the Qur'ānic verses 90 (*al-balad*): 8–12, he repeatedly stressed that human beings are called upon to use their own God-given faculties in understanding and responding to revelation, thence going on to argue that Islam both encourages and provides necessary parameters for the exercise of human reason.[48]

In the notes accompanying the published text of his 1957 Constituent Assembly address, Natsir points out the origins of such an approach to natural law in the work of the Roman Catholic theologian, Thomas Aquinas

[45] *Islam and the Panca Sila*, 19ff. See also Yusril Ihza, "Modernisme Islam dan Demokrasi: Pandangan Politik Mohammad Natsir," in: Harjono, *M. Natsir*, 143–44.

[46] For a sense of the range of contemporary Natural Law theories see, for example, Randy E. Barnett, "A Law Professor's Guide to Natural Law and Natural Rights," *Harvard Journal of Law and Public Policy* 20 (1997): 655.

[47] For more on such modern conceptions of 'natural law' in the Western tradition, see Brian Bix, "Natural Law Theory: The Modern Tradition," in *Handbook of Jurisprudence and Legal Philosophy*, ed. Jules L. Coleman and Scott Shapiro (Oxford University Press, 2000), 3–4.

[48] Natsir, *Islam dan Akal Merdeka*, 16.

(d. 1274).[49] The implications of the link here between medieval Christian and modern Islamist thought are interesting for a number of reasons. For one, it once again raises issues of the impact of Western formulations of "religion" – and Islam in particular – upon modern Muslim thinking about Islam. Mention has already been made of the importance of Gibb's statement on the nature of Islam for Natsir's project of conceptualizing Islam as an ideology. Well beyond this, however, throughout his voluminous writings on Islam, Natsir also drew far more from works of European Orientalism than he did from either classical Arabic sources or modern Indonesian publications. His colonial education gave him access to modern studies of Islam and Muslim societies written in English, German, and French, as well as Dutch. Works of this type are cited extensively as the sources for his essays on medieval Muslim thinkers such as Ibn Rushd, Ibn Tufayl, and Miskawayh, reprinted in his *Capita Selecta*.[50]

Well beyond this general point, however, Natsir's citation of a medieval Roman Catholic theologian in establishing his conception of Natural Law raises questions about just what he had in mind when deploying such a reference and, more generally, what he found appealing in certain forms of Western natural law reasoning. Modern neo-Thomist revivals and other reinterpretations of Natural Law theory flourished in the middle decades of the twentieth century, not only in Europe and the United States, but in many parts of the world in contexts informed by processes of decolonization in many parts of Asia and Africa.[51] These developments have had some of their most lasting impact in modern Muslim societies through their influence on the formulation and proclamation of the 1948 United Nations Universal Declaration of Human Rights.[52] Prominent in discussions of this was the notion of "fundamental rights," a concept that Natsir also appealed to with the Indonesian terminology *hak-hak asasi* in arguing for

[49] For an introduction to Aquinas' thought on natural law and related issues, see John M. Finnis, *Aquinas: Moral, Political, and Legal Theory* (Oxford University Press, 1998).

[50] *Capita Selecta* I, 3–36.

[51] For brief overviews of these developments, see, e.g. T. Payzs, "Human Rights," and "Natural Law," in *New Catholic Encyclopedia* (New York: McGraw-Hill, 1967), VII, 209–14 and X, 251–71, respectively.

[52] The provisional Indonesian constitution of 1950 was one of the first national constitutions to incorporate the text of the *Universal Declaration*. Crowe, Michael Bertram, *The Changing Profile of the Natural Law* (The Hague: Martinus Nijhoff, 1977), 251. For a discussion of the impact of decolonization on the formulation of the UN declaration, see Johannes Morsink, *The Universal Declaration of Human Rights: Origins, Drafting, and Intent* (Philadelphia: University of Pennsylvania Press, 1999), 96–102.

what he considered to be "the Islamic position" on the relationships between individuals and the state.[53]

Another religious intellectual who was deeply involved with the broader international conversations on such topics in the middle decades of the twentieth century, and whose views intersect at certain key points with those of Natsir, was the Roman Catholic philosopher Jacques Maritain (d. 1973).[54] In formulating his approach to Natural Law, Maritain argued that its most basic principles could be known not through reason or any rational method, but rather "connaturally" or "by inclination"; and that these impressionistic bases for right are ultimately incontestable.[55] Modern Muslim appeals to analogous conceptions of natural law created new spaces for the impressionistic elaboration of agendas based upon implicit but unexamined assumptions about the Way of God. This givenness was expressed by Natsir in rhetorical reductions such as "Islam, you know . . . it's Islam" (*Islam itu . . . ialah Islam*).[56] Natsir's assumptions about an essentialized Islam dovetailed with his understanding of Muslim majoritarianism as legitimizing the implementation of his own particular model for the modern Indonesian state.

In his published writings and public speeches, Natsir appeared to take for granted that just as the essence of Islam could be impressionistically appealed to, so the Muslim character of Indonesian society, could be assumed in this emerging Indonesian Islamist discourse. The argument here made by Natsir and other Masjumi activists appealed to raw demographic data reporting near 90 percent of the population of the archipelago identifying themselves as Muslims. Analogous positions have also been advanced by modern Christian religious thinkers in other countries, while some of their critics have characterized such reasoning as tending toward

[53] *Demokrasi di bawah Hukum*, 5–7.

[54] While there are some points of similarity in some aspects of this approach, it should be recognized that as a religious thinker Maritain differed from Natsir in a number of significant ways. This is particularly evident in Maritain's deep mastery of medieval religious thought, and in particular of the work of Thomas Aquinas. For a broader historical overview of twentieth-century developments of Natural Law thinking in which Maritain was situated, see David Hollenbach, *Claims in Conflict: Retrieving and Renewing the Catholic Human Rights Tradition* (New York: Paulist Press, 1979), 41–106.

[55] Jacques Maritain, *Natural Law: Reflections on Theory and Practice*, ed. and introduced William Sweet (South Bend, IN: St. Augustine's Press, 2001), 9. An excellent short introduction to Maritain's life and works can be found in William Sweet, "Jacques Maritain," in *The Stanford Encyclopedia of Philosophy* (Spring 2004), ed. Edward N. Zalta, http://plato.stanford.edu/archives/spr2004/entries/maritain/. For more on his work in relation to the UN declaration, see David Hollenbach, *The Global Face of Public Faith: Politics, Human Rights, and Christian Ethics* (Washington, DC: Georgetown University Press, 2003), 242–48.

[56] Natsir, *Capita Selecta* I, 24.

authoritarianism. However mid-twentieth-century advocates for conceptions of natural law – often recast in the language of "natural right" – were by no means uniformly religious. In fact, one of the most influential voices in the modern revival of appeals to natural right was the political philosopher Leo Strauss (d. 1973) who, in defense of his own conception of the absolute truth of natural right, argued that "transcendence is not a preserve of revealed religion. In a very important sense it was implied in the meaning of political philosophy as the quest for the natural or best political order."[57]

Elsewhere Strauss argued that philosophy sought "The Way" in nature, the basic order of the cosmos, rather than in mere human custom – a position that would have been well received among the modern Muslim reformists of Natsir's *Masjumi*. The Straussian and Islamist perspectives would appear to share a number of other affinities as well, including their radical rejection of historicism, their fixations with conceptualizing "the best regime," and their appeals to certain forms of reason characteristic of a modern intellectual elite.[58] As Strauss once wrote, commenting on the work of Rousseau, "The people do not always see the good of the people. The general will is therefore in need of enlightenment."[59] Developments of such analogous trends between movements of modern social thought among both Muslim and non-Muslim ideologies have barely begun to be explored.

What can be said here is that in the particular case of Indonesia, one clear corollary to such a Natural Law vision of the Sharīʿa has been the deprivileging of complex, historically contextualized textual reasoning in favor of an approach to knowledge of the law that is impressionistic and potentially quite arbitrary. Such an orientation to discussions of Islamic law can be seen throughout Natsir's writings on the subject. For example, in one of his published discussions on the subject of *ijmāʿ*, Natsir makes only a brief acknowledgment of the theoretical complexity of this aspect of Islamic jurisprudence before going on to argue that there is really no need to make things unnecessarily difficult as the meaning of Islam and its law should be clear to those who know.[60]

[57] Hilail Gildin, ed., *Political Philosophy: Six Essays by Leo Strauss* (Indianapolis: Pegasus, 1975), 137.

[58] Leo Strauss, *Natural Right and History: A Cogent Examination of one of the Most Significant Issues in Modern Political and Social Philosophy* (Chicago: University of Chicago Press, 1950), 82–83, 140–55.

[59] Strauss, *Natural Right and History*, 286. Indeed, such sentiments were expressed extensively in the literature produced by Masjumi leadership following their failures in the 1955 general elections. See, for example, *Muktamar Masjumi ke VIII – 22–29 Des. 1956 di Bandung*. (Jakarta: N. V. Pertjetakan Gunung Sahari, 1956).

[60] *Islam sebagai Dasar Negara*, 9.

Another way in which such unwritten understandings of Sharī'a have tended to foster paternalistic, if not outright authoritarian, proclivities among modern Islamists such as Natsir is in their apparent eagerness to forbid even licit things if in them one perceives the danger of leading to sin. In classical Islamic jurisprudence, the mechanism for such cautionary prohibitions is discussed in terms of "blocking the means [to prohibited acts]" (*sadd al-dharā'i'*).[61] The area where this is most developed in Natsir's writings on issues related to Islamic law and society is in his frequent discussions of *amr makruf nahi munkar* ("enjoining the right and forbidding the wrong").

Natsir considers this duty to be an absolute (*syarat mutlak*) for all people, and not merely the *'ulamā'* or intellectuals (*tjendekiawan*). However, the ways in which Natsir conceived of the duty to "command right and forbid wrong" were not necessarily those processes of determining law undertaken by classically trained Muslim jurists. As Michael Cook has noted in his monumental study of interpretations of this concept in Islamic intellectual history:

> the core of modern conceptions of forbidding wrong has become the organised propagation of Islamic values. This insistent concern with organisation is very much a sign of the times; it is the result of living in a world in which the competition tends to be far more organised than ever before.[62]

Natsir also contended that the making of law in a formal sense is not enough, for in his opinion, "mere law" was insufficient in itself to change people's character.[63] From the late 1960s onward, he increasingly stressed that what was needed was a more comprehensive – and organized – program for creating a society of people who could readily recognize and appropriately respond to the Natural Law of the Sharī'a.

Nearly a decade after his 1957 address, Natsir revisited discussions of natural law but in doing so largely dropped his references to *ḥudūd*, choosing instead to develop his ideas under the rubric of *Sunnatullah* (literally, the Way of God). Significantly, he glossed this term in Indonesian as *undang-undang alam*, which carries resonances of "laws of nature" perhaps more

[61] For an introduction to these discussions in classical Islamic jurisprudence, see Mohammad Hashim Kamali, *Principles of Islamic Jurisprudence* (Cambridge: Islamic Texts Society, 1991), 310–20.

[62] Michael Cook, *Commanding Right and Forbidding Wrong in Islamic Thought* (Cambridge University Press, 2001), 516.

[63] M. Natsir, *Demokrasi di Bawah Hukum* (Jakarta: Penerbit Media Da'wah, 2002), 3. This booklet is based upon lectures given in 1966.

than Natural Law.[64] However he specifically argues that these 'laws of nature' hold also to govern the behavior of human beings in society.[65] While Natsir was elaborating these arguments, he was also advocating the formal implementation of the Sharīʿa as positive law enforceable by the Indonesian state. However, in the realities of New Order Indonesia, he was forced to withdraw from direct political participation and instead lay the groundwork for the establishment of Islamic law through less formal channels – focusing on the transformation of individual Muslims in order to prepare for the broader realization of Sharīʿa in society:

> The power to preserve social welfare and stability in society is rooted in society itself. That is, by empowering 'conscience' (*ḍamīr, hati nurani*), individual hearts for the conscience of society, and by empowering independent activism to repress and to wipe out wrongdoing for the salvation of society as a whole.[66]

The means to achieve this eventually came to be seen as most strategically pursued not through politics, but through propagation of a particular vision of Islam (*daʿwa*).

Natsir's understanding of *daʿwa* is a distinctly modern one, envisioning the Sharīʿa in ways both comfortable and comprehensible to a certain kind of educated twentieth-century Muslim.[67] That is, one who held deep faith commitments to Islamic ideals and strong individual identification with the Muslim community, but who lacked a substantial background in

[64] Over the past decade, the usage of *sunnatullah* has become increasingly common in Indonesian Muslim public discourse as a gloss for "laws of nature." One example of this can be found in a 2002 essay published by a Madurese student studying in Cairo, where in a discussion of diversity and pluralism one reads, "Difference is a law of nature (*sunnatullah*)." Ahmad War'ie Karim, "Toleransi Antarumat: Usaha Mencari Titik Persamaan, mengenal Pemikiran Dr. Muhammad Imarah," in *Kontekstualisasi Islam dalam Peradaban*, ed. Mas Guntur Romli and Shofia Tidjani (Cairo: FOSGAMA, 2002), 250.

[65] Natsir, *Demokrasi di bawah Hukum*, 8.

[66] Natsir, *Demokrasi di bawah Hukum*, 17.

[67] Something of the way in which this was envisioned can be seen in the 120-page glossy photo-book entitled, *Hidup Bahagia* that Natsir, along with his colleague A. S. Nasroen, published during his tenure as minister of information. This text outlines a rationalized and systematic presentation of Islamic religious duties and cultural values, and emphasizes the importance of modern organizational structures and technologies for advancing the ideals of Islam and the Indonesian nation. In a short essay on the Qur'ān near the end of the volume, the reader is told that although the truths of Islam are "deep and very broad" (*dalam dan luas sekali*) its basic teachings are nonetheless "short and easy" as the entirety of the Qur'ān can be boiled down to three major themes: the oneness of God (*Ke-Esa-an Tuhan*) and the ways to worship Him, moral and ethical teachings, and stories and examples from the history of the world of how people have related to God's word. The packaging here is streamlined, squeezing out differences of interpretation and technical details to create a unified and comprehensible Islam that could be easily accessed and accepted by modern, educated Muslims. M. Natsir and A. S. Nasroen, *Hidup Bahagia* (Bandung: Penerbitan Vorkink van Hoeve, 1954), 108ff.

the traditional texts and methodologies of the Islamic religious sciences; one for whom Islamic law was conceived of in relation to a personal faith commitment rather than as an inherited tradition of juristic practice or as a body of technical scholarship. In other words, people like Natsir and his colleagues in Masjumi, particularly those who remained after NU split from the organization in 1952, and who later moved into the formally depoliticized cadres of the Dewan Dakwah Islamiyah Indonesia (DDII).

## *IJTIHĀD* AND ISLAMIST POLEMIC

Within the 'limitations' (*ḥudūd*) of Natsir's conception of natural law, *ijtihād* was ideally a controlled mechanism for applying the Sharīʿa across space and time. It thus allowed for adaptation to changing circumstances, but also for means by which understandings of Islam could be consolidated against what he perceived to be the grave threats to the integrity of the *umma*. Already in his days writing for the PERSIS periodical *Pembela Islam*, Natsir invested considerable energy in responding to perceived insults to Islam and its Prophet.

The Communist threat in particular was something that certain segments of the Indonesian Muslim community were increasingly concerned about during the 1950s–60s. As local Islamic teachers and community leaders across the archipelago were busy calling for coordinated religious propagation efforts (*daʿwa*) to combat Communism and Marxist/Leninist ideology on both the national and local levels, Natsir railed against what he perceived to be the looming danger of Communism and other ideologies of secularism in print, as well as in public speeches.[68] Only "religion" (read "Islam") he argued, could provide the moral order necessary for the Indonesian nation to face the challenges of modernization. As he expressed it in one popular publication:

> [Secularism] conceives of moral issues as personal, private matters. But matters of the licit (*ḥalāl*) and the forbidden (*ḥarām*) are religious issues! In secular societies, religion is restricted to the areas of mosque and church, marriage office and

[68] For an example of one such regional agenda from Kalimantan, see Hasbullah Mursjid, "Approach Daʿwah Islamijah terhadap Komunisme/Marxisme-Leninisme: Pidato Hari Lahir ke-II, Institute Agama Islam Negeri Djamiʿah Antasari" (Bandjarmasin: unpublished MS/ KITLV Bibliotheek 01774452, 20 Nov. 1966), 15. Masjumi as an organization also exerted considerable energy in this effort, for example by disseminating booklets addressed to Muslims with Communist sympathies containing polemical essays and a *fatwā* from the Madjlis Sjuro Masjumi that pronounced Communism to be "unbelief" (*kufur*). See *Kami Memanggil* (Jakarta: Dewan Pemimpin Partai Masjumi Bahagian Penerangan, 1955), 14.

cemetery. Beyond that all other areas of life are "religiously neutral." There is no religion in the markets, or in those places for public bathing. This gives rise to great opportunities for a person's lust to "play with fire".[69]

However, for Natsir not just any religion would do to prevent the dangers of secularization, as he perceived Christianity to be potentially just as great a danger to Islam and Muslims in Indonesia.[70] A constant theme throughout Natsir's many other writings on this subject was a perception of the ways in which Muslims were being forced (*terpaksa*) to convert to Christianity through "enticements and monetary incentives" (*bujuk dan dana*).[71] Natsir and his colleagues campaigned aggressively for government intervention, and such continuing pressure eventually forced President Suharto to issue a decree on the issue of proselytization in 1968 that called for a toning down of Christian missionary activity in predominantly Muslim areas of the country.

Nevertheless, tensions over this issue continued through the late 1960s and into the 1970s, not just in Indonesia, but worldwide. On the international level, a conference on missionary activity was held in 1976 at Geneva, with delegations from Islamic *daʿwa* groups and the World Council of Churches led by Ismail Faruqi and Kenneth Cragg, respectively. This assembly issued a resolution on the misuse of *diakonia* ("social services") for purposes of evangelization.[72] Despite the Geneva resolution, however, in the years that followed Indonesian media continued to report extreme incidents of over-aggressive missionizing work on the part of Christians in Indonesia. One striking example of this, commented upon at length by Natsir, was an incident from 1978 when three Adventist missionaries in Pasuruan (East Java) went to the point of allegedly proselytizing to death one H. Achmad Al Amudi. Feeling uncomfortably coerced in his own

[69] M. Natsir, *Fiqhud-Daʿwah: Djedjak Risalah – Dasar2 Daʿwah* (Jakarta: Penerbit Madjalah Islam "Kiblat", 1969), 64.

[70] Many of Natsir's occasional pieces containing his views of the strained relations between Muslims and Christians in Indonesia were collected into a volume first published in 1969. M. Natsir, *Islam dan Kristen di Indonesia* (Jakarta: Peladjar/Bulan Sabit, 1969).

[71] Such complaints about the influence of international Christian organizations in funding such means for missionizing were often cast within the mode of a narrative of victimization centered on the Muslim community. See M. Natsir, *Mencari Modus Vivendi antar Ummat Beragama di Indonesia* (Jakarta: Media Daʿwah, 1980), 7–8.

[72] Natsir, *Modus Vivendi*, 33–34. Many Muslim activists apparently came to understand this restriction as implying that certain strictures would be applied to Christian missionary activities, but rarely (if ever) to their own public *daʿwa* initiatives. Although Islam had a long history of charitable institutions throughout the Middle Ages, more modern types emerged in different areas of the Muslim world in the twentieth century. For example, the Muṣṭafā Maḥmūd Society in Cairo, whose activities were a prominent early example of Muslim *daʿwa* organizations taking up such social-service projects as part of their broader missionizing programs.

sitting room, he had asked the Christian missionaries to leave, and thence a tussle ensued in the front yard, where the Haji reportedly dropped dead of "shock."[73]

The public uproar caused by such sensational stories in the media led to further Indonesian government decrees in 1978 and 1979 that required any 'foreign' support of religious missions to be approved by the Indonesian minister of religious affairs, which was of course a highly politicized position invariably held by an Indonesian Muslim appointee.[74] Unsatisfied with such measures, however, some Muslims took matters into their own hands in the form of such militant actions as church burnings. Commenting on this disturbing situation, Natsir and other Islamists elaborated public arguments along lines that, while admitting that such acts of violence were illegal, also stressed that they would not have happened if only the Christians had not been so flagrantly violating existing government restrictions on their missionary activities.[75]

In the face of such conflict, Natsir argued that national harmony could only be achieved if each religious community not only preserves its own "identity" (*identitas*), but also is respectful of the 'identities' of other groups.[76] Along these lines he developed his arguments that Christian proselytization in Indonesia had to be restricted so that "the *identitas* of Muslims is not disturbed."[77] Natsir's arguments on this point were frequently elaborated in an idiom that could be characterized as a siege mentality, and in commenting on one of Natsir's early essays for PERSIS, Ajip Rosidi has recognized the way in which he used this type of defense posturing to successfully inspire Muslim mass mobilization.[78]

During the struggle for Indonesian independence, such thinking about the power of reactionary defensiveness for an Islamic vision of nationalism was carried over into Masjumi. For example, in the 1946 publication of its booklet on the Masjumi "program of struggle" (Dt. *Strijdprogram*/Ind. *Program Perdjoeangan*):

[73] Natsir, *Modus Vivendi*, 77–78.
[74] Natsir, *Modus Vivendi*, 57. The texts of these decrees appear as appendices at the end of this booklet.
[75] Natsir, *Modus Vivendi*, 23. In this Natsir remained consistent with positions earlier in his career as, for example, evidenced in his reluctance to condemn Katrosuwirjo's Darul Islam campaigns. Federspiel, *Islam and Ideology*, 201.
[76] Natsir, *Modus Vivendi*, 9–10. Elsewhere in this same text (p. 16), Natsir glosses *identitas* as *ṣibgha* – the indelible "dye of God" that is described as a mark of believers in the Qur'ān 2 (*al-baqara*): 138.
[77] Natsir, *Islam dan Kristen*, 2.
[78] Ajip Rosidi, *M. Natsir: Sebuah Biografi I* (Jakarta: Girimukti Pasaka, 1990), 127.

The defense of truth and justice, according to the dictates of Islam, oblige the *umma* to struggle in the path of God (*Sabilillah*), that is to elevate the Word of God that is so commonly insulted and disparaged today.[79]

Over the decades that followed, Natsir's own struggles toward these goals took several radical turns. After publicizing his calls on the pages of PERSIS periodicals, he moved to the forefront of national efforts to establish Islam as the constitutional basis for the Indonesian state through party politics. When such efforts began to appear hopeless, Natsir took the radical step of joining the "revolutionary" rebel government known as the PRRI (Pemerintah Revolusioner Republik Indonesia) in 1958.

At that time, increasingly tense relationships between Masjumi and the Soekarno government eventually drove a number of Islamist leaders, including Sjafruddin Prawiranegara, Burhanuddin Harahap, and Natsir to leave the Indonesian capital and join the PRRI rebellion in Sumatra. Natsir was made vice-president of their opposition government until 1961 when he and other Masjumi leaders surrendered under an Indonesian offer of an amnesty.[80] Masjumi had by that time been declared illegal and ceased to be a contender in national politics, as much of its leadership had been marginalized for refusing to condemn its members, including Natsir, who had actively sided with the PRRI rebellion.[81]

By that time the political atmosphere of Indonesia had decisively changed in ways that served – for a time at least – to significantly limit the scope of public discussions on the implementation of Islamic law. On July 5, 1959 Soekarno consolidated power under the aegis of his "Guided Democracy" and issued a presidential decree that put an end to the work of the Konstituante by officially returning to the Indonesian constitution of 1945.[82] This document acknowledged that while the Jakarta Charter, "inspired (*menjiwai*) the 1945 Constitution," the substance of the fact remained that Soekarno had thus re-established the constitution with the version of the

[79] *Anggaran Dasar dan Rentjana Perdjoeangan Masjoemi Partai Politik Indonesia* (Bukit Tinggi: Dewan Pemimpin Daerah Masjoemi Soematera Barat, 1946: 17). The paragraph following this quotation in the text specifically mentions armed struggle in terms of *Perang Sabil*. The text also includes an entire separate section on the formation and organization of Barisan Sabilillah (28–30) financial support for the same (Fonds Sabilillah, 30–36), Hizboellah (36–39), Gerakan Pemuda Islam Indonesia (GPII, 39–45), and its women's organization, Moeslimaat (22–28).

[80] Federspiel, *Islam and Ideology*, 222.

[81] Herbert Feith, *The Decline of Constitutional Democracy in Indonesia* (Ithaca: Cornell University Press, 1962), 588. For more on the broader politics behind these developments, see Audrey R. and George McT. Kahin, *Subversion as Foreign Policy* (New York: The New Press, 1995), 140ff.

[82] Boland, *Struggle*, 86–105.

preamble that did *not* include the by then infamous "seven words" ("with the obligation that Muslims observe the Sharī'a").[83]

These measures were deeply resented among certain Muslim sectors, particularly among Masjumi supporters. Some came to criticize the legal regime of Soekarno's Guided Democracy as drawing on the symbolism of *adat* institutions, rather than Islamic law, in the construction of its authority.[84] Natsir viewed the establishment of Guided Democracy as a great sacrifice of the *umma* at the hands of the Indonesian nationalist government led by Soekarno.[85] In these changing political circumstances it became increasingly clear to Natsir that public political discussions of Islamizing the state were no longer feasible. Thus he began exploring new avenues for the further Islamization of Indonesian society. His most extensive efforts in this direction were undertaken in the establishment of the DDII.

## DEWAN DAKWAH ISLAMIYAH INDONESIA (DDII)

Within their own, emic historical narratives, the DDII viewed the period from the end of the Constituent Assembly to the fall of Soekarno as "the darkest time in the national history of Indonesia."[86] The successive failures of Islamist politicians in their attempts to establish an Islamic state during that period had left some Indonesian Muslims with the sense that the struggle of the revolution had not yet reached its goal.[87] The turbulent toppling of Soekarno's government following a failed coup attempt in 1965 was followed by mass killings, especially on the islands of Java and Bali, that resulted in the deaths of tens (possibly hundreds) of thousands of suspected Communists (among others), in which some Muslim organizations played a significant role.

[83] *Dekrit Presiden Undang-Undang Dasar 1945 Piagam Djakarta* (Jakarta: P. N. Penerbit Pradnjaparamita, 1963), 3.

[84] Peter Burns argues for recognizing the role of the Leiden-trained *adatrecht* scholar Supomo in inspiring the ideology of Soekarno's guided democracy in *The Leiden Legacy: Concepts of Law in Indonesia* (Jakarta: PT Pradnya Paramita, 1999), 297–308. M. C. Ricklefs has also emphasized the more direct influence of the ideology of Taman Siswa schools on these developments (personal communication).

[85] Natsir, *Pendidikan, Pengorbanan*, 33.

[86] Lukman Hakiem and Tamsil Linrung, *Menunaikan Panggilan Risalah: Dokumentasi Perjalanan 30 Tahun Dewan Dakwah Islamiyah Indonesia* (Jakarta: DDII, 1997), 7.

[87] Such sentiment was reflected, for example, in the reading of the Ikrar Pemuda Islam Indonesia before the minister of religious affairs at a commemoration of the anniversary of the Piagam Jakarta in 1963, in which it was proclaimed that "The unity of the *umma* is an absolute requirement for bringing to fruition the struggle of the Indonesian people in completing the national revolution (*menyelesaikan revolusi nasional*) in the interest of religion and the nation." Mas'uddin Noor, *Piagam Djakarta Mendjiwai Undang-undang Dasar* (Jakarta: Departemen Agama, 1963), 24.

In the wake of this turmoil, a military officer named Suharto seized power as president and declared a *New Order* (*Orde Baru*) for Indonesian society. With this decisive defeat of Communist aspirations in Indonesia, many Muslims who had struggled against them looked forward to playing a more prominent role in national affairs. In the early years of the New Order, however, the government's drive to consolidate power resulted in the continued political disenfranchisement of Muslim political parties and organizations. In such circumstances Natsir and others from the old Masjumi leadership began to redirect their activities to other fields, such as social welfare and education. These then increasingly became central areas for a number of formally apoliticized programs for furthering the Islamization of the social and cultural spheres of Indonesian life in the later twentieth century. These new efforts in the fields of education and especially preaching (*tablīgh*) for the deepening Islamization of Indonesian society in the 1960s and 1970s were elaborated under the rubric of *daʿwa/dakwah*.[88]

In February1967, Natsir proposed a discussion of *daʿwa* at a gathering attended by members of the former Masjumi leadership, where the decision was made to establish a foundation (*yayasan*) to further the deepening Islamization of Indonesian society. This was the birth of the DDII. Natsir expressed the under-the-radar role that he envisioned for the organization in a 1978 interview in which he likened it to a small electric generator that is buried behind a house. There it cannot be heard running and thus can serve to 'enlighten' the Muslim community without raising a loud voice that would entangle itself in politics.[89] As expressed in a phrase that DDII activists themselves attribute to Natsir, "Before we conducted *daʿwa* through politics, now we pursue politics through *daʿwa*."[90] This agenda was pursued aggressively through various means, including publishing ventures and preaching activities. In this mode DDII established and maintained communication with broad networks of Muslim preachers, teachers, and activists aligned with a range of pietistic, populist, and Islamic nationalist sentiment across the Archipelago.[91]

Given the antagonism of Natsir and his associates toward Christian missionaries, the extent to which they themselves have adapted modern

[88] Boland, *Struggle*, 190–96.

[89] *Pesantren* 4.4 (1978) – reported in Hakiem and Linrung, *Menunaikan Panggilan Risalah*, 15.

[90] Hakiem and Linrung, *Menunaikan Panggilan Risalah*, 8.

[91] An example of one such local figure who interacted with aspects of the broader *daʿwa* movement can be found in the Sumatran preacher Zaini Kunin. Attached to an admiring biography of this figure are letters of appreciation for his involvement in various Islamic causes, including one from Natsir in his capacity as head of the DDII. Fakhrunnas Jabbar, MA, *Buya H. Zaini Kunin: Sebutir Mutiara dari Lubuk Bendahara* (Pekanbaru: Universitas Islam Riau Press, 1990), 137–39.

Christian conceptions of missionary activity and organization is striking.[92] As one contemporary Indonesian observer has put it, the new vision of *da'wa* pioneered by Natsir in the DDII was: "inspired by Christian missionary social programs, [as] Natsir believed that *da'wa* activities had to focus on both religious and social well-being of the Muslims since economic development was as important as their religious observance."[93]

Natsir's modern approach to Muslim missionary work is most extensively and systematically expounded in a book with the curious title of *Fiqhud-Da'wah* – a volume based upon the lecture notes that he used in training courses for *da'wa* preachers (*muballigh*), gathered and edited by his colleague Saleh Umar Bajasut.[94] Despite its title, this work little resembles a traditional work of Muslim jurisprudence and is not a *fiqh* book in the technical sense of the term. Rather than dealing with specific legal issues, it contains rather general guidelines on things like the value of family and the importance of maintaining proper relationships with one's neighbors. Likewise the text does not refer to any works of medieval or modern works of *fiqh* proper in its nearly three hundred pages. Most of the book, in fact, is devoted to practical advice for modern preachers (*da'i*), with discussions of issues such as the relationship of evangelism to religious freedom (Ind. *kemerdekaan beritiqad*), and the qualifications needed to become a responsible *muballigh*. In his training sessions for these *da'wa* preachers Natsir stressed the need for them to be well informed about Islam and fortified with strong argumentation to refute skeptics and ideological opponents, and placed great emphasis on the obligation for all believers to actively purify and propagate Islam, that is to perform *da'wa*.[95]

Both Natsir's *Fiqhud Da'wah* and the DDII as an organization also placed considerable emphasis on media and communications as powerful tools for proselytization. Natsir himself was quick to realize the power of the media as an instrument of modern politics and social change, going so

[92] Natsir began one of his 1938 essays with the exclamation: "The best way to oppose an enemy is with his own weapon!" See "Suara Adzan dan Lontjeng Geredja: 'Islam' dalam Conferentie Zending," reprinted in M. Natsir, *Islam dan Kristen di Indonesia* (Jakarta: Peladjar/ Bulan Sabit, 1969), 49. Only very recently have *dakwah* activists in Southeast Asia begun to reflect critically on such a strategy. In a recent report on the "Cross-Cultural Dakwah" held at Jakarta in November, 2004, Ahmad F. Yousif (University of Brunei Darussalam) remarked, "We also know that there are Christian groups that attempt to convert other religious believers. We must not repeat their mistakes" (M. Taufiqurrahman, "Scholars Prefer Religious Dialog to Islamic Proselytization," *The Jakarta Post* online (www.thejakartapost.com/detailheadlines.asp? fileid=20041130.A01 & irec=4)

[93] Husin, *Philosophical and Sociological Aspects of Da'wah*, 90.

[94] M. Natsir, *Fiqhud-Da'wah: Djedjak Risalah – Dasar2 Da'wah* (Jakarta: Penerbit Madjalah Islam "Kiblat," 1969).

[95] Natsir, *Fiqhud-Da'wah*, 97–152.

far as to state that the press and mass media in practice occupy a position as a "fourth estate" in the system of state alongside the formal governmental branches of the legislative, executive, and judicial powers.[96] Over the nearly four decades of its existence, the DDII has maintained a very active publication enterprise that produces hundreds of books, including translations of Islamic books from outside Indonesia. Such titles include not only Middle Eastern texts, but also some others produced in cooperation with the International Institute of Islamic Thought (IIIT) in Washington, DC.[97] Beyond this, however, they also publish a number of locally produced, well-circulated periodicals, including a monthly magazine for preachers, *Serial Khutbah Jum'at*, a weekly *Bulletin Da'wah* sent to over 200,000 mosques across the country each Friday, and its flagship magazine, *Media Dakwah*.[98] One prominent feature of this last-mentioned journal has been the amount of attention dedicated to stories and issues important for a global Islamist, rather than merely Indonesian Muslim interests.

This aspect of *Media Dakwah*'s presentation reflects an important facet of the DDII, as Nastir also used the foundation to raise public consciousness of international Islamist issues among Indonesian Muslims, such as solidarity with Muslim minority populations in the southern Philippines.[99] However the most striking case of Natsir's publicizing of an "international Islamic issue" can be found in his calls for Muslim support of the Palestinian cause. After encountering Middle Eastern discussions of the issue through his involvement in the international conferences held by the Islamic World League, Natsir began publicizing the Palestinian cause through lectures in Indonesia and eventually in a booklet published in 1971.[100] In this work he characterizes Zionism as a religious (*sic*) movement of imperialist expansion, and goes on to insist that the struggle of Palestinians against the state of Israel is "an Islamic cause" deserving the concern and solidarity of Muslims in Indonesia.[101]

96 Natsir, *Pendidikan, Pengorbanan*, 19.

97 Hakiem and Linrung, *Menunaikan Panggilan Risalah*, 26.

98 In fact, *da'wa*-inflected journalism was considered to be so crucial to the success of the movement that special attention was directed toward "press coaching" and other means of bringing the modern media into the service of Islam. See, for example, Ajip Rosidi, *Beberapa Masalah Umat Islam di Indonesia* (Bandung: Bulan Sabit, 1970), 29–35.

99 Lukman Hakiem, *Menjawab Panggilan Risalah: 70 Tahun H. Buchari Tamam* (Jakarta: Media Da'wah, 1992), 92–93.

100 M. Natsir, *Masalah Palestina* (Jakarta: Penerbit Hudaya, 1971).

101 This is a remarkably early assertion of the "Islamic" nature of the Palestinian cause, as at that time it was still often conceived of in terms of Arab nationalism in the Middle East and elsewhere. Indeed, Natsir himself apparently realized that there might be more to the issue than its religious dimension. Thus when he praised the "Fedayeen" as the gleaming hope in the future of the struggle

Natsir's international Islamist concerns had developed gradually over the course of his career. His first contacts of this type came in 1951, when he made his first trip abroad as Indonesian prime minister on a state visit to Pakistan. Natsir devoted increased attention to fostering such connections in the 1970s, when he began working in earnest to invite financial support from Islamic countries in the Middle East, and especially from the oil-rich nations of the Persian Gulf, who continue to fund some DDII activities to this day.[102] International cooperation on DDII projects has been most heavily dominated by Kuwait and Saudi Arabia, but through the 1990s the DDII also maintained active relationships with Muslim organizations in Abu Dhabi, Dubai, Egypt, Pakistan, Malaysia, and the United States.[103]

Despite such active encouragement of global Muslim solidarity, however, most DDII constituents are not primarily proponents of conceptions of a global *umma* without national borders, or linguistic or ethnic divisions.[104] Rather they have largely continued to imagine Islam as integrally related to an exclusive Indonesian nationality, and this in turn has been an important aspect in the way in which DDII activists have framed their visions of Islamic law and the ideal relationship between the Sharīʿa and the modern Indonesian nation-state. Such a combination of nationalist sentiment with the 'ideologization' of Islam and an aggressive *daʿwa* agenda of personal piety and public moralism has made for a powerful cocktail, which continues to intoxicate some Indonesian Islamists to this day.

## DEVELOPMENTALISM AND *DAʿWA* UNDER THE NEW ORDER

Over the last decades of the twentieth century, significant reconfigurations in understandings of Islam in Indonesian society were facilitated by the

with their spirit of jihad (*semangat djihad*) he is forced to recognize that, "Not all the Fedayeen are Muslims . . . Among them there are Christians as well as a number of 'adventurers' (*avonturir*)," 67–68.

102 Husin, *Philosophical and Sociological Aspects of Daʿwah*, 91–92; and Anthony Bubalo and Greg Fealy, *Joining the Caravan: The Middle East, Islamism, and Indonesia* (Alexandria, NSW: Lowy Institute, 2005), 59.

103 In funding the DDII program of sending *daʿi* to transmigration areas, for example, 55 of 272 were funded by Kuwait's Ministry of *Waqf* and *Bayt al-Zakāt*, and from 1992 to 1997, DDII built over 150 mosques with funds from Kuwait, and 180 other projects in cooperation with Saudi Arabian organizations. Since the 1990s the DDII has also been increasingly active in fostering connections with the OIC, as well as with particular Muslim groups in various countries. Examples of this include DDII calls for solidarity with Bosnian Muslims during the war there. During this period they frequently received official visits from foreign Muslim leaders including the Pakistani Inamullah Khan, secretary general of the Muktamar Alam Islami and Ahmad Shah who at the time of his visit (1992) was the interior minister of the Taliban government in Afghanistan. Hakiem and Linrung, *Menunaikan Panggilan Risalah*, 28, 35, 42–46, 182.

104 Ihza, "Modernisme Islam dan Demokrasi," 137–38.

success of the New Order's economic developmentalist agenda. During that period, economic growth and the restructuring of the national education system produced a burgeoning new class of literate Indonesian Muslims who were keen on mainstream religious revitalization. As early as 1978, Herbert Feith remarked that some members of this 'middle class' including but by no means limited to Muslim activists were at the same time disillusioned with the progress of developmentalism under Suharto's regime. This led some educated young activists to support populist student movements for cleaner government, more even distribution of the country's new wealth, and "a search for leaders with a broader social vision."[105] In a much more recent and extensive analysis of these developments, Robert Hefner has documented the ways in which, during the late 1970s and 1980s, the ranks of Indonesia's educated middle class expanded dramatically, and new Muslim print media flourished in the country. During that period, Indonesia witnessed an Islamic resurgence in some ways analogous to the "Islamic Awakenings" of other countries such as Egypt and Iran. While this seems to have initially caught some of the New Order leadership off guard, by the end of the 1980s an expanding Islamic revival had established itself centrally on the national scene.[106]

These transformations occurred in spite of earlier attempts on the part of the New Order regime to further marginalize the place of Islam in national life. Indeed some DDII leaders have remarked on what they perceive to have been the unintended Islamizing effects of government measures such as the 1983 decree requiring all organizations in the country to assert *Pancasila* as their sole ideological foundation (*asas tunggal*).[107] Others, such as Bahtiar Effendy, have emphasized instead an apparent pattern of increasingly accommodative steps through which the Indonesian government courted Muslim sympathies since the 1970s. In the legal sphere this has been evidenced in the passing of legislation supportive of certain Muslim interests in the areas of marriage law (1974), religious endowments (1977), national education (1989), Islamic religious courts (1989), and the promulgation of the Indonesian "Compilation" (KHI) of Islamic law on marriage, divorce, inheritance, and *waqf*, as well as the minister's collective decision on *zakāt* institutions, and the reversal of government policies discouraging Muslim

105 Herbert Feith, "*The Indonesian Student Movement of 1977–78*," unpublished typescript, 1978 (KITLV Bibliotheek 0219 8149), 9.

106 Hefner, *Civil Islam.*

107 Harjono, *Perjalanan Politik Bangsa*, xvi.

women from wearing headscarves (*jilbab*) in 1991, not to mention the abolishment of a sports lottery in 1993.[108]

Throughout the 1980s–90s, then, Indonesian Islamism and its vanguard of the DDII continued to gain strength. All the while, however, the organization called for the need to improve the quality of *da'wa* in order to confront what they saw as ongoing challenges from "other religions and belief systems (including anti-God worldviews that still survive underground), Catholics, Protestants, Hindus, Buddhists, and others."[109] Such antagonistic positions on the development of *da'wa* in late twentieth-century Indonesia characterized the views of Anwar Harjono who ascended through the ranks of the DDII in the 1980s, eventually to become the general head of the organization upon Natsir's death in 1993.

At the turn of the twenty-first century Natsir's reputation in Indonesia is enjoying something of a renaissance in posthumous popularity, with a series of retellings of and reflections on his life,[110] as well as reprintings of a number of his own writings, and a flurry of popular publications praising him as a pioneer of Islamic Nationalism.[111] In the re-invigorated political atmosphere following the fall of Suharto, Natsir has been hailed as a hero by those claiming to carry forward the Masjumi legacy of advancing agendas of Islamizing the modern Indonesian state and its system of laws.[112]

A rather different degree of posthumous popularity has been the lot of Natsir's successor at the head of DDII, Anwar Harjono (d. 1999). While his written work is not as widely read today as that of Natsir, an examination of his published writings reveals important aspects of DDIIs *da'wa* agenda during the 1980s–90s as well as a broad outline of visions of the relationship between Islam, law, Indonesian nationalism, and the state that continue to inform contemporary debates. Taking Harjono as our focal

[108] The controversies surrounding this case will be discussed in chapter 5.

[109] Hakiem and Linrung, *Menunaikan Panggilan Risalah*, 9.

[110] Striking examples of this can be found in the essays by Deliar Noer aimed at rehabilitating Natsir's image in the *Reformasi* period. See *Membincangkan Tokoh-tokoh Bangsa* (Bandung: Mizan, 2001), 170–200.

[111] As explicitly stated, for example in the prefaces to recent reprints of Natsir's *Islam sebagai Dasar Negara*, *Agama dan Negara dalam Perspektif Islam*, and *Demokrasi di bawah Hukum*. In the preface to the reprint of the last of these titles, the editors of Media Dakwah publications make it clear that they are rereleasing these writings of Natsir, "So that the mistakes of the past are not repeated, particularly in this time of transition."

[112] Prominent examples of this have included Deliar Noer, who wrote an appreciative preface to a new edition of Natsir's "Islam as the Foundation of the Nation," *Islam sebagai Dasar Negara* (Jakarta: DDII, 2000). The leadership of the Partai Keadilan Sejahtera, quoted this same edition of Natsir's classic essay in the official outline of their own program for establishing the Sharī'a in contemporary Indonesia. For more on this, see H. Nandang Burhanudin, *Penegakan Syariat Islam Menurut Partai Keadilan* (Jakarta: Al-Jannah, 2003), 119.

point here, however, is not to conflate his writings with the official positions of DDII as an organization, nor of Indonesian Islamist movements as a whole.[113] Nonetheless, in his published books and articles are found more extensive elaborations of Indonesian Islamist arguments about the role of Sharīʿa in society than are usually found in the shorter, and increasingly numerous pamphlets, articles, and political cartoons produced by the country's burgeoning Islamist popular media, both within and beyond the circles of DDII.

## ANWAR HARJONO

Harjono was born in 1923 to a pious *priyai* family from a village near Sidoarjo, East Java, that had a reputation as home to devout Muslims.[114] He grew up studying Islam under his father and the *kyai* of the local mosque before attending a Taman Siswa school. He then continued on past primary education in a Muhammadiyah vocational training school and, after stints working as a teacher and librarian, studied for a period at the famous NU *pesantren* Tebuireng in Jombang.[115] After a short time there, Harjono moved to Jakarta and studied at the Sekolah Tinggi Islam, where he became involved in the Indonesian independence movement and with Masjumi.[116] It was during this early period of his activism on the national level that Harjono first met Natsir. To the end of his days, Harjono maintained that his life's work was primarily that of a "continuer" (*pelanjut*) of the efforts toward the further Islamization of Indonesian society pioneered by Natsir.[117] However, these two leaders of the DDII differed in a number of significant ways. Harjono did not command the personal charisma so often attributed to Natsir, and has not left the same kind of inspirational

113 To do so would require an entire monograph of its own examining literally thousands of short texts.

114 He added the "Anwar" to his name when he was twenty-two years old in order to avoid the kind of suspicion that his single Javanese name was perceived to have aroused in his interactions among pious Muslim circles. Lukman, Hakiem, *Perjalanan Mencari Keadilan dan Persatuan: Biografi Dr. Anwar Harjono*, SH (Jakarta: Media Daʿwah, 1993), 41.

115 Husin, *Philosophical and Sociological Aspects of Daʿwah*, 94–95. Throughout his later career, Harjono attempted to use these school ties to both Muhammadiyah and NU schools to portray himself as a figure acceptable to both modernist and traditionalist Muslims in Indonesia. Harjono's "adventures" among the traditionalists are celebrated in Hakiem, *Perjalanan Mencari Keadilan dan Persatuan*, 34–41.

116 Details of his activities can be found in Hakiem, *Perjalanan Mencari Keadilan dan Persatuan*, 125–92.

117 Husin, *Philosophical and Sociological Aspects of Daʿwah*, 107. The problems of the lack of a clear successor to Natsir's leadership, however, is discussed in Thohir Luth, *M. Natsir: Dakwah dan Pemikirannya* (Jakarta: Gema Insani, 1999), 134–35.

legacy among contemporary Indonesian Muslims. In the field of law, it was Harjono who had the advantage, having earned his law degree (*Sarjana Hukum*) from Universitas Islam Djakarta in 1963 and then a Ph.D. in Islamic legal studies under the direction of Hazairin and H. M. Rasjidi in 1968.

His dissertation was entitled "*Hukum Islam: Keluasan dan Keadilannya*,"[118] and in its pages Harjono elaborated his vision of Islamic law, some elements of which have become standard components of the ideology of several Indonesian Islamist groups. The discussion of Hazairin in the last chapter might lead one to imagine that his legacy in Indonesia would generally be one of a localization and indigenization of Islamic legal thought. A number of his students, associates and admirers, however, drew on Hazairin's work and cited his authority for rather different ends. Or, rather, they emphasized certain elements of Hazairin's own intellectual lineage that were not at the forefront in Hazairin's published writings, such as his Dutch teacher Ter Haar's thoughts on the need for the exercise of state power in order to transform cultural values into positive law.[119]

On the very first pages of his dissertation, Harjono acknowledges the formative influence that both Hazairin and Hasbi had on framing his own approach to Islamic law[120] – one that revolves around a perceived discrepancy between understandings of the Sharīʿa and the cultural realities of modern Indonesia.[121] However from that point, Harjono departs in a direction rather different than that of those two proponents of the creation of an Indonesian *madhhab*, as in this work he is not so much concerned with how the law is to be interpreted and applied, as he is with the nature of Islamic law itself. This is made clear in the paragraphs immediately following his acknowledgments of Hasbi and Hazairin.

There Harjono also states that the work of his dissertation was also stimulated by the proceedings of the "Week of Islamic Law," a conference of Orientalists convened at Paris in the summer of 1951. Harjono characterized the findings of this conference as extolling the richness of Islamic law and its potential to fulfill all the needs of a modern life, and filled the pages of his introductory chapter with a lengthy quotation in French

[118] Later that same year this work was published as a book by Penerbit Bulan Bintang.

[119] For a short summary of Ter Haar's *beslissingenleer*, see Burns, *Leiden Legacy*, 246–47.

[120] A sense of the degree to which the work of Hazairin and Hasbi framed Harjono's thinking about Islamic law can also be seen in his short, English-language essay: Anwar Harjono, "The Future of Islamic Law in Indonesia," *South East Asia Journal of Theology* 14.2 (1973): 56–60.

[121] Harjono, *Hukum Islam*, 11–12, 21. This is not only a problem for Indonesia, for nowhere according to Harjono is Islamic law truly being implemented.

summarizing the conference's conclusions.[122] Taking this statement in an essentialized manner, Harjono argues that if all had gone as it should have in the history of Muslim societies there would be no need for the positions of Hasbi and Hazairin. That is, the problem according to Harjono is not that the law of Islam needs to be adjusted to modern Indonesian contexts, but that modern Indonesian society needs to be more fully Islamized in order to enjoy the benefits that the Sharīʿa can bring. Thus if there appears to be a conflict between Sharīʿa and contemporary social realities, it is not the law of Islam that must bend to fit the context, but rather various times and places must pull themselves into line with the law of Islam.[123]

## "CAPTURING THE SPIRIT" OF THE SHARĪʿA

Harjono conceived of the Sharīʿa in scripturalist terms while at the same time, however, acknowledging that the text of the Qurʾān does not provide a detailed legal code, but rather a set of "norms and principles" to establish justice in all times and places.[124] In this mode Harjono argued that God's law, as made known through the Qurʾān and *Sunna*, must be appealed to directly and established as a "living law" through the practice of a kind of intuitive *ijtihād* – rather than relying on the man-made *fiqh* of the established schools. Rather than a formalized system of jurisprudence, Harjono calls for a scripturalist project of "capturing the spirit" of the Qurʾān and *Sunna* in a way that is "impressionistic and always up to date."[125]

Harjono refers to this unarticulated, tacitly understood 'spirit' of Islamic law as *Sunnatullah*, and worked to further develop the Natural Law discourse on the Sharīʿa pioneered by Natsir.[126] In this conceptualization of Islamic law, it appears that Harjono is never really searching for God's law,[127] but often arguing in a way that takes particular conceptualizations of the

[122] Harjono, *Hukum Islam*, 12–13. Here, as was the case with Natsir, it was Orientalist notions of the nature of Islam and Islamic law that were fundamental in framing the essentialized conception of Sharīʿa central to modern Islamist thought.

[123] Harjono, *Hukum Islam*, 14–17.

[124] Harjono, *Hukum Islam*, 93. Nevertheless, Harjono later maintained that while the Qurʾān does not provide a ready "constitution," its ethical and social imperatives need to be "made law" through work in the sphere of politics (*Indonesian Kita*, 84, 134).

[125] Harjono, *Hukum Islam*, 101.

[126] Indeed, the roots of Harjono's thoughts on the Natural Law of God in Natsir's statements peculiar usage of *ḥudūd* can be seen in Harjono's discussion of *Sunnatullah* as imposing "limits" on the use of reason. Harjono, *Indonesia Kita*, 27.

[127] I borrow this phrase as a way of referring to the practice of classical Islamic jurisprudence from the title of Bernard Weiss' interpretation of the work of the thirteenth-century Shāfiʿī jurist, Sayf al-Dīn al-Āmidī (Salt Lake City: University of Utah Press, 1992).

Shari'a for granted. In one of his later essays, Harjono elaborated on this understanding of *Sunnatullah* as: "A Law that is not made by human beings, but influences and in fact serves to order human society, with or without their agreement to it."[128] Harjono developed this conception of *Sunnatullah* within a particular political context, that being one of great disappointment over the deletion of the "Seven Words" of the Jakarta Charter, and the dismantling of Muslim political parties such as Masjumi that had advocated their reinstatement. Such appeals to the fundamental nature of a Natural Law of God could thus serve to support agendas for the Islamization of Indonesian society through any and all means possible.[129]

## ISLAMISM AND THE ECLIPSE OF JURISPRUDENCE

Harjono came to work more closely with Natsir in the context of the DDII, and as several of the first generation of that organization's leaders passed away in the 1970s and early 1980s, Harjono rose rapidly through the ranks.[130] In a 1983 reshuffling of the DDII leadership, Harjono received his first major appointment as a high official in the organization, and by 1997 he was formally acknowledged as general chairman.[131] Throughout this period, the DDII came to serve as something of an unofficial patron of various Islamist groups in Indonesia that maintained low profiles under the New Order.[132] The respective social, legal, and political agendas of these various groups were considerably diverse, and many of them shared a basic view of Islamic law as a tool for social engineering enacted through the political commitments and personal piety of individual believers.[133] In particular, the DDII played a considerable role in the transmission and translation of ideas and institutions developed in the Middle East by the Muslim Brotherhood, as well as those of other groups advancing agendas in various shades of *Salafi* scripturalism.[134] As discussed in chapter 2 a major early exponent of the latter line of thought in the archipelago was A.

128 He further comments, curiously enough, that this is what Thomas Aquinas had referred to as *lex divina* (Harjono, *Indonesia Kita*, 26).

129 The range is expressed by Harjono in his definition of politics, "The art of the possible, plus the Will of God." Harjono, *Hukum Islam*, 274.

130 Dr. Anwar Harjono, S.H., *Perjalanan Politik Bangsa: Menoleh ke Belakang Menatap Masa Depan* (Jakarta: Gema Insani Press, 1997), xiii.

131 In this rank he was complimented by two other Ketua – K. H. M. Rusjad Nurdin and Prof. Dr. H. M. Rasjidi (a founding member and Natsir's original Wakil Ketua in 1967). However, it was Harjono who was most involved in running the DDII's day-to-day operations. Lukman and Linrung, *Menunaikan Panggilan Risalah*, 10–14.

132 Personal communication: Ismail Yusanto, Jakarta, June 2004.

133 Harjono, *Indonesian Kita*, 132.

134 Bubalo and Fealy, *Joining the Caravan*, 59.

Hassan, and the inspiration that Natsir found in him – and thence Natsir's own subsequent tremendous influence on Indonesian Islamism as a whole – has thus been instrumental in the shaping of modern conceptions of Islam and Islamic law in the country.

One continuing legacy of such reformism in Indonesia is the continuing dominance of *'ibādāt* issues in contemporary discourses about Islamic law and society. Indeed, browsing the *fiqh* section at the DDII central Media Dakwah bookstore in Jakarta, one finds rather little there on any other aspect of jurisprudence – be it *mu'āmalāt* or *uṣūl.* Furthermore, the lion's share of titles on sale there are Indonesian translations of *fatwā* issued by Arab *'ulamā'* of various *Salafi*-Islamist perspectives ranging from those of the neo-Ikhwānī Yūsuf al-Qaraḍāwī to the neo-Wahhābī clerics 'Abd al-'Azīz b. Bāz (d. 2000), Muḥammad Ṣāliḥ 'Uthaymīn, 'Abd Allāh b. 'Abd al-Raḥman al-Jubrin, and Ṣāliḥ b. Fawzān b. 'Abd Allāh Āl Fawzān.[135]

All of the Indonesian Muslim reformists discussed in chapters 2 and 3 were active in formulating new methodologies for determining Islamic legal rulings. Similar concerns, however, are largely absent from the agendas of *da'wa* activists influenced by popularizations of the kind of Islamic Natural Law developed in the work of Natsir and Harjono. In these discussions, technical debates over matters of jurisprudence were increasingly seen as potentially dangerous distractions from their primary agenda of propagating "Islam" as a good in itself. The technical details of legal interpretation were thus relegated to positions of minor importance, as the Believers realize that (as Natsir had put it) "Islam is Islam."[136] The orientation of public debates over Islamic law in Indonesian society in these Indonesian Islamist discourses has thus undergone a significant shift from those in which Hassan, Chalil, Hasbi, and Hazairin were participants.

These earlier figures and their colleagues were engaged in involved conversations over the sources, jurisprudential methodology, and particular rulings of Islamic law in the face of rapidly changing contemporary society. For all of them, regardless of their background training or institutional affiliation, the content and substance of Islamic law were areas that required

[135] This list of translated Arabic works should be seen against a second popular group of readings among Indonesian Islamists – that of translations of a rather stable, albeit eclectic canon of Western writers. For example, during the same visit to Media Dakwah in which the above observations were made on the shelves of the *fiqh* section (June 2004), I saw stacks of translations of another popular title near the cashier – Hart's *100 Tokoh* – in which Muḥammad figures prominently. Alongside this work one could list Maurice Bucaille's *La Bible, Le Coran, et la science*, and others including the works of Gibb and Stoddard mentioned above. The impact of this curious canon on modern Indonesian Islam, and the conceptions of authoritative knowledge that appeals to these titles implies, deserves to be the subject of a substantial study in its own right.

[136] Natsir, *Capita Selecta* I, 24.

extensive elaboration. However this was not primarily the case with Natsir, and even less so with Harjono and later Indonesian Islamists. For them, the issue has been increasingly not the interpretation of Islamic law in relation to contemporary Indonesian society, but rather with Islam as the formal identity for the law of the Indonesian nation-state. Increasingly, Indonesian Islamists had less and less patience for the kind of complex debates over Islamic legal reasoning engaged in by the *'ulamā'* of the traditional *pesantren* community. The latter's deliberations over various issues were not seen as valuable for the development of an efficient, modern Islamic nation, and their proclivity toward, and relative recognition of, difference of opinion within the *umma* was viewed as a hindrance to the unification and solidarity of the Muslim community by many Indonesian Islamists.[137]

## STATE POWER AND SOLIDARITY IN CONCEPTIONS OF THE *UMMA*

As mentioned above, when formal political action was no longer an option for the heirs of Masjumi under Suharto's New Order, the DDII pursued their aspirations for the Islamization of Indonesia in a variety of other, 'cultural forms'; i.e. in the field of *da'wa*. The compromises to this changed political context are seen, for example, in the way that Harjono described his vision of a society under Sharī'a as not necessarily contradicting the official state ideology of *Pancasila*.[138] In fact, a major characteristic of Harjono's thought is the combination of Islamist and Indonesian nationalist interests.[139] This comes through in his repeated discussions of the

[137] Such concerns are reflected, for example, in the *Anggaran Dasar/ Rumah Tangga* of the DDII, that stress the importance of cooperation between Muslims and the avoidance of internal arguments in the interests of streamlining and unifying the community in the face of external challenges. Husin, *Philosophical and Sociological Aspects of Da'wah*, 142.

[138] Harjono, *Indonesian Kita 96*; Anwar Harjono, *Perjalanan Politik Bangsa: Menoleh ke Belakang Menatap Masa Depan* (Jakarta: Gema Insani Press, 1997), 67.

[139] During the last years of his life, Harjono also devoted considerable attention to the development of a new Islamic nationalist historiography in works such as an edited volume on the life and work of Natsir that includes the reprinting of a newspaper column from *Republika* calling for the formal recognition of Natsir as a national hero (Ind. *pahlawan nasional*), and a book entitled *On the Birth of the Republic: The Devotion of the Sekolah Tinggi Islam and the Balai Muslimin Indonesia to their Nation*. The latter work, that was written together with his close associate Lukman Hakiem, was published with prefaces from both the new leadership of the DDII (H. Ahmad Muflih Saefuddin and H. Hussein Umar), the minister of religious affairs Tarmizi Taher, and by President Suharto himself as part of a campaign to designate the site of the Balai Muslimin Indonesia in Jakarta (Jl. Kramat Raya, no. 19) as a national historic site. Anwar Harjono *et al.*, *M. Natsir: Sumbangan dan Pemikirannya untuk Indonesia* (Jakarta: Penerbit Media Da'wah, 1995), 99–102; Anwar Harjono and Lukman Hakiem, *Sekitar Lahirnya Republik: Bakti Sekolah Tinggi Islam dan Balai Muslimin Indonesia Kepada Bangsa* (Jakarta: DDII, 1997), i–vi.

Jakarta Charter, which he considered to be not only "an inseparable part of the 1945 constitution," and an artifact representing national *ijmā'*, but also a document with implications for the lives of Muslim Indonesians in this life and the next.[140] The upshot of all this, for Harjono, was that the essence of Indonesian national identity is '*Ke-Islam-an*' – a reified abstract construction that might be rendered in English as "Islamicity" or "Islamness."[141]

Given this equation of Islam and Indonesianness, Harjono had to constantly contend with a consternation similar to that of the Masjumi leadership following the 1955 elections. Why, he asks, with the vast majority of Indonesians being Muslim, is not Islamic law the law of the land?[142] He attributed this situation to a combination of internal and external factors, but reacted most sharply to perceived outside influences impeding the application of Islamic law in Indonesian society. Prominent among those to be blamed for the present sorry state of affairs, according to Harjono, are the political and social legacies of European colonialism, and the continuing domination of Muslim lands by the the West through its technological and economic supremacy.

In the overview sketch of the history of Islamic law forming part of his dissertation, Harjono points to European colonial intervention as introducing Christian ideas of church/state distinctions into Islam, weakening Islamic law and allowing foreign legal systems to prosper at its expense.[143] This, however, was only part of the problem that Harjono had with Christianity. For in his view the Islamic identity of the Indonesian nation faced an ever-increasing threat of 'Christianization' (*Kristenisasi*).

The idea that such an overwhelming majority might feel threatened by the expansion of a rather small and internally diverse minority may at first appear implausible, but becomes somewhat more comprehensible when one explores the kind of presentation of Christianity to which Islamist activists like Harjono and Natsir were responding. One widely circulated example of this came to the archipelago from an Evangelical press in

[140] Harjono, *Indonesia Kita*, 89, 96,123–24.

[141] Anwar Harjono, S. H., *Perjalanan Politik Bangsa: Menoleh ke Belakang Menatap Masa Depan* (Jakarta: Gema Insani Press, 1997), 16.

[142] Harjono, *Indonesia Kita*, 260.

[143] Harjono, *Hukum Islam*, 268–70. However, Harjono also directs considerable attention to factors within the history of the Muslim community itself which have contributed to contemporary dilemmas within the *umma*. Primary among these in Harjono's view are the delimitation of Sharī'a jurisdiction and the subordination of Islamic courts to the executive power of the caliph during the Umayyad period, as well as the much bemoaned – if elusive – "closure of the gate of *ijtihād*," and the ways in which sectarian factionalism has impeded attempts for the codification of Islamic law. The second of these is illustrated with the example of developments in Khedival Egypt, 263.

southern California in the 1970s. The missionary author of this tract proclaimed his message in a tone of imminent triumphalism:

> Many of the events I have experienced in Indonesia can be explained only if one believes that they were shaped by God's hand. But God wears gloves. His hand is often hidden though his actions are evident in the events that affect us – politics, culture, society, and of course, religion . . . What has been billed as 'the Indonesian revival' is in reality a Christward movement that has been gaining momentum since 1931. For decades God wove the threads of revolution, independence, and the building of a nation together with his redemptive acts to create a receptivity to the gospel.[144]

Continuing on in this same text, the missionary author even explicitly linked then recent Indonesian 'successes' in Christian proselytization with the great suffering of the country that was still a painfully recent memory at the time his book was published, "Traumatic events from 1965 to 1968 changed the face of Indonesia – politically, socially, and religiously – and produced instability that aided the growth of Christianity."[145] Such insensitive statements as these – published less than a decade after that great national trauma – continued to provide fodder for the proliferation of "defenses" of Islam against outside threats of the kind that were so vital to the enlistment of popular support for Indonesian Islamist agendas for the formal implementation of the Sharīʿa.

In his position as leader of the DDII, Harjono grew increasingly outspoken in his railings against the perceived threat of *Kristenisasi* and other dangers to Islam (especially Communism, atheism, and secularism) in the last years of his life. This was particularly the case during the 'honeymoon' (*bulan madu*) between Suharto's government and Islamist groups toward the end of the New Order.[146] Within a matter of months after Suharto stepped down, his appointed successor B. J. Habibie was hosting a high-profile gathering of DDII activists and supporters at the presidential palace, where Anwar Harjono was seen as a particular focus of the president's attentions. Habibie also used the occasion to remark on what he saw as the contribution of Natsir to strengthening the national unity of Indonesia. Harjono and other leaders of the DDII at the time, including the organization's current head, Hussein Umar, used the same occasion to press their

[144] Avery T. Willis, Jr., *Indonesian Revival: Why Two Million Came to Christ* (Pasadena: William Carey Library, 1977), xv.

[145] Willis, Jr., *Indonesian Revival*, 82.

[146] Hakiem, *Perjalanan Mencari Keadilan dan Persatuan*, 419–34.

advocacy for a *da'wa*-oriented program of "total reform" encompassing the moral, economic, political, and legal spheres of Indonesian life.[147]

These were not the only conversations on Islam being developed by Indonesians during the second half of the twentieth century, however. In fact it was these very same decades that witnessed the development of a remarkable, broad-based movement for the "renewal" (*pembaharuan*) of Indonesian Islam led by figures such as Nurcholish Madjid (d. 2005). For their provocative presentations of such ideas as "secularization" and "inter-religious *fiqh*," Madjid and other *Pembaharuan* thinkers have been continually subjected to strident criticisms in Indonesian Islamist publications such as *Media Dakwah*. There have been a great many examples of this over recent decades as can be seen, for example, in the December 1992 special issue dedicated to blasting Madjid's ideas and attacking his character by, *inter alia*, attempting to link his ideas to an imagined 'Zionist Freemasonry Movement.'[148]

Contemporary enthusiasts for such conspiracy theories have kept alive the siege mentality characteristic of Natsir and especially Harjono's worldviews, and continue to rail against the perceived threats of secularism, Communism, and missionary Christianity spreading in contemporary Indonesia.[149] To combat these dangers, Islamist activists have called for intensified campaigns of education and campus activism to propagate a vision of knowledge that will capitalize on selective, attractive aspects of modernity which can be considered "Islamic."[150] However Madjid continually voiced critiques of such Islamist apologetics, which he saw as "a sign of a lack of self-confidence."[151] The differences in understandings of Islam and Islamic law between this scholar – who, in his student days of the 1970s, was hailed by some of his Indonesian contemporaries as 'the young Natsir' – and the majority of those who today see themselves as carrying on Natsir's legacy are considerable, as will be discussed in chapter 5.

[147] *Silaturrahmi Nasional dan Peluncuran Home Page Keluarga Besar Dewan Dakwah*, Jakarta, November, 1–2 1998 (Jakarta: DDII, 1998), 9–17.

[148] For an English-language overview of the contents of this particular issue, see Darul Aqsha, Dick van der Meij, and Johan Hendrik Meuleman, *Islam in Indonesia: A Survey of Developments from 1988 to March 1993* (Jakarta: INIS, 1995), 354–56.

[149] For the relationships between the DDII and other Indonesian Islamist organizations such as KISDI that emerged at the end of the New Order Period, see Hefner, *Civil Islam*, 109–10.

[150] Husin, *Philosophical and Sociological Aspects of Da'wah*, 257.

[151] Nurcholish Madjid, *Islam: Kemoderenan and Keindonesiaan* (Bandung: Mizan, 1987), 240.

CHAPTER 5

# *New Muslim intellectuals and the "re-actualization" of Islam*

> As religion and the civil laws should aim principally to make good citizens of men, one sees that when either of these departs from this end, the other should aim more toward it.
>
> Montesquieu, *De l'esprit des lois*

The Islamic revival of late twentieth-century Indonesia was to a considerable extent facilitated by the very success of the New Order's developmentalist agenda. Economic growth and the restructuring of the national educational system produced a burgeoning new middle class of literate Indonesian Muslims, who have become a significant factor in the nation's political and socio-cultural dynamics since the 1970s.[1] In the early years of the New Order, Suharto's drive to consolidate power energized a new wave of policies directed toward the systematic disenfranchisement of Muslim political parties. As discussed in chapter 4 in relation to the burgeoning *da'wa* movements of Indonesia during the 1970s–90s, outside the sphere of politics proper, however, new Muslim social movements experienced considerable growth during this same period.[2] Abdurrahman Wahid,[3] the

[1] Between 1965 and 1995, the general literacy rate in Indonesia rose from 40 percent to 90 percent of the country's population. This great expansion of the potential reading public facilitated the rapid growth of the market for Muslim books and periodical publications. See Graeme J. Hugo *et al.*, *The Demographic Dimension in Indonesian Development* (Singapore: Oxford University Press, 1987), 60–67; Terence H. Hull and Gavin W. Jones, "Demographic Perspectives," in *Indonesia's New Order: The Dynamics of Socio-Economic Transformation*, ed. Hal Hill (Honolulu: University of Hawaii Press, 1994), 123–78.

[2] The political aspects of these developments have been extensively described and analyzed in Hefner's *Civil Islam*.

[3] Wahid was born in 1940 into one of the most prominent NU families in Java, and pursued an eclectic course of advanced studies abroad in Egypt and Iraq. His complex, ever-changing, and at times even apparently contradictory views on religious and social issues hinder the possibility of any systematic and fully representative description of his thought, and studies of his political career have already filled the pages of many books and articles. For an overview on some of his work in relation to that of the thinkers described in this chapter, see Greg Barton, "Indonesia's Nurcholish Madjid and Abdurrahman Wahid as Intellectual Ulama: The Meeting of Islamic Traditionalism and Modernism in Neo-Modernist Thought," *SI* 4.1 (1997): 29–82. The author of this article has

charismatic NU leader who worked closely with a number of liberal Muslim thinkers during this period, expressed the aspirations of some segments of the Muslim community at that time in these terms: "democracy constitutes the hope of those who reject the use of the state to serve religious interests, while at the same time democracy is able to create space for religion in society."[4]

The debacles of Islamic party politics in the decade before the fall of Soekarno and the rise of the New Order led many Indonesian Muslims of diverse ideological orientations to begin looking for other means through which to bring their religious ideals into engagement with the rapid social transformations of the period and the new course of national development. The *da'wa* movements described in chapter 4 were multifaceted, pursuing their agendas for the reform of Islam in Indonesia through a broad array of media on multiple levels of society. Islamic activism was on the rise in many parts of the Muslim world in the late 1960s–70s, and some of the most fruitful fields of *da'wa* activity in the early years of the New Order were to be found on 'secular' college campuses. In the Middle East, these developments are most often regarded by contemporary scholars as a reaction to the crushing defeat of Arab armies by Israel in the 1967 war. As Issa Boullata has succinctly expressed it, in the years that followed:

> Islam, as a comprehensive ideological discourse began to loom as an appealing system of ideas and beliefs to increasing numbers of Muslim Arabs searching for secure moorings in a rapidly changing world and for a means to oppose the prevailing Arab regimes.[5]

In Indonesia, the immediate political effects of the Palestinian–Israeli conflict may not have been so keenly felt, but disillusionment with the policies of a local repressive regime provided fertile grounds for the reception of Islamist ideologies among some of the nation's highly educated youth.

Some of the impacts of such developments on Islamic revivalism in Southeast Asia have been examined by Judith Nagata in her pioneering work on *da'wa* movements in Malaysia, in which she noted ways in which *da'wa* movements were integral to the formation of an alternative youth culture in Malaysia, which to various degrees expressed concerns over issues

also produced a book-length biography of Wahid, written mostly during his brief and tumultuous presidency. *Abdurrahman Wahid: Muslim Democrat, Indonesian President* (Honolulu: University of Hawaii Press, 2002).

4 Abdul Ghofur, *Demokratisasi dan Prospek Hukum Islam di Indonesia: Studi atas Pemikiran Gus Dur* (Semarang: Pustaka Pelajar, 2002), vi.

5 Issa Boullata, *Trends and Issues in Contemporary Arab Thought* (Albany: SUNY Press, 1990), 153–54.

of social justice.[6] While no parallel study of comparative length yet exists for Indonesia we do know that analogous developments did take place in the Archipelago during the same period, particularly under the rubric of "training" (*tarbiyah*) on "secular" campuses such as that of the Bandung Institute of Technology (ITB).[7] Muslim student activism there was centered on ITB's Salman Mosque, which emerged as a center of national importance for Islamic revivalism in the 1970s–80s, associated with popular preachers such as Muhammad Imaduddun Abdulrahim.[8] The mosque itself, appropriate for its congregation on the campus of a college of engineering, was named after an early Persian convert to Islam who is remembered for his role in introducing new military technologies to the Muslim community of Medina on the eve of the Battle of the Trench in 627.

Some students turned to contemporary developments in the Middle East for inspiration, finding attractive elements in sources ranging from Saudi Arabia's reactionary Wahhābism to Iran's revolutionary Shī'ism, and the mobilization models of Egypt's Muslim Brotherhood in attempting to formulate alternative visions to New Order politics.[9] Brotherhood influences had already been a factor in the development of Indonesian Islam among Masjumi and DDII circles before this time. With the success of the 1979 Iranian revolution, however, new visions of Islam's potential role in social and political transformations began to enter into Indonesian conversations. Despite New Order policies of censorship and concern over the possible destabilizing effects of this new revolutionary Islamist ideology, Indonesian translations of 'Alī Sharī'atī (d. 1977) and Ayatullah Khomeini (d. 1989), as well as locally produced commentaries on their work began circulating among campus activists.[10] Aside from this, however, one of the most important means by which aspects of modern Iranian Muslim thought entered into Indonesian conversation was through the work of Jalaluddin Rakhmat.

[6] Judith Nagata, *The Reflowering of Malaysian Islam: Modern Religious Radicals and their Roots* (Vancouver: University of British Columbia Press, 1984), 125.

[7] Martin van Bruinessen, "Post-Suharto Muslim Engagements with Civil Society and Democratisation," paper presented at the Third International Conference and Workshop, Indonesia in Transition, organized by KNAW and Labsosio, Universitas Indonesia, August 24–28, 2003. This text is available online at www.let.uu.nl/~martin.vanbruinessen/personal/publications/Post_Suharto_Islam_and_civil_society.htm

[8] A selection of his sermons from the Salman mosque in 1977 has been frequently reprinted as *Kuliah Tawhid* (Jakarta: Yayasan Pembina Sari Insan, 1990). See also Achmad Tirtosudiro, *Bang 'Imad: pemikiran dan gerakan dakwahnya* (Jakarta: Gema Insani Press, 2002).

[9] Ken Miichi, "Islamic Youth Movements in Indonesia," *IIAS Newsletter* 32 (November 2003): 22.

[10] See, for example, Yusuf Abdullah Puar, *Perjuangan Ayatullah Khomeini* (Jakarta: Pustaka Antara, 1980).

## JALALUDDIN RAKHMAT

Jalaluddin Rakhmat was born in 1949 at Bandung, West Java, where he attended Universitas Pajajaran and later worked as a schoolteacher while serving in a number of offices for the local branch of the Muhammadiyah. He describes his own progression from being a modernist of the Muhammadiyah stripe as developing out of a growing realization that the charges of *bid'a* that were being launched by various reformists against their fellow believers were not based on any objective stance toward the scriptural sources of Islam, but rather upon differing interpretations of the corpus. Therefore the criticisms launched by the classical modernists were in fact not the absolute condemnations which they purported to be, but instead amplified statements of personal or scholarly opinion.

Rakhmat claims to have overcome such a narrowness of view through more extensive reading of the traditional sources and an increased appreciation of their variety and richness.[11] In the late 1970s, he went on to do graduate work in the United States, studying Communications at Iowa State University.[12] It was during his student days there that Rakhmat was invited by Haidar Bagir[13] to join a conference on Islamic Unity in Sri Lanka to participate on panels discussing relevant aspects of Islamic jurisprudence. This experience of encountering Muslims from diverse backgrounds heightened his awareness of alternative modes of Islamic thought and practice, and in the process Rakhmat became particularly attracted to the new formulations of activist Shī'ism then being developed in the Middle East.

Upon his return to Indonesia, Rakhmat took a position as lecturer in Communications at his Bandung *alma mater*, and over the course of the 1980s he became increasingly prominent as a popular preacher (*da'ī*) and lecturer on Islamic topics at other local campuses, including the prestigious Bandung Technology Institute (ITB) and the local branch of IAIN (Gunung Jati). In one of his most recent books, Rakhmat tells of his early Islamist sympathies, his activities with campus *da'wa* groups, and his clashes with the "Renewalist" thinker Nucholish Madjid (discussed below) whom he viewed at that time as "someone who hated the Sharī'a." Rakhmat also criticized figures such as Fazlur Rahman and the Indonesian jurist Ibrahim

11 Jalaluddin Rakhmat, *Menjawab Soal-soal Islam Kontemporer* (Bandung: Mizan 1998), 207–9

12 Where Rakhmat completed a thesis entitled, "A Model for the Study of Mass Media Effects on Political Leaders" in 1984.

13 Bagir (b. 1957), was also active with Islamic organizations on the campus of ITB and later went on to do graduate work in Middle Eastern Studies at Harvard (1990–92), and completed his Ph.D. at the University of Indiana. He is currently director of Mizan in Bandung, one of the largest publishers of books on Islam and Muslim society in Indonesia.

Hosen (see chapter 6) for what he regarded as their preoccupation with the "spirit of the text," sometimes at the expense of its clear outward meaning. Following this, however, he narrates his own change of heart after traveling to other Muslim countries where he was disappointed to discover that "the Sharīʿa by itself does not necessarily bring prosperity."[14]

In his attempts to develop a new, more effective model of Islamic revivalism, Rakhmat drew on approaches from his formal studies in Communications. In one of his essays entitled, "Para Daʿi versus Globalisasi," for example, he not only deals with the aspects of spreading the word of Islam in a formalist sense, but also makes an appeal to preachers to go beyond communication to practice a kind of therapy: "For *daʿī*, in addition to being educators are also "Doctors of the Soul" and their patients are the victims of Globalization." One way of doing this, he suggests, would be for modern *muballigh* to "take a lesson from the methods of the Sufis."[15] Rakhmat's appreciation of a more "spiritualized orientation" – in a distinctly modern sense – toward Islam may be seen as part of a broader movement for a new appreciation of Sufism in Indonesia over the past three decades.[16] Where earlier modernist reformers were often unsparingly harsh in their criticisms of Sufi practices, by the mid-1980s some Indonesian authors had become willing to reconsider even the traditional 'orders' (*ṭarīqa*) as positive agents of social change and a counterbalance to the perceived ill-effects of purely scripturalist models of Islamic reform.[17] As Rakhmat expresses it:

> Scripturalism pushes the mystical experience to the margins of religious life. The Sufis, who try and capture the inner meaning of the Qur'ānic texts, are deemed to be heretics. Religious practices that are not explicitly delineated in scripture are seen as "blameworthy innovations" (*bidʿa*). By marginalizing the mystical, the scripturalists have done away with emotional religious experiences; their followers can no longer enjoy religion and thus some of them are left spiritually unsatisfied.[18]

[14] Jalaluddin Rakhmat, *Dahulukan Akhlak di atas Fikih* (Bandung: Muthahhari Press, 2002), 79–80.

[15] Jalaluddin Rakhmat, *Islam Aktual: Refleksi-Sosial Seorang Cendekiawan Muslim* (Bandung: Mizan, 1991), 70–71.

[16] For an overview of these developments, see J. D. Howell, "Sufism and the Indonesian Islamic Revival," *Journal of Asian Studies* 60.3 (2001): 701–29. A recent, extensive statement of Rakhmat's own participation in these conversations can be found in his *Reformasi Sufistik: 'Halaman Akhir' Fikri Yathir* (Bandung: Pustaka Hidayah, 1998).

[17] See, for example, Moeslim Abdurrahman, "Kesyahduan Sufi dalam Transformasi Sosial: Suatu Pengamatan Perkembangan Tarket," *Pesantren* 2.3 (1985): 49–59; Nurcholish Madid, "Tasauf sebagai Inti Keberagamaan," *Pesantren* 2.3 (1985): 3–9.

[18] "Tinjauan Kritis atas Sejarah Fiqh: Dari Fiqh al-Khulafa al-Rasyidin Hingga Madzhab Liberalisme," in *Kontektualisasi Doktrin Islam dalam Sejarah*, ed. Budhy Munawar-Rachman (Jakarta: Yayasan Wakaf Paramadina, 1994), 288–89. Quotes such as this clearly display the influence of the Muhammadiyah-affiliated promoter of modern Muslim mysticism, Hamka (d. 1981), and his conceptions of "Modern Sufism" and its emphasis on the quality of *bahagia* ("Happiness"). See Hamka, *Tasauf Modern* (Jakarta: Bulan Bintang, 1983).

In an oft-reprinted 1985 campus lecture on "Sufism and Poverty" Rakhmat further questioned the idea that mysticism is a source of passivity and fatalism in Islam, arguing instead that Sufism can in fact be seen as a potential source of "dynamism and even militancy."[19] Rakhmat himself remains actively engaged with modern forms of Sufism to this day, particularly through his association with the Jakarta-based Sufi study circle Yayasan Tazkiya Sejati.[20]

Nevertheless he is most widely known not for his Sufism, but for his role in promoting public discussions of modern Shīʿite thought in Indonesia.[21] In his written works and public lectures Rakhmat has often elaborated upon such traditional Shīʿite doctrines as the occultation (*ghayba*) of the twelfth Imām and the belief that Fāṭima's spiritual purity was physically evidenced by her freedom from the "defilement" of menstruation.[22] This being said, it is important to keep in mind that Rakhmat is no simple Shīʿite sectarian. For the works of Islamic scholarship upon which he draws in the formulation of his own ideas include a greater number of more generally Sunni authors than specifically Shīʿite ones. A simple review of his textual citations and bibliographies reveals a wide range of sources that includes the works of such established Sunni scholars as Ibn al-Qayyim (d. 1350), al-Ghazālī, and al-Suyūṭī alongside modern Shīʿite authors such as Bāqir al-Ṣadr (d. 1980) and ʿAlī Sharīʿatī (d. 1977). Thus while Rakhmat's thought has been deeply influenced by certain aspects of Shīʿism, it would be a gross over-simplification to label him as a 'Shīʿite thinker.'[23]

As perceived Shīʿite leanings would have been a serious political liability in New Order Indonesia – particularly after the 1979 Iranian revolution –

[19] Jalaluddin Rakhmat, *Islam Alternatif: Ceramah-Ceramah di Kampus* (Bandung: Mizan, 1986, 5th reprint, 1993), 98. See also his *Membuka Tirai Kegaiban* (Bandung: Mizan, 1994).

[20] Rakhmat's own understanding of this simultaneous involvement with both Sufi and Shīʿite-oriented organizations is reflected in his essay, "Tasawuf dalam Perspektif Syi'ah" (*Islam Alternatif*, 259–70), in which he draws considerably on S. H. Nasr's works on the esoteric and mystical dimensions of Shīʿite thought.

[21] For an overview of contemporary Shīʿism, see Moojan Momen, *An Introduction to Shi'i Islam* (Yale University Press, 1985), 246–99. More detailed studies of some of the most influential Shi'ite thinkers in modern times include: A. A. Nayed, "The Unitary Qur'ānic Hermeneutics of Muhammad Baqir al-Sadr," *Islamic Studies* 31.4 (1992); Chibli Mallat, *The Renewal of Islamic Law: Muhammad Baqer as-Sadr, Najaf and the Shi'i International* (Cambridge: Cambridge University Press, 1993); Richard A. Norton, "Musa al-Sadr," in *Pioneers of Islamic Revival*, ed. Ali Rahnema (London: Zed Books, 1994), 184–207; and Ibrahim M. Abu-Rabi, "Toward an Islamic Liberation Theology: Muhammad Husayn Fadlallah and the Principles of Shi'i Resurgence," in *Intellectual Origins of Islamic Resurgence in the Modern Arab World* (Albany: SUNY Press, 1996), 220–47.

[22] See, for example, Rakhmat, *Menjawab Soal-soal Islam Kontemporer*, 249–65.

[23] However, there have been other modern Indonesian Muslims who more formally identify with Shīʿism and its traditions of learning. A small number studied at Qum in the 1970s, and their number has expanded considerably since the 1990s. For a brief overview of these developments, see Zulkifli, "Seeking Knowledge unto Qum: The Education of Indonesian Shi'i ustadhs," *IIAS Newsletter* 38 (September 2005): 30.

Rakhmat intentionally downplayed the more radical political rhetoric of this in favor of a more intellectualized elaboration of Shīʿite ideas on social justice, law, and society.[24] Like many other governments of countries with a large Muslim population, the New Order was somewhat uncomfortable with the possibility of a spread of post-revolutionary Iranian preaching among their citizens.[25] During the 1980s several radical preachers were persecuted for their alleged links with an international Shīʿite network.[26] By the end of that decade, however, the publication of works associated with Shīʿite thinkers such as Khomeini and Sharīʿatī began expanding considerably without significant government restriction. Since the 1990s, a variety of houses ranging from the radical Media Dakwah to the more moderate Mizan of Bandung have undertaken the publication of translations of works by these authors and secondary works deriving from them.[27] Mizan become the primary sponsor of Rakhmat's work, thus affording him access to an extensive nationwide audience.

Since 1988 Rakhmat has also served as head of the Yayasan Muthahhari at Bandung. Named after the prominent modern Shīʿite scholar Murtaḍā al-Muṭahharī (d. 1979), this Institute offers a number of local services, including a well-known school which supplements the standard national curriculum with vocational, computer training, and English-language study in addition to Arabic and Islamic subjects covering a broad range of studies of comparative studies of legal schools of thought. When questioned on the Shīʿite bias of this school in the popular Indonesian news weekly *Gatra*, Rakhmat answered, "We study all of religion, one cannot say whether it is

[24] Rakhmat seems to have been especially attracted by what he perceived as the "this worldly" orientation of Shīʿism and its concern for the rights and dignity of the oppressed classes. Rakhmat sees this as reflected not only in scholarly texts, but also in popular devotional practices such as the mourning rites for Ḥusayn b. ʿAlī (*Islam Aktual*, 243–58). Some parts of Indonesia have their own traditions for Muharram observances, but none seem to display the kind of intense focus on redemptive suffering that has been observed in similar celebrations in Iran and South Asia. See, for example, R. Michael Feener, "Muharram Observances in the History of Bengkulu," *SI* 6.2 (1999).

[25] One observer in the early 1980s noted that Indonesian affinities for the rhetoric of the Iranian revolution were generally not directed toward particular aspects of Shīʿism such as the role of religious leadership for the imams. Rather, what seemed to be attractive to a number of young Indonesian Muslims was, "its demonstration that popular will united under the banner of Islam could overcome a despotism backed by military might and Western favour." Ruth McVey, "Faith as the Outsider: Islam in Indonesian Politics," in *Islam in the Political Process*, ed. James P. Piscatori (Cambridge: Cambridge University Press, 1983), 220

[26] Fred von der Mehden, *Two Worlds of Islam: Interaction between Southeast Asia and the Middle East* (Gainesville: University Press of Florida, 1993), 68. Cf. *Indonesia: Muslims on Trial* (London: Tapol, 1987), 81ff.

[27] Examples of such publications include Ali Syariʿati, *Islam Agama Protes*, trans. Satrio Pinandito (Jakarta: Pustaka Hidayah, 1993).

Sunni or Shīʿa."[28] In his campus lectures, many of which were later published in volumes of collected essays, Rakhmat worked to introduce other new streams of contemporary Islamic thought into Indonesian-language discussions of Islamic law and related issues, arguing that the introduction of Shīʿi, as well as Ẓāhirī, arguments into the evolving discourse on *ijtihād* should be further pursued for their potential valuable contributions to the ongoing development of Islamic intellectualism in Indonesia.[29]

Rakhmat tends to follow the Jaʿfarī ("twelver" Shīʿite) school in rejecting *ḥadīth* texts transmitted by a number of the Prophet's companions whom they regard as unreliable or antagonistic toward members of the Prophet's household in the line of ʿAlī b. Abi Ṭālib (*Ahl al-bayt*). In this regard he has directed particularly caustic criticism toward the Prophet's companion and second caliph of Islam, ʿUmar b. al-Khaṭṭāb (d. 644).[30] As will be discussed below, ʿUmar has become a modern hero for reformers appealing to the spirit of the law over particularistic rulings that they see as impeding the interpretation of Islam in terms of contemporary conceptions of justice. This has been a particularly prominent trend among thinkers associated with the Indonesian "Renewalist" (*Pembaharuan*) movement. Rakhmat, however critiqued the work of this modern "*madhhab of ʿUmar*" on three specific points:

> (1) it focuses attention almost exclusively on the Qur'ān, (2) it tends to emphasize *ra'y* [personal opinion] over the Sunna, and (3) it stresses the concept of *maqāṣid al-sharīʿa* with too little connection to the clear and outward meaning of the Qur'ānic text.[31]

[28] "Mereka yang Dituding Syiah," and "Saya Bingung, Apa Saya Syiah," *Gatra* 47.3 (October 11, 1997). Rakhmat is perhaps the most prominent figure in what might be referred to as a growing Shīʿite movement in Indonesia. For information on some of the institutions that have developed in connection with this, see Nurujulianti and Arief Subhan, "Lembaga-lembaga Syiʿah di Indonesia," *Ulumul Qur'an* 6. 4 (1995): 20–26.

[29] See, for example, Rakhmat, *Islam Alternatif*, 242–58.

[30] See, for example, Jalaluddin Rakhmat, "Ijtihad: Sulit diperlakukan, tetapi Perlu," in *Ijtihad dalam Sorotan* (Bandung: Mizan, 1988), 184–86. In much of Rakhmat's writing, ʿUmar is portrayed as a rash, overbearing despot who was known to neglect the tradition of the Prophet in cases where it best suited more immediate ends. Such harsh criticism of a figure who is considered by many to be an early hero of Islam is often associated with a Shīʿite point of view which regards ʿUmar, and the other caliphs before ʿAlī as usurpers.

[31] "Tinjauan Kritis atas Sejarah Fiqh," 293. Elsewhere Rakhmat gives a much more abbreviated historical sketch of the development of *fiqh* in which he generally divides developments along the lines of two general trends: that of ʿUmar who placed *ra'y* over textual proofs, and that of ʿAlī who stuck more closely to the scriptural sources. He refers to these two groups as the *Manhaj Iraqi* (*ʿUmari*) and the *Manhaj Hijazi* (*ʿAlawi*), respectively. See Jalaluddin Rakhmat, "Sistem Pengambilan Hukum oleh Aimmatu al-Madzahib (Tanggapan atas Ceramah K. H. Ali Yafie)," in *Kontroversi Pemikiran Islam di Indonesia*, ed. Muhtar Gandaatmadja *et al.* (Bandung: PT Remaja Rosdakarya, 1990/reprinted 1993), 21–24.

Despite this sharp divergence of opinion on the interpretation of the legacies of key figures in early Muslim history, however, Rakhmat has come to share a number of basic ideas and affinities with key *Pembaharuan* figures such as Nurcholish Madjid (d. 2005).[32] In particular, both of these authors have devoted a significant amount of energy to producing historical sketches of the development of various schools of Islamic thought designed to show the origins of sectarian splits within the community.[33] Based upon this historicist recognition of the contingent origins of these divisions, they both agree with the basic conclusion that, "it is clearly absurd . . . to absolutize the claims of one Islamic religious 'sect' over another."[34]

Rakhmat once proposed that the *umma* might be more harmoniously united in a spirit of *ukhuwwa* (brotherhood) under the aegis of what he refers to as the "*Mazhab Ali*"[35] – something that he is careful to differentiate from "Shī'ism" more generally.[36] Rather he argued that in fact not all "Shī'ites" are of the "*Mazhab Ali*," and that what distinguishes a Muslim as belonging to this group is his or her faith and actions in the broadest sense, rather than any particular points of doctrine or ritual.[37] In support of this Rakhmat quotes from 'Alī himself as well as the sixth Shī'ite Imam Ja'far al-Ṣādiq (d. 765) in defining a true follower of the *Ahl al-bayt* (people of the [Prophet's] house) as one who, through both moral character and ethical behavior, is an "ornament to their faith, and does not simply take their faith as an ornament."[38] Thus while drawing on

[32] See, for example, Rakhmat's essays, "Konsep Asbab al-Nuzul dan Relevansinya bagi Pandangan Historis Segi-segi Tertentu Ajaran Keagamaan" (24–41); "Masalah Ta'wil sebagai Metodologi Penafsiran al-Qur'an" (11–23); and "Tradisi Syarah dan Hasyiyah dalam Fiqh dan Masalah Stagnasi Pemikiran Hukum Islam" (311–18). These could be compared to those of Nurcholish in the same volume, Nurcholish Madjid, "Sejarah Awal Penyusunan dan Pembakuan Hukum Islam," in *Kontekstualisasi Doktrin Islam dalam Sejarah*, 237–520. Cf. *Islam: Doktrin dan Peradaban: Sebuah Telaah Kritis tentang Masalah Keimanan, Kemanusiaan, dan Kemoderenan* (Jakarta: Yayasan Wakaf Paramadina, 1992), 238ff.

[33] "Tinjauan Kritis atas Sejarah Fiqh", 278–79.

[34] Nurcholish Madjid, "Skisme Dalam Islam: Tinjauan Singkat Secara Kritis-Historis Proses Dini Perpecahan Sosial-Keagamaan Islam," in *Kontekstualisasi Doktrin Islam dalam Sejarah* (Jakarta: Yayasan Paramadina, 1994), 687.

[35] *Islam Aktual*, 36. Elsewhere Rakhmat refers to followers of this approach as the *kaum Alawi* or "Alid group." "Tinjauan Kritis atas Sejarah *Fiqh*," 273.

[36] The use of the term *madhhab* here is looser even than that of Hasbi Ash Shiddeiqy and Hazairin. As will be discussed in chapter 7, the term has over the past two decades come to be used well beyond its jurisprudential sense to be applied informally to various "schools of thought" in contemporary Indonesia.

[37] In this Rakhmat's "*mazhab Ali*" is also differentiated from other forms of non-Shī'ite 'Alid piety known in Indonesia such as the *'Alawiyya ṭariqa*. This Sufi order is prominent among the descendents of the Hadrami Arabs across the Indonesian archipelago, particularly those claiming "*sayyid*" status as descendents of the Prophet.

[38] Rakhmat, *Menjawab Soal-soal Islam Kontemporer*, 239–40.

pre-eminent Shīʿite authorities, Rakhmat is careful to distinguish his positions from those popular Indonesian understandings of Shīʿism in its narrowly sectarian sense. Rakhmat's distancing of himself from any association with formal institutions of modern Shīʿism became even more pronounced after having spent time in Iran during 1994–95. Over the course of this visit, his regard for the Iranian *mullahs* changed from one of considerable esteem to great disappointment as he witnessed the corruption that ensued upon their taking control of government and their apparent arrogation of Divine authority.

More recently, Rakhmat has shifted even further the emphasis in his writings away from technical aspects of the formal Islamic religious sciences. This sea change was announced with the publication of his *Prioritize Ethics over Fiqh* (*Dahulukan Akhlak di atas Fikih*), which quickly went through three printings within two years of its initial publication.[39] In the preface to this text, he bemoans what he sees as the reduction of Islam to "mere" *fiqh* in a way that has made it possible that one can be quite learned in the intricacies of the law, and yet unable to muster the moral judgment necessary to confront complex contemporary issues. He posits one possible means to address this through a reorientation toward what he refers to as the "beauty" of ethics[40] that he sees having its historical roots in the teachings of the Prophet's family and the twelve imams of *ithnā ʿasharī* Shīʿism as "the founders of the *madhhab* of *akhlāq*."[41] Rakhmat then attempts to assert an alternative vision to what he refers to as the "religious paradigm" (*paradigma diniah*) of *fiqh*, one that can serve to help Muslims recognize the ethical insights of Islam's religious teaching in their daily lives.

In doing this he criticizes not only the medieval Muslim jurists so often scapegoated by modern Muslim reformists for their perceived "stagnation" of Islamic thought, but also modern authors such as the Sayyid Sābiq (d. 2000), whose *Fiqh al-Sunna* has gained worldwide popularity through translations into a number of languages since its initial Arabic publication in the 1970s. Within Indonesia, the *Fiqh al-Sunna* has gained considerable

[39] Jalaluddin Rakhmat, *Dahulukan Akhlak di atas Fikih* (Bandung: Muthahhari Press, 2002).

[40] In thus framing this introduction to the argument of his book, Rakhmat draws on the same horrifying incident – the March 2002 death of Saudi schoolgirls who were prohibited from leaving a burning building by religious authorities who would not allow them in public without required covering – that was reacted to by Khaled Abou El Fadl in the introduction to his essay "The Ugly Modern and Modern Ugly: Reclaiming the Beautiful in Islam," in *Progressive Muslims*, ed. Omid Safi (Oxford: OneWorld, 2003). It appears that each of them – from West Java and the West Coast of the United States, respectively – came to this reaction independently of the other in a way which reinforces the sense of how developments across the contemporary Muslim world are increasingly part of immediate, global conversations.

[41] Rakhmat, *Dahulukan Akhlak*, vi–xi.

importance in public discourses on Islamic law over the past two decades. The prominent NU *kyai* Ali Yafie has voiced high regard for this work, and recent research into the practice of Islamic Religious Court justices in contemporary Indonesia has revealed Sayyid Sābiq's work to be the text most often studied by aspiring judges in preparing for their examinations, and a frequent point of reference in their administration of Islamic law.[42] Rakhmat, however, sees the *Fiqh al-Sunna*, and other modern works of this kind, as exhibiting dangerous tendencies toward narrow and exclusivistic conceptions of "true Islam" based upon selective citation of scriptural sources, rather than a broader appreciation of the richness and diversity of traditional scholarship.

Lamenting the impact that this has had on young Indonesian Muslim readers who take their understandings of Islam from such sources alone, he writes:

> They elevate the *fiqh* of Sayyid Sābiq to the level of the *Sunna* itself. Because the *fiqh* of Sayyid Sābiq is [entitled] the *Fiqh al-Sunna*, it comes to be regarded as the only true *fiqh*. Any other *fiqh* is thus [by implication] the *fiqh* of *bid'a*.[43]

Instead of such exclusionary conceptions of truth in matters of Islamic law, Rakhmat vigorously promotes the recognition of internal Muslim diversity of opinion as a key characteristic of his '*akhlak* paradigm.'[44] An important part of this for Rakhmat is knowing the range of traditions within Islam to both broaden one's perspective and to humble those who would presume to know the true meaning of Islam as if they had some special insight into the mind of God. After a review of a history of "stagnation" of Islamic legal thought, Rakhmat comments on the dead end of scripturalism as a solution to this, and looks forward appreciatively to the work of "liberal" Muslim thinkers who have attempted to move beyond a strictly literal reading of authoritative texts to arrive at a better understanding of the "meaning" (*makna*) and "essence" (*esensi*) of the law.[45]

[42] Euis Nurlaelawati, "Modernization, Tradition, and Identity: The Compilation of Islamic Law and Legal Practices in the Indonesian Islamic Courts" (Leiden University Thesis, 2006).

[43] Rakhmat, *Dahulukan Akhlak*, 16. Later in this same text Rakhmat further develops this discussion with reference to juristic distinctions between different kinds of differences under the rubrics of *ikhtilāf* and *khilāf* (97–115).

[44] Rakhmat, *Dahulukan Akhlak*, 33ff. Rakhmat adds something new to the equation here that develops out of his affinity for aspects of *ithnā 'asharī* Shī'ite thought. That is that one effective means by which a relative harmony amidst internal Muslim divisiveness on various legal issues might be achieved is through the concept of *taqiyya*, which he glosses as "setting aside our *fiqh* in the interest of preserving a sense of 'brotherhood' (*persaudaraan*) within Muslim circles."

[45] Rakhmat, *Dahulukan Akhlak*, 153–217.

In doing this he critically reviews the work of modern Muslim scholars from Indonesia and around the world who have pursued such projects in various ways.[46] Similarly, he advocates the historical study of Muslim intellectual and religious legacies in ways that again highlight how his agendas intersect with those of Madjid and other *Pembaharuan* thinkers, as well as with the work of Haidar Bagir, and even Luthfi Assyaukanie and other young Indonesian intellectuals associated with the Liberal Islam Network (JIL).[47] At the same time, however, his calls for such openness to diverse views as an essential part of *akhlaq* are set alongside critiques of what he calls the "*fiqh* paradigm"; referring to the way in which legal rulings are viewed by ordinary Muslims ("those who do not know and do no know that they do not know") rather than to the jurisprudential reasoning of classically trained religious scholars. Thus while acknowledging that *fiqh* texts often reproduce more than one position on a given issue, Rakhmat nevertheless argues that this openness to multiple solutions to a given problem is not recognized by non-specialists, who tend to hold whatever particular ruling they have been told as absolute, and in the process regard all alternatives as invalid.[48]

Although strenuously asserting the need for a continuous exercise of *ijtihād* in order to allow Muslims to adapt themselves to the constantly changing needs of society, Rakhmat does not believe that simply anyone is qualified for such an undertaking. Instead he maintains that *ijtihād* may only be exercised by those possessing the proper prerequisites, advocating a hierarchical model of "*Ijtihād* for the *'ulamā'*, and *taqlīd* for the masses."[49] Placing such restrictions on the kind of mass appeals for *ijtihād* advocated by earlier generations of autodidact reformists such as Hassan, Rakhmat calls for an awareness of the need for specialization and a new concept of professionalism for those engaged in the interpretation of Islamic law. The demands imposed upon such specialists should be stringent, he argues, because the work that they do is so important for the welfare of the

[46] This includes critiques of the "*fiqh* of 'Umar," whom Rakhmat refers to here as the "primadonna" of those who elevate mere "opinion" (*ra'y*) over "revelation" (*wahyu*). Rakhmat, *Dahulukan Akhlak*, 222.

[47] Ind. *Jaringan Islam Liberal.* This group will be discussed in chapter 7.

[48] Rakhmat, *Dahulukan Akhlak*, 108, 19.

[49] Jalaluddin Rakhmat, "Skisma dalam Islam: Sebuah Telaah Ulang," in *Kontektualisasi Doktrin Islam dalam Sejarah*, ed. Budhy Munawar-Rachman (Jakarta: Yayasan Wakaf Paramadina, 1994), 706. This position, however, does not seem to restrain Rakhmat himself from acting in something of the capacity of *Mufti* in response to religious and social questions posed to him. For some of Rakhmat's own remarks to the effect that he is not a *fiqh* (scholar trained in Islamic jurisprudence), see *Menjawab Soal-soal Islam Kontemporer*, 147, 158–64, 240; and *Islam Alternatif*, 255.

community. As a title of one of his essays reads, "*Ijtihād* is Difficult to Carry Out, but Necessary."[50]

Important to note here, however, is the point that the "specialists" Rakhmat elevates here are not traditional Muslim jurists in the mould of either Sunni *ʿulamāʾ* or the Shīʿite clergy. Rather he appears to have in mind here scholars like himself who combine personal piety and an interest in traditional Muslim learning with advanced degrees in "modern sciences." Those with such training should, he argues, be able to approach contemporary questions from a perspective beyond that of particular rulings on individual issues to broader conceptions of the intent behind the law (*maqāṣid al-sharīʿa*).[51] Ironically, this is precisely the approach that Rakhmat had in earlier years castigated as "the *madhhab of* ʿUmar," an orientation toward the "aims (*maqāṣid*) of the Sharīʿa" that has been characteristic of the Indonesian 'Renewalist' movement known as *Pembaharuan*.

## "RENEWAL" AND INDONESIAN "NEO-MODERNISM"

General aspects of *Pembaharuan's* intellectual agenda, as well as the impact of New Order development ideology on its formulations and reception, have already been treated extensively elsewhere, first by the Indonesian scholars Factry Ali and Bahfiar Effendy,[52] and later by international scholarship in the works of Greg Barton and others.[53] The brief discussion of the *Pembaharuan* movement in this chapter takes a different tack in focusing on the implications that it had for the development of Indonesian discourses on Islamic law and society during the last decades of the twentieth century. *Pembaharuan* thinkers themselves tended to avoid discussions of Islamic law and Muslim jurisprudence in favor of other areas of religious scholarship, especially that of "theology" (*kalām/ uṣūl al-dīn*). Even though they did not engage directly with issues of legal thought, their work did play an important role in opening up new conversations on Islam in modern Indonesia that reoriented the frameworks for a range of contemporary Muslim discourses on law and society.

50 Jalaluddin Rakhmat, "Ijtihad: Sulit diperlakukan, tetapi Perlu," in *Ijtihad dalam Sorotan* (Bandung: Mizan, 1988), 173–201.

51 Rakhmat, *Dahulukan Akhlak*, 150.

52 Fachry Ali and Bahtiar Effendi, *Merambah Jalan Baru Islam: Rekonstruksi Pemikiran Islam Indonesia Masa Orde Baru* (Bandung: Mizan, 1986), 144ff.

53 On the origins and development of *Pembaharuan* in Indonesia, see Greg Barton, "The International Context of the Emergence of Islamic Neo Modernism in Indonesia," in *Islam in the Indonesian Social Context*, ed. M. C. Ricklefs (Clayton: Monash University Centre of Southeast Asian Studies, 1991), 69–82.

In certain respects, *Pembaharuan* had much in common with the *da 'wa* movement that was rapidly expanding across Indonesia at the same time. Both, for example, spent more time speaking of 'Islam' in an abstract sense than of the technicalities of jurisprudence, and both advocated the Islamization of society by imbuing individuals with Islamic values that would inform their actions in both the private and the public spheres. But *Pembaharuan* promoted an alternative vision of Islam to that of the former Masjumi cadres involved with the DDII, many of whom never fully abandoned their aspirations for the establishment of a formally Islamic Indonesian state, even after being forced out of party politics. Indeed, rather than envisioning the *umma* as a totalising body politic ambivalent or antagonistic toward non-Muslim citizens, *Pembaharuan* thinkers embraced the demographic realities of the country through appeals to democracy and pluralism informed both by universal ideals and the historical traditions of the region.[54]

As discussed in chapter 4 the social orientation of Harjono and the DDII tended to be rather confrontational toward non-Muslims and even toward Muslims who disagreed with them on various religious and social issues. Their emphasis was often on the formal delimitation of confessional community boundaries defined in the idiom of new, reformist models of public and personal piety. *Da 'wa* activists tended to package their platforms for social transformation by redeploying a symbolic vocabulary of formal Islamic ideology and institutions, often inflected with hyper-Arabicized neologisms. *Pembaharuan* writers, on the other hand, often presented their Indonesian readers with English-derived technical terminology from the Social Sciences that they argued expressed the substantive ideals of "true" Islam.[55] Both of these approaches to understanding Islam, however, are modern formulations which to different extents are selectively framed by certain essentialist assumptions and categories developed in the religious and social thought of the Euro-American tradition. Nevertheless, proponents of *da 'wa* and *Pembaharuan* adopted very different orientations toward the presentation of their positions as 'authentically' Islamic.

Significant elements of the foundations of the *Pembaharuan* movement were first formulated within the context of the "Limited Group" discussions held in the 1960s at Yogyakarta under the direction of A. Mukti

[54] For an extended discussion of *Pembaharuan* thinkers' engagement with issues of pluralism and democracy in New Order Indonesia, see Hefner, *Civil Islam*.

[55] Indeed, the only major English-language collection of essays by Madjid was published under the title *The True Face of Islam: Essays on Islam and Modernity in Indonesia* (Ciputat: Voice Center Indonesia, 2003).

Ali (d. 2004). In these circles younger Indonesian Muslim thinkers such as Djohan Effendi, Manshur Hamid, Dawam Rahardjo, and the Ahmad Wahib (among others)[56] were free to explore sometimes radical ideas in a search for new ways in which Islam could be interpreted and implemented with greater relevance to conditions in contemporary Indonesia.[57] The head of this group, Mukti Ali, had studied in Dutch colonial schools, the "modern-style" *pesantren* at Termas (Java), and the Universitas Islam Indonesia before going on to pursue graduate degrees abroad at the University of Karachi and McGill University. Over the course of his earlier studies in Indonesia, Mukti Ali moved away gradually from his family's association with the NU toward affiliation with the Muhammadiyah, and this experience of moving across such internal divisions of the Indonesian *umma* helped his rise through the political ranks of the young Indonesian Republic, holding a number of positions in the Department of Religious Affairs before eventually being appointed as Minister.

Serving in that position from 1971 to 1978, he both reinvigorated existing institutions such as the Inter-religious Dialogue Consultation (Musyawarah Antarumat Beragama), and played a role in the creation of new Muslim organizations. The most influential of these organizations has been the Majelis Ulama Indonesia (MUI), which was founded by the Suharto government in 1975 as a national body for the production of *fatwā* to advise the Muslim community – and the Indonesian government – on issues facing contemporary society.[58] As minister of religious affairs, Mukti Ali also oversaw a series of new developments in the IAIN system that had a marked impact upon the ways that Islam and Islamic law were taught in these institutions. In particular, he worked to further integrate these

[56] See, for example, Ismed Natsir and Djohan Effendi, eds., *Pergolakan Pemikiran Islam: Catatan Harian Ahmad Wahib* (Jakarta: LP3ES, 1981). For an English-language discussion and analysis of Wahib's writings, see A. H. Johns, "An Islamic System of Islamic Values? Nucleus of a Debate in Contemporary Indonesia," in *Islam and the Political Economy of Meaning*, ed. W. R. Roff (London: Croom Helm, 1987), 54–280.

[57] Other sometime participants in these discussions included: Syu'bah Asa, Saifullah Mahyudin, Djauhari Muhsin, Kuntowijoyo, Syamsuddin Abdullah, Muin Umar, Kamal Muchtar, Simuh, and Wadjiz Anwar. Bahtiar Effendi, "Islam and the State in Indonesia: Munawir Sjadzali and the development of a New Theological Underpinning of Political Islam," *SI* 2.2 (1995): 102.

[58] For more on the history of the MUI, treatments of some of its *fatwās*, and its place within the broader context of *iftā* ' in the region, see Mohamad Atho Mudzhar, *Fatwa-Fatwa Majelis Ulama Indonesia: Sebuah Studi tentang Pemikiran Hukum Islam di Indonesia, 1975–1988* (Jakarta: INIS, 1993); M. B. Hooker, *Indonesian Islam: Social Change through Contemporary Fatāwā* (Honolulu: University of Hawaii Press, 2003); Moch. Nur Ichwan, "*'Ulamā '*, State and Politics: Majelis Ulama Indonesia after Suharto," *ILS* 12.1 (2005): 45–72; and C. van Dijk, "Religious Authority, Politics, and *Fatwā* in Contemporary Southeast Asia," in Feener and Cammack, eds., *Islamic Law in Contemporary Indonesia*.

schools into the national education system and to develop them as centers for the quality training of religious intellectuals who would be attuned to the contemporary needs of the nation's social and economic development. Mukti Ali's own formal academic training was in the comparative study of religions – especially under the influence of W. C. Smith at McGill – and upon his return to Indonesia he worked to establish a new tone of religious pluralism in Indonesian public discourses on Islam that situated religious issues within the development and modernization agendas of the New Order state.[59]

The contrast between *Pembaharuan* and the religious and social visions of Natsir and Harjono as discussed in chapter 4 are clear, as the former flatly rejected the idea that because a majority of its population is Muslim this necessarily implied a mandate for the formal implementation of the Sharī'a as the law of the Indonesian nation-state. Since 1947, however, a younger generation of thinkers and activists sympathetic to the Masjumi legacy had organized themselves into a Muslim student union called the Himpunan Mahasiswa Islam (HMI), a prominent early leader of which was Nurcholish Madjid. It was in his decisive break from the formalist Islamizing agenda of the Masjumi legacy that the *Pembaharuan* movement made its dramatic entrance into Indonesian public discourses on Islamic law and society.

## NURCHOLISH MADJID

Madjid was born into a prosperous family at Jombang, East Java, in 1939.[60] At the age of fourteen, he entered a local NU-affiliated *pesantren*, but after two years Madjid moved on to pursue further studies at the "Modern Pesantren" of Gontor. At this institution, emphasis was placed on training in English and Arabic, and his increasing proficiency in these languages gave him access to vast literatures that he continued to explore for the rest of his life. In 1968, he visited the United States on the invitation of the State Department, and before returning to Indonesia, he also visited

[59] Biographical sketches of Mukti Ali can be found in Howard Federspiel, *Muslim Intellectuals and National Development in Indonesia* (Commack, NY: Nova Science Publishers, 1992), 19–22; and Azyumardi Azra, Saiful Umam *et al.*, eds., *Menteri-Menteri Agama RI: Biografi Sosial-Politik* (Jakarta: INIS, 1998), 269–319. For more on his religious thought, see Ali Munhanif, "Islam and the Struggle for Religious Pluralism in Indonesia: A Political Reading of the Religious Thought of Mukti Ali," *SI* 3. 1 (1996): 79–126.

[60] The biographical sketch given here is based for the most part upon that found in Greg Barton "Neo-Modernism: A Vital Synthesis of Traditionalist and Modernist Islamic Thought in Indonesia," *SI* 2.3 (1995): 13–17, supplemented with material from interviews with Madjid in June 2004.

France, Turkey, Lebanon, Syria, Egypt, the Sudan, Saudi Arabia, Pakistan, and Iraq. Writing of these travels, Madjid admitted to being impressed by his time in America, however he considered himself to have been more heavily influenced by the meetings and discussions he shared with fellow Muslims during his return trip through the Middle East. For it was during that time that he came into more contact with diverse currents of modern Islamic reformism.

After his return to Indonesia Madjid became most widely known for his controversial call for "*sekularisasi*."[61] He had intended this term to convey the idea that if Islam was to be reformed and thus made a more vital and dynamic part of Indonesian religious life, Muslims would have to examine their tradition critically with an eye towards "de-sacralizing" outmoded human institutions that mistakenly came to be seen as divinely sanctioned ones. This, Madjid argued, would allow them to make clearer distinctions between the eternal message of revelation, and the human accretions on and interpretations of this as they had developed over time. Such a position would of course have tremendous implications for those advocating the establishment of an "Islamic State," and his use of *sekularisasi* provoked angry reactions from Islamists who equated his calls for "secularization" with ideological "Secularism".[62]

In 1973 Fazlur Rahman and Leonard Binder visited Indonesia seeking participants for an extended seminar to be held at the University of Chicago.[63] The controversy surrounding Madjid at that time had put him in the spotlight, and he was invited to attend the Chicago seminar in 1976 and then he returned again from 1978 to 1984 to complete a dissertation on the fourteenth-century Ḥanbalī scholar Ibn Taymiyya under the direction of Fazlur Rahman. While the congruences of Rahman's thought with that of Madjid and other advocates of *Pembaharuan* are clear, Greg Barton has argued that they developed along their own individual tracks:

> Fazlur Rahman was not, despite the strong congruence of his ideas with those of Madjid, Ahmad Djohan *et al.*, the originator of Neo Modernism in Indonesia.

[61] For an overview of Nurcholish's ideas on *Sekularisasi*, see Greg Barton, "Indonesia's Nurcholish Madjid and Abdurrahman Wahid as Intellectual Ulama: The Meeting of Islamic Traditionalism and Modernism in Neo-Modernist Thought," *SI* 4.1 (1997): 18–24.

[62] Some of the most strident criticisms of Nurhcolish's ideas were put forward by H. M Rasjidi and Mohamad Roem. See H. M. Rasjidi, *Koreksi terhadap Drs. Nurcholish Madjid tentang Sekularisasi* (Jakarta: Bulan Bintang, 1977). Later, a compilation of correspondence between the latter and Madjid on the matter was published as Agus Edi Santoso, ed., *Tidak Ada Negara Islam: Surat-surat Politik Nurcholish Madjid – Mohamad Roem* (Jakarta: Penerbit Djambatan, 1997).

[63] Nurcholish's ideas seemed quite amenable with the interests of this scholar. See, for example, Leonard Binder, *Islamic Liberalism: A Critique of Development Ideologies* (Chicago: University of Chicago Press, 1988), 210.

The fundamentals of Indonesian Neo Modernism were established by late 1969. In 1970 *Pembaruan Pemikiran* emerged from a fiery public birth, and by late 1972, battle hardened after three years in the public arena it was already well developed. It was not until 1973, when he visited Indonesia for the first time, that Madjid and Djohan knew anything about Fazlur Rahman.[64]

Madjid's Neo-Modernism is perhaps most apparent in his attempts to reevaluate Muslim tradition in a constructive reformulation that draws upon Islamic ideals in ways viewed to be most beneficial and relevant to the needs of contemporary society. While drawing on examples of figures and ideas from the rich intellectual and religious history of Islam, however, the approach to these materials taken by Madjid and other *Pembaharuan* thinkers is one that places interpretations of Muslim history squarely in the service of contemporary concerns.

Madjid asserted that while justice, pluralism, civility, and egalitarianism are fundamental principles underlying all aspects of Islam and especially its law, *fiqh* has historically tended to emphasize detailed discussions of rulings on outwardly manifest actions, rather than the inner meaning of the law.[65] As advocate of the 'Renewal' of Islamic thought, Madjid places great importance on the concept of *ijtihād*, working within the modern tradition of Muhammad Iqbal's vision of it as the "principle of movement within Islam."[66] Such dynamic and evolving conceptualizations of *ijtihād*, however, are older than Iqbal, and Madjid often centers his discussions of *ijtihād* on an even earlier figure, the second (Sunni) Caliph 'Umar b. al-Khaṭṭāb.[67]

Admiring descriptions of 'Umar and his approach to *ijtihād* have made for a popular trope in modern discussions of Islamic law in many countries, at least since the publication of the Aligarh scholar Shibli Nu'mani's *'Umar al-Farūq* in 1898.[68] The recent rise in popularity of the "*fiqh* of 'Umar"

[64] Barton, "Emergence of Islamic Neo Modernism in Indonesia," 81.

[65] See, for example, *Islam Doktrin dan Peradaban*, 247, 574–61.

[66] Muhammad Iqbal, *The Reconstruction of Religious Thought in Islam* (London: Oxford University Press, 1934). Iqbal's conception of the role of *ijtihād* in Islamic history influenced many contemporary Indonesian advocates of *Pembaharuan*. See, for example, Haidar Bagir, "Dua Bentuk Respon Atas Pembaruan Islam," *Ulumul Qur'an* 4.1 (1993): 3. For more on the life and work of this important modern Muslim thinker, see Annemarie Schimmel, *Muhammad Iqbal, Prophetischer Poet und Philosopher* (Munich: E. Diederichs, 1989).

[67] Madjid, *Kontekstualisasi Doktrin Islam dalam Sejarah*, 339–41.

[68] An English-language abridgment of the original Urdu text is now available: Shibli Numani, *Umar* (London: I. B. Tauris, 2004). For an overview of his treatment of 'Umar as a major figure in the development of Islamic law, see pp. 101–06, 114–29. In his introduction to this edition, Jamil Qureshi notes that Numani's view of the importance of 'Umar for the development of Islamic law draws upon the ideas of the eighteenth-century Indian scholar Shah Waliullah al-Dihlawī (p. x), who as we have mentioned in chapter 3, also had an indirect influence on Hasbi's understandings of Islamic legal change.

is cleary evidenced in the number of essays, popular addresses, and full monographs on the subject that have been produced all across the Muslim world.[69] Madjid wrote repeatedly of the appeal of 'Umar's "principles of *ijtihād*."[70] In one specific discussion of the "*fiqh* of 'Umar," he quoted extensively a letter from 'Umar to his governor of Iraq, Abū Mūsā al-Ash'arī, extracting from this document what he understood to be five principle aspects of 'Umar's criteria for establishing valid Islamic legal rulings: (1) authenticity; (2) development; (3) the progressive revision of existing legal decisions; (4) the conviction with which important decisions are executed; and (5) the necessity of sincere intention.[71]

Madjid's own conception of *ijtihād*, however, is one which could be characterized as more theological than jurisprudential.[72] That is, he and other *Pembaharuan* thinkers have tended to be more concerned with macro-level discussions of 'reinterpretation' than they have with particular technical aspects of Islamic legal reasoning.[73] This is clearly evidenced, for example in the relative emphasis he places on discussions of the "wisdom" (*ḥikma*) behind various rulings as a means of evoking the broader moral and ethical principles that he sees as underlying the law as a whole. In one of his articles on the subject Madjid begins by establishing the etymological links between *ḥikma* and other permutations of the Arabic root, *ḥ-k-m* with the Indonesian word *hukum* ("law").[74] Elsewhere he places more emphasis on connecting his own understandings of *ḥikma* with other terms from the technical vocabulary of *fiqh* used to refer to the anterior groundings of

[69] A number of modern Arabic works on the *ijtihād* of 'Umar have found new readerships in Indonesian translation, including Muḥammad 'Abd al-Azīz al-Halawī, *Fatwa dan Ijtihad Umar bin, Khaththab: Ensiklopedi berbagai persoalan fiqih* (Surabaya: Risalah Gusti, 1999) Arabic original is *Fatāwa wa aqḍiya amr al-mu'minin 'Umar b. al-Khaṭṭāb* (Cairo: Maktaba al-Qur'ān, 1986).

[70] For an overview of his general argument in this direction, see *Persoalan Taqlid dan Ijtihad*, 1–4.

[71] Following this abstracted list, Madjid then contrasts the glory of such a paragon of progressivism with a sketch of later Islamic history that follows the well-known model of greatness and decline so often employed by Muslim reformists and Orientalists alike. Madjid, *Kontekstualisasi Doktrin Islam*, 339–41.

[72] The ascendancy of what might be termed "theology" in modern Muslim religious discourses is unprecedented in the earlier history of Islam, in which *kalām* – at least since the *mihna* of the early ninth century – had been relegated to a position on the margins of a *fiqh*-centered tradition. Over the second half of the twentieth century, however, the number of theses, dissertations, articles, and books produced by Muslims on "Islamic theology" in Indonesia and elsewhere has been remarkable. These developments, and the role of Western academic and religious preoccupations with them, deserve an extensive study of their own.

[73] Nucholish Madjid, "Taqlid dan Ijtihad: Masalah Kontinuitas dan Kreativitas dalam Memahami Pesan Agama," in *Kontekstualisasi Doktrin Islam dalam Sejarah* (Jakarta: Yayasan Paramadina, 1994), 346–49.

[74] "Konsep 'Hukum' dalam al-Qur'an" Antara Ketgaran Menegakkan Keadilan dan Kelembutan Rasa Kemanusiaan," in *Islam Doktrin dan Peradaban*, 312–27.

Islamic legal rulings such as the *'illa* (ratio legis) and especially the *maqāṣid* ("intentions" or "goals") of the *Sharī'a*.[75]

Madjid and most of his colleagues involved in the *Pembaharuan* movement more generally have understood one of the primary "intentions" or "goals" of the *Sharī'a* to be *maṣlaḥa* ("benefit" or "welfare") broadly conceived. This has fostered the opening and rapid expansion of conversations on the extent to which *maṣlaḥa* can serve as the foundation for legal decisions, even when taken to inform rulings independent of specific scriptural references (*maṣāliḥ mursala*). Considerations of social welfare or public benefit framed in terms of achieving *maṣlaḥa* (*istiṣlāḥ*) have thus come to dominate much of the philosophical and public discourses on Islamic legal change over the past two decades.[76] During the late New Order period, it also received a considerable degree of official sanction from various quarters, including that of the Minister of Religious Affairs, Munawir Sjadzali (d. 2004).

## MUNAWIR SJADZALI

Sjadzali was born in Klaten in 1925 and educated at Islamic schools in Central Java, gaining a proficiency in Arabic and Islamic religious texts that he later put to the service of the Arab Section of Indonesia's Ministry of Foreign Affairs. He also held other positions in the Ministry's diplomatic postings to London and Washington, which enabled him to pursue graduate degrees in Political Science from Exeter and Georgetown.[77] In these studies he continued to pursue an interest in the relationships between Islam and politics that he had been extensively exploring since the early years of Indonesian independence.[78]

In 1983, Sjadzali was appointed to the first of his two terms as Indonesian Minister of Religious Affairs (1983–93). During his tenure the administration of Islam by the New Order state underwent a remarkable degree of consolidation with the establishment of *Pancasila* as the sole ideological

75 Nurcholish Madjid, *Persoalan Taqlid dan Ijtihad* (Jakarta: Yayasan Wakaf Paramadina, 1987), 10–14.

76 This has become a dominant trend not only in Indonesia, but across much of the Muslim world, some of the jurisprudential consequences of which have been discussed by Wael Hallaq in *A History of Islamic Legal Theories: An Introduction to Sunnī Uṣūl al-Fiqh* (Cambridge: University Press, 1997), 214–31.

77 Biographical sketches of Munawir Sjadzali can be found in "Dari Lembah Kemiskinan," *Kontekstualisasi Ajaran Islam: 70 Tahun Prof. Dr. H. Munawir Sjadzali*, ed. Muhammad Wahyuni Nafis *et al.* (Jakarta: Paramadina, 1995), 1–118; and Azyumardi Azra, Saiful Umam *et al.*, eds., *Menteri-Menteri Agama RI: Biografi Sosial-Politik* (Jakarta: INIS, 1998), 369–412.

78 One of his early published works on the subject is M. Sj. Ibnu Amatillah, *Analyse: Mungkinkah Negara Indonesia Bersendikan Islam?* (Semarang: Usaha Taruna, 1950).

basis for all organizations within the country in 1984,[79] the restructuring of the Islamic religious courts in 1989,[80] and the promulgation of an official compilation of Islamic legal rulings on marriage, inheritance, and charitable trusts in 1991.[81] All of these measures had the effect of further establishing the authority of the New Order over potential political, governmental, and legal challenges by Muslims eager for the establishment of alternative arrangements for the institution of Islamic law in the Indonesian state.

In line with these broader trends, the IAIN underwent a series of changes during this period that were intended to redefine its legal status in the national Ministries of Education and Religious Affairs, as well as to enhance its curriculum and pedagogical approaches in ways more amenable to the needs of contemporary Indonesian society.[82] By the time of Sjadzali's tenure as minister, IAIN enrollments were swelling and came to include an increasing number of students educated in the *pesantren* milieu who went on to become active participants in academic and popular debates over issues of religion, law, and society.[83] The level of these conversations was transformed and to a considerable extent directed toward formally depoliticized orientations as various IAIN branches were expanded to include postgraduate studies and other programs to upgrade the skills of the teaching staff for the Religious Sciences (*ʿulūm al-dīn*) in an interdisciplinary format.

In formulating his program for further changes in the IAIN system, Sjadzali appealed to outside experts for their input on the present state of the system and suggestions for improvement. The two most prominent such advisors were Muslim scholars whose disciplines and approaches were forged largely under a Western model of higher education: the Turkish intellectual Serif Mardin and the Pakistani Fazlur Rahman. Both of them visited Indonesia in the summer of 1985, when they toured a number of IAIN campuses before submitting reports to the Minister of Religious Affairs. The main thrust of both their reports was advocating a greater

[79] Faisal Ismail, "Pancasila as a Sole Basis for all Political Parties and for all Mass Organizations: An Account of Muslim Responses," *SI* 3.4 (1996).

[80] Mark Cammack, "Indonesia's 1989 Religious Judicature Act: Islamization of Indonesia or Indonesianization of Islam?" *Indonesia* 63 (1997): 143–68.

[81] The text of this document is available in English as *The Compilation of Islamic Laws in Indonesia* (Jakarta: Republic of Indonesia Department of Religious Affairs, 1996).

[82] Zaini Muchtarom, "Kebijakan Pendidikan Islam di Departemen Agama," *Kontekstualisasi Ajaran Islam: 70 Tahun Prof. Dr. H. Munawir Sjadzali*, ed. Muhamad Wahyuni Nafis *et al.* (Jakarta: Yayasan Wakaf Paramadina, 1995), 516–32.

[83] For a report on the state and development of IAIN during Sjadzali's tenure as minister, see *Information on State Institute for Islamic Studies (IAIN)* (Jakarta: Departemen Agama RI, 1988/89).

openness to Western academic approaches in order to promote further studies toward a "critical religious history of Islam."[84]

This advice was implemented, to an extent, and such programs had a marked effect on the kinds of religious scholars produced in Indonesia during the last decades of the twentieth century. In fact a marked shift in the orientation of IAIN can be observed between the earlier years when faculty were being exchanged with Egypt[85] and the later period when IAIN began looking more to the West for training and methodological approaches. This started with the sending of trainees to the United States, the Netherlands, Canada, and Australia in the 1970s, but greatly increased during the 1980s under Sjadzali's tenure as minister.[86] At that time Sjadzali began working together with then American Ambassador to Indonesia Paul Wolfowitz in creating programs for sending young IAIN teaching staff to the United States for graduate studies.

The changes of orientation at the IAIN and the ascendancy of development ideology under the New Order were integral to the creation of a new corps of intelligentsia that approached religious questions from a viewpoint radically different from that of either the *'ulamā'*, or the generation of Muslim reformists before them. Many of these 'new intellectuals' had advanced training in such fields as communications, economics, and the social sciences, and some of the most prominent among them held advanced degrees in Islamic Studies from universities in Europe and North America. These returning students exercised a considerable influence through their transmission and translation of some of the approaches and conceptual categories from the academic study of religion and Islamic Studies into the mainstream of Indonesian public religious discussions.[87]

[84] For the English text of Rahman's report see Muchtarom, "Kebijakan Pendidikan Islam di Departemen Agama," 520–23.

[85] Said Mahmud *et al.*, eds., *15 Tahun Institut Agama Islam Negeri Jami'ah Ar-Raniry Darussalam Banda Aceh* (Banda Aceh Panitia Harijadi ke-XV IAIN Jami'ah Ar-Raniry, 1978), 50–51, 114. These changes were directly noted by members of the Indonesian student community in Cairo who voiced their concerns over these developments in an article published in the popular Indonesian news weekly *Tempo*. See "IAIN Beralih Kiblat?" No. 40, Th. XV (November 30, 1985).

[86] The number of Indonesian students at the McGill Institute for Islamic Studies eventually grew to the point where they published their own official handbook for new colleagues, which includes information on everything from the application process and class registration to the basic needs of getting settled in a new city and cultural environment. Akh Minhaji and Iskandar Arnel, *Petunjuk Praktis Belajar di Institute of Islamic Studies, McGill University, Montreal, Kanada* (Yogyakarta: Permika, 1997).

[87] In the field of Islamic law, one important thinker who has advised a number of Indonesian students at McGill, and whose influence is starting to be noticed within Indonesia is Wael Hallaq. See Akh Minhaji, "Kontribusi Dr. Wael B. Hallaq dalam Kajian Hukum Islam," in *Pengalaman Belajar Islam di Kanada*, ed. Yudian W. Asmin (Yogyakarta: Permika and Titian Ilahi, 1997), 115–42. For one

Far more than for his work on the reform of the IAIN, however, Sjadzali is known for his ideas on the "Re-actualization" (*Reaktualisasi*) of Islamic law.[88] In the mid 1980s Sjadzali used his position as minister to broadcast an appeal to reinterpret Islamic law in light of his model of a "contextual hermeneutic" for undertaking *ijtihād*.[89] This new approach to the tradition had become necessary, he argued, because of the increasing number of Indonesian Muslims who were choosing to simply ignore various aspects of Islamic law in their everyday practice. In connection with this, Sjadzali noted that in areas such as bank interest, inheritance, and laws concerning slavery, legal prescriptions considered to be "out of date" or impracticable in contemporary society were often simply ignored. He then began to speculate on the possible consequences of such a phenomenon if it were left to develop unchecked; would a piecemeal abandonment of individual legal precepts eventually lead to the dissolution of Islam as a meaningful moral force in the lives of Indonesian Muslims? In response to this question Sjadzali argued that maintaining the relevance of Islam and its message in contemporary society required a "re-actualization" (*Reaktualisasi*) of Islamic law.

Sjadzali centered his initial proposals for *Reaktualisasi* on the three issues of bank interest, slavery, and inheritance law mentioned above.[90] For example, he viewed the various verses referring to slavery in the text of the Qur'ān to be now obsolete, as contemporary society has realized the negative aspects of this institution and abolished it, thus making any Qur'ānic statements on the treatment, marriage, and manumission of slaves in effect dead letters. He also points out, however, that Muḥammad did not pronounce a total abolition of slavery during his lifetime on account of his consideration of

former student's reflections on the experiences of studying Islamic law at both McGill and the IAIN, see Ratno Lukito's essay in that collection, 143–64.

88 One common version of the text in which he publicly proclaimed his program can be found in Munawir Sjadzali, "Reaktualisasi Ajaran Islam," in *Polemik Reaktualisasi Ajaran Islam* (Jakarta: Pustaka Panjimas, 1988), 1–11. This text is also available in Juhaya S. Praja, ed., *Hukum Islam di Indonesia: Perkembangan dan Pembentukan* (Bandung: PT Remaja Rosdakarya, 1991), 83–94. It appears, however, that the minister had already tried these ideas out on audiences abroad before publishing them to a wider Indonesian public. In December 1985, he attended an international Seminar on "Sharī'a and Codification" at Colombo, Sri Lanka, in which he outlined his interpretation of Islamic law as being "dynamic and adaptable" in nature. Munawir Sjadzali, "Syariah: A Dynamic Legal System," reprinted in *Islam: Realitas Baru dan Orientasi Masa Depan Bangsa* (Jakarta: Universitas Indonesia Press, 1993), 9–15.

89 Munawir Sjadzali, "Ijtihad dan Kemaslahatan Umat," in *Ijtihad dalam Sorotan*, ed. Haidar Bagir dan Syafiq Basri (Bandung: Penerbit Mizan, 1988), 121–22.

90 An overview of the main issues addressed in Sjadzali's program of Reaktualisasi in comparative perspective can be found in Atho Mudzhar, "Letak Gagasan Reaktualisasi Hukum Islam Munawir Sjadzali di Dunia Islam," in *Kontekstualisasi Ajaran Islam: 70 Tahun Prof. Dr. H. Munawir Sjadzali*, ed. Muhammad Wahyuni Nafis *et al.* (Jakarta: Paramadina, 1995), 311–20.

public reaction to what would have been perceived as such a radical proposal at the time. Sjadzali then asks, "If the Prophet himself regarded public opinion and practice as a valid consideration in such legal matters, should not we, as the Prophet's community (*umma*), learn from the wisdom of our great exemplar?"[91]

Responses to Sjadzali's positions on the individual issues discussed in his proposals for *Reaktualisasi* varied widely; from a majority support for his ideas concerning the formal and final abolition of slavery, to strident criticism for his views on the position of women in society. For, while the ruling on slavery was largely in accordance with the near total majority of Muslim sympathies, other positions which Sjadzali arrived at in similar ways were not. Perhaps the most controversial of these was his advocacy of an equal 1:1 ratio of males to females in matters of inheritance, which swept aside the standing verses of revelation which call for a ratio of 2:1.[92] Here, as with the verses on slavery, Sjadzali was apparently willing to simply overlook Qur'ānic proof-texts when they seemed out of concert with contemporary ideas of justice. Such an apparently cavalier attitude toward what many Muslims view as a clear scriptural statement on the issue opened his program of *Reaktualisasi* up to criticism from traditionalist *'ulamā'* and scripturalist reformers alike.

Sjadzali characterized his approach to the interpretation of the Qur'ān as *kontekstual*, as distinguished from the purely "textual" approaches of the classical exegetes. In this regard Sjadzali could be grouped along with other writers who have established contextualized approaches as the dominant theme in the late twentieth-century Indonesian literature of Qur'ānic interpretation.[93] What distinguished his program of *Reaktualisasi* from this broader trend, however, was his radical understanding of the principle of *naskh* ("abrogation") in the Qur'ān.[94] This interpretive device implicitly assumed an evolution and perfection of the message over the course of Muḥammad's prophetic career. Established Muslim consensus has determined that this progressive revelation had come to completion just prior to Muḥammad's death in 632, marking the "seal" (*khatm*) on the long line of Abrahamic prophecy. Thus while over the centuries the *'ulamā'* employed

[91] Sjadzali, "Ijtihad dan Kemaslahatan Umat," 120–21.

[92] A position that he maintained in later publications even after his tenure as Minister of Religious Affairs. See Munawir Sjadzali, *Ijtihad Kemanusiaan* (Jakarta: Yayasan Paramadina, 1997), 7.

[93] See, for example, Taufik Adnan Amal and Syamsu Rizal Panggabean, in *Tafsir Kontekstual Al-Qur'an: Sebuah Kerangka Konseptual* (Bandung: Mizan, 1989); and the enormously popular M. Quraish Shihab, *"Membumikan" Al-Qur'an: Fungsi dan Peran Wahyu dalam Kehidupan Masyarakat* (Bandung: Mizan, 1992) (15th reprint, 1997).

[94] See, for example, Munawir Sjadzali, "Ijtihad dan Kemaslahatan Umat," 118–19.

the principle of *naskh* to determine rulings from among apparently conflicting verses revealed during the Prophet's life, no attempt was made to propose that Qur'ānic verses could be "abrogated" (*mansūkh*) by subsequent historical developments. Indeed, such an approach would seem to directly contradict the firmly held Muslim conviction that, as the eternal word of God, the Qur'ān must be accepted in its entirety.

Sjadzali, however, offered his own radical re-interpretation of the very verse used by traditionalist scholarship to support *naskh* in order to justify overlooking or neglecting Qur'ānic injunctions which he saw as incommensurate with contemporary social needs and conceptions of justice. In support of his program for the radical exercise of *ijtihād* through the device of *naskh*, Sjadzali, like Madjid and other *Pembaharuan* thinkers, took as his exemplar 'Umar b. al-Khaṭṭāb. He explained 'Umar's departures from literal meaning of scriptural texts as a means of better realizing the intention (*maqṣūd*/ pl. *maqāṣid*) behind the law, and maintained that likewise contemporary Indonesian Muslims had to look beyond purely 'textual' understandings of the law and instead search for the "spirit" (*jiwa*) of a just ruling in light of contemporary contexts.[95]

A number of Muslim public figures, including the prominent NU *kyai* Ali Yafie, were highly critical of Sjadzali's use of *naskh*, asserting that there is no abrogation of Qur'ānic verses after the death of the Prophet.[96] The critiques he received from "traditionalist" *'ulamā'* on this technical point of methodology were compounded by others launched from Islamists who viewed Sjadzali's extremely liberal application of *naskh* as an affront to their scripturalist understandings of the law.[97] One of the most extensive critiques of the use of *naskh* in Sjadzali's work is Ahmad Husnan's polemic monograph, *Hukum Islam Tidak Mengenal Reaktualisasi*. After demonstrating what he saw as the liberties taken by Sjadzali with the established processes of Muslim textual interpretation, Husnan characterizes the "sloppy reasoning" of *Reaktualisasi* as "immature and brutal." However, these particular criticisms of Sjadzali and his program of Islamic religious renewal are also situated in what for Husnan is a broader cause, that of maintaining what he sees as the integrity of Islamic law as an essentialized abstraction of Islamic identity. Thus an entire section of this polemical monograph is

95 "Ijtihad dan Kemaslahatan Umat," 122.

96 Ali Yafie, "Antara Ketentuan dan Kenyataan," in *Polemik Reaktualisasi Ajaran Islam*, ed. Iqbal Abdurrauf Saimima (Jakarta: Pustaka Panjimas, 1988), 92–102.

97 Some of the reactions provoked by Sjadzali's ideas are included in two published collections: *Polemik Reaktualisasi Ajaran Islam* (Jakarta: Pustaka Panjimas, 1988); and *Ijtihad dalam Sorotan*, ed. Haidar Bagir and Syafiq Basri (Bandung: Penerbit Mizan, 1988).

dedicated to arguing that attempting any change to "Islamic law" (*hukum Islam*) represents deviant religious thinking that would have the result of damaging its totality, perfection, and systematic applicability to all times and places.[98]

Sjadzali's ideas on *Reaktualisasi*, and the various reactions to them, highlight a number of significant themes in the history of Islamic legal thought in twentieth-century Indonesia. In some ways, it may serve as an illustration of the potential consequences of the processes described in the first chapter which served to open debates on Islamic legal issues up to a much wider range of participants, many of whom had little familiarity with the tradition of Muslim textual reasoning. It may also be seen as the continuation of an increasing emphasis on considerations of public interest (*istiṣlāḥ*), taken to their most radical extreme.[99] Several key aspects of Sjadzali's program for *Reaktualisasi* are shared more generally with other Indonesian advocates of Islamic religious "Renewal" (*Pembaharuan*). One of the most central of these is found in their shared concern for history and its importance for a contextualized interpretation of law in society. Sjadzali sees the development of Islamic law as a reflection of the historical realities that the Muslim community has faced over the last 1,400 years. This history is important and must be taken account of in reformulations of law that can continue to develop in accordance with the course of a society's progress.[100]

Like Madjid and other *Pembaharuan* thinkers, Sjadzali also maintains a significant place for the role of reason in the interpretation of religious texts. There is, however, one significant qualification that signals a considerable distinction between the views of Sjadzali as a minister of the New Order government and his colleagues employed in academia and various nongovernmental organizations. For Sjadzali, the exercise of reason in religious and legal matters must not come into conflict with a more fundamental concern for stability of the social order. Thus he argued that the use of reason in the re-interpretation of religious texts is not the right of individual thinkers, but rather something that must be carried out collectively by a

98 Ahmad Husnan, *Hukum Islam Tidak Mengenal Reaktualisasi* (Solo: C. V. Pustaka Mantiq, 1989), 7–8, 68–83.

99 The secularizing tendencies of utilitarian appeals to considerations of public interest in modern Muslim debates on Islamic law has been remarked upon more generally by Wael Hallaq, *A History of Islamic Legal Theories* (Cambridge University Press, 1997), 214–27. The relationship of this to agendas for the codification of Islamic law in various Arab countries has been further explored by Aharon Layish, "The Transformation of the Shari' from Jurists' Law to Statutory Law in the Contemporary Muslim World," *WI* 44.1 (2004): 85–113.

100 Munawir Sjadzali, "Ijtihad dan Kemaslahatan Umat," in *Ijtihad dalam Sorotan*, ed., Haidar Bagir and Syafiq Basri (Bandung: Penerbit Mizan, 1988), 117.

recognized and responsible body,[101] while maintaining that this is necessary as a guarantee against anarchy and a safeguard of the unity of the Muslim community (*umat*) and the Indonesian nation (*bangsa*).[102] This concern with the integrity of the existing state, and the authority of the sitting government, is revealed especially clearly in what is perhaps a slip of the pen in one of his later publications. There, in referring once again to ʿUmar as an exemplary *mujtahid*, he states, "In the historical development of Islamic law and doctrine, one finds many rulers (*penguasa*) who were courageous enough to institute policies that were not in accordance with a literal reading of the Qurʾānic text or the *ḥadīth* reports."[103]

That Sjadzali postulates *ijtihād* as the realm of worldly rulers rather than that of the *ʿulamāʾ* or, more generally, jurists and other thinkers is a very revealing insight into some of the political realities informing his thinking about the nature and interpretation of Islamic law. Here it should be kept in mind that in first putting forward his ideas on *Reaktualisasi*, Sjadzali was not speaking as an independent scholar of *fiqh* or a Muslim public intellectual but rather as Indonesia's Minister of Religious Affairs; a position which carries with it important considerations of state policy that impinge upon his more intellectualized religious concerns. Thus aside from its position in the intellectual development of Indonesian Muslim discourse, *Reaktualisasi* should also be seen in relation to the political context of increasing openness toward a depoliticized "cultural" Islam by the late New Order government. Sjadzali himself remarked on this, noting that, "Suharto has only allowed greater government attention to Islam because he perceives that most Muslims no longer question *Pancasila*."[104]

The *Reaktualisasi* agenda thus held very real political implications for the New Order government as it provided a model for interpreting Islamic law that could be easily reconciled with the exigencies of the development program toward which the state was primarily oriented.[105] One clear example of this can be found in the minister's remarks to an international conference on Islam and population issues held at Cairo in 1987. There Sjadzali boasted of the way in which Indonesian *ʿulamāʾ* had helped to provide

[101] Sjadzali, *Ijtihad Kemanusiaan*, 50–54, 76.
[102] Sjadzali, "Ijtihad dan Kemaslahatan Umat," 125.
[103] Sjadzali, *Ijtihad Kemanusiaan*, 57.
[104] Douglas E. Ramage, *Politics in Indonesia: Democracy, Islam, and the Ideology of Tolerance* (London: Routledge, 1995), 188.
[105] See, for example Munawir Sjadzali, "Relevansi Hukum Keluarga Islam dengan Kebutuhan Masa Kini," in *Dimensi Hukum Islam dalam Sistem Hukum Nasional*, ed. Amrullah Ahmad *et al.* (Jakarta: Gema Insani Pres, 1996), 223–26.

legitimation for government birth control programs through the issuance of *fatwās* on the subject by the national *Majelis Ulama Indonesia* (MUI).[106] Elsewhere in numerous public speeches and printed essays, he also stressed the compatibility of Islamic ideals with modern development.[107] Indeed, through a wide range of programs with which his Ministry was involved, Sjadzali attempted to demonstrate on behalf of the New Order that a great deal of social and religious progress for the Muslim community could be made once Islam had disassociated itself from the 'dangerous and distracting' realm of party politics.[108]

Sjadzali's conceptions of Islamic reform were officially endorsed by President Suharto, who instructed Sjadzali to, "Use the IAIN to mold (*mencetak*) scholars who will agree with your way of understanding."[109] The government's concern with the success of *Reaktualisasi* was more than purely academic, as Sjadzali himself acknowledges that his ideas on this were first put forward simultaneously and in conjunction with the launch of the government's project for the compilation of Islamic law. The program was backed by a number of prominent figures from government circles, including the MUI. K. H. Ibrahim Hosen, then chair of the organization, provided a public endorsement of the minister's program by publishing an extensive commentary on (or rather 'apology' for) *Reaktualisasi* that attempted to support its various positions with extensive Arabic quotations from the classical corpus of *fiqh* scholarship.[110] In the end, however, Sjadzali's proposed,

106 Munawir Sjadzali, "The Role of Muslim Religious Leaders (Ulama) in the Solution of the Population Problem," in *Islam: Realitas Baru dan Orientasi Masa Depan Bangsa* (Jakarta: Universitas Indonesia Press, 1993), 67–73. In this particular case the MUI first issued a *fatwā* legalizing birth control in general, but prohibiting the use of IUDs as it could possibly involve the situation in which a non-*muḥrim* male doctor would have to look at a woman's *awra* for the initial procedure. However, this ruling of the MUI was later reversed after the government determined that the IUD was the most effective and least expensive of their birth control options. For more on such politically informed MUI *fatwā* decisions, see Mohammad Atho Mudzhar, *Fatwa-Fatwas Majelis Ulama Indonesia: Sebuah Studi tentang Pemikiran Hukum Islam di Indonesia, 1975–1988* (Jakarta: INIS, 1993).

107 See, for example, the essays: "Asas Pancasila, Aspirasi Umat Islam, dan Masa Depan Bangsa" (1986); "Wawasan Perjuangan Muslim Indonesia" (1990); and "Beberapa Keberhasilan Pemerintah Orde Baru, Khususnya Kabinet Pembangunan V dalam Pembangunan Bidang Agama" (1992), all of which are reprinted in *Islam: Realitas Baru dan Orientasi Masa Depan Bangsa* (Jakarta: Universitas Indonesia Press, 1993).

108 As he most directly claims in "Aspirasi Umat Islam Terpenuhi tanpa Partai Islam," in *Islam: Realitas Baru dan Orientasi Masa Depan Bangsa* (Jakarta: Universitas Indonesia Press, 1993), 61–66. In the closing section of this essay, Sjadzali quotes with enthusiastic acceptance Nurcholish Madjid's slogan, "Islam yes, Islamic Party no!"

109 The verb choice in this sentence is quite telling; as the Indonesian *mencetak* literally means to "imprint" or "stamp" in the sense of printing copies (Sjadzali, 1995: 97).

110 Ibrahim Hosen, "Beberapa Catatan Tentang Reaktualisasi Hukum Islam," in *Kontekstualisasi Ajaran Islam: 70 Tahun Prof. Dr. H. Munawir Sjadzali*, ed. Muhammad Wahyuni Nafis *et al.* (Jakarta:

"re-actualized" rulings on issues such as inheritance law were dropped from the *Kompilasi* in compromises with more formalist segments of the Indonesian Muslim community.

The influence of Sjadzali's political positions on his conceptualization of *Reaktualisasi* should not be underestimated. The most substantial presentation of his understanding of the relationship between Islam and the state can be found in his *Islam dan Tata Negara*.[111] This work was originally composed as a textbook for students in the postgraduate seminars on 'Political Law in Islam,' that he put together at IAIN Jakarta in consultation with Nurcholish Madjid and the rector of the university, Harun Nasution. In it Sjadzali recounts the political history of the Prophet's administration of the early community (*umma*) through the period of the "Rightly Guided Caliphs" (*al-khulafā 'al-rāshidūn*), and through medieval and modern works of Isalmic political theory, as well as sketches of the political systems of some "sectarian" interpretations of Islam (e.g. Shī'ism, Khārijism, and Mu'tazilism) and case studies of a number of contemporary Muslim countries such as Saudi Arabia, Egypt, Turkey, and Pakistan.

Of all of these various interpretations of Islam and politics, however, Sjadzali cites with greatest approval not any of the "classical" statements on the subject, but rather the views of modern Egyptian author, Muḥammad Ḥusayn Haykal (d. 1956).[112] Haykal, following 'Abd al-Rāziq, maintained that Islam established no particular form of government and emphasized basic principles and moral values over detailed legal rulings. Sjadzali found such positions particularly well-suited to the New Order's vision of a depoliticized Islam and its conceptualization of the Indonesian state based on *Pancasila* as "neither religious, nor secular" (*bukanlah negara agama, tetapi juga bukan negara sekuler*).[113] Thus drawing upon Haykal, Sjadzali argued that there was no obstacle to the full realization of Islam for believers living within the structure of the Pancasila state.[114]

Paramadina, 1995), 251–84. Hosen's place in broader developments of Islamic legal thought in Indonesia will be discussed in chapter 6.

111 Munawir Sjadzali, *Islam dan Tata Negara: Ajaran, Sejarah, dan Pemikiran* (Jakarta: Universitas Indonesia Press, 1990). This work has since become available in English translation as *Islam and Governmental System* (Jakarta: INIS, 1991).

112 This earlier twentieth-century Egyptian author is perhaps best known for his modern style biography of the Prophet (*Hayāt Muḥammad* (Cairo: Dār al-Ma'arif, 1935)). For a short biographical sketch, see Louis Awad, *The Literature of Ideas in Egypt, part 1* (Atlanta: Scholars Press, 1986), 123–25.

113 Sjadzali, *Islam dan Tata Negara*, 210.

114 As one observer has noted, "With these theologico-political underpinnings, Sjadzali, like many other proponents of the new Islamic intellectualism and activism is actually advancing a 'middle

### *PEMBAHARUAN* AND THE *PESANTREN*

For many Indonesian Muslims during the New Order period, however, living within the *Pancasila* state did not prevent them from seeking alternative institutional frameworks for furthering their own ends. Working within the parameters possible under the authoritarian Suharto regime, a number of non-governmental organizations (NGOs) were established for social and economic development programs. In the process, some have argued, they also began contributing to the establishment of civil society and to processes of democratization in Indonesia.[115] During the late 1960s Oxfam as well as Community Aid Abroad (Australian), World Neighbor (American), and Nihon Kensei Kai (Japanese) organizations had begun investing in agricultural programs through *pesantren* in West Java.[116] However it was not until the 1970s that Muslim communities as such became more deeply involved in such projects. At that time the Indonesian minister of religious affairs, Mukti Ali, began promoting the idea of involving *pesantren* in projects of community development.[117] This top-down reorientation complemented, and to a certain degree can be seen as a reaction to, the work that was begun by Muslim intellectuals and activists in various areas of the country who were at that time already formulating new ideas on how Islamic ideals and/or institutions might become involved with rural development projects.[118]

The Muslim NGO known as LP3ES (Lembaga Penelitian, Pendidikan dan Penerangan Ekonomi dan Sosial) was formed in 1972 by a group of activists who had previously been associated with the (by then defunct) Masjumi as well as from the Indonesian Socialist Party (PSI). It attracted foreign funding, much of which initially came from the Friedrich Naumann Stiftung, which was later phased out through measures designed to foster more domestic support. Over the course of the 1970s, LP3ES

way' of Islamic political theorizing" (Effendi, "Islam and the State in Indonesia," 115). Such an orientation was maintained by Sjadzali's successor as Minister of Religious affairs, Tarmizi Tahir, who advanced his ideas on the subject in numerous Indonesian speeches and essays, as well as in an English-language monograph, *Aspiring for the Middle Path: Religious Harmony in Indonesia* (Jakarta: CENSIS, 1997).

115 Philip J. Eldridge, *Non-Government Organizations and Democratic Participation in Indonesia* (Kuala Lumpur: Oxford University Press, 1995); Bob S. Hadiwinata, *The Politics of NGOs in Indonesia: Developing Democracy and Managing a Movement* (New York: RoutledgeCurzon, 2003).

116 M. Saleh Widodo, "Pesantren Darul Fallah: Experimen Pesantren Pertanian," in *Pesantren dan Pembaharuan*, ed. Dawam Rahardjo (Jakarta: LP3ES, 1974), 122–23.

117 Muhammad Munib Huda, *Mutiara Nahdlatul Ulama* (Jakarta: Fatma Press, 1998), 128.

118 See, for example, A. Surjadi, *Da'wah Islam dengan Pembangunan Masjarakat Desa* (Bandung: Rivanty, 1971).

gained a prominent national profile by directing considerable attention to the educational needs of economic and social development, looking to available local options such as *pesantren* for potential resources and working on pilot programs for vocational training and cooperative projects with the Indonesian Ministry of Religious Affairs.[119]

A major figure in bridging the worlds of Islamic education and modern NGOs in this period was Dawam Rahardjo. He was born at Solo in 1943, and in his youth became affiliated with Masjumi and the HMI, where he came to know Nurcholish Madjid. He was also a participant in the 'Limited Group' discussion circle founded by Mukti Ali. Like Madjid and other *Pembaharuan* figures, Rahardjo tended to avoid technical discussions of Islamic law and jurisprudence, which were often perceived in such circles as a medieval legacy that appeared obsolete in the face of the complexities of the problems facing modern Indonesia. Instead he worked to redirect the attention of religious leaders and activists away from *ʿibādāt*-dominated discussions of *fiqh* and toward conversations involving social-scientific approaches to economy and society.

In the early 1970s Rahardjo became involved with NGO circles at Jakarta that had at that time already begun to engage projects that involved Islamic religious educational institutions.[120] Later, as director of LP3ES, Rahardjo worked to further develop avenues of cooperation with former student activists from ITB and other campuses interested in projects focused on the dissemination of appropriate technologies for village-level development projects. In this vein he also became increasingly involved with projects that focused on *pesantren* as national resources potentially contributing to social and economic development in ways informed by Islamic religious values.[121] Such interest is reflected, for example, in his role in a joint LP3ES/IAIN Syarif Hidayatullah project studying nine such institutions in West Java in the early 1970s.[122]

NGO-*pesantren* cooperation at that time was pursued through a number of rather high-profile experiments such as that of the "modern *pondok*" at

[119] Irchamni Sulaiman, "Pesantren Mengembangkan Teknologi Tepat Guna," in *Pergulatan Dunia Pesantren: Membangun dari Bawah*, ed. M. Dawam Rahardjo (Jakarta: P3M, 1985), 245–63; Eldridge, *Non-Government Organizations*, 92–97.

[120] M. Dawam Rahardjo, "Perkembangan Masyarakat dalam Perspektif Pesantren," in *Pergulatan Dunia Pesantren*, vii–xxii.

[121] Dawam Rahardjo, "Dunia Pesantren dalam Peta Pembaharuan," in *Pesantren dan Pembaharuan*, ed. Dawam Rahardjo (Jakarta: LP3ES, 1974), 1–38.

[122] Dawam Rahardjo *et al.*, *Profil Pesantren: Laporan Hasil Penelitian Pesantren al-Falak dan Delapan Pesantren Lain di Bogor* (Jakarta: LP3ES, 1974). This text went through at least three printings before 1982.

Gontor[123] and the "Agricultural *pesantren*" Darul Fallah at Bogor.[124] Thereafter an increasing number of *pesantren* became partners in a wide range of projects with NGOs that came to focus increased attention on what Abdurrahman Wahid had described as the *pesantren* "sub-culture."[125] Working with Wahid, Rahardjo not only brought NGO activists to local *pesantren*, but also invited religious scholars to participate in projects extending well beyond their village base. This milieu was seen as particularly attractive for Indonesian economists and other social scientists such as M. M. Billah who were at that time looking for potential 'push factors' in processes of 'social engineering' that would be grounded in some sense of cultural authenticity.[126]

It should be noted, however, that the rising profile of *Pembaharuan*-inspired NGO activists in the *pesantren* milieu came at the same time to be viewed as a threat by Muslims associated with the *da'wa* organizations described in chapter 4.[127] Despite such Islamist opposition, however, interest in *pesantren* as loci for various conceptions of development continued to grow during the 1970s–80s and during that period a number of Muslim NGOs were founded specifically to deal with social issues relevant to development agendas, including a number that focused on issues of women and the family. In 1979 the Lembaga Konsultasi Bantuan Hukum Wanita dan Keluarga (LKBWHK) was founded at Jakarta with a charter for research and education on women's issues in Islamic family law. With the support of the Ford and Asia foundations in the 1980s, it also established branch offices in Bandung, Yogya, Palembang, and Banda Aceh.[128]

The role of women outside of the domestic sphere also began receiving increased attention with the founding of organizations such as the Yayasan Pendidikan Islam's women's cooperative in Tasikmalaya, which combined Islamic education with marketable skills such as machine embroidery. Such

[123] Ali Saifullah HA. "Darussalaam, Pondok Modern Gontor," in *Pesantren dan Pembaharuan*, 134–54. More on the driving force behind the institutional and curricular innovations of this *pesantren*, Imam Zarkasyi, and selections from his own writings on Islamic education can be found in Ahmad Fuad Effendi, Amir Hamzah Wiryosukarto *et al.*, *K. H. Imam Zarkasyi dari Gontor: Merintis Pesantren Modern* (Ponorogo: Gontor Press, 1996).

[124] M. Saleh Widodo, "Pesantren Darul Fallah: Expserimen Pesantren Pertanian," in *Pesantren dan Pembaharuan*, 121–33.

[125] Abdurrahman Wahid, "Pesantren sebagai Subkultur," in *Pesantren dan Pembaharuan*, 39–60.

[126] See, for example, M. M. Billah, "Pikiran Awal Pengembangan Pesantren," in *Pergulatan Dunia Pesantren: Membangun dari Bawah*, ed. M. Dawam Rahardjo (Jakarta: P3M, 1985), 289–98. For more on Billah's involvement with the *pesantren* NGO scene, see Huda, *Mutiara Nahdlatul Ulama*, 38–42.

[127] See, for example, M. Rusli Karim, *HMI – MPO dalam Kemelut Modrenisasi Politik di Indonesia* (Bandung: Mizan, 1997), 147–78.

[128] Eldridge, *Non-Government Organizations*, 162–63.

projects of religious revival engaged with social and economic transformation in the *pesantren* milieu have made some of the most immediately visible impacts of a new way of thinking about Islam that came to be referred to within traditionalist circles as *Fiqih Sosial.* A number of prominent NU *kyai* have been involved in formulating the reconceptualizations of Islamic jurisprudence involved in these developments, which will be discussed in chapter 6.

CHAPTER 6

# *The new* ʿulamāʾ

> The teacher then leads the student back over the discipline a second time. He gives him instruction in it on a higher level. He no longer gives a summary but full commentaries and explanations. He mentions to him the existing differences of opinion and the form these differences take all the way through to the end of the discipline under consideration. Thus the scholarly habit is improved.
>
> Ibn Khaldūn (d. 1406), *al-Muqaddima*

In the introduction to his volume anthologizing writings characterized as texts of "Liberal Islam" from all across the Muslim world, including Indonesia, Charles Kurzman identified a central preoccupation of liberals without orthodox religious education as being that of "who may speak," or who holds the legitimate authority to exercise *ijtihād*.[1] This description could in fact be applied more broadly to nearly all of the major figures discussed in chapter 5 – as well as to the Islamist autodidacts and modern-schooled reformers in chapters 2, 3, and 4.[2] Such issues of authority on religious matters, however, were configured differently for the scholars whose works will be examined in this chapter, as they had formed their understandings of Islamic law within the milieu of *pesantren* education and were deeply immersed in the texts and interpretive praxis of traditional Muslim scholarly authority.

As discussed in chapter 1, *pesantren* and the orientations toward Islam which they preserved and disseminated had been the target of a series of Muslim reformist critiques in Southeast Asia since the turn of the twentieth century. Despite such calumny, however, many *pesantren* persevered in their traditions of Shāfiʿī *fiqh* study throughout the twentieth century to a greater degree than did their counterparts in many other twentieth-century Muslim

[1] Charles Kurzman, ed., *Liberal Islam: A Sourcebook* (New York: Oxford University Press, 1998), 23.
[2] The only major exception to this being Moenawar Chalil, as discussed in chapter 2.

societies.[3] Over the last three decades, the Indonesian *pesantren* milieu has experienced a remarkable renaissance thanks in part to their increased interaction with Indonesian government programs, NGOs, *Pembaharuan* intellectuals, and other Muslim reformists.[4] These developments within the traditionalist organization Nahdlatul Ulama (NU) were also in part facilitated by the development of a growing appreciation of the traditional corpus of Muslim scholarship by Indonesian Neo-Modernists, as they came to recognize the shortcomings of "classical modernism" and were searching for new sources of depth and authenticity in their approach to Islam. The intellectual and specifically jurisprudential aspects of these developments will be discussed at length below; however, before that can be done, we must first recall something of the broader context in which they arose.

## ABDURRAHMAN WAHID AND NU'S "RETURN TO THE *KHITTAH*"

Most rural Javanese *pesantren* and many analogous Muslim schools in various parts of Indonesia are affiliated with the NU. Throughout the struggle for independence and the first twenty years of the Republic, the NU had tended to support Soekarno, even through much of his flirtation with Socialism and Communism. This pattern of cooperation with the Indonesian government was considerably altered in the early years of the New Order period as Muslim frustrations mounted in response to what was perceived as the gradual disenfranchisement of formalized Muslim interests in the structure of the Indonesian state. Popular resentment over such issues as the proposed 1973 marriage law, which attempted to create a civil administration for marriages, removed from any particular religious law, fueled this – as did reconfigurations of national politics in this period. The state-mandated merging of all Muslim political parties into one nominal opposition party (PPP) eventually led to an NU parliamentary walkout in 1978, and through the early 1980s NU's political difficulties with the New Order regime brought the organization to a point of crisis. These debacles on the political front ultimately had the effect of stimulating a new assertiveness of the *'ulamā*'s authority within the organization relative to that of its political operators.

[3] For descriptions and analyses of comparable developments in South Asia and the Middle East, see Muhammad Qasim Zaman, *The Ulama in Contemporary Islam: Custodians of Change* (Princeton: Princeton University Press, 2002).

[4] Andrée Feillard, "Traditionalist Islam and the State in Indonesia: The Road to Legitimacy and Renewal," in *Islam in an Era of Nation States: Politics and Religious Renewal in Muslim Southeast Asia*, ed. Robert W. Hefner and Patricia Horvatich (Honolulu: University of Hawaii Press, 1997), 143.

In these turbulent political times Abdurrahman Wahid, Achmad Siddiq, and other prominent NU *kyai* began promoting the idea of redirecting the organization's activities toward education and social programs rather than party politics. Thus, as was the case earlier in Islamist circles following the disbanding of Masjumi once political activities had become closed to them, NU activists began redirecting their energies into other channels, especially in the area of education.[5] This turn away from formal participation in oppositional Islamic party politics was framed in terms of a "Return to the *Khittah*," – reorientation of the NU toward the "original design" and "religious foundations" of the organization as it was established in 1926. These changes coincided with the development of a new appreciation within the NU of the unique potential value of its central sources of cultural capital: *kyai* with "broad vision and deep understandings of religious knowledge."[6] The Return to the *Khittah*, however, should not be understood as a decision to abandon politics completely, but rather a means of tempering what was viewed as an excessive preoccupation with party politics and a strategic redirection of the organization's activities.

The NU's Return to the *Khittah* was formalized during its national conference (*Musyawarah*) held in December, 1983 at the *pesantren* of one of Java's most respected senior *kyai*, As'ad Syamsul Arafin in Situbondo, East Java. The setting was to serve as a symbol of a return to the initial tradition of those educational settlements, and it was there that the 500 *kyai* assembled formalized a new program for the NU in which the *ʿulamāʾ* previously centered in the organization's deliberative council (*Syuriyah*), rather than the political functionaries who had dominated the executive council (*Tanfidziyah*), would direct the future of the organization.[7] The

[5] See, for example, Masdar Farid Masʿudi, Mohamad Ichwan Syam, and Slamet Effendy Yusuf, *Dinamika Kaum Santri: Menelusuri Jejak dan Pergolakan Internal NU* (Jakarta: CV. Rajawali, 1983), 135.

[6] Masʿudi *at al.*, *Dinamika Kaum Santri*, 144. A number of important outside studies of these developments are available, and the reader is referred to them for more in-depth discussions. See Martin van Bruinessen, *NU: Tradisi, Relasi-relasi Kuasa, dan Pencarian Wacana Baru* (Yogyakarta: LKiS, 1994); Andrée Feillard, *Islam et Armée dans l'Indonésie Contemporaine* (Paris: Editions l'Hartmann, 1995); Greg Barton and Greg Fealy, eds., *Nahdatul Ulama: Traditional Islam and Modernity in Indonesia* (Clayton: Monash Asia Institute, 1996); Robin Bush, "Redefining 'Political Islam' in Indonesia: Nahdlatul Ulama and Khittah '26," *SI* 7.2 (2000): 59–88.

[7] François Raillon, "The New Order and Islam, or the Imbroglio of Faith and Politics," *Indonesia* 57 (1994): 198–217. It must be borne in mind, however, that neither of these two groups was composed exclusively of either politicians or *kyai*, and that there was a certain amount of crossover between them. See Feillard, *Islam et Armée*, 169–70; Martin van Bruinessen, "Traditions for the Future: The Reconstruction of Traditionalist Discourse within NU," in *Nahdatul Ulama: Traditional Islam and Modernity in Indonesia*, ed. Greg Barton and Greg Fealy, 163–89 (Clayton: Monash Asia Institute, 1996), 181.

agreement at Situbondo in 1983 paved the way for the NU's acceptance of the presidential mandate of 'sole foundation' (*asas tunggal*) to *Pancasila* as the official ideology of the Indonesian state in 1984.[8] More immediately relevant to the development of discourses on law and society, however, it allowed the NU to begin to reassert its authority to interpret Islam and direct its course of action on both the local and national levels.

The reorientation of the NU's primary focus away from oppositional party politics and toward religious and social activities, combined with a new appreciation of the intellectual heritage of Islam among urban *Pembaharuan* circles, facilitated a reascendancy of the *'ulamā'* to developments on the national level. The participation of these *fiqh* specialists in conversations on broader social issues in turn fostered a new spirit of open inquiry into religious questions among some *kyai* and younger *santri*.[9] Thus while the NU is often labeled as a "traditionalist" Muslim organization, this characterization must be qualified considerably. For, while the NU continues to place considerable emphasis on the "tradition" of Muslim scholarship and the importance of following the jurisprudence of one of the established Sunni *madhhabs*, a number of its *kyai* and their students have come to do so in innovative ways that have brought about a reorientation of what it means to identify with the "tradition" of *fiqh*.

A leading role in these transformations was played by Abdurrahman Wahid, who was elected to head the organization's newly reconstituted *Tanfidziyah* at the Situbondo meeting.[10] Wahid had since the 1970s been rising to increasing prominence as one of the most visible, national-level advocates of a "cultural" rather than "formalist" vision of Islam in Indonesia.[11] Well beyond NU circles, he was leading new initiatives directed

[8] For an overview of various Muslim reactions to this New Order policy, see Faisal Ismail, "Pancasila as the Sole Basis for All Political Parties and for All Mass Organizations: An Account of Muslim Responses," *SI* 3.4 (1996): 1–92.

[9] Many of the contemporary scholars working in this area have worked to convey something of the intellectual depth and dynamism of thinkers associated with this "traditionalist" organization. As Martin van Bruinessen has written, "Ironically, in the late twentieth century, traditionalist *'ulamā'* often appear more flexible than the spokesmen for reformist Islam, many of whom have not evolved beyond the positions taken at the beginning of this century." Martin van Bruinessen, "Traditions for the Future: The Reconstruction of Traditionalist Discourse within NU," in Barton and Fealy, *Nahdatul Ulama*, 163–89.

[10] Ken Miichi, "Kiri Islam, Jaringan Intelektual dan Partai Politik: Sebuah Catatan Awal," *Tashwirul Afkar: Jurnal Refleksi Pemikiran Keagamaan dan Kebudayaan* 9 (2000): 163.

[11] See, for example, his *Muslim di Tengah Pergumulan* (Jakarta: Lappenas, 1981). For a short statement of his views more specifically on the subject of Islamic Law: "Pengaruh Perubahan Sosial Pada Perkembangan Hukum Islam," *Aula: Majalah Nahdatul Ulama* 17.3 (March 1995): 34–46. For a more recent collection of his reflections on "cultural" Islam as facilitating a pluralistic and tolerant attitude toward tradition, see Abdurrahman Wahid, *Tuhan tidak Perlu Dibela* (Yogykarta: LKiS, 1999).

toward cooperation with other segments of the Muslim community such as, for example, fostering the ties between certain segments of NU and thinkers and activists associated with the *Pembaharuan* movement, as well as those working in the NGO sector as described in chapter 5. In particular, he had come to play a pivotal role in the development of various NU-affiliated and indirectly related institutions such as the Lakpesdam, and the Yogyakarta NGO, LKiS. These organizations, and others that sprang up in NU circles over the 1980s–90s advocated approaches to religion, law, and society that pursued the substantive realization of Islamic ideals within existing social institutions and political structures. Their various agendas for the revivification of jurisprudence are thus generally directed not toward the implementation of some fixed code of normatively "Islamic" positive law, but rather primarily along lines of the promulgation of cultural values that can be regarded as "Islamic in substance" even without the "formalist" trappings so often viewed as potent markers of Islamic identity.[12]

## RETHINKING *ASWAJA*

In this atmosphere several NU *kyai* have undertaken various projects for the re-evaluation of the traditional corpus of Muslim scholarship as well as more general reconstructions of the idea of Islamic tradition. In contemporary Indonesian the latter has increasingly come to be referred to in terms of *Aswaja*; an acronym compressed from the Arabic phrase *Ahl al-sunna wa'l-jamā ʿa* ("the People of the Tradition [of the Prophet] and [the] Community"). In the last years of the New Order, the NU began articulating the need, for the first time, to produce a systematic statement of what exactly was meant by this term, and in 1995 the central leadership of the organization passed a resolution calling for the compilation of a "handbook" of *Aswaja*.[13] In an important sense, this reformulation of the concept of tradition reflects the culmination of a process of rethinking the role of classical Islamic learning in contemporary Indonesia that was

[12] Writings on "substantive" *vis-à-vis* "formalist" orientations toward Islam in contemporary Indonesia now comprise a vast literature in the popular press and Indonesian Muslim academic periodicals that extends well beyond the confines of NU circles. One frequent point of reference in these discussions is the collection of essays by Azyumardi Azra published under the title *Islam Substantif: Agar Umat Tidak Jadi Buih* (2000). Azra comes out of a Muhammadiyah background in West Sumatra. His work both as a scholar and as the Rektor of the IAIN Syarif Hidayatullah/UIN Jakarta will be discussed in chapter 7.

[13] For an account of the process in which this was set in motion, see "Upaya Membakukan Buku dan Membukukan Baku Aswaja," *Aula: Majalah Nahdatul Ulama* 19.3 (March 1997): 12–22.

initiated by the NU thinkers discussed in the pages that follow. It was also, however, a reflection of the new intellectual climate of Indonesian Islam that had been reshaped by the activities of Madjid and the *Pembaharuan* movement.

The most influential statement of the new NU understanding of the term has been that published by Said Agiel Siradj in 1997.[14] In this short booklet the way of the *ahl al-sunna wa'l-jamā 'a* is described as preeminently the way of moderation (Ind. *tawassuth*/Ar. *tawassuṭ*), characterized by the cardinal virtues of "balance" (*tawazun*), and "equity" (*tasamuh*).[15] Siradj argues that the "moderate" nature of *Aswaja* can be seen clearly in its approach to formulating Islamic legal decisions (*instinbāth*), in which neither the literal statements of authoritative texts (*naṣṣ*), nor the use of human reason (Ind. *akal*/, Ar. *'aql*) are completely excluded or exclusively decisive. With specific reference to Muslim jurisprudence, the implications of such an understanding of *Aswaja* include a rethinking of one's orientation to the established traditions of *madhhab* allegiance.

In this vein Siradj also counseled moderation in one's devotion to any particular school of legal thought so as to avoid the charges of "*madhhab* fanaticism" that were so often launched against *pesantren*-based scholars by modern Muslim reformists. He argues the *taqlīd manhaji* of *Aswaja 'ulamā'* is in no way the kind of "blind imitation" (*taklid buta*) critiqued by earlier generations of Muslim reformists in Indonesia and elsewhere. Rather he asserts that critically engaging with the methodologies of Islamic jurisprudence developed in the established schools of *fiqh* (*madhhab*) comprises the legitimate means by which to undertake *ijtihād* in informed and responsible ways. The difference here between reformist understandings of *ijtihād* and traditionalist understandings of *taqlīd* are thus, according to Siradj, reduced to terminological misunderstandings. As he puts it, "although the *'ulamā'* were not prepared to call themselves *mujtahids*, their decisions can nonetheless be viewed as the products of *ijtihād*."[16]

[14] H. Said Agiel Siradj, *Ahlussunnah wal Jama'ah dalam Lintas Sejarah* (Yogyakarta: LKPSM, 1997).

[15] Such a view has since become a staple of NU *Aswaja* discourses, and can be seen repeated, for example, in some of the popular newspaper columns of Sahal Mahfudh, among others. See *Dialog Dengan Kiai Sahal Mahfudh: Solusi Problematika Umat* (Surabaya: Ampel Suci, 2003), 464–67. It was also, however, characteristic of late New Order positions defining Islam as the "Community of Moderation," as seen for example in the work of Tarmizi Taher, who has continued to advocate ideas along this line well after the conclusion of his tenure as Minister of Religious Affairs (1993–98). See, for example, *Menjadi Muslim Moderat: Beragama di Tengah Peradaban Global* (Bandung: Hikmah, 2004).

[16] Siradj, *Ahlussunna*, 88.

In his more specific statements on adherence to an established *madhhab*, Siradj maintains a distinction between two types of *taqlīd*: one textual and particularistic (*qauli*), and the other contextual and programmatic (*manhaji*). The term *manhaj* used in these conversations has within NU circles increasingly been used as a gloss for "*metodologi*," i.e., to *uṣūl al-fiqh* and its various sub-fields, approached with an historically contextualized awareness of the tradition's diversity and flexibility. In this, such Indonesian *manhaj* discourses are distinct from most modern Muslim discussions employing such terminology, which tend to be the preserve of Islamists espousing a totalizing and systematic view of Islam that is both essentialistic and fundamentally opposed to the kind of historically conscious approach advocated by Siradj and his colleagues in the NU.[17]

In his preface to Siradj's *Aswaja* booklet, then NU Chairman Abdurrahman Wahid emphasized the importance that such an understanding of *Aswaja* is to remind Muslims of the fact that differences of opinion within the Muslim community should be viewed as a blessing (*ikhtilāf al-umma, raḥma*). In this the NU's reformulation of *Aswaja* fits well the broader agendas of democracy and pluralism that Wahid was exploring during the 1990s.[18] It also, however, may have been a way of attempting to engage with the considerable diversity that was becoming increasingly apparent within the NU since the 1980s. This ran the gamut from strictly Shāfiʿī jurists working in essentially formalist modes to young *santri* captivated by the writings of Gramsci, and from *kyai* working closely with foreign NGOs to others actively participating in state-directed development programs and working within government institutions.

Following the 1983 Situbondo conference and the official acceptance of *Pancasila* as its sole ideological foundation, the new NU's leadership's relations with the New Order government grew increasingly warm. As a result of this, new government subsidies became available for Islamic education, although they were somewhat limited and not without their own complications for the organization.[19] More importantly, these changes in the relationship between the NU and the New Order state created a situation in which some of the organizations prominent figures were increasingly willing to lend their religious authority in support of

[17] One of the classic formulations of such Islamist *manhaj* discourses can be found in Sayyid Quṭb's *ʿAdala al-ijtimāʿiya fī 'l-Islām*. See William E. Shepard, *Sayyid Qutb and Islamic Activism: A Translation and Critical Analysis of Social Justice in Islam* (Leiden: E. J. Brill, 1996).

[18] Examples of the role that Wahid's support played in the development of Siradj's thought are highlighted in Muhammad, Munib Huda, *Mutiara Nahdlatul Ulama* (Jakarta: Fatma Press, 1998), 55–59.

[19] Feillard, *Islam et Armée*, 227–29.

government-sponsored development programs, including those considered religiously controversial, such as family planning.[20] Two of the most prominent NU *'ulamā'* involved in such projects of religiously legitimizing New Order government programs were Ibrahim Hosen and Ali Yafie.

## ALI YAFIE

Ali Yafie was born into a family of Muslim religious scholars at Donggala, Central Sulawesi, in 1928.[21] After completing rudimentary studies in religious subjects with his father, he studied at various *pesantren*-type schools in South Sulawesi. Later, when the Japanese occupation put an end to the Dutch domination of the Archipelago, Yafie accepted a position as a preacher (*muballigh*) working for the administration of the occupational government. After the war he went to Pare-Pare where he worked in the then recently formed *Dār al-Da'wa wa'l-Irshād* (DDI) under his former teacher Shaykh Firdaws and the renowned Buginese scholar, 'Abd al-Raḥmān Ambo' Dalle (d. 1997).[22] There, Yafie also became involved and increasingly active in the NU, and through this organization became first active in government as a member of the local People's Representative Assembly (DPRD) in 1953. From 1959 to 1962 he also served as judge for the Muslim Religious Court at Ujung Pandang, followed by a three-year term as inspector for the religious court system of Eastern Indonesia. Aside from these duties, however, he also continued work in the traditional mode of South Sulawesi *'ulamā'* during that period, composing two basic teaching texts in *lontar* script Buginese on Qur'ānic exegesis and jurisprudence, respectively.[23] After moving to Makassar in 1959, he taught and served as dean of the IAIN branch campus there until 1970, when he left for Jakarta

[20] Some *kyai* had been involved in such work even earlier, such as in the case of the Indonesian government's family planning initiative (*Keluarga Berencana*/ KB) in the 1970s. One of the most prominent public supporters of this program from NU circles has been Ali Yafie. See, for example, his essay, "Doktrin *Fiqh* dalam Program Kependudukan," in *Teologi Sosial: Telaah Kritis Persoalan Agama dan Kemanusiaan* (Yogyakarta: LKPSM, 1997), 29–40. Further discussion of Ali Yafie's work can be found below.

[21] This biographical sketch is based largely upon that found in the recent *Festschrift* published in commemoration of Ali Yafie's seventieth birthday: Jamal D. Rahman, ed., "Biografi dan Visi Seorang Ulama," in *Wacana Baru Fiqih Sosial: 70 Tahun K. H. Ali Yafie* (Bandung: Mizan, 1997), 3–48, supplemented with information from an interview in June, 2004.

[22] For a short introduction to the life and work of Ambo' Dalle, see Jajat Burhanuddin and Ahmad Baedowi, *Transformasi Otoritas Keagamaan: Pengalaman Islam Indonesia* (Jakarta: Gramedia, 2003), 199–204.

[23] Yafie claims that these works were taught at some traditionalist Muslim schools in South Sulawesi until the 1980s, when they came to be replaced by modern works in Roman script Bahasa Indonesia (personal communication, June 2004).

to serve his first term as a representative of NU in the DPR, an office he served until 1987.

In 1970 he also attended the general congress (*Muktamar*) of the NU in Surabaya, where he was elected as chair of the *ʿulamāʾ* council (*Rois Syuriyah*), and over the years that followed he became increasingly associated with the 'political' activities of NU. Yafie offered his support to a number of government proposals by lending his stamp of authority as a *kyai* to such New Order programs as Family Planning[24] and the establishment of the Bank Muʿamalat Indonesia.[25] His ability to convincingly interpret classical Islamic texts in accordance with the needs of national development programs came to be greatly appreciated by the New Order state. Using his considerable knowledge of the traditional literature of *fiqh*, Yafie was able to elaborate substantial justifications for various government projects and policies that lend to them an air of legitimacy.[26] Yafie described his position on such rulings as "*Fiqh Sosial*," a rubric now used in Indonesia to describe a diverse array of approaches to legal rulings on contemporary issues, but which for Ali Yafie had from the beginning a connection to the legitimation and implementation of government policies and development initiatives.

He published a collection of essays on this new model of Muslim jurisprudence 1994, in which he put considerable emphasis on re-elaborating a distinction between *ʿulamāʾ* trained in the technical sciences of Islamic textual reasoning and the social scientists and technocrats who had by then come to dominate public discourse on Islam in Indonesia.[27] Yafie has a highly developed awareness of technical matters of definition and methodology that is evident throughout his writings on Islamic law and legal theory and he is critical of those who attempt *ijtihād* without the proper credentials in Muslim jurisprudential scholarship, including advocates of *Pembaharuan*

[24] Yafie has written a number of articles and essays on this subject, including: "Pendekatan Maslahah dalam Menelaah Masalah Kependudukan dan Keluarga Berencana," in *Menggagas Fiqih Sosial* (Bandung: Mizan, 1994), 179–92.

[25] For an appreciative assessment of Ali Yafie's work in this area, see Karnaen H. Perwataatmadja, "Pembangunan dan Upaya Perbaikan Taraf Hidup: Sekilas Pandangan K. H. Ali Yafie," in *Wacana Baru Fiqih Sosial*, ed. Jamal D. Rahman (Bandung: Mizan, 1997), 273–85. More generally on the history of the BMI, see Robert W. Hefner, "Islamizing Capitalism: On the Founding of Indonesia's First Islamic Bank," in *Toward a New Paradigm: Recent Developments in Indonesian Islamic Thought*, ed. Mark R. Woodward (Tempe: Arizona State University Program for Southeast Asian Studies, 1996), 291–322.

[26] See, for example, his essays collected in *Teologi Sosial: Telaah Kritis Persoalan Agama dan Kemanusiaan* (Yogyakarta: LPKSM, 1997), 1–82.

[27] Ali Yafie, *Menggagas Fiqih Sosial: Dari Soal Lingkungan Hidup, Asuransi hingga Ukhuwah* (Bandung: Mizan, 1994), 66.

and *Reaktualisasi* who advance programs of religious and legal reform without demonstrating what he would consider to be a proper understanding of the foundational texts or jurisprudential methods of Islamic legal theory.[28] He nevertheless maintains that the work of the latter is important for the development of society. In fact, the services of such specialists in fields of expertise outside of the Islamic religious sciences have been an absolute necessity to facilitate the New Order development programs of which Yafie was such a prominent supporter.[29]

Yafie maintains that such modern academic and technological advances should not be conflated with *ijtihād* in the sphere of Islamic law, which can only be carried out by trained experts, and which should be primarily oriented toward a "renewal of religious faith" (*tajdīd al-īmān*).[30] In contradistinction to this, Yafie describes the work of modern specialists in economic, educational, and technological developments as a particular kind of 'renewal' with the Arabic phrase *tajdīd 'urfi*. Yafie claims to take this terminology from the work of al-Māwardī (d. 1058), one of the most prominent Muslim political theorists of the medieval period. His signature work, *al-Aḥkām al-sulṭāniyya*, focuses on the problem of reconciling divine imperatives to rule according the Sharī'a with the actual political conditions of a society in which the reigning government tended to act according to other, more worldly, standards and motivations.[31]

Well-worn classical Sunni justifications of political quietism in the tradition of al-Māwardī were given repeated public reiterations by Indonesian Muslims under the New Order. Yafie also worked within this mode when discussing the politically sensitive issues of the codification and official enforcement of Islamic law. Recognizing global political developments in the modern period including the establishment of the nation-state as the standard form of political organization, Yafie described the contemporary

[28] See, for example, Ali Yafie, "Nasikh Mansukh dalam al-Qur'an," in *Kontekstualisasi Doktrin Islam dalam Sejarah*, ed. Budhy Munawar-Rachman (Jakarta: Yayasan Paramadina, 1994), 42–50; Ali Yafie, "Antara Ketentuan dan Kenyataan," in *Polemik Reaktualisasi Ajaran Islam*, ed. Iqbal Abdurrauf Saimima (Jakarta: Pustaka Panjimas, 1988), 92–102.

[29] Yafie supports this position with reference to such classical sources as the writings of al-Ghazālī, who advocated an appreciation of the sciences of mathematics and medicine, "because all such knowledge is needed in the creation of a good society," *Menggagas Fiqih Sosial*, 162.

[30] Ali Yafie, "Reaktualisasi Hukum Islam di Indonesia," in *Kontekestualisasi Ajaran Islam: 70 Tahun Prof. Dr. H. Munawir Sjadzali*, ed. Muhammad Wahyuni Nafis *et al.* (Jakarta: Yayasan Wakaf Paramadina, 1995), 305.

[31] For more on al-Māwardī's political thought, see Ann K. S. Lambton, *State and Government in Medieval Islam* (Oxford: Oxford University Press, 1981), 83–102. For Ali Yafie's interpretations of al-Māwardī: "Pengertian Wali al-Amr dan Problematika Hubungan Ulama dan Umara, " in *Kontekstualisasi Doktrin Islam dalam Sejarah*, ed. Budhy Munawar-Rachman (Jakarta: Yayasan Paramadina, 1994), 595–605.

period as the "era of *taqnīn*" (codification).[32] However, he also added that any project of establishing a formal code of Islamic law must address the needs of Muslims in specific areas of ordering society, and that it must be achieved through constitutional means. In 1985, the Indonesian Ministry of Religious Affairs set up a special team to work on a unified compilation of Islamic legal rulings on matters of marriage, divorce, inheritance, and religious endowments (*waqf* ).[33] Yafie was appointed co-chair of the section assigned to work on marriage law, and became one of the most prominent public *ʿulamāʾ* arguing for the legitimacy of this New Order government project.

His proclivities toward producing politically informed Islamic legal rulings are even more apparent in his work on a 2003 publication entitled *Free Market Fiqh* (*Fiqih Perdagangan Bebas*), which was published in cooperation with the Office of the Vice President (and conservative NU politico) Hamzah Haz.[34] Most of its pages constitute a sort of primer on technical business terms and international economic organizations. However there are also short sections dedicated to 'non-economic' factors, including attempts at constructing an Islamic understanding of the social functions of property and the encouragement of religious considerations to inform Indonesian consumerism with a sense of "rightness" (*ke-thayyib-an*). All of this is elaborated within the clearly stated mission of the project as a whole, that is of serving 'national interests' that appear to be generally equated with political agendas of certain segments of the Indonesian Muslim community. The rhetoric here is one which combines a paternalistic concern to 'protect' the Muslim community of Indonesia with a penchant for conspiracy theories invoking, among other demons, "the economic hegemony of Jews and the yellow-skinned race, i.e. the Chinese."[35]

Under the New Order, Yafie's writings on *Fiqih Sosial* often contained reflections of then-popular interpretations of *Pancasila* emphasizing pluralism and diversity. In lending his authority to these more recent reversals of orientation toward confessional identity politics, Yafie presents what is

[32] Ali Yafie, "Konsep-Konsep Hukum," in *Kontekstualisasi Doktrin Islam dalam Sejarah*, ed. Budhy Munawar-Rachman (Jakarta: Yayasan Paramadina, 1994), 85–96.

[33] Their work eventually resulted in a document promulgated by a special 'presidential instruction' (*Inpres*) in 1991, the text of which is available in English and Arabic, as well as Indonesian. Post-Suharto critiques of this form of Islamic legislation will be discussed in chapter 7.

[34] Ali Yafie *et al.*, *Fiqih Perdagangan Bebas* (Jakarta: Teraju, 2003). Yafie is not the sole author of this text, but rather served as the head of a team of writers for this project, made up of a combination of Muslim intellectuals and activists as well as economists, journalists, and Indonesian government officials.

[35] *Fiqih Perdagangan Bebas*, 226.

perhaps the most striking example of the way in which he has been willing to craft Islamic legal rulings commensurate with the evolving exigencies of contemporary politics. Even more explicitly jurisprudential statements of deference to political necessity can be found in the work of another prominent contemporary NU *kyai*, Ibrahim Hosen.

## IBRAHIM HOSEN

Ibrahim Hosen was born at Bengkulu, Sumatra, in 1917 and first studied *fiqh* in traditional *pesantren*-type schools in the region.[36] Later he supplemented this early education with studies at al-Azhar in Cairo. He became involved early on in the New Order as a representative from the *'ulamā'* who would cooperate with the Suharto government on various issues, and spent most of his career in government service, holding various offices within the Department of Religious Affairs as well as teaching and administrative positions at IAIN campuses in Palembang, Riau, Medan, and Jakarta.[37] In these various positions he has also joined delegations to various meetings and seminars in Malaysia, Pakistan, Egypt, and Jordan, while at home in Indonesia he worked with various institutions of higher education.[38] In line with his deep involvement with government and state politics, Hosen is quite clear about what he sees as the proper relationship between the *'ulamā'* and the *Ulil Amri*, an Indonesian term for "those in authority" derived from the much discussed Qur'ānic verse 4 (*al-nisā'*): 59 (. . . *ulī 'l-amri min-kum*). Hosen glosses *Ulil Amri*, for his immediate purposes, as the government (*pemerintah*) of the modern nation-state of Indonesia, and argues that his deference as a scholar to those who happen to be in political power is religiously justified by a consensus (*ijmā'*) on the necessity of obedience to religious authority.[39]

[36] For more detailed biographical information on Hosen, see Hasbullah Bakri *et al.*, *Prof. KH. Ibrahim Hosen dan Pembaharuan Hukum Islam di Indonesia* (Ciputat: CV Putra Harapan, 1990), 1–90.

[37] For example, in 1970, he was serving as a vice-chair of the steering committee for the "All Indonesia *'Ulamā'* Conference" of the *Pusat Da'wah Islam Indonesia*, whose theme that year was the participation of the *'ulamā'* in fostering unified Islamic social projects in the service of national development. See "Materi Musjawarah Alim Ulama Se-Indonesia" (Jakarta: unpublished MS/ KITLV Bibliotheek 01774270), September 28, 1970.

[38] He founded his own schools for Qur'ānic studies in 1971 (Pergurauan Tinggi Ilmu al- Qur'an) and 1977 (Institut Ilmu al-Qur'an). The second in particular has become an important center for training female reciters and scholars of Qur'ānic Studies. For a profile of some of the women who have studied there, see Mursyidah Thahir and Musthafa Helmy, eds., *Aku dan IIQ: Peran dan Kiprah Wanita IIQ antara Ide dan Fakta Kelangkaan Ulama Wanita* (Jakarta: Institute Ilmu al-Qur'an, 2002).

[39] Ibrahim Hosen, *Analyse: Ma huwa al-maysir/ Apakah Judi Itu?* (Jakarta: Lembaga Kajian Ilmiah Institut Ilmu al-Qur'an, 1987), pp 60–62. Here he leans on a well-established tradition among

In 1980 Hosen was appointed as the head of MUI *fatwā* commission, where he played an important role in the formulation of a number of controversial rulings on issues ranging from fasting and alms-giving to birth control, organ transplants, and bank interest.[40] In producing such decisions, Hosen emphasized the importance of developing smooth, dynamic, and accommodative processes of legal change that combined aspects of the contextualism promoted by *Pembaharuan* thinkers with a deeper familiarity with the technical aspects of traditional *fiqh* methodologies.[41] The most elaborate published statement of his own methodology was produced in relation to his much-debated ruling on the permissibility of participating in state lotteries (SDSB, and the unfortunately abbreviated *Porkas*).[42] Hosen ruled that there was no legal prohibition of such activity, for which he was chastised on a number of fronts, including the political, as some critics pointed to the fact that President Suharto's family held a considerable stake in the lottery.

The most extensive criticism, however, was advanced in the idiom of *fiqh*, particularly in a book published by an association of West Javanese *ʿulamāʾ* who demanded that Hosen be more clear in explaining the way that he arrived at a decision that was to them so clearly contrary to a Qurʾānic prohibition on gambling.[43] Hosen responded to this with a book of his own, in which he laid out an extended justification for his decision, starting with the very question of whether or not the lottery was actually to be considered "gambling" in the Qurʾānic sense (*maysir*).[44] He pursues this question through a detailed examination of the various components of a legal ruling, elaborating upon the technical distinctions drawn between *dalīl* (indicator), *ḥukm* (judgment), *ʿilla* (*ratio legis*), and *ḥikma* (the "wisdom" behind a particular ruling). After setting up these general categories, he applies them to the case of the lottery, arguing that it does not fit what

Sunni jurists that stretches back to work of al-Māwardī, al-Juwaynī, and al-Ghazālī. For more on this, see Ann K. S. Lambton, *State and Government in Medieval Islam – An Introduction to the Study of Islamic Political Theory: The Jurists* (Oxford: Oxford University Press, 1981), 83–129.

40 Hasbullah Bakri *et al.*, *Prof. KH. Ibrahim Hosen dan Pembaharuan Hukum Islam di Indonesia* (Ciputat: CV Putra Harapan, 1990), 101–210.

41 See, for example, Ibrahim Hosen, "Memecehkan Permasalahan Hukum Baru," in *Ijtihad dalam Sorotan*, ed. Haidar Bagir and Syafiq Basri (Bandung: Mizan, 1988), 23–45.

42 For an overview of the controversy surrounding this case, see Darul Aqsha, Dick van der Meij, and Johan Hendrik Meuleman, *Islam in Indonesia: A Survey of Developments from 1988 to March 1993* (Jakarta: INIS, 1995), 63–65, 68–69, 71–73, 75–78.

43 Badan Kerja Sama Pondok Pesantren Jawa Barat, *Fatwa Lengkap tentang Porkas* (Jakarta: Pustaka Panjimas, 1986).

44 Something of the sense of the range of ways in which the Qurʾānic prohibition of *maysir* was interpreted and/ or simply ignored can be gleaned from Franz Rosenthal, *Gambling in Islam* (Leiden: E. J. Brill, 1975).

he understands to be the *'illa* of the Qur'ānic indicator (al-Ma'ida: 90–91) *ḥukm* (prohibition) on *maysir* (betting face-to-face with competitors), the *ḥikma* of which is to prevent giving rise to feelings of animosity and hatred, as well as to prevent distraction from remembrance of God.[45]

Hosen then seeks to ground his decision upon the authority of those of earlier jurists who had addressed the issue of lotteries, appealing in particular to the rulings of Muḥammad Abduh and Aḥmad Sūrkatī.[46] However in doing so he had to acknowledge that while he was in agreement with Abduh on the permissibility of playing the lottery, he differed in opinion with the Egyptian shaykh's position that winners should not be allowed to claim their prizes. This selective appropriation of elements from various legal opinions for the construction of a particular desired ruling can be viewed as an extreme example of *talfīq*. This practice, as it has popularly come to be viewed as a means of shopping around for easy solutions (*rukhaṣ*), has been a target for *talfīq*'s critics in the modern period as such measures have become increasingly productive means for the production of contemporary rulings.[47] This has been the case particularly for jurists interested in developing particular rulings adapted to the needs and interests of modern governments.[48] For Hosen this has been a major attraction of *talfīq*, both for his MUI *fatwās* and his later work on the committee that produced the Indonesian government's 1989 compilation of Islamic laws on marriage, inheritance, and endowments (*waqf/wakaf*).

Hosen holds an extremely liberal position on *talfīq*, allowing in it a wide range of cases save for where it would contradict rulings that have been enforced by government.[49] Indeed, he is reported to have been so openly proud of the flexibility of *fiqh* provided by this device that he once boasted that he could formally concoct arguments for almost any opinion as well as its opposite.[50] Such positions, however, have opened him up to critique by scholars of a wide range of dispositions and approaches to jurisprudence.

[45] Hosen, *Ma huwa al-maysir*, 10.

[46] The Arabic text of Sūrkatī's 1919 (1337H.) opinion on the matter is included in an appendix (*Ma huwa al-maysir*, 70–77).

[47] Birgit Krawietz, "Cut and Paste in Legal Rules: Designing Islamic Norms with *Talfīq*," *WI* 42.1 (2002): 2–40. The tactic, however, is often employed on both sides of any given debate. In this case quite literally, as in the critique of Hosen published by the West Javanese *'ulamā'* mentioned above, where the proof texts in support of their argument from medieval and modern scholars in both English and Arabic have obviously been photocopied and set in place by hand within the body of the Indonesian text.

[48] Aharon Layish, "The Transformation of the Sharī'a from Jurists' Law to Statutory Law in the Contemporary Muslim World," *WI* 44.1 (2004).

[49] Ibrahim Hosen, *Persoalan Taqlid dan Ijtihad* (Jakarta: Yayasan Wakaf Paramadina, 1987).

[50] Martin van Bruinessen, "Muslims, Minorities and Modernity: The Restructuring of Heterodoxy in the Middle East and Southeast Asia (Inaugural Lecture at Utrecht, November 21, 2000).

Jalaluddin Rakhmat, for example, sees in this a prime example of the ways in which the practice of *fiqh* can come to be displaced from its function of determining rulings in the service of Islamic ethical ideals and instead enlisted in the service of providing justifications for state power politics.[51] Within the NU as well, over the past two decades there have been significant developments among scholars resisting the subservience of jurisprudence to state interests and promoting the methodologies of *fiqh* as rich resources to be brought to bear on the pursuit of greater autonomy, authenticity, and social justice.

## NEW SANTRI STUDY CIRCLES

Much of the work in this direction has grown out of the milieu of a new type of study circle, referred to as *halqah* (from the Ar. *ḥalqa*), discussions that were fostered by certain senior NU *kyai* in the 1980s. In these *halqah* young, *pesantren*-educated thinkers came together to re-examine traditional *fiqh* texts from various new, "contextualizing" approaches.[52] Emphasis was placed on the critical rereading of texts of the *pesantren* curricula (*kitab kuning*) that looked beyond the detailed rulings on particular matters to the dynamics of the underlying methods of analysis that these texts established for jurisprudential reasoning.[53] The overall goal of this project was the construction of new discourses on religion and society in which *fiqh* could be brought into conversation with contemporary issues in ways that recognized the problems and possibilities of contemporary political and economic realities.[54] Among the most prominent *kyai* supporting such developments was Sahal Mahfudh, who encouraged young *santri* to take the initiative in this work, as they were in his view best positioned as potential mediators in conversations that needed to be developed between modern specialists in the technical and social aspects of contemporary problems and the religious ideals of Islam as elaborated in scripture and classical *fiqh* scholarship.[55]

[51] Rakhmat, *Dahulukan Akhlaq*, 232–35.

[52] An example of one such lecture can be found on a microfilm at the KITLV in Leiden: Sahal Mahfudh, "Kitab Kuning di Pesantren – Makalah untuk munazfarah pengembangan ulumud diniyah melalui telaah kitab kuning secara siyaqiyah (kontekstual) di Pondok Pesantren Darussalam Watucongol" (Magelang: December 15–17, 1988).

[53] Hairus Salim and Nuruddin Amin, "Ijtihad dalam Tindakan," Introduction to Sahal Mahfudh, *Nuansa Fiqih Sosial* (Yogyakarta: LKiS, 1994), viii.

[54] Van Bruinessen, *NU*, 220–34.

[55] Sahal Mahfudh, *Pesantren Mencari Makna* (Jakarta: Pustaka Ciganjur, 1999), 172.

Some of the ideas formulated in such study groups have had repercussions well outside of their small circles. For instance, the 1991 National Congress of the NU held at Bandar Lampung, Sumatra, included special forums dedicated to the discussion of new methodologies in legal interpretation for the organization, some of which were formally adopted by the organization at the 1994 national NU Conference (*Muktamar*) at Cipasung, West Java.[56] One of the primary ideas to emerge from the new NU *halqah* of the 1980s–90s is that of a new understanding of *taqlīd* in the sense of adherence to a tradition of scholarship as a disciplined interpretive methodology, rather than merely an acceptance of particular established legal rulings.

This is an orientation which has come to gain considerable acceptance in some NU circles and more recently a generation of younger scholars has been pursuing increasingly sophisticated efforts to distinguish adherence to a particular *madhhab* methodology from the sort of "blind imitation" (*taklid buta*) criticized by many reformists. In 2001, for example, Lahmuddin Nasution published an historically contextualized study of the thought of al-Shāfiʿī (d. 819) that was directed largely toward demonstrating aspects of the development of al-Shāfiʿī's positions between his earlier work produced in Baghdad (*qawl qadīm*), and that of his later life in Egypt (*qawl jadīd*). He then uses this historical reconstruction to support the broader contemporary argument that from its very founding, the *madhhab* methodology outlined in the work of al-Shāfiʿī is "dynamic" and thus always capable of dealing with contemporary challenges.[57] In this same year, Abdul Mun'im Saleh published a revised version of his MA thesis from IAIN Sunan Ampel, Surabaya, dealing with the historical development of the place of considerations of public interest (*maṣlaḥa*) within the Shāfiʿī *madhhab*. This work is composed largely of a critical review of major Shāfiʿī jurists from the eponymous founder of the *madhhab* through such luminaries as al-Juwaynī (d. 1067), al-Ghazālī (d. 1111), ʿIzz al-Dīn b. ʿAbd al-Salām (d. 1261), and al-Subkī (d. 1369) to al-Suyūṭī (d. 1505) in ways that deliberately highlight the internal diversity and dynamism of traditional *fiqh* methodology.[58]

[56] For overviews of these discussions and the jurisprudential programs that were suggested in them, see A. Malik Madaniy, "Cara Pengambilan Keputusan Hukum Islam dalam Bachtsul Masail Nahdlatul Ulama (Sebuah Alternatif Pengembangan)," *Aula: Majalah Nahdatul Ulama* 13.12 (December 1991): 53–63; "Ijtihad dalam Kemantapan Hidup Bermadzhab (Dari Halqah-halqah di *Pesantren* sampai dengan Munas Alim Ulama NU di Bandar Lampung)," *al-Jamiah* 51 (1993): 21–33; and Zamhuri, *Wacana Fikih Sosial NU: Studi atas Hasil Muktamar Cipasung 1994* (Semarang: Fakultas Syari'ah IAIN Wali Songo, 1998).

[57] Lahmuddin Nasution, *Pembaruan Hukum Islam dalam Mazhab Syafʿī* (Bandung: Rosda, 2001).

[58] Abdul Mun'im Saleh, *Madhhab Syafiʿi: Kajian Konsep al-Maslahah* (Yogyakarta: Ittaqa Press, 2001).

Since the 1980s, the *halqah* milieu and the work that scholars involved in it have produced in such directions has been supported in general institutional and political terms within the NU by the prominent presence of Abdurrahman Wahid. The more technical aspects of such projects of reinterpreting the legacies of traditional Muslim jurisprudence, however, were fostered not by Wahid's eclecticism, but rather through the disciplined training and socially engaged scholarship of *kyai* such as Sahal Mahfudh.

## SAHAL MAHFUDH

Mahfudh was born in 1937 at Kajen, Central Java, to a family with long-established ties to the networks of traditionalist Javanese *ʿulamāʾ*. He studied Shāfiʿī *fiqh* at a number of *pesantren* in both Central and East Java, and returned to Kajen in 1963 to become head of *Pesantren Maslakul Huda*. In that position he rose to prominence in the local NU *Syuriah* council and, in the 1970s, Mahfudh became one of the first local *kyai* to involve his *pesantren* in educational reforms and other social and economic welfare programs then being organized by the local government and the Ministry of Religious Affairs, as well as by the Jakarta-based NGO, LP3ES (Lembaga Penelitian, Pendidikan, dan Penerangan Ekonomi-Sosial/ Institute for Socio-Economic Research, Education, and Information).[59] In the 1980s he began to attract wider notice among NU *kyai* for his ability to relate traditional *fiqh* scholarship to the realities of village social contexts. As he matured into a *kyai* in his own right, Mahfudh became increasingly active within local branches of the NU and eventually through the ranks to become general head of the *Syuriah* Council (1999–2004).

As a scholar trained in the Islamic religious sciences and head of a *pesantren*, Mahfudh remains deeply immersed in the Arabic tradition of Shāfiʿī *fiqh* scholarship as an established discipline of scholarship and textual analysis. He has himself written a number of works within this tradition in the form of Arabic commentaries on earlier Shāfiʿī texts, [60] as

[59] Eldridge, *Non-Government Organizations*, 177–83; Arief Mudatsir, "Kajen Desa Pesantren," in *Pergulatan Dunia Pesantren: Membangun dari Bawah*, ed. M. Dawam Rahardjo (Jakarta: P3M, 1985), 197–218.

[60] Including one on al-Shīrāzī's (d. 1083) *al-Lumʿa*, entitled *al-Bayāan al-mullamaʿ*, and another on Zakariyyāʾ al-Anṣārī's (d. 1520) *Ghāyat al-wuṣūl*, entitled *ṭarīqat al-ḥuṣūl* (Surabaya: Diantama, n.d.). I have heard from a number of *santri* in Java that this text has been used in the curriculum of the popular *madrasa* of Habib ʿUmar in Tarīm, which draws students from Southeast Asia and around the world to this small city in the Hadramawt (Yemen). Mahfudh's own involvement with the tradition of Hadrami Shāfiʿī scholarship is also apparent in his *Fayḍ al-ḥijā ʿalā nayl al-rajā manẓuma safīnat al-najā* (Semarang: Aneka Ilmu, 1421H/ 2000 CE).

well as other guides to the classical texts and interpretive methodologies of traditional Muslim jurisprudence.[61] This concern with fostering a deeper understanding of the technical aspects of *fiqh* methodology is also evident in Mahfudh's Indonesian-language publications, particularly in the adaptation of an Arabic *Encyclopedia of Ijmā ʿ* that he published together with another leading NU *kyai*, Mustofa Bisri.[62]

Mahfudh calls for a new look at the tradition that recognizes and appreciates both the subtleties of jurisprudential methodology, and the diversity of opinion present within the history of *fiqh* – calling attention to the fact that a considerable pluralism of interpretations can be found not only between various *madhāhib*, but also within each school. In his commentarial work on traditional Shāfiʿī *fiqh* texts, one can see an example of the active, self-conscious selection of authors and arguments for teaching purposes within his *pesantren*, and in his Indonesian-language writings for Muslim intellectuals he repeatedly calls attention to aspects of the tradition such as *ikhtilāf* (differences of legal opinon on various issues). Along these lines he maintains that the traditional corpus of Muslim scholarship (*kitab kuning*) should continue to be used, although in ways less normatively than they have been in the past. Mahfudh characterizes the dominant mode of study of these materials in the *pesantren* as merely "*tekstual*," emphasizing the technical minutiae; of their contents rather than the broader theological and epistemological contexts in which they are situated. These, he argues, should receive new attention through reconsidering the tradition from *kontekstual* perspectives, that is through a conscious recognition of the historically contingent, human construction of *fiqh* as an ongoing project working toward the understanding of God's law in changing times.[63]

Mahfudh's popular writings on particular religious issues have been published in weekly question and answer (*soal-jawab*) columns for the Semarang-based *Suara Merdeka*, and other newspapers.[64] These popular press "Dialogues" generally consist of carefully reasoned, but nonetheless rather straightforwardly presented, practical answers to readers' questions

[61] For example, *Al-thamra al-hājayniyya fī al-iṣṭilāḥāt al-fiqhiyya* (Kediri: Dār al-salām, 1422H/2001 CE).

[62] Sahal Mahfudh and Mustofa Bisri, *Ensiklopedi Ijmak: Persepakatan Ulama dalam Hukum Islam – Berdasarkan Karya Sa'di Abu Habieb* (Jakarta: Pustaka Firdaus, 1987, 2nd edn 2003).

[63] Sahal Mahfudh, *Nuansa Fiqih Sosial* (Yogyakarta: LKiS, 1994), 268ff.

[64] A selection of these can be found in Sahal Mahfudh, *Dialog dengan KH MA Sahal Mahfudh: Telaah Fikih Sosial* (Semarang: Yayasan Karyawan Suara Merdeka, 1997); with more recent pieces also appearing in Sahal Mahfudh, *Dialog Dengan Kiai Sahal Mahfudh: Solusi Problematika Umat* (Surabaya: Ampel Suci, 2003).

about the details of religious practice and regulations concerning ritual purity. That is, the questions posed to him by these readers are for the most part concerned with particular matters of *ʿibādāt*. In response to some, Mahfudh takes the opportunity of using particular cases as opportunities for the re-examination of the relationship between individual legal rulings (*furūʿ*) and the systematic jurisprudential methodologies (*uṣūl*) behind them. For the most part, however, his more theoretical reflections on the interpretation of Islamic law have been published in the form of a collection of essays entitled *Nuansa Fiqih Sosial*.[65] The general appeal in these pages is for the revivification of Islamic law in society by means of a thorough, critical, and appreciative re-evaluation of the tradition of *fiqh* scholarship so as to maintain its relevance to the lives of contemporary Muslims.

Throughout *Nuansa Fiqih Sosial*, Mahfudh contends that the substantive integration of *fiqh* into contemporary processes of social change involves more than simply "bringing things up to date"; as if *fiqh* were some concrete corpus that simply needs tinkering with here and there. Rather, he argues, *fiqh* should not be thought of as "a second closed body of scripture beside the Qurʾān," but rather as a dynamic "counter discourse" to the hegemonic thought structures of modernity that have come to frame dominant discourses on Islam along with most other issues in the Indonesian public sphere. In resistance to this, Mahfudh advocates a reconceptualization of *fiqh* itself as an interpretive methodology (*perangkat hermeneutika*) that can be taught within the *pesantren* milieu, as he envisions such schools to be vital alternatives to modern, formal, and market-driven educational institutions.

Mahfudh writes that *pesantren* have traditionally been a place of *tafaqquh fī ʾl-dīn* (religious understanding), while asserting that *dīn* should not be defined too narrowly as simply "religion." Mahfudh prefers to understand this term in the broader sense of "the set of Divine directives that urge anyone with a healthy sense of reason to do the right thing for themselves in this world and the next."[66] Unfortunately, Mahfudh continues, one of the great problems facing a number of traditionally-trained religious scholars today is that they are unacquainted with contemporary social developments and thus unable to provide meaningful advice for the community facing them. He thus laments what he perceives to be an ever-increasing isolation of religious knowledge from the discussion of contemporary social issues

[65] The dates given for the individual pieces contained in this collection range from throughout the decade prior to the book's publication, i.e., from the mid-1980s when Mahfudh began to involve himself with the younger *santri* who formed some of the first *halqah* of the type mentioned above.

[66] *Nuansa Fiqih Sosial*, 315.

and urges his fellow *'ulamā'* to better equip themselves to deal with the issues that face the community today and not to be content to simply leave certain issues up to 'secular' intellectuals.

Mahfudh argues that, through a "living" conceptualization of *sosial fiqh* as developed in the intellectual milieu of more dynamic *pesantren*, society can become more deeply infused with the spirit of (*terjiwai*) the principles that animate Muslim jurisprudence.[67] One such principle that Mahfudh employs extensively throughout his work is that of *maṣlaḥa*, although recognizing that traditionally the Shāfi'ī *madhhab* has not taken this legal indicator into account to the extent that it has been in the other established Sunni schools.[68] However, he carefully addresses this issue by means of an examination of its potential place within the established methodological parameters of the Shāfi'ī *madhhab*. This is accomplished in part through an argument for the recognition of the various ways in which much of what he perceives to be the substance of matters referred to in other *madhāhib* under the rubric *istiṣlāḥ* are already discussed by Shāfi'ī scholars in terms of the legal reasons (*'illa*) and understandings (*ḥikma*) underlying various rulings.

In considering cases in which there is no clear scriptural statement to inform a ruling, Mahfudh maintains that the jurist is allowed to evaluate its contextualized particulars in terms of the broader axioms (*qawā 'id*) of, "Avoiding that which is damaging before working toward a benefit," and "the benefit which is immediately apparent must take precedence over that which is not yet clear."[69] In this way he attempts to demonstrate that even within the established interpretive traditions of the Shāfi'ī school there are established methods of interpretation and argumentation by which the eternal law of God can be contextualized to meet the ever-changing needs of society. Mahfudh emphasizes the need for the flexible and dynamic potential of *fiqh* methodology to be both intellectually sophisticated and concretely integrated into approaches to questions important to the community and to the actual, lived reality of individuals.

67 *Nuansa Fiqih Sosial*, 23–24.

68 Mahfudh explains that his interest in *maṣlaḥa* developed out of his own independent program of studies of *fiqh* texts from other *madhabs*, and in particular the *Muwafaqāt* of the fourteenth-century Mālikī scholar al-Shāṭibī. In recent years a number of younger scholars associated with the NU have devoted significant efforts toward the elaboration of new understandings of *istiṣlāḥ*. See, for example, the essays devoted to this subject by Ust. Nuruddin Marbu Banjar Al-Makky, Mukhlash Hasyim, Chariri Ma'mun, and Ahmad Nadhif Mudjib and Afifuddin Harisah in the January 1996 electronic edition of the journal *Nuansa* (www.muslims.net/KMNU).

69 "*Dar'u al-mafāsid muqaddam ala jalb al-maṣāliḥ*" and "*al-maṣlāḥa al-muhaqqaqa muqaddama ala al-maṣlāḥa al-mutawahhama*," respectively; See *Nuansa Fiqih Sosial*, 43–45.

In explaining the contextual relationship of *fiqh* to social life, Mahfudh repeatedly reminds his readers that the first two institutions built by Muḥammad at Medina were the mosque and the marketplace.[70] According to Mahfudh this shows that the Prophet was keenly aware of the need to balance the concerns of this world with those of the world to come. He points out, for example, that even in classical Islamic thought, a scholar of *fiqh* was required to "understand questions pertaining to both God and the world."[71] Mahfudh argues that solutions for the pressing issues facing Indonesian society today must take into account both religious and technical aspects of the problem in order to ensure the well-being of the community in this life and the next.

Such a socially engaged understanding of jurisprudence requires a certain amount of political action, and in general Mahfudh agrees with the statement of Munawir Sjadzali that "Religion and State are not separate, but also not one and the same either" (*Agama dan Negara tidak berpisah, tetapi tidak jadi satu juga*).[72] Through the 1990s, he had tended to resist the temptation to lend his knowledge of *fiqh* to direct support of government development programs to the extent of Ali Yafie and Ibrahim Hosen, maintaining that some degree of separation between religious scholarship and state politics was necessary if the *'ulamā'* were to remain "integrative and accommodative" to the needs of the community at large. Thus, for example, he reportedly advised Abdurrahman Wahid against running for president in the 1999 election,[73] and once wrote that the pursuit of power politics is like chewing gum, "it is habit-forming and those already hooked on it will continue to chew long after its flavor is gone."[74]

However, in 2000 Mahfudh accepted an appointment to lead Indonesia's government advisory *fatwā* council (MUI).[75] In the first weeks of his second term in that office (July 2005) the MUI issued a dramatic, eleven-point *fatwā* directed broadly against a range of perceived dangers to the Indonesian Muslim community including the Aḥmadiyya sect, interreligious marriages, "Shamanism," and the ideological influences of secularism, pluralism, and liberalism. The announcement sparked intense public reaction; while it elicited favor from those supporting formalist visions of Islam in Indonesia it was met with shock and dismay by other Muslims. This was particularly the case for a number of thinkers and activists who

[70] *Nuansa Fiqih Sosial*, 158 *et passim*. [71] *Nuansa Fiqih Sosial*, 315.
[72] Personal communication May 3, 2004 at Kajen (Central Java).
[73] Andrée Feillard, "Indonesian Traditionalist Islam's Troubled Experience with Democracy (1999–2001)," *Archipel* 64 (2002): 121–22.
[74] *Nuansa Fiqih Sosial*, 216. [75] See *20 Tahun Majelis Ulama Indonesia* (Jakarta: MUI, 1995).

had become engaged in projects for developing 'liberal' interpretations of Islam in the spaces of *halqah*-NGO interaction that Mahfudh had earlier been so influential in developing.

## NGOS AND THE NU

As discussed at the end of chapter 5, since the 1970s *pesantren* have come to be seen as potential partners in various development projects sponsored by Indonesia's burgeoning NGO sector. Under the direction of Dawam Rahardjo LP3ES in particular began engaging in creative ways with *pesantren kyai* and other NU leaders, foremost among whom was Abdurrahman Wahid. Wahid served as an important bridge between the *pesantren* and NGO communities at this early stage, writing extensively for the LP3ES journal *Prisma* and facilitating the invitation of *kyais* across Java to join in discussions on various programs. It was also at his family's *pesantren* at Tebuireng (East Java) that one of the first new NGO-sponsored institutions was established within such a school, a library built upon the private collection of the *kyai* that was organized according to the Dewey decimal system and administered by staff trained in modern library science by experts brought in from Yogyakarta.[76] Using these new facilities, Tebuireng became an early center for a new model of study and research within the *pesantren* milieu in which students began approaching traditional materials in new ways that informed the *halqah* discussions that were then beginning to take shape within certain NU circles.

Analogous initiatives were soon introduced into other *pesantren*.[77] In Central Java, Kajen was also emerging as a significant site for increased NGO–*pesantren* interaction for grass-roots development projects under the influence of Sahal Mahfudh.[78] There were more than a dozen *pesantren* in the area during the mid-1980s, and well beyond Kajen such cross-fertilization of ideas and programs between the NGO sector and NU *pesantren* contributed to a remarkable renaissance within Indonesia's 'traditionalist' Muslim community. The ranks of *pesantren* students swelled, *kyai* began gaining a new prominence in the public sphere, and a number of new NGOs were formed by a new generation of social activists with NU

[76] M. Dawam Rahardjo. "Perkembangan Masyarakat dalam Perspektif Pesantren," in *Pergulatan Dunia Pesantren: Membangun dari Bawah*, ed. M. Dawam Rahardjo (Jakarta: P3M, 1985), vii–xxii.

[77] See, for example, "Da'wah bil Hal Gaya Pesantren," in *Pergulatan Dunia Pesantren*, 219–44.

[78] Arief Mudatsir, "Kajen Desa Pesantren," *Pergulatan Dunia Pesantren*, 197–218. Mahfudh's own thoughts on such programs were laid out succinctly in an article that he published for the LP3ES journal. See Sahal Mahfudh, "Membangun Harus dari Bawah," *Prisma* 8.3 (1979).

backgrounds. For example, the Lembaga Kajian dan Pengembangan Sumberdaya Manusia (Lakpesdam/Institute for the Resarch and Development of Human Resouces) was founded at Yogyakarta in 1986 to undertake "scientific research in the fields of religion and development." One of its most prominent public programs was the dissemination of its findings through publications, seminars, and training sessions. Similar activities have characterized the work of another Yogya-based NGO, the Lembaga Kajian Islam dan Sosial (Institute for Islamic and Social Studies/LKiS), that has pursued an ambitious program of publishing Indonesian translations of the work of critical modern Muslim thinkers from around the world as well as original works by Indonesian scholars in a similar vein since the early 1990s.

One of the most influential of these new NGOs rooted in NU backgrounds for the development of Islamic legal thought through the 1990s was the Perhimpunan Pengembangan Pesantren dan Masyarakat (P3M/Society for *Pesantren* and Community Development). It was founded in 1983 as an independent organization whose membership nonetheless came largely from the NU, and which was financially supported by the Friedrich Naumann Stiftung and the Ford Foundation. A number of its founding leaders had been active within LP3ES *pesantren* programs, including Abudrrahman Wahid and Sahal Mahfudh. Its emphasis was explicitly placed upon projects with a bottom-up orientation administered through NU-affiliated *pesantren*, and one of its most central mandates was to serve as a forum for communication and cooperation between various *pesantren* involved in such programs. It also, however, placed considerable emphasis on research and education through a series of publications, seminars, and workshops.[79]

These spaces for discussion provided opportunities for *pesantren*-trained scholars to engage with issues of Islamic law and society in new ways. In this they were guided by senior *kyai* and particularly by Mahfudh, who served both as assistant director from 1983 to 1990 and as the general editor of this organization's journal, entitled *Pesantren*. A major emphasis in the work of P3M came to be the formulation of "religiously grounded" and "culturally authentic" responses to contemporary social and economic issues through a reconfiguration of the intellectual and institutional legacies of traditional Islamic education in Indonesia. In particular, it emphasized the need for informed, critical, and contextualized re-evaluations of the traditional texts

[79] Manfred Oepen and Wolfgang Karcher, eds., *The Impact of Pesantren in Education and Community Development in Indonesia* (Berlin: Fredrich-Naumann Stiftung, 1988). For more on the later history of P3M, see van Bruinessen *NU*, 244–48, and Eldridge.

of the *pesantren* curriculum known as *kitab kuning*, which was promoted in a series of workshops.

These workshops were hosted at various *pesantren* and developed a series of recommendations of *kyai* to consult on issues such as economic justice, social equality, administrative consultation, and representative deliberation.[80] Some of these points were informed by discussions of contemporary intellectual approaches to issues of religion, law, and society being developed elsewhere in the Muslim world, such as Abdullahi an-Na'im's work toward a discourse of rights in contemporary Islamic legal thought. In this vein P3M also pioneered efforts within NU–NGO circles to address issues of women's status and particularly women's education, experimenting with new formats such as workshops, role-playing sessions, and other outreach programs, to promote new models of gender-inclusive studies of Islam. A significant role in these developments during the 1990s was played by P3M's young director, Masdar F. Mas'udi.

### MASDAR FARID MAS'UDI

Mas'udi was born at Purwokerto, Central Java, in 1954 and, after completing elementary school, studied at the *Pesantren* of Kyai Khudlori in Tegalrejo. This was followed by six more years of study (1969–75) under Kyai Ali Ma'shum at the *Pesantren* Krapyak, during which time he also began working with Sahal Mahfudh in *halqah* discussions. After that he went on to the Sharīʿa Faculty of IAIN Sunan Kalijaga (Yogyakarta), graduating in 1979. Upon completion of these studies, he worked for a time as a journalist contributing essays to a number of edited volumes dedicated to various aspects of Islam, and in 1983 he joined the staff of the newly founded P3M to work on its *Pesantren* journal, and later took on a leadership role within the organization.

Under Mas'udi's directorship P3M held workshops on a variety of topics that promoted constructive conversations between traditionally trained Muslim scholars, social scientists, and NGO activists on such issues as nationalism, pluralism, human rights, and military rule.[81] P3M continues to pursue such agendas in a number of areas, turning more recent

[80] See, for example, Masdar F. Mas'udi, *Seri Halqah: Fiqh Permusyarawatan/ Perwakilan Rakyat* (Cipasung: P3M, 1992).

[81] Proceedings from one of these workshops have been published in cooperation with the NGO LKiS in Yogyakarta; Ahmad Suaedy, ed., *Pergulatan Pesantren dan Demokratisasi* (Yogyakarta: LKiS, 2000).

attention to issues of government and business corruption.[82] Recurrent themes throughout these discussions over the past two decades have been the enduring potential value of the *kitab kuning* as a resource for confronting contemporary issues and appeals to traditional *fiqh* discourses for their purported dynamism and flexibility. In particular, Masʿudi's contributions to these developments emphasized the importance of familiarizing oneself with the internal diversity of classical Muslim jurisprudence for holding in check modern proclivities toward the formation of prematurely absolutist positions on various issues. As he once expressed it, "As far as differences of opinion arise in relation to questions that are not fundamental (*ushul – dasar*) one is constantly reminded to refrain from the tendency to pronounce 'black and white' judgements (*putusan*)."[83]

At the same time, however, Masʿudi insisted that such an appreciation for nuance within traditional Muslim jurisprudence is in no way a mandate for outright relativism. Rather he emphasized the grounding of diverse *fiqh* positions in the ultimate authority of revelation in a way expressed in terms of a vision of Islam as a Middle Way that was increasingly popular in late New Order Indonesia. In Masʿudi's own words, "Islam is the balancing point between the tendency toward the absolutism of "everything is certain" on one hand, and the trend toward the relativism of "nothing is certain" on the other."[84] This, however, is only one aspect of Masʿudi's work on the critical reevaluation of Muslim religious epistemologies. On a more detailed level he explored some of the intellectual, legal, and social implications of the traditionally dominant Ashʿarite theology, which he understood as having fostered within Islam an overly atomistic world view characterized by piecemeal, *ad hoc* approaches to issues (*juzʾiyya*) rather than a more integralistic vision of human life.[85] This, he argues, has led

[82] Here too they have promoted the potential relevance of *fiqh* to this issue and produced compilations of guidelines addressing frequently asked questions on the topic. See, for example, *Keputusan Bahtsul Masail Nasional Membangun Fiqh Anti-Korupsi* (Jakarta, Hotel Kaisar, May 11–13, 2004).

[83] Masdar F. Masʿudi, "Mengenal Pemikiran Kitab Kuning," in *Pergulatan Dunia Pesantren: Membangun dari Bawah*, ed., M. Dawam Rahardjo (Jakarta: P3M, 1985), 55–70.

[84] Masdar F. Masʿudi, *Islam and Women's Reproductive Rights* (Kuala Lumpur: Sisters in Islam, 2002), 9.

[85] *Agama Keadilan*, 5, 34–41. However such a critique of Ashʿarism should in no way be thought of as a counter-argument for a "Neo Muʿtazilism" of the kind that has been advanced by some Muslim reformers in Indonesia and elsewhere over the past century. In fact, Masʿudi has written a substantial critique of this school of traditional Islamic theology as well, see Masdar F. Masʿudi, "Telaah Kritis atas Teologi Muʿtazilah," in *Kontektualisasi Doktrin Islam dalam Sejarah*, ed. Budhy Munawar-Rachman (Jakarta: Yayasan Wakaf Paramadina, 1994), 123–30.

to a limitation of perspective that has had detrimental social effects on the Muslim community at large.

Masʿudi has attempted to counter such trends in his work toward constructing a coherent methodology for the reinterpretation and reformulation of Islamic law. The figures discussed in previous chapters of this book also called for sweeping agendas of the reinterpretation of Islam. Masʿudi, however, argues that much of what was called *ijtihād* by earlier reformists was actually not really *ijtihād* at all, and he distinguishes his own *pesantren* tradition-based approach from the programs of such reformists by stipulating that, "Opening the gate of *ijtihād* is one thing, actually entering into it is something else."[86] As has been noted in chapter 2, many of the debates initiated by reformers like A. Hassan and Moenawar Chalil centered around religious practices for which they could find no authoritative basis in scripture. However, as Masʿudi points out, such debates centered almost exclusively on the relative evaluation of different Qurʾānic verses and the lines of transmission for the *ḥadīth* texts that were used to support a given practice. Speaking from the perspective of the technical sciences of Muslim jurisprudence, he argues, such questions are actually matters for *tarjīḥ* ("choosing the position of strongest evidence"), and not *ijtihād* proper.

The foundation for Masʿudi's more comprehensive vision of *ijtihād* is his re-evaluation of *qaṭʿī* (absolute) and *ẓannī* (relative) as categories in Islamic legal theory. These terms have come to be most often used with reference to particular textual statements used to inform rulings on concrete issues. For example, the meaning of one "clear" Qurʾānic verse on, say, inheritance law would be taken as *qaṭʿī* and thus non-negotiable, while other verses might be more ambiguous in their legal import and thus subject to diverse human interpretations (*ẓannī*). Masʿudi rejects this 'textual' model, and instead calls for a fundamental re-evaluation of common understandings of absolute and relative considerations in the determination of Islamic law. Instead, he argues for a more holistic understanding of the Sharīʿa in which, "What is immutable (*qaṭʿī*) and non-negotiable . . . is justice"[87] rather than any particular practice, obligation, legal sanction, or decontextualized excerpts of scriptural text.

Masʿudi insists that *ijtihād* is not needed in order to determine whether or not justice is required under the law. Rather *ijtihād* is necessary in the

[86] Masdar F. Masʿudi, "Menuju Keberagamaan yang Pluralistik: Reorientasi Pemikiran Keagamaan Nahdhatul Ulama-Muhammadiyah," in *Muhammadiyah dan NU: Reorientasi Wawasan Keislaman*, ed. Yunahar Ilyas (Yogyakarta: Kerjasama LPPI UMY, LPKSM NU & PP Al-Muhsin, 1993), 188.

[87] *Islam and Women's Reproductive Rights*, 18–19.

formulation of evolving understandings of justice in diverse contexts and for determining how best to establish it through specific rulings on cases as they arise. The promotion of social justice through the medium of Islamic law is, moreover, not merely an intellectual exercise for Masʿudi, but one which he insists must be 'actualized' through concrete implementation.[88] Here, however, the model of "implementing" the absolute values of Islamic law are understood by Masʿudi in a way significantly different from those who advocate the establishment of Sharīʿa law in an institutional sense. In his own words:

> I understand the Sharīʿa not as a goal to be reached, but rather as a method. Therefore the Islamic quality of a given society, in for example its economic aspects, does not have to be measured by such indicators as "Do they pay *zakāt*?" but rather "Have they yet achieved economic justice or not?"[89]

It is precisely this issue of the relationship between *zakāt* and economic justice that stands at the center of Masʿudi's magnum opus, *Agama Keadilan* (*Religion of Justice*).

His efforts toward reformulating conceptions of *zakāt* into the context of the modern Indonesian state stand out as perhaps the single largest and most original contribution to the public discussions of *zakāt* and taxation that were increasingly prominent in the later years of the New Order. In 1990 the Majelis Ulama Indonesia (MUI) issued a ruling on the issue that *zakāt* and taxation were separate but equally obligatory for Indonesian Muslims.[90] Masʿudi, however, had been developing an alternative conception of the issue that highlighted the ethical dimensions of *zakāt* and its redistribution, with particular emphasis on the proper relationship of government policy to the moral and legal obligations imposed on authorities who receive and redistribute alms given to fulfill this "pillar of Islam."[91]

In doing this he calls attention to the fact that the Qurʾān explicitly and repeatedly links *zakāt* with *ṣalāt* (obligatory daily prayers), something

88 Masdar Masʿudi, "Hak Milik dan Ketimpangan Sosial: Telaah Sejarah dan Kerasulan," in *Kontekstualisasi Doktrin Islam dalam Sejarah*, ed. Budhy Munawar-Rachman (Jakarta: Yayasan Paramadina, 1994), 659.

89 Masdar F. Masʿudi, "Memahami Ajaran Suci dengan Pendekatan Transformasi," in *Polemik Reaktualisasi Ajaran Islam* (Jakarta: Pustaka Panjimas, 1988), 189.

90 In 1991, an edited volume on *zakāt* and taxation appeared that contained essays by a number of prominent Muslim intellectuals with strong government ties, including Munawir Sjadzali and Ibrahim Hosen. Many of these were adapted from earlier seminar papers that had come to serve as the basis for the 1990 MUI decision. B. Wiwoho *et al.*, eds., *Zakat dan Pajak* (Jakarta: PT Bina Rena Pariwara, 1991).

91 Masdar Masʿudi, "Konsep Harta yang Bersih," in *Kontekstualisasi Doktrin Islam dalam Sejarah*, ed. Budhy Munawar-Rachman (Jakarta: Yayasan Paramadina, 1994), 423–29.

that he regards as reflecting two essential and inseparable aspects of Islam. That is, whereas *ṣalāt* is linked to personal spirituality and the individual's relationship with God, *zakāt* is concerned more with the moral and ethical dimensions of social life.[92] Because of its engagement with the issue on this rather 'theological' (or, at least, theoretical) macro-conceptualization of *zakāt*, Mas'udi does not consider *Agama Keadilan* to be a technical work of *fiqh*. Instead of dealing with specific legal rulings on the amounts of *zakāt* assessment, collection, procedures, and distribution requirements, he presents instead an "entry into a broader discussion of the Social Vision of Islam"[93] which focuses on *zakāt* because he sees it as addressing some of the most profound injustices resulting from the dramatic changes brought on by the advent of modernity in Indonesian society. Mas'udi thus regards mandatory alms giving in Islam in terms of the redistribution of wealth rather than as a ritual act to be a truer reflection of what he understands to be the *ḥikma* behind the Qur'ānic pronouncements on the obligation of *zakāt*, i.e., "so that wealth is not always circulated only among the rich."[94]

Mas'udi's arguments, however, are not scripturalist but rather elaborated to a considerable extent through a kind of anecdotal genealogy of considerations of political authority in Muslim society. After a discussion which seeks to concretize abstract principles of sovereignty and worldly authority into particular examples of Prophetic precedent, he goes on to demonstrate the ways in which the faith of the community in its leader as an *imam* who is qualified to administer *zakāt* in the form of taxation, has all but disappeared.[95] With this loss of moral and religious authority to administer *zakāt*, he argues, the successive political leaders of the *umma* instituted additional taxes such as the *kharaj* and *jizya* in order to supplement their coffers. Because these levies carried no scriptural sanctions as to how such moneys were to be spent, they involved no restrictions on the use of the rulers' revenues. As such developments progressed, *zakāt* became increasingly distanced from governmental concerns and adjusted itself to a number of more informal settings. Mas'udi understands these adverse developments in the history of *zakāt* administration to be symptoms of a much deeper problem, which he insists must be dealt with on the fundamental plane of conceptual reformulation rather than in a piecemeal fashion of adjusting individual rulings on particular issues.[96]

[92] *Agama Keadilan*, 29–30. [93] *Agama Keadilan*, 6–7. [94] *Agama Keadilan*, 3.
[95] *Agama Keadilan*, 93–97. [96] *Agama Keadilan*, 58.

Viewing this marginalization of *zakāt* from the formal leadership of the community as a source of corruption and economic injustice, Masʿudi offers a model of rectification that emphasizes a moral responsibility for the use of public funds through a reintegration of conceptions of *zakāt* and taxation. In short, he argues that Muslims living within a modern nation state such as Indonesia should be able to consider the monies they pay in government taxes (or at least a portion thereof) as comprising their *zakāt*. Such a rethinking of the institution would have economic and political benefits for the community on a number of levels. For those "paying" their *zakāt* this way, they are spared the "double burden" of owing obligations to both "mosque" and "state," which can help to advance the economic conditions of individual Muslims and their families. Masʿudi, however, devotes more attention to the implications that this would have for state policy, insisting that if Muslims were to consider their taxes as *zakāt* the government could then be obliged to utilize this revenue only in "appropriate" ways; i.e. those that serve to advance the spirit of justice that animates the Islamic religious obligation of alsmgiving.

Beyond his work on *zakāt* and taxation, Masʿudi has also pursued the concern with religiously legitimated demands for social justice and the application of his reformulated understandings of *qaṭʿī* and *ẓannī* to other issues, and in the 1990s Masʿudi had collaborated extensively with women activists associated with various *pesantren* and NGOs in efforts to establish Islamic conceptions of gender equality and reproductive rights.[97] In particular, he worked to foster the critical re-examination of texts from the *kitab kuning* tradition that had been used to support practices that disadvantaged women in marriage and family relationships, as well as in Indonesian society at large.[98] In 1995–96, Masʿudi and other activists associated with P3M, along with Lies Marcoes, Husein Muhammad, and others, organized specialized training courses on women's reproductive rights held at *pesantren* in Muslim communities throughout Java and Madura.[99] In connection

[97] For more on contemporary Indonesian activities of this type connected to Masʿudi and P3M, see A. Feillard, "Indonesia's Emerging Muslim Feminism: Women Leaders on Equality, Inheritance, and Other Gender Issues," *SI* 4.1 (1997): 83–112.

[98] See Masdar F. Masʿudi, "Perempuan di antara Lembaran Kitab Kuning," in *Wanita Islam dalam Kajian Tekstual dan Kontekstual*, ed. Lies M. Marcoes-Natsir and J. H. Mueleman (Jakarta: INIS, 1993), 155–64.

[99] Masdar F. Masʿudi, Lies Marcoes, and Rosalia Sciortino, "Learning from Islam: Advocacy of Reproductive rights in Indonesian *Pesantren*," *SI* 4.2 (1997): 83–103. The work of Marcoes and Muhammad will be discussed further in chapter 7.

with this collaborative work, Mas'udi compiled a short book entitled *Islam and Women's Reproductive Rights.*[100]

The text is framed as a discussion of "gender justice" in the form of an idealized dialogue between the wife of a rather liberal *kyai* and a female Muslim student covering a number of issues including marriage, sexual enjoyment and obligations, birth control, pregnancy, child rearing, reproductive leave, and divorce. Over the course of their conversations, the wise woman teacher explains that one way of working toward justice on gender issues in Islam is through the critical discussion of issues important to women that focus on rights, rather than exclusively on duties and prohibitions. In particular, this character advances the position that Muslim women must be guaranteed rights of three types: rights to safety and health, rights to well-being and welfare, and rights to participate in decision-making on issues related to reproduction.[101]

Building on his earlier work in redefining the categories of *qaṭʿī* and *ẓannī*, Mas'udi critiques the popular penchant for fragmented (*juzʾiyya*) rulings on issues related to women's rights and responsibilities derived by appeals to particular proof-texts, rather than a more holistic approach to the "underlying principles and foundations" of Islamic revelation. As the senior partner in this didactic dialogue explains, traditional understandings of the former type, "have made our religious understanding too literal, and in the end have resulted in our *fiqh* loosing its dynamism."[102] By making a contextualized orientation toward the implementation of justice the absolute criterion for understanding various obligations and entitlements, this approach allows for a conceptual regrounding of discussions of such basic elements of contemporary debates as the responsibility of mothers to care for children and perform household chores, and the idea that the primary aim of marriage is for reproduction.

Of all the gender issues discussed in this book, however, there is no treatment whatsoever of polygamy – a topic that has long been at the center of debates on women's issues in Indonesia and many other Muslim societies in the modern period. The silence on this issue in Mas'udi's work grew even more deafening between the publication of the original Indonesian text (1996) and its English translation (2002), as in 2000, Mas'udi himself took the unexpected step of taking a second wife. This move has put him

[100] This text, sponsored in part by the Ford Foundation and published at Jakarta by P3M in 1996, was later also published in English translation at Kuala Lumpur by the Sisters In Islam as *Islam and Women's Reproductive Rights* (2002).

[101] *Islam and Women's Reproductive Rights*, 31–37.

[102] *Islam and Women's Reproductive Rights*, 5, 17–19.

at odds with many of his former colleagues in Muslim NGO circles, and since then he has generally refrained from formulating public positions on issues of Islam and gender. In a May 2004 interview, Masʿudi remarked that polygamy is not only a sensitive issue, but that it also marks a fundamental parting of ways between Islam and the modern West – and one that became a touchstone issue as a function of modernization and its different trajectories in various parts of the Muslim world. In relation to this issue, he has himself made a considerable break from the agenda of his earlier work on the reinterpretation of formalist Islamic institutions in light of contextualized approaches to the implementation of social justice, arguing that since the practice of polygamy is sanctioned in an explicit Qurʾānic textual statement human beings have no right to prohibit something which God has made licit.

Masʿudi's assertion of such a highly charged symbol of contemporary conceptions of religious identity and ideology presents a striking example of the rapid re-configurations of the positions of several prominent Indonesian Muslim figures in recent years. Chapter 7 will highlight some of the major dynamics of these reformulations of Muslim discourses on Islamic law in the era of *Reformasi*. The dramatic developments of Islamization in the Indonesian public sphere over the past decade have made "religion" a pervasive category in contemporary discourses on law and society. Nevertheless, the visions of Islamic law at play in these conversations are diverse and by no means restricted to the formalist symbols of Sharīʿa that are perhaps most often associated with the much-touted resurgence of Islam in contemporary societies. In fact what many Indonesian Muslims have increasingly come to refer to as 'substantivist' as opposed to 'formalist' conceptions of Islam in general and *fiqh* in particular have become prominent in the work of a number of young scholars and activists associated with both modernist and traditionalist circles in recent years.

# CHAPTER 7
# *Next generation* fiqh?

> Laws . . . are not merely something external for us, as are sensible objects, so that we can leave them behind or pass them by; rather, in their externality, they also ought to have, for us subjectively, an essential, subjectively binding power. When we grasp or recognize the law, when we find it rational that crime should be punished, this is not because law is positive, but rather because it has an essential status for us.
>
> G. W. F. Hegel, *Lectures on the Philosophy of Religion*

The chapters preceding this one have included relatively detailed discussions of the written work of a limited number of modern Indonesian thinkers. This final chapter, however, will be constructed somewhat differently. Rather than in-depth treatments of a handful of individuals, these last pages will briefly present an introduction to a broader range of materials from some of the many new voices that are just beginning to emerge in Indonesian public discussions of Islam, law, and society at the turn of the twenty-first century. Many of them are still quite young, and thus it is impossible to give a full accounting of the contributions that they may eventually make to Islamic thought and Indonesian culture. Rather, the aim here is to present an overview of the diversity of contemporary Indonesian Islamic thought in order to indicate at least some of the different directions in which conversations have been carried by a new generation of scholars and activists, working in the post-Suharto era.

## *REFORMASI*, DEMOCRACY, AND NGO ISLAM

These lively contemporary conversations on issues of Islamic law in Indonesia had their origins in the transitional times of the late New Order and subsequent *Reformasi* period. Through the late 1990s, movements for social, religious, and political reform had been gaining ground due to a variety of factors including the growth of the Indonesian middle class, the rapid development of NGOs in the country, the spread of liberalization accompanying globalization, and the internal fragmentation of the ruling elite. The failure of the New Order in addressing these various internal challenges through the early 1990s fostered a gradual erosion of its earlier hegemonic authority, in which a number of groups and individuals perceived new spaces in which to voice a variety of alternative views on politics, law, and society.[1]

Over the last years of New Order rule, the NU leader Abdurrahman Wahid emerged as one of Indonesia's most prominent opposition figures. Wahid's support of the causes of democratization and religious pluralism in the early 1990s had taken a number of forms, including the formation of the Forum Demokrasi (*Fordem*) in 1991, and by the time the Asian financial crisis hit Indonesia in 1997, Wahid had decisively emerged from a period of relative reconciliation with the New Order regime to become one of the most visible national voices demanding democratic reform.[2] At the same time, two of the other leading Indonesian opposition figures, Megawati Sukarnoputri and Amien Rais, began negotiating with Wahid and with each other in attempts to form an alliance with enough support to push forward aspects of their respective agendas for reform as well as their own political aspirations.

After the fall of Suharto in 1998 and the brief interim term of Suharto's former vice-president, B. J. Habibie, Wahid became the Republic of Indonesia's fourth president in 1999. Despite the almost millennial expectations that some had for this presidency, Wahid's turbulent year in office was marked by internecine strife and scandal. Challenges from various sectors, including opposition from within the NU itself, eventually led to his fall and replacement by his own vice-president, Megawati Sukarnoputri. While Wahid and other senior Muslim public intellectuals became increasingly preoccupied with politics, however, a new generation of Indonesian thinkers and activists – including many from within the NU who had been nurtured by Wahid's work within the organization – found their own disillusionment with the machinations of the Indonesian state and, in a now familiar pattern, turned their primary attention elsewhere.[3] In this context,

[1] Arief Budiman, "Indonesia: Transisi ke Arah Demokrasi?," in *Indonesia dalam Transisi*, ed. Hanafi Sofyan (Jakarta: Halmahera Foundation, 1995), 12–14; and Pramono U. Tanthowi, "Islam dan Reformasi: Oposisi Islam Terhadap Orde Baru Dasawarsa 1990-an," *Jauhar: Jurnal Pemikiran Islam Kontekstual* 3.1 (2002): 3–5.

[2] Pramono U. Tanthowi, "Islam dan Reformasi: Oposisi Islam Terhadap Orde Baru Dasawarsa 1990-an," *Jauhar: Jurnal Pemikiran Islam Kontekstual* 3.1 (2002): 12.

[3] Andrée Feillard, "Indonesian Traditionalist Islam's Troubled Experience with Democracy (1999–2001)," *Archipel* 64 (2002): 144.

the work of NGOs and other organizations with financial support from both within and outside the country have continued to play an important role in Indonesian developments both within and well beyond the *pesantren* milieu.

As discussed in chapters 5 and 6, since the 1970s NGOs have become increasingly involved with the development of Islam in Indonesia, advancing a variety of social agendas with the support of foreign as well as domestic funding. In fact, many of the most prominent figures in Indonesian Muslim public debates have benefited at different times in their careers from the largesse of foreign monetary support, while developing their own distinctive visions of the role of Islamic law in contemporary Indonesian society. Acknowledgment of this fact, however, is problematic for many of those involved, as vitriolic accusations of the infiltration of 'foreign' values into the country have often been launched at those working with organizations such as the Ford and Asia foundations by those advocating more 'formalist' or Islamist agendas. Ironically, however, these same critics often refuse to acknowledge the simultaneous widespread influence of funding and institutional support of Islamist groups from the Middle East and elsewhere for their own organizations.[4]

On both sides, then, outside financial and institutional support is being deployed to develop and disseminate particular visions of religion, law, and society developed elsewhere. As we shall see below, the effect of such financial support and the imported ideologies they advocate sometimes produce rather unexpected results. This was the case, for example, with the scholarships and doctrinal education provided by a Saudi-sponsored college in Jakarta (LIPIA) for Ahmad Baso and Ulil Abshar Abdalla, both of whom had earlier studied in NU *pesantren*, and both of whom ultimately went on to develop interpretations of Islam in direct opposition to that promoted by the imported Islamist ideology of that school.

## SOCIAL AND GENDER JUSTICE AGENDAS WITH *PESANTREN* ROOTS

Benefiting from the pioneering work of *kyai* such as Sahal Mahfudh, a new generation of *pesantren*-based scholars and activists has been attempting to envision new possibilities for the role of religion in society along a wide range of agendas. A considerable amount of their energies has been directed toward discussion of issues grouped under the rubric of

[4] Some of these sources of support have been discussed in chapter 4.

"social justice" (*keadilan sosial*), and there has been a prolific production of books and articles in this vein since the publication of Mas'udi's work on *zakāt*. One recent example of this literature, a volume edited by Zuhairi Misrawi and published by the Ford Foundation in 2003, argues for approaches to contemporary social issues based upon a "humanist vision of Islam" (*pandangan Islam humanis*). This is defined as an orientation to the tradition that encourages empathy and fosters the pursuit of solutions based upon principles of equality (Ind. *kestaraan*/Ar. *al-musāwāt*), liberty (Ind. *pembebasan*/Ar. *al-ḥurriyya*), non-violence (Ind. *anti-kekerasan*/ Ar. *salām*), tolerance (Ind. *toleransi*/Ar. *tasamuh*), and human solidarity (*al-ukhuwwa al-bashariyya*). This agenda is argued as a direct refutation of what the authors refer to as "*fundamentalisme*" – defined with reference to "reductionalistic" approaches to Islam that combine literalist understandings of the textual tradition with the political ideologization of religious symbols.

Their first line of attack here is through the examination of case studies of societies that have recently experimented with the formal implementation of the Sharī'a, including Saudi Arabia, the Islamic Republic of Iran, Taliban Afghanistan, and Aceh. From there the authors move through familiar, *Pembaharuan*-type appeals to viewing *fiqh* with an eye toward the universal principles of the *maqāṣid al-sharī'a*, rather than particularistic rulings before getting to the direct discussion of the issues at hand. The bulk of this text, however, is composed of more detailed discussions in the form of a series of explorations of contemporary social issues, including the legalization of abortion, domestic violence, child prostitution, and treatment for drug addiction. In each of these sections, the format is the same: a critical examination of the texts from the Qur'ān and *ḥadīth* often used to justify what the authors view as unjust reactions to these problems, and quotations of "representative opinions" on these matters from Indonesian Muslims (mostly from East Java and Lombok). Building upon this material, the authors of this study proceed to develop inter-disciplinary approaches to religious and social issues that can "put a more human face to Islam."[5]

Issues related to sexuality and reproductive health in particular have been the subject of considerable attention from a number of young *pesantren*-based Muslim scholars in Indonesia in recent years. Some of their work has been undertaken within the contexts of new organizations dedicated to

[5] Zuhairi Misrawi *et al.*, *Dari Syariat menuju Maqashid Syariat: Fundamentalisme, Seksualitas, dan Kesehatan Reproduksi* (Jakarta: KIKJ/Ford Foundation, 2003), 138–46.

developing models for the local cultural contextualization of conceptions of "gender justice" in Muslim Indonesia. The Yayasan Kesejahteraan Fatayat (YKF), for example, began in 1991 through work on a project entitled, "Raising Gender Awareness among Young NU Activists". Through the 1990s, the YKF built upon the momentum of more general developments of liberal trends within the NU, and the work of P3M in particular, to begin forming new public discourses on issues such as domestic violence and HIV/AIDS that drew their inspiration from elements of the *pesantren* tradition.[6]

Pursuing initiatives set into motion by scholars such as Sahal Mahfudh and Masdar Mas'udi, the YKF actively pursues programs for the critical study of established texts from *pesantren* curricula, read in light of contemporary conceptions of "gender justice." Among them particular attention has been directed to the *'Uqūd al-lujjayn* of Muḥammad Nawawī (Banten), a scholar from West Java active in Mecca at the end of the nineteenth century.[7] This text, traditionally popular in some *santri* circles, has recently come under considerable criticism from a number of prominent NU *kyai*, and in 2001, a team of *pesantren*-trained scholars produced a new study of the *'Uqūd al-lujjayn* that critiqued various assumptions and arguments of that text, as well as the soundness of the various *ḥadīth* used by Nawawī to support his positions on various issues related to a woman's proper role in a Muslim family and society.[8]

YKF has also been innovative in the continuing development of new media through which to disseminate its message, including student essay contests, radio broadcasts, television shows, promotional give-aways, and even the commissioning of a novel written to address women's issues.[9] Their work on these various fronts has been complemented by that of other contemporary gender activists from *pesantren* backgrounds who have worked in other spaces ranging from religious voluntary associations and NGOs to government offices in the Ministry of Religious Affairs. A number of them have prepared for these careers in academia with theses and dissertations produced at IAIN and other universities that often emphasize practical

[6] Nelly van Doorn-Harder, "Re-considering Authority: Indonesian *Fiqh* Texts about Women," in Feener and Cammack, eds., *Islamic Law in Contemporary Indonesia*.

[7] *Sharḥ 'Uqūd al-lujjayn fī bayān ḥuqūq al-zawjayn* (Singapore: al-Ḥaramayn, n.d.). For a first-hand description of Nawawī in Mecca, see C. Snouck Hurgronje, *Mekka in the Latter Part of the Nineteenth Century* (Leiden: E. J. Brill, 1931).

[8] *Wajah Baru Relasi Suami-Istri: Telaah Kitab 'Uqud al-Lujjayn* (Yogyakarta: LKiS, 2001); see also Husein Muhammad, *Fiqh Perempuan: Refleksi Kiai atas Wacana Agama dan Gender* (Yogyakarta: LKiS, 2001, reprinted 2002), 171–83.

[9] Van Doorn-Harder, "Re-considering Authority." The novel referred to there is Abidah el Khalieqy, *Perempuan Berkalung Sorban* (Yogyakarta: YKF, 2001).

aspects of developing agendas of gender justice in Indonesian society.[10] Increasingly, these scholars are also involved in projects where they work alongside NGO activists who come from non-*pesantren* backgrounds, one of the most influential of whom in this area has been Lies Marcoes.

She was born at Ciamis (West Java) in 1959 and raised in circles affiliated with the Muhammadiyah, rather than in the traditionalist *pesantren* milieu. As a student she conducted field research in West Java focusing on the social roles of female preachers (*muballigha*) as leaders of study groups (*majlis ta'līm*), and in particular on the development of Peristri, the women's auxiliary to PERSIS.[11] In the course of her research, Marcoes observed that although these women were active in discussions of religion, they did not on the whole actually seek to make women more aware of their rights, or to engage religious teachings with contemporary social justice issues.[12] Determined to change this aspect of female religious participation in Indonesian Islam, she has worked for over a decade on various related programs for NGOs in Indonesia, and it was through these networks that she became increasingly involved with the work of certain *pesantren* circles through projects involving P3M.

Marcoes has been associated with the Asia Foundation office in Jakarta coordinating work with other sectors of the *pesantren*-NGO community on the preparation of materials for the workshops and courses on "Islam and Gender for Women Activists" such as those organized through the Fahmina Institut at Cirebon, West Java. She clearly sees her own work as having international, as well as local dimensions. When presenting her views on the history of developments in the area of gender justice in Indonesian Islam, Marcoes draws an elaborate graph of the development of various organizations that she has been involved with in relation to agendas put forward in global discussions such as those of the 1994 International Conference on Population and Development in Cairo, and the 1995 Women's Summit in Beijing. Much of her work has, accordingly, been in the area of working to root an awareness of these global developments into the culture of local *pesantren*. Her networks within the NU community are now extensive,

[10] A number of them have subsequently been published. See, for example, Khoiruddin Nasution, *Status Wanita di Asia Tenggara: Studi Terhadap Perundang-undangan Perkawinan Muslim Kontemporer di Indonesia dan Malaysia* (Jakarta: INIS, 2002).

[11] Lies M. Marcoes-Natsir, "Profil Organisasi Wanita Islam Indonesia: Studi Kasus Peristri," in *Wantia Islam Indonesia dalam Kajian Tekstual dan Kontekstual*, ed. Lies M. Marcoes-Natsir and Johan Hendrik Meuleman, (Jakarta: INIS, 1993), 95–110.

[12] Lies M. Marcoes, "The Female Preacher as a Mediator in Religion: A Case Study in Jakarta and West Java," *Women and Mediation in Indonesia*, ed. Sita van Bemmelen *et al.* (Leiden: KITLV Press, 1992), 203–28.

and she works closely with a number of prominent *kyai* including Husein Muhammad who has established the Fahmina Institut at his *pesantren* in Cirebon where several of Lies' programs have been held.

Husein Muhammad is best known for his "reflections on discourses of religion and gender" in a book entitled *Fiqh Perempuan* (*The Fiqh of Women*).[13] In the main body of this work, he attempts to come to an understanding of gender difference in a way that will foster the development of "more just and humane" views on related issues of Islamic law and society. His vision is one of a new, socially engaged *fiqh* that brings the intellectual heritage of Islamic jurisprudence into conversations with contemporary needs and concerns.[14] It is an agenda that is 'progressive' in the sense that it views human history as developing in directions of an ever-advancing openness and increasing rationality in addressing human realities.

The pages of *Fiqh Perempuan* repeatedly call attention to the extant differences of opinion among medieval and modern Muslim jurists on various issues, and the way that these may be seen as reflections of the social realities of their particular situations. As the author himself puts it, "*fiqh*, as a human intellectual project, is actually always tied up with its historical situations."[15] With this historical awareness, he hopes to convince his readers that even long-held understandings of the law purportedly based on communal consensus (*ijmā'*) can change over time in accordance with evolving conceptions of communal welfare (*kemashlahatan*).[16] Citing the position of a prominent medieval Muslim interpreter of the Qur'ān, Fakhr al-Dīn al-Rāzī (d. 1210), he advocates a greater attention to 'empirical facts' in the formulation of legal opinions on contemporary issues so as to ensure the relevance of *fiqh*-based rulings in rapidly changing times. The touchstone for finding answers to new questions is the Qur'ān, which Husein Muhammad views as advocating a "universal humanism" (*kemanusiaan universal*) that is grounded in the fundamental moral values of Islamic ethics (*akhlāq*). He thus makes an explicit point of the need to begin discussions of women's issues in Islamic jurisprudence from Qur'ānic universals, rather than from the handful of decontextualized verses that are commonly cited as authoritative statements on women's issues.[17]

[13] This text was published through his own NGO Rahima, with the cooperation of the Yogyakarta-based LKiS and the Ford Foundation office at Jakarta, and includes substantial prefaces by both Sahal Mahfudh and the French scholar Andrée Feillard.

[14] K. H. Husein Muhammad, *Fiqh Perempuan: Refleksi Kiai atas Wacana Agama dan Gender* (Yogyakarta: LKiS, 2001), 7.

[15] *Fiqh Perempuan*, 137. [16] *Fiqh Perempuan*, 152. [17] *Fiqh Perempuan*, 11, 16.

From this perspective, he goes on to explore ways in which these principles of religious ethics – including concerns for basic human rights (*hak-hak asasi manusia*) – can be grounded in the lived relationships between men and women. Muhammad maintains that women are the equal of men, and that:

> This reality must become a certainty to the point that all traditions, teachings, and views that disparage, discriminate, or insult women must be swept away. In this way the religious texts that serve as foundations for thinking on such issues should be those concerned with the ideal principles of Islam on justice, equality, welfare, and compassion for all, regardless of their sex.[18]

In this mode, then, he goes on to re-evaluate established *fiqh* rulings on issues ranging from the propriety of women leading communal prayers and becoming heads of state, to practices of genital incision (Ind. *khitan*), women's rights in the context of marriage, and the rapes and other acts of violence toward women that gained prominent public attention following the 1998 riots that eventually resulted in the fall of Suharto.

## "INTER-RELIGIOUS *FIQH*"

NGO-affiliated programs on issues of Islam and gender are, however, only some aspects of the diverse contemporary projects of young scholars coming out of NU backgrounds. One activist in these circles, Muhammad A. S. Hikam, has commented on the internal diversity of NU as one of the significant ways in which the dynamics of the *pesantren* community differ from those of some Islamic modernist organizations.[19] One example of another track within these circles can be found in the work of Mun'im Sirry. He comes from a *pesantren* background in Madura and later studied at the International Islamic University in Islamabad, Pakistan, as well as the IAIN Syarif Hidayatullah in Ciputat (Jakarta). He went on to study at UCLA and Arizona State University. While at Ciputat, he produced a booklet for the IAIN Center for Languages and Cultures (Pusat Bahasa dan Budaya/PBB) that argues against a formalist implementation of the Sharīʿa in Indonesia by emphasizing the distinction between "religion" (*agama*) and human understandings of religion. He then advocates an historical approach to Islamic law that takes into account the "reciprocal

[18] *Fiqh Perempuan*, 26.

[19] Muhammad A. S. Hikam, "NU, Civil Society, dan Proyek Pencerahan," in *Pergulatan Pesantren dan Demokratisasi*, ed. Ahmad Suaedy (Yogyakarta: LKiS, 2000), 50. However, as will be discussed below in relation to the young Muhammadiya group JIMM, there is considerable internal diversity to be found there as well.

patterns between Islamic law and other legal systems."[20] Along these lines Sirry maintains that any law that maintains moral values in the interest of public welfare cannot be considered to be opposed to Islam, but rather as a manifestation of Islamic law itself – that is "Islamic" in substance, rather than in a purely formalistic sense.

Sirry is perhaps most widely known today for editing a controversial collaborative volume entitled *Inter-religious Fiqh* (*Fiqih Lintas Agama*), published by the Paramadina Press.[21] This book represents a remarkable Indonesian exercise in the radical reconceptualizations of *fiqh* in contemporary Islamic thought. It departs from the polemical position that, "*Fiqh*, both explicitly or implicitly, has been used to justify hatred and suspicion toward other religions,"[22] and then goes on to argue that this need not be the case. The authors advocate "dynamizing" *fiqh* as a necessary step toward the "deconstruction" of the Sharīʿa as a static and exclusive concept, and its reconstruction in a more dynamic, inclusive, and egalitarian mode.[23] Examples of what such a *fiqh* would look like are provided in this volume through a series of discussions of a number of issues which have become central to public debates about inter-religious relations among Indonesia's Muslim community, including: use of Islamic greetings with non-Muslims, attending celebrations and exchanging wishes for the celebration of Christmas and other non-Muslim holidays, and the permissibility of non-Muslims entering mosques. A considerable portion of the text is, however, devoted not to jurisprudence, but to theology.

In this, *Fiqih Lintas Agama* reflects the approach of some of the older *Pembaharuan* thinkers involved in the project, including Nurcholish Madjid. However a significant shift in their orientation is apparent here as well, in that rather than framing their discussion in terms of *kalām*, the authors turn to *fiqh* as the "practical theology" of Islam.[24] That is, *fiqh* has now come to be seen by them as "occupying a strategic position in clarifying *kalām* in particular ways that address questions faced in everyday life"; in other words, they have come to see *fiqh*, as "perfecting *kalām*." The "perfection" being aimed for by the authors of *Fiqih Lintas Agama* is the social welfare (*maṣlaḥa*) of the entire community, Muslim and non-Muslim, conceived of broadly as an ideal that can be approached through

[20] Mun'im A. Sirry, *Hukum Barat pun Islam: Membongkar Argumen Kejumudan Syariat* (Jakarta: Pusat Bahasa dan Budaya UIN Syarif Hidayatullah Jakarta, 2003), 14.

[21] Mun'im A. Sirry, ed., *Fiqih Lintas Agama: Membangun Masyarakat Inklusif-Pluralis* (Jakarta: Yayasan Wakaf Paramadina, 2004). The team which produced this book included such senior figures as Nurcholish Madjid and Masdar F. Masʿudi.

[22] *Fiqih Lintas Agama*, 2. [23] *Fiqih Lintas Agama*, 7–8, 12–13. [24] *Fiqih Lintas Agama*, 65.

a flexible *fiqh* directed toward the goals (*maqāṣid*) of fostering "universal human values."[25] In their own words, "a *fiqh* that advocates democracy, pluralism, and egalitarianism will facilitate the formation of a society that is just and civilized."[26] This vision of a new *fiqh*, and in particular one with a more pluralist orientation, has, however, not been welcomed by all Indonesian Muslims, and its attempts at constructing a theological basis for pluralism have evoked harsh critiques of *Inter-religious Fiqh* from various sectors. Predictably, Indonesia's Islamist media was filled with energetic refutations of *Fiqih Lintas Agama* in the months following its publication.[27]

## YOUNG *SANTRI* IN A "HYBRID CULTURE"

Despite such public polemics, projects of reorienting discussions of Islamic law to include issues of pluralism and democracy have attracted the attention of an increasing number of young Muslims, many of whom have come out of *pesantren* backgrounds. Some of these contemporary *santri* have already made some significant efforts toward rooting their concerns for social justice in actual lived practice and the work of social transformation. This phenomenon of a generation of *santri* active in projects well beyond *pesantren* walls has been referred to as a new Hybrid Culture (*Kultur Hibrida*) by some of those involved. After more than three decades of NU engagement with NGOs, *Pembaharuan* thinkers, and the broader Indonesian public sphere, a new generation of *santri* have begun exploring their own ways to develop the tradition of *fiqh* without having to be traditional in the sense of uncritically following the directives of previously established rulings.[28] In the process, a considerably diverse constellation of thinkers, artists, and activists has moved well beyond their *pesantren* studies into a wider world of social critique and grass-roots activism.[29] Moreover, these figures have emerged not only from Jakarta, but from across the archipelago, with important regional centers embodying considerable autonomy and

25 *Fiqih Lintas Agama*, 8–10. 26 *Fiqih Lintas Agama*, 176.

27 For example in *Media Dakwah*, which advertised its refutation of *Fiqih Lintas Agama* on the front cover of its May–June 2004 issue (no. 355).

28 See Hairus Salim HS and Muhammad Riwan, eds., *Kultur Hibrida: Anak Muda NU di Jalur Kultural* (Yogyakarta: LKiS, 1999), 2.

29 Portraits of young Muslim activists in these circles can be found in the chapters of Syafi' Alieha, Sri Hadayati, Arif Ruba'i, Ahmad Bahrudin, Hana Mufida, and Nurlaila Diryat in the *Kultur Hibrida* volume.

contributing to internal Muslim pluralism, such as the Pondok Pesantren al-Amien Preduan of Sumenep on the island of Madura.[30]

A recent volume of autobiographical essays by *santri* of this generation is subtitled, "Young NU on the cultural track" (*Anak Muda NU di Jalur Kultural*). What is meant here is, loosely, a tendency to pursue projects of social reform outside of party politics, in ways that might be seen as functionally analogous to those pursued by *da'wa* activists following the dissolution of Masjumi, as well as by the *Pembaharuan* movement. However, the aims of these young "hybrid" *santri* have generally been rather different – being aimed primarily not toward the cultivation of personal piety and cultural "Islamization," but rather toward agendas of social and economic justice and advocacy of the rights of underprivileged groups in Indonesian society, sometimes irrespective of their religious "identities." Such projects are being pursued in a wide variety of ways, ranging from literary experiments and intellectual reformulations of the relation between religious norms and social values, to campus demonstrations and programs of social work with farmers, factory workers, women, and homeless orphans.

On the intellectual front Ahmad Baso has drawn on European postmodern thinkers such as Focault, Derrida, and Lyotard in formulating cultural critiques of *Pembaharuan* intellectualism.[31] He writes that in the early 1990s he was introduced to Abdurrahman Wahid, Masdar Mas'udi, and Ulil Abshar Abdalla through a study group called Kajian 164 in Jakarta, while he was there studying Islamic law at the Institute for Islamic and Arabic Studies (LIPIA), an institution affiliated with Riyadh-based Muḥammad ibn Sa'ūd University.[32] As he came to find the intellectual atmosphere of the campus stifling, he eventually left LIPIA and worked for a while as a journalist before becoming a student once again, taking up the study of philosophy at a Roman Catholic college in Jakarta.[33]

One of Baso's most influential contributions to contemporary discussions came through his work of translating a collection of articles by the

[30] For a brief overview of the intellectual milieu of young Madurese *santri*, see M. Aunul Abied Shah, "Santri Madura di Tengah Pusaran Peradaban," in *Kontekstualisasi Islam dalam Peradaban*, ed. Mas Guntur Romli and Shofia Tidjani (Cairo: FOSGAMA, 2002), 257–61.

[31] See, for example, Ahmad Baso, "Problem Islam dan Politik: Perspektif *Kritik Nalar Politik* Mohammed Abed al-Jabiri," *TA* 4 (1999).

[32] For observations on the impact of LIPIA on the development of Islamism in contemporary Indonesia, see Madinier, "Du temps des chameaux," 151–52; Fealy and Bubalo, *Joining the Caravan*, 57–58.

[33] Ahmad Baso, "Dari Kritik Wacana Agama Menuju Rasionalisme," in *Kultur Hibrida: Anak Muda NU di Jalur Kultural*, ed. Hairus Salim HS and Muhammad Riwan (Yogyakarta: LKiS, 1999), 19–44.

contemporary Moroccan philosopher Muḥammad 'Ābid al-Jābirī.[34] Baso's enthusiasm for Jābirī's project of developing a new epistemology to serve as a basis for contemporary conceptualizations of Islamic law is one that is shared with a number of other young Indonesian Muslim thinkers. The openness to such views within NU circles in particular is something that Baso attributes in part to the influence of Abdurrahman Wahid. Such developments are often viewed by those directly involved as part of a broader movement referred to as *Post-Tradisionalisme*, a phrase which also happens to be the title given to Baso's Indonesian translation of al-Jābirī's work.[35] Baso put forward more of his own ideas on this approach in a special edition of the NU Lakpesdam's flagship journal on the subject of "Post Traditionalist Islam: Ideology & Methodology."[36] The idea of *Post-Tradisionalisme*, however, is one that is being developed simultaneously by an expanding number of "new *santri*."[37] *Post-Tradisionalisme* attempts to move forward in the engaged study of Islam through works of epistemological critiques (*kritik nalar*) in order to open up new areas for critical social thought.

One broadly shared item on the agenda of many of them are calls for a more extensive and programmatic (*manhaji*) engagement with *uṣūl al-fiqh* that would privilege general legal axioms over the particularistic rulings that had become standardized within the tradition.[38] For example, another "Post-Traditionalist," Zuhairi Misrawi, defines the movement as:

34 Ahmad Baso, "Postmodernisme sebagai Kritik Islam: Kontribusi Metodologis 'Kritik Nalar' Muhammad Abed al-Jabiri," in Muhammad Abed al-Jabiri, *Post-Tradisionalisme Islam* (Yogyakarta: LKiS, 2000). This volume is but one example of the great number of Indonesian translations of works dealing with religion, law, and society published by LKiS in Yogyakarta. In addition to publishing original works by Indonesian Muslim intellectuals, they also are committed to enriching Indonesian conversations through introducing the work of such international thinkers as Ḥasan Ḥanafī, Nasr Abu-Zayd, Fatima Mernissi, Mohammed Arkoun, and Abdullahi an-Na'im.

35 Baso, "Dari Kritik Wacana," xxvi.

36 Ahmad Baso, "Dari Tradisionalisme Menuju Post-Tradisionalisme Islam: Geliat Pemikiran Baru Islam Arab," *TA* 9 (2000): 47–61.

37 The term "new *santri*" (*santri baru*) has been used as the title of a recent book by Nur Khalik Ridwan that critically discusses broad developments across an entire generation, ranging from Islamic liberals and deconstructionists to radical Islamists and even violent terrorists. In this chapter, however, I use the term in a much more narrowly defined sense to refer to the young men and women from *pesantren* backgrounds embracing the "Hybrid Culture" of the NU, NGOs, academia, the arts, and non-violent social activism. Cf. *Santri Baru: Pemetaan, Wacana Ideologi dan Kritik* (Jogjakarta: Gerigi Pustaka, 2004). Ridwan's work is part of a rich and evolving body of Indonesian Muslim culture critique that deserves a separate study of its own.

38 E.g. in Afifudin Muhajir and Imam Nahe'i, "Fungsionalisasi Ushul Fiqih dalam *Bahtsul Masa'il NU*," in *Kritik Nalar Fiqih NU: Transformasi Paradigma Bahtsul Masa'il*, 243–63.

A new way to liberate and further expand the potential of humanity by building a society that values difference, upholds the law, and develops understandings of pluralism and democracy. In this way *Post-tradisionalisme* affirms that the critical study of tradition is the best way to build a culture and a way of thinking that can stimulate social transformation and change on a practical level.[39]

In discussing inspirations for this movement, Misrawi mentions a number of modern and contemporary Muslim thinkers other than Jābirī that he regards as having influenced the thinking of NU's "post-traditionalists" on matters not only of *fiqh*, but also philosophy, poetry, literary criticism, aesthetics, politics, and human rights. Their diverse sources of inspiration include, according to his list: Ṭāriq Bishrī, Nawāl Sa'dāwī, 'Alī Mabrūk, Anwar Mughīth, Maḥmūd Amīn al-'Ālim, Muḥammad al-Ghazālī, Sayyid Ṭanṭāwī, Sa'īd Ashmāwī, 'Abd al-Raḥmān Badawī, Zakī Najīb Maḥmūd, Jābir 'Uṣfūr, Sālim Yafut, Sulaymān al-Askarī, Sa'īd Ḥawwā, and even Christian Arab thinkers such as Mīlād Ḥannā for his thoughts on economic and social justice issues.

Of course some contemporary Arab Muslim thinkers have held more attraction than others for the new *santri*. For example, the work of Jamāl Bannā on the "deconstruction of *fiqh*" is something that fits well with the kind of *Post-Tradisionalisme* reform agendas developed among young NU scholars. The latter have, however, elaborated their own work along these lines in terms of a "critique of *fiqh* reasoning."[40] This project takes as its starting point the position that the products of traditional Islamic jurisprudence are 'subjective and relative' (*ẓannī*), as developed most prominently in the earlier work of Masdar Mas'udi. From there the new *santri* involved in this work have undertaken a variety of critical explorations of the ways in which over time a derationalization of *fiqh* (*nalar naqli*) has marginalized the role of reason (*'aql*) to the extent that *fiqh* finds itself reaching conclusions that are "far from the spirit of the Qur'ān."[41] Drawing selectively and critically on the work of Mohamed Arkoun, Nasr Abu-Zayd, and al-Jābirī, the Indonesian 'critique of *fiqh* reasoning' stresses the need for more flexible and comprehensive approaches to Islamic religious thought that further develop *Pembaharuan* approaches oriented toward historical contextualization and the consideration of public interest, but in ways that more subtly and critically engage both classical Muslim jurisprudence and a broad range of international developments in contemporary thought.

[39] Misrawi, *Dari Syariat menuju Maqashid Syariat*, 57.
[40] See, for example, Rumadi, "Kritik Nalar: Arah Baru Studi Islam," *TA* 9 (2000): 62–77.
[41] Muhammad Abidun, "Kritik Nalar Fiqh," *Nuansa: Jurnal Pemikiran Keagamaan* 12 (July–September 2003): 31–41, 35.

THE "ISLAMIC LEFT" IN CONTEMPORARY INDONESIA

One of the contemporary Arab Muslim thinkers most popular among young Indonesians today is Ḥasan Ḥanafī.[42] Since a discussion of his work by Nurcholish Madjid and other Indonesian Muslim intellectuals published by the then-new journal *Studia Islamika* in 1993, interest in Ḥanafī's work has grown considerably among modernists and traditionalists in the country alike.[43] For *Pembaharuan* thinkers one of the main attractions of Ḥanafī's work was his reassessment of the "heritage" (*turāth*) of Islamic thought through the critical study of the intellectual history. Among the new *santri*, other aspects of Ḥanafis oeuvre have come into the conversation, particularly in the form of an engagement with his program for 'the Islamic Left' (*al-yasār al-Islāmī*), generally glossed in Bahasa Indonesia as "*Islam Kiri*" and/or "*Kiri Islam.*"[44]

*Al-Yasār al-Islāmī* was the title of a one-issue journal that Ḥanafī published in 1981. Its central theme was the critique of 'capitalist liberal democracy' as a system of power, constructed upon what Ḥanafī refers to as 'three pillars of the Islamic renaissance': a revivification of classical Islamic intellectual legacies, the study of occidentalism as a challenge to 'the worldwide myth of Western civilization', and empirical analysis of the lived conditions of contemporary Muslim societies.[45] In one recent Indonesian discussion of Ḥanafī's work, Mas Guntur Romli reads Ḥanafis "left" as a general rubric for, "rational, progressive, critical, revolutionary, social justice, reformist, democratic, humanist, and liberation-oriented" approaches to Islam. All of these interests so central to the work of Romli and his "new *santri*" colleagues are then set in stark contrast to the "right," identified with "irrationality, conservatism, textualism, despotism, theo-centrism, colonialism, and oppression."[46] Here 'the Islamic Left' (*Kiri Islam*) has come to serve as a broadly conceived term of reference for an alignment of interests that

[42] For a brief introduction to his life and work, see John L. Esposito and John O. Voll, *Makers of Contemporary Islam* (Oxford: Oxford University Press, 2001), 68–90.

[43] "Forum Dialog," *SI* 1.1 (July–September 1993).

[44] These recent developments, it should be noted, are genealogically distinct from the various forms of "Islamic Communism" or "Communist Islam" advocated by figures such as Hadji Misbach and Hadji Datoek Batoeah in the early years of the twentieth century. For an overview of those developments, see C. van. Dijk, "'Communist Muslims' in the Dutch East Indies," in *State and Islam*, ed. C. van Dijk and A. H. de Groot (Leiden: Research School CNWS, 1995), 77–95.

[45] For an overview of Ḥanafī's "Islamic Left," see Shimogaki Kazuo, *Between Modernity and Post-Modernity: The Islamic Left and Dr. Hasan Hanafi's Thought, a Critical Reading* (Japan: I. U. J. Institute for Middle Eastern Studies, 1988).

[46] Mas Guntur Romli, "Menelusuri Post-Tradisionalisme Islam: Mengkaji Proyek Pembaruan Hassan Hanafi," in *Kontekstualisasi Islam dalam Peradaban*, ed. Mas Guntur Romli and Shofia Tidjani (Cairo: FOSGAMA, 2002), 215.

has over recent years become a popular one among some circles of socially engaged and intellectually imaginative young Indonesian Muslims.[47]

Indonesia's *Islam Kiri* has thus come to involve a broad array of young thinkers and activists for whom Islam is a source of inspiration for social change, and who at the same time draw on a range of non-Muslim thinkers from Gramsci to Foucault in developing visions of greater social justice. They often cast their own efforts at reinterpreting tradition in terms of struggles against both the shibboleth of Islamist imaginings of Islam as a static and uniform system of beliefs and practices and the hegemonic formalization of Islam within the coercive structures of the state. In this regard they have much in common with other young NU activists who have incorporated post-modern perspectives on Muslim tradition developed by scholars working in the Middle East, Europe, and North America in formulating critical approaches to dominant understandings of Islam, law, and society.[48]

## *KOMPILASI* AND ITS CRITICS

One of the major late-New Order artifacts relevant to contemporary critical discussions of Islamic law and society is a collection of rulings on matters related to marriage, inheritance, and religious endowments (*waqf*) that gained prominence through a special "presidential instruction" (*Inpres*) in July, 1991. The legal status of this compilation (Ind. *Kompilasi*) thus was not one of formal legislation, but rather as a document whose 'circulation' was officially endorsed by the president for use as a guide to decisions in the country's system of Islamic religious courts (*pengadilan agama*). Since the fall of Suharto, this document and its legitimacy as a guide to legal decisions in the nation's Islamic courts has been opened to new criticism on several fronts, including a monograph by two young, NU-affiliated writers, Marzuki Wahid and Rumadi.

Following a theoretical introduction outlining Gramsci's understanding of 'hegemony' for a contemporary Indonesian audience, the authors move on to an historical treatment of the formulation of the *Kompilasi* within the politics of Suharto's authoritarian rule. Whereas the *Kompilasi* was hailed by some Muslim groups as a high point of success in "Islamizing" the

[47] For an early survey of these developments, see Ken Miichi, "Kiri Islam, Jaringan Intelektual dan Partai Politik: Sebuah Catatan Awal," *TA* 9 (2000): 155–69.

[48] The work of three such figures, Imam Aziz, Anom Suryaputra, and Syafi' Alieha, is described in Miichi Ken, "Indonesia-ni okeru isuramu saha to chisikijin netowaku," *Tōnan Ajia Kenkyu* 40.1 (June 2002): 42–73.

Indonesian state during the late New Order, the authors of this critique argue that it actually should be seen as a legal product of an authoritarian regime promoted to serve a particular set of political interests. Thus instead of a triumph of the pious aspirations of the Muslim community in Indonesian society, they read the document as an instrument imposing an artificial hegemony upon a pluralistic jurisprudential discourse that was viewed as a potential impediment to the developmentalist agenda of the New Order state and its totalitarian claims to authority.[49]

In the post-Suharto era of *Reformasi*, some Indonesian Muslims reacted to the problematic legal position of the enactment of this presidential instruction by attempting to secure more firm legal footing for the *Kompilasi* in formal legislation. However, at the same time there are others addressing the situation from a significantly different tack, calling instead for the thorough revision of the *Kompilasi* before any firmer implementation of the document is pursued. Work in this direction was undertaken by a team of scholars working under the direction of Siti Musdah Mulia, a prominent woman in the 'Expert Staff' (Staf Ahli) at the central office of the Department of Religious Affairs (Departemen Agama). In 2004, they produced a counter-draft to the original presidential instruction that sparked intense debate in Indonesia's Muslim media.[50] In presenting their counter draft, Musdah Mulia and her team argued that a number of the sections of the *Kompilasi* contain statements that contradict basic, universal principles of Islamic justice, and that furthermore the overall approach to Islamic law evident in the *Kompliasi* is one taken wholesale from Middle Eastern understandings of *fiqh*, and not engaged with the issues and conversations relevant to the Indonesian context.

Their program was not conceived of as one of merely technical revisions, but as part of a broader agenda of social justice. For example, in their critique of the section dealing with marriage law, they began with the very way in which the institution itself is defined in the *Kompilasi*, which includes both dimensions of a binding contract (*mithaqan ghalizan*), and of a religious act (*ibadah*). However they point to the fact that within *fiqh*, marriage is dealt with as a contract (*'aqd*) without any implication that it is an essentially 'religious' act. Musdah Mulia and her team thus argued for a kind of 'de-sacralization' of accepted understandings in light of the flexibility

[49] Marzuki Wahid and Rumadi, *Fiqih Madzhab Negara: Kritik Atas Politik Hukum Islam di Indonesia.* (Yogyakarta: LKiS, 2001), revised edn.

[50] For an early report on reactions to this document, see "Draf Kompilasi Hukum Islam Picu Kritik," *Republika On-line*, www.republika.co.id/ASP/online_detail.asp?id=174636&kat_id=3

and historically contingent nature of traditional *fiqh*,[51] while maintaining that such critical reevaluations of established positions must be carried out under the guiding principle of social benefit (*maṣlaḥa*) underlying the aims (*maqāṣid*) of the Sharīʿa. Their proposed revisions thus comprised not a piecemeal tinkering with established positions, but rather a critique of their underlying epistemological assumptions and jurisprudential methodology. In doing this, they called into question what they regarded as its dangerous truth claims implied by the literalistic readings of scripture and its normative understandings of *fiqh*, and advocated instead more critical appeals to the tradition in light of the complex social realities of contemporary Indonesia.[52]

The sharp public criticisms that the team received for their work, however, were overwhelmingly focused on specific changes to individual rulings rather than such overarching epistemological and methodological points. By way of appeals to established Indonesian government regulations prohibiting discrimination toward women passed in 1984,[53] as well as Indonesia's ratification of the international Convention on the Elimination of All Forms of Discrimination Against Women in 1999, Mulia's team had taken head on what they perceived to be the inherent gender bias of the current *Kompilasi*.[54] In order to correct this they proposed substantial revisions to nearly all sections of the text, but with a special emphasis on articles which they viewed as contributing to significant social problems such as child marriage, 'secret' (*sirri*) or unregistered marriages, inequality in divorce and inheritance rulings, and polygamy.[55] These were precisely the hot-button issues that nearly guaranteed controversy, and which had the ultimate effect of defeating any chance the counter-draft had of becoming law.

## INVESTIGATING *ISTIṢLĀḤ*

Musdah Mulia is also active on issues of Islam and 'gender justice' well beyond the Department of Religion, and is associated with a number of

[51] Siti Musdah Mulia, "Revisi KHI," unpublished MS, May 2005.

[52] Major aspects of this critique of the *Kompilasi* are discussed in an interview with Ulil Abshar-Abdalla, "Dr. Siti Musdah Mulia, MA – Kompilasi Hukum Islam sangat Konservatif!," available at http://islamlib.com/id/page.php?page=article&mode=print&id=408

[53] UU nomor 7, 1984.

[54] Kelompok Kajian KHI – Tim Pokja Pengarusutamaan Gender Departemen Agama, "Memantapkan Posisi Kompilasi Hukum Islam (KHI) dalam Masyarakat Indonesia yang Demokratis," unpublished MS.

[55] Musdah Mulia herself has written a popular booklet on this subject that addresses some of the negative social implications of polygamy, critiques existing Indonesian government policy related to this, and argues that "in striving for justice, the foundational principle of marriage outlined by Islam is monogamy, not polygamy." *Pandangan Islam tentang Poligami* (Jakarta: LKAJ/ Perserikatan Solidaritas Perempuan/Asia Foundation, 1999), 65.

Muslim women's organizations and inter-religious dialogue groups, including the Fatayat and Muslimat NU, and the Indonesian Conference on Religion and Peace. At the same time she is the director of the *Lembaga Kajian Agama dan Jender* (LKAJ/Institute for Religious and Gender Studies) and works closely together with other religious intellectuals and social activists, including Lies Marcoes. Another important figure active within these same circles is Nahe'i, who provides an excellent example of the kind of critical rethinking of traditional Islamic jurisprudence that is going on simultaneously on the local, as well as the international, level.[56]

After completing his *pesantren* education in East Java, Nahe'i went on to pursue graduate work in Islamic Studies at the Universitas Islam Malang. There he wrote a thesis critically comparing the theories of *istiṣlāḥ* in the works of two fourteenth-century Islamic thinkers who have become increasingly popular in Indonesia since the second half of the twentieth century: the Mālikī jurist al-Shāṭibī and the Ḥanbalī al-Ṭūfī.[57] Through the deployment of a tripartite model of *maṣlaḥa* and the further refinement of understandings of one of its major categories (*mursala*) he is able to resituate the conversations of *qaṭʿī* and *ẓannī* as developed by Masʿudi within more extensively documented traditions of classical Muslim jurisprudence. Since completing this work, Nahe'i has written on other technical aspects of Muslim jurisprudence. In an essay on *uṣūl al-fiqh* in the NU *Bahtsul Masa'il* co-written with Afifuddin Muhajir, he has argued that to this point *uṣūl* has still not really been utilized as a means by which to develop new understandings of Islamic law in these circles. Thus he calls for more nuanced understandings of *fiqh* concepts like *maṣlaḥa*, as well as more consequential commitment to the idea of practicing *ijtihād* based on contextualized interpretations of general legal axioms (*qawāʿid al-fiqh*) rather than simply "raping" (*memperkosa*) classical texts for particularistic rulings that would conveniently fit predetermined outcomes.[58]

Aside from such methodological concerns, Nahe'i has also contributed to movements for the progressive reform of *fiqh* in response to various social

[56] His name has been spelt in a bewildering number of various ways on his published works, including Nahoe'i, and Nakho'i in addition to Nahe'i.

[57] He writes that one of the motivations in undertaking this study was to construct a model of *maṣlaḥa* that could support Sjadzali's position on the equality of inheritance shares of Muslim daughters and sons. Thus he re-reads the much-discussed Qur'ānic verse 4: 2 as being superseded in its textual particulars by the broader conception of welfare that he shows to have greater precedence in the interpretive hierarchy. Nahe'i, "Madzhab Maslahah: Studi Analysis Komparatif Konsep Maslahah Asy-saytibi dan Najmuddin Ath-Thufi sebagai Upaya Membangun Madhzhab Kemaslahatan" (Malang: Universitas Islam Malang MA Thesis, 2002), 217

[58] Afifudin Muhajir and Imam Nahe'i, "Fungsionalisasi Ushul Fiqih dalam *Bahtsul Masa'il NU*," in *Kritik Nalar Fiqih NU: Transformasi Paradigma Bahtsul Masa'il*, ed. M. Imdadun Rahmat (Jakarta: Lakpesdam, 2002), 243–63.

issues, and gender concerns in particular. He has written a number of short papers on these topics for the Asia Foundation's program for Islam and Civil Society in Indonesia, and has also become a prominent participant in discussions and seminars held by the Fahmina Institute where he has worked closely with Husein Muhammad and Faqihuddin Abdul Kodir in presenting critical assessments of historical and methodological dimensions of *uṣūl al-fiqh*.[59] Back in East Java, moreover, Nahe'i is also a teacher affiliated with the Maʿhad Aly, an institute for the advanced study of *fiqh* at Pondok *Pesantren* Salafiyah Syafiʿiyah Sukorejo in Situbondo.[60]

## THE MAʿHAD ALY

The Sukorejo *pesantren* has been a prominent traditionalist institution for decades under the leadership of Kyai H. As'ad Syamsul Afirin. This teacher is remembered among Java's *pesantren* community for a number of reasons, but for the advanced students at Sukorejo, one of his most important legacies has been his involvement in the development of what has been described as "post-*fiqh* thought" (*pemikiran post-fiqih*). What is meant by this is a tendency to frame decisions not strictly in terms of textual arguments from traditional *fiqh* texts, but rather through a process of "encounters with concrete social realities." His admiring biographers have described As'ad's thought as "very rational and always oriented toward considerations of the public good (*kemaslahatan – res publica*) as the guiding principle for determining authoritative Islamic teachings."[61] Under the direction of As'ad, a new institute was founded within the Sukorejo *pesantren* for the advanced study of *fiqh* within the framework of a three-year Master's degree (S2) program.

This is known as the Maʿhad Aly, which was formally opened for its first class of students in 1990 and which was accredited to award

[59] I would like to thank Lies Marcoes for providing me with copies of a number of such presentations from 2003–04, including "Karakteristic Metode Berfikir Ushul Fiqih Klasik," and "Sejarah Kelahiran dan Perkembangan Fiqh Perspektif Perempuan," by Nakhe'i; "Mengggugat Konsepsi Seksualitas Perempuan dalam Literatur Klasik Islam," and "Kontekstualisasi Hadis: Metoda Memahami Hadis-Hadis Relasi Laki-laki dan Perempuan," by Abdul Kodir; and "Tafsir al-Qur-an dalam Perspektif Perempuan," by Husein Muhammad.

[60] The combination of "Salafi" and "Shāfiʿī" in the name of this school may strike some as unusual, and thus requires some explanation. "Salafi" is used here to refer to something rather different from its use by modern reformist groups working in the tradition of Rashīd Riḍā and has in fact come to be used by a number of NU *pesantren*. In such cases, the two terms can be understood as relating to different aspects of the mission of the school: the former implying the avocation of an intentionally simple lifestyle, while the latter denotes the school's methodologically aware approach to *fiqh* and *uṣūl*.

[61] A. H. Syamsul, *Kharisma Kiai As'ad di Mata Umat* (Yogyakarta: LKiS, 2003), xi.

graduate degrees in 2005. In conceptualizing the form and curriculum of the Ma'had Aly, the *kyai* invited a number of leading NU thinkers to Sukorejo for a seminar in which plans for the institution were discussed. Prominent in these discussions were some of the *'ulamā'* discussed in the preceding chapter, including Ali Yafie and Sahal Mahfudh.[62] The mission statement of the Ma'had Aly calls for the establishment of a center for the comprehensive study of *fiqh* and *uṣūl al-fiqh*, but also for the development of *pesantren* education in ways that will prepare *santri* to address contemporary religious and social problems in a manner informed by modern intellectual developments. Some of the major ways in which this is to be pursued reflects the model of NU *halqah*, such as the reorientation to traditional *fiqh* texts as setting out interpretive methodologies rather than particularistic rulings. However the Ma'had Aly also has some more distinctively focused emphases, such as a critical attention to the historical development of *fatwā* in changing social contexts, and a tendency toward prioritizing universal (*kulliyya*), rather than particularistic (*juz'iyya*) rulings.

Their overall program of reinvigorating discussions of social issues in terms of traditional Islamic jurisprudence is most often summed up by the members of the Ma'had Aly themselves in terms of a three-point program: (1) the revitalization of *fiqh* methodology; (2) the diversification of Islamic texts studied in the *pesantren* milieu; and (3) the widening of the sphere of *ta'wīl* (non-literal interpretation). When talking with students there and reading some of their published discussions of various issues, however, what comes most strikingly to the fore is their emphasis on evoking the principle of *maṣlaḥa* as a guiding – one might even say overriding – principle in determining Islamic legal rulings. In doing this, they have a rather clear set of social agendas and are frank in acknowledging that:

> as a body of knowledge that grows within concrete historical contexts, the discipline of *fiqh* is not neutral. It is understood that *fiqh* is always influenced by its relation to certain powers to such an extent that it may not be "sacralized" in order to prevent questions that ask, "For whose social, economic, and political benefit?" is a particular legal ruling being made.[63]

The evocation of *maṣlaḥa* in the arguments offered by the Ma'had Aly can at times even serve to trump explicit textual rulings from the Qur'ān and *ḥadīth*, a move which they defend by arguing that, "often statements

[62] *Profil Ma'had Aly li al-Ulum al-Islamiyah Qismi al-Fiqh* (Situbondo, Jawa Timur: Pondok *Pesantren* Salafiyah Syafi'iyah Sukorejo, 2003), 2.

[63] *Fiqih Rakyat*, vi.

that are taken to be unambiguous and legally binding (*qaṭ ʿī*), when put into practice, will actually be set against the sociological facts of a given society."[64] Here the importance of Nahe'i's work on *maṣlaḥa* for the Maʿhad Aly is clearly evident, since its agenda explicitly identifies itself with the "*fiqh* of ʿUmar" that has been increasingly popular in Indonesia since it was developed by *Pembaharuan* thinkers in the 1980s.[65]

The results of some of the Maʿhad Aly discussions on a wide range of issues have been published in a locally produced newsletter entitled *Tanwirul Afkar*. The first issue of this four-page, single-sheet weekly was published in early August 1997, and has since then appeared regularly each Friday. At present the total circulation is just around 2,000, mostly within the *pesantren* community of Situbondo and its environs. Each edition of *Tanwirul Afkar* is devoted to the discussion of one particular issue, and the topics have varied widely over the past seven years – ranging from labor strikes to oral sex, from Valentine's Day cards to suicide bombers. To date, compilations of various *Tanwirul Afkar* discussions have been gathered into two volumes. The first, entitled *Fiqih Rakyat* (*People's Fiqh*), was published at Yogyakarta in 2000. The second collection, entitled *Fiqih Pembebasan (Liberation Fiqh)* was more modestly produced, and has thus enjoyed only a very limited circulation outside Situbondo.[66] However, some discussion of this material is justified in this survey not only because of its intrinsic interest, but also as a remarkable example of the kind of work being produced by engaged scholars within the tradition at the local, rather than the national level.

The Maʿhad Aly's approach to Islamic legal thought challenges traditional *pesantren* approaches to *fiqh* focused on the transmission and application of *furūʿ* rulings. Following Masdar Masʿudi in maintaining that "99 percent of *fiqh* decisions are *ẓannī*," they also challenge the predominance of Shāfiʿī tradition in this milieu and call for greater freedom in moving between the established Sunnī *madhabs* in seeking out elements for the construction of new methodologies.[67] This openness toward greater room for a variety of opinions and internal Islamic debate on the nature of Islamic law is viewed by these students not just as an intellectual exercise, but as a requisite for the religious and social development of the Muslim community at large:

[64] *Fiqih Rakyat*, xx.

[65] Ibid., 103–09. Significantly, however, they generally avoid discussing this in terms of *naskh* (abrogation) which, as discussed in chapter 5, drew significant criticism upon Munawir Sjadzali's program of *Reaktualisasi*.

[66] *Rancang Fikih Pembebasan: Hasil olah pemikiran crew 'Tanwirul Afkar' Lembaga Kader Ahli Fikih Maʿhad Aly* (Sukorejo: Situbondo, 2003).

[67] *Fiqih Rakyat*, 182–87.

Opening the fonts of knowledge for the *umma* about the variety of legal opinions held by the *'ulamā'* will help to make the *umma* more mature, more wise, more accustomed to difference, more democratic, and proud of the richness of their religion.[68]

Bringing this non-formalist perspective to bear on discussions of the relationship between the Sharī'a and modern systems of positive law, the Ma'had Aly editors of *Tanwirul Afkar* maintain a distinction between what they see as the defining principle of a law (*mabda*) and its "operational form" (*bentuk operasional*). From there they argue that non-Islamic forms of positive law, including those derived from European legal traditions, can be regarded as upholding and preserving some of the essential values and principles of Islamic law, even when the operational forms (say in the area of criminal punishment) may appear quite different.[69]

The Ma'had Aly might be viewed as 'progressive' in their critical approach to traditional jurisprudential methodologies, as well as for their positions on issues such as the establishment of flexible 'productive *waqf*' and the government's role in environmental protection.[70] At the same time, however, they might also appear strikingly 'conservative' to some observers in relation to other issues, especially those connected with the role of women.[71] The complexity of positions and tensions between their opinions on various questions thus challenges Western typologies such as traditional/modern, conservative/ liberal. However, there is more than just intellectual typology involved in these apparent incongruities.

I have asked a number of figures associated with the Ma'had Aly about this, and received one of the most insightful responses from a young teacher there who called attention to the fact that many of the *kyai* themselves are involved in multiple marriages, a longstanding tradition in the *pesantren* community.[72] Thus opposing polygamy would *de facto* put the *santri* in direct opposition to their *kyai*. Furthermore, because the Prophet himself had multiple marriages, some supporters of polygamy argue that forbidding it would be tantamount to condemning the person and character

[68] Ibid., 193.

[69] "Hukum Positif *vis-à-vis* Hukum Islam," *Tanwirul Afkar* (118): September 22, 2000. The argument here runs parallel in a number of ways to that of Mun'im Sirry discussed above.

[70] *Tanwirul Afkar* (180) June 14, 2002; and (164) February 1, 2002.

[71] *Fiqih Rakyat*, 245–50, 176–81.

[72] Of course, not all *kyai* are so resistant to reforming both the theory and practice of gender relations in contemporary Indonesian Islam. K. H. Husein Muhammad, for example, has repeatedly criticized what he sees as a lack of democratic values such as liberty (*kebebasan/ al-ḥurriya*) and equality (*kesetaraan/ al-musāwā*) within the institutional culture of the NU. See Husein Muhammad, "Tradisi istinbath Hukum NU: Sebuah Kritik," in *Kritik Nalar Fiqih NU: Transformasi Paradigma Bahtsul Masa'il*, ed. Imdadun Rahmat (Jakarta: Lakpesdam, 2002), 26–35.

of Muḥammad. This particular senior *santri* moved to avoid that trap by arguing that, in his legal opinion, the prohibition of polygamy is not *li-dhātihi*, but rather *li-ghayrihi*, i.e. not a ruling based on the "essence" of polygamy itself, but rather on the tendency of it to lead to unfortunate consequences – something which he argues is clearly apparent when one actually witnesses the real suffering caused to women and children by such relationships. Faced with the institutional inertia that still holds back the implementation of their innovative intellectual formulations, a number of younger thinkers, including several increasingly prominent figures associated with the Ma'had Aly, remain critical of the slow pace of change within the NU as a whole. At the same time, however, they continue to hold *fiqh* not only as the "queen of the sciences," but also as an important avenue for change within NU.

## NEW DIRECTIONS IN MUHAMMADIYAH

Because of the dynamic development of some sectors within the 'traditionalist' *pesantren* community over the past three decades, the NU has attracted substantial outside scholarly attention in recent years. This represents a significant shift from the situation prior to that when the NU was of little interest to most foreign observers. Writing in 1985, François Raillon remarked on the unusual scholarly work of Allan Samson at that time, whom he characterizes as arguing "that Western scholars only know NU through the unfavorable views of reformist Muslims. So far NU has failed to correct this negative image, and it still has little communication with non-Muslims."[73] Shortly thereafter, however, a dramatic sea-change occurred as the NU became not only more deeply involved with foreign NGOs, but also the subject of the work of a number of international scholars who formed strong ties with many of those involved in the organization's *pesantren* as well as its politics.[74] In a paper recently presented at Singapore, Greg Fealy has critiqued this trend (and even his own involvement in it), cautioning that it has resulted in a tendency for observers to overlook developments in other sectors of the Indonesian Muslim community, including the Muhammadiyah.[75]

[73] The French-language original was published in 1985 (*Archipel* 30: 229–61). This article later appeared in English translation as François Raillon, "The New Order and Islam, or the Imbroglio of Faith and Politics," *Indonesia* 57 (1994): 207, n.15.

[74] These included many of the most recognized scholarly authorities on Islam in modern Indonesia such as Robert Hefner, Andrée Feillard, Martin van Bruinessen, Greg Barton, and Greg Fealy.

[75] "After the Cheering: A Critical Appraisal of Nahdlatul Ulama's 'Pluralism' and Western Scholarly Perceptions," in Political Legitimacy in Islamic Asia Conference (Singapore, Asia Research Institute, April 25, 2005).

Doing so would be a considerable oversight in a treatment of contemporary Indonesian Islamic thought, as over the past few years internal movements for the reform of Muhammadiyah have also made significant contributions toward the revitalization of Islamic intellectualism in contemporary Indonesia. At the forefront of this has been a group of young thinkers and activists, many of whom have come through the IAIN and have thus been exposed to a broad range of ideas on *Pembaharuan*, contextualization, and *Fiqih Sosial* in their studies of Islam. While they remain a somewhat marginal constituency of the Muhammadiyah at large, their work has found support from various sectors within the organization, and particularly in the grass-roots activist circles associated with Moeslim Abdurrahman.

In his 1995 book entitled *Islam Transformatif* Abdurrahman voiced a critique of the current state of the Muhammadiyah and called for a reorientation of the movement in order to more responsibly fulfill its founding mandate for religious revival and social transformation. In the essays published there, he rebuked the organization for directing overwhelming attention to the modernist obsessions with 'peripheral matters' such as the audible pronunciation of *niyya*, and the permissibility of men and women shaking hands. Beyond this, however, he also challenged what he considered to be the elitist nature of Islamic modernism as well as the tendencies toward the ideologization and politicization of Islam that he sees as having led to the spread of reactionary conservatism within 'modern reformist' organizations such as Muhammadiyah. In looking for ways to overcome these problems, Abdurrahman drew inspiration from the work of critical Muhammadiyah scholar Kuntowijoyo (d. 2005) in seeking a new, '*profetis*' format for the social sciences that could be put into the service of ethical endeavors for the improvement of society.[76] This, Abdurrahman argues, would require cooperative efforts with preachers, *'ulamā'*, and social scientists to transform the *umma* through the application of new, socially engaged ideas on religion and society. To further their work of "collective *ijtihād*" he calls for the establishment of a new center for the study of Islam, complete with an information center and library facilities for documentation. He has since begun some work in that direction himself on a modest scale in a converted house that now serves as the headquarters for a group calling themselves the Young Muhammadiyah Intellectual Network (Jaringan Intelektual Muhammadiyah Muda/ JIMM).

[76] See, for example, Kuntowijoyo, *Paradigma Islam: Interpretasi untuk Aksi* (Bandung: Mizan, 1991); and *Intelektualisme Muhammadiyah: Menyongsong Era Baru* (Bandung: Mizan, 1995).

Abdurrahman has become a kind of mentor for younger thinkers and activists associated with JIMM intent on transforming the Muhammadiyah from within with an emphasis on social engagement.[77] In describing the project of JIMM in the preface to a collection of essays produced by its members, he has highlighted what he sees as three major characteristics: (1) a new openness of approach to hermeneutics; (2) an emphasis on 'liberation' and 'resistance to hegemony' and (3) a sense of practical engagement with "the New Social Movement."[78] Despite such over-arching characterizations, however, JIMM itself is internally diverse, some of its members have even come to it from out of NU backgrounds. Most of those affiliated with the movement share an intellectually imaginative orientation toward Islam and an affinity for grass-roots social activism. They pursue these interests through an array of overlapping methods ranging from forms of social critique building upon the work of Gramsci, as well as that of Roman Catholic liberation theologians,[79] to new models of scriptural exegesis[80] and a critical re-evaluation of the ways in which conceptions of gender are operative within the ideals and institutions of Muhammadiyah.[81]

In ways that, in their rhetorical form, reflect concerns within the NU to create a model of *Post-traditionalism*, the young activists associated with JIMM call for the development of a *Post-Puritan* vision for the Muhammadiyah.[82] For example, Abd. Rohim Ghazali and Zakiyuddin Baidhawy have called for a reappraisal of Muhammadiyah's fundamental concern with what its adherents commonly refer to as 'TBC' (*Takhayul, Bid'ah*, and *Churafat*). Rather than seeing the real targets of reform as these 'imaginations, innovations, and superstitions (respectively)' in religious beliefs

[77] See, for example, M. Hilmi Faiq and Pradana Boy ZTF, *Kembali ke al-Qur'an Menafsir Makna Zaman: Suara-suara Kaum Muda Muhammadiyah* (Malang: Universitas Muhammadiyah Malang, 2004), 279–93.

[78] Moeslim Abdurrahman "Pengantar," in M. Hilmi Faiq and Pradana Boy ZTF, *Kembali ke al-Qur'an Menafsir Makna Zaman: Suara-suara Kaum Muda Muhammadiyah* (Malang: Universitas Muhammadiyah Malang, 2004), vii–xviii.

[79] To this end they have organized discussions of the work of both major figures in the development of this movement such as Paolo Freire and major Indonesian interpreters of liberation theology in relation to local contexts such as Wahono Nitiprawiro's *Teologi Pembebasan* (Yogykarta: LKiS, 2000).

[80] See, for example, Ahmad Fuad Fanani, "Hermeneutika dan Alternatif Konstekstualisasi al-Qur'an," *Tanwir: Jurnal Pemikiran Agama dan Peradaban* 1.2 (July 2003): 177–89; and M. Hilmi Faiq and Pradana Boy ZTF, *Kembali ke al-Qur'an Menafsir Makna Zaman: Suara-suara Kaum Muda Muhammadiyah* (Malang: Universitas Muhammadiyah Malang, 2004).

[81] Tuti Alawiyah Surandi, "Dakwah Kultural dan Posisi Perempuan di Indonesia," in *Muhammadiyah sebagai Tenda Kultural*, ed. Moeslim Abdurrahman (Jakarta: Ideo Press, 2003), 93–108.

[82] Hilman Latief, "Post-Puritanisme Muhammadiyah: Studi Perfulatan Wacana Keagamaan Kaum Muda Muhammadiyah, 1995–2002," *Tanwir: Jurnal Pemikiran Agama dan Peradaban* 1.2 (July 2003): 43–102.

and practices, the thinkers and activists associated with JIMM argue for a new, religiously based critique of such 'idolatrous' dangers to the community as "corruption, nepotism, and the cult of individualism."[83] Thus in place of what Moeslim Abdurrahman has critiqued as a stultified emphasis on *da'wa* as a form of 'propaganda'[84] JIMM directs its work toward the development of what have come to be referred to as 'alternative cultural *da'wa*' strategies that are both 'new' and at the same time true to their understandings of the "original, dynamic vision of Muhammadiyah" put forward by the organization's founder K. H. Ahmad Dahlan.[85]

Among proponents of this movement there is a developing discourse on issues such as 'tolerance', 'pluralism', and 'multiculturalism' – issues that have not previously been central in established Muhammadiyah paradigms of rationalizing reform and the purification of religious practice. A glimpse into some of ways in which this new orientation toward local cultures (*budaya lokal*) has been reimagined by young Muhammadiyah thinkers in the early twenty-first century can be seen in the recent publication of several volumes of collected essays with such titles as *Religion and the Plurality of Local Cultures*[86] and *The Synergy of Religion and Local Culture*.[87] The latter volume, developed out of presentations and discussions of the Halaqah Tarjih in cooperation with the Majlis Tarjih dan Pengembangan Pemikiran Islam PP Muhammadiyah at the January 2002 Muhammadiyah conference in Bali, contains a preface by Komaruddin Hidayat that signals some of the remarkable recent changes that have occurred within the Muhammadiyah in their attitude toward local cultural practices.[88]

83 Moeslim Abdurrahman, ed., *Muhammadiyah sebagai Tenda Kultural* (Jakarta: Ideo Press, 2003).

84 See, for example, Moeslim Abdurrahman, *Islam sebagai Kritik Sosial* (Jakarta: Penerbit Erlangga, 2003), in which he argues for the need to reenergize the Muhammadiyah "movement of social liberation" with a more "open and substantial" vision, rather than a stultified emphasis on *da'wa* as a form of propaganda.

85 Ahmad Fuad Fanani, "Membendung Arus Formalisme Muhammadiyah," in *Muhammadiyah sebagai Tenda Kultural*, pp. 15–29. More recently, a number of senior Indonesian Muslim figures have also publicly promoted such views of a perceived discrepancy between the ideals of the Muhammadiyah's founder and the current state of affairs. In June 2005, for example, former Minister of Religious Affairs Tarmizi Taher published an article along these lines in the national Muslim daily *Republika* entitled, "Memetik Nilai-nilai Pluralisme dari KH Ahmad Dahlan." Coming from such an established figure, the piece attracted considerable criticism from some Islamist factions, including Hidayatullah: www.hidayatullah.com/index.php?option=com_content&task=view&id=1946&Itemid=0

86 Abdul Manan, *Agama dan Pluralitas Budaya Lokal* (2002).

87 M. Thoyibi *et al.*, eds., *Sinergi Agama dan Budaya Lokal: Dialektika Muhammadiyah dan Seni Lokal* (Surakarta: Muhammadiyah University Press, 2003).

88 Komaruddin Hidayat, "Prolog: Budaya Lokal dalam Perspektif Baru," in *Sinergi Agama dan Budaya Lokal.*

In reading some other new Muhammadiyah writings on approaches to *budaya local*, however, there are clearly divergent tendencies between those who advocate a general openness to cultural diversity in local understandings of Islam, and those who advocate familiarizing one's self with 'culture' in order to use it strategically as a tool for conducting *da 'wa* with the aim of eventually bringing those '*lokal*' forms of Islam more in line with the modernist Muslim standards of Muhammadiyah. Those associated with JIMM have tended to critique Muhammadiyah exponents of the latter, 'strategic' approach to local cultures, marking a significant divide within the organization that is currently being played out on both the intellectual and institutional levels.[89]

An analogous division within the organization is being played out in debates over Muhammadiyah's understanding of Islamic law and its jurisprudential practices. In the 1930s the Majelis Tarjih Muhammadiyah was founded as the locus for *fiqh* discussions within the organization.[90] Since then, however, some critical observers have seen this body as contributing to a rigid formalism in the Muhammadiyah's interpretation of Islam.[91] In response to critiques of this kind, the Majelis Tarjih has issued a number of official statements on particular reforms of methodology and procedure since the mid-1980s.[92] However, as its name indicates, the primary function of this body is *tarjīḥ*, in the technical sense of selecting the 'most correct' scriptural indicator upon which to base an Islamic legal ruling, thus perpetuating an orientation to the production of Islamic law that is essentially scripturalist.[93] At the 1995 Muhammadiyah conference in Banda Aceh, however, the name of the board assigned the task of determining Islamic legal rulings was officially changed from *Majelis Tarjih* to

[89] Abd Rohim Ghazali, "Dari Dogmatis ke Kultural: Refleksi Kritis Dakwah Muhammadiyah," and Zakiyuddin Baidhawy, "Dakwah Kultural *vs.* Supremasi Islam Murni," in *Muhammadiyah sebagai Tenda Kultural*, 1–14, 77–92. At the same time, however, the work of JIMM has raised concerns in other segments of the Muhammadiyah community; see, for example, Samsul Nizar "Pluralisme dan Toleransi: Ada yang Perlu Diwaspadai," and the articles by Abd Rohim Ghazali, Zuly Qodir, Hilman Latief, and Achmad Fedyani Saifuddin in *Tanwir: Jurnal Pemikiran Agama dan Peradaban* 1.1 (May 2003): 7–146. Critiques of JIMM have also been featured in *Tabligh: Menyatukan Visi dan Misi Umat*, which ran its critique of their "deviant" ideas of "liberalisme, pluralisme, and inklusivisme" as the lead article of its April 2004 issue (2.9).

[90] For a general introduction to this *fatwā* institution, see Syamsul Anwar, "*Fatwā*, Purification and Dynamization: A Study of *Tarjīḥ* in Muhammadiyah," *ILS* 12.1 (2005): 27–44.

[91] See, for example, Syafii Anwar, "Muhammadiyah, Organisasi Pembaharu yang Jalan di Tempat," in *Muhammadiyah sebagai Tenda Kultural*, 119.

[92] H. Asjmuni Abdurrahman, *Manhaj Tarjih Muhammadiyah: Metodologi dan Aplikasi* (Yogyakarta: Pustaka Pelajar, 2002), 105, 10–12.

[93] See, for example, M. Fathurrahman Jamil, *Metode Ijtihad Majelis Tarjih Muhammadiyah* (Jakarta: Logos, 1995).

*Majelis Tarjih dan Perkembangan Pemikiran Islam* ('Assembly for *tarjīḥ* and the development of Islamic Thought'). The addition to this name was intended to signal a broader mandate for the development of new interpretations of Islam than had previously been the case, however it was formally retracted in 2005 and the wider mandate apparently abandoned at the national level.[94]

Despite this relative reversal of the trend toward greater openness, some Muhammadiyah thinkers and activists, including those involved with JIMM, continue to advocate moving beyond 'classical modernist' approaches and to reconceptualize the very practice of *ijtihād* within the organization.[95] In formulating their new approaches to Islamic legal reasoning, Muhammadiyah thinkers have drawn on the work of the contemporary Moroccan philosopher Muḥammad 'Ābid al-Jābirī.[96] In particular they have taken up his tripartite categorization of *ijtihād* as: *bayāni, qiyāsi,* and *istiṣlāḥi* as referring to rulings based respectively upon clear scriptural texts (*naṣṣ qaṭ'ī*), those from texts which do not directly provide a clear ruling, and those based upon the 'spirit' (*jiwa*) of the text in the interest of the common social good (*maṣlaḥa*). This has allowed them to establish a basic vocabulary in which to carry on their discussions on the development of a *Post-Puritan* agenda for the Muhammadiyah.

Alongside this revitalization of activity among young thinkers and activists associated with the two long-standing Indonesian Muslim organizations of NU and Muhammadiyah, the turn of the twenty-first century has also introduced other new individuals and institutions onto the national stage to participate in expanded debates on religion and society. These are myriad, and a complete survey of them is simply not possible within the scope of this chapter. However, to get some sense of the range of orientations of these emerging voices, the following pages will set forth brief discussions of two much smaller Muslim groups: the Jaringan Islam Liberal (JIL) and the Hizbut Tahrir Indonesia (HTI). These two groups espouse radically different visions of Islam and its role in shaping social transformation. Their respective agendas are so disparate, in fact, that they might be viewed as

94 The guidelines for pursuing such work were further set out at the National *Tarjīḥ* Conference held at Jakarta in July 2000, where the Muhammadiyah announced a new comprehensive methodology of *tajdīd* and *ijtihād*. Abdurrahman, *Manhaj Tarjih Muhammadiyah*, 105.

95 Anjar Nugroho, "al-Ijtihad al-Mu'ashir: Paradigma Pengembangan Pemikiran Islam di Muhammadiyah," in *Kembali ke al-Qur'an Menafsir Makna Zaman*, 297–316.

96 Amin Abdullah, rector of the IAIN Yogyakarta, is often credited with introducing al-Jābirī's thought to the Muhammadiyah, after having himself becoming acquainted with it during studies in Ankara. As discussed above, al-Jābirī's works have also been influential for young thinkers and activists within the NU, although sometimes they have been attracted to significantly different aspects of his work than have their Muhammadiyah counterparts.

bookends marking opposite outer limits of the continually swelling shelf of Islamic texts produced in contemporary Indonesia. The views of neither JIL nor HTI can thus be taken as being in any way representative of mainstream Muslim public opinion in the country. Nevertheless, mapping their respective views on Islam – and on Islamic law in particular – can provide some sense of perspective on the wide expanse of middle ground upon which ongoing discussions are taking place.

## JARINGAN ISLAM LIBERAL

The Jaringan Islam Liberal (JIL/Liberal Islam Network) is a loosely affiliated community of scholars, artists, and activists dedicated to open interpretations of Islam on issues of pluralism and democracy. Many of JIL's early participants were young Muslims who had come out of *pesantren* backgrounds or had other NU affiliations, and it was initially formed through discussions of Islam taking shape on an on-line mailing list (*islamliberal@yahoogroups.com*) in 2001. JIL entered into the broader Indonesian public sphere the following year when one of the organizers of this group, Ulil Abshar Abdalla, wrote an article on the *Paramadina* edition of Charles Kurzman's anthology *Liberal Islam* for the prominent national newspaper *Kompas*.[97] JIL's increasingly ambitious public assertion of a Liberal Islam platform had the effect of triggering a barrage of critiques in the Muslim and broader national media and catapulted Abdalla to public prominence.[98]

He was born at Kajen, Central Java, in 1967 and first studied in *pesantren* there, including some time at the Madrasah Mathali'ul Falah under the direction of Sahal Mahfudz. There he was inspired by the openness of that *kyai* in working together on community development projects with NGOs, as well as by the range of texts that he gained access to through Mahfudh's private library. During this period Abdalla began to read not only classical Arabic texts of the *pesantren* milieu (*kitab kuning*), but also modern works by Muslim thinkers including Fazlur Rahman, Mawdudi, and Sayyid Quṭb alongside issues of the LP3ES journal *Prisma*. He recalls the excitement in the air for many young *santri* at that time as Abdurrahman Wahid rose to prominence at the 1984 NU Muktamar in Situbondo and works by Sahal

97 Daniel S. Lev, "Menciptakan Kembali Indonesia," in *Wajah Islam Liberal di Indonesia*, ed. Luthfi Assyaukanie (Jakarta: JIL, 2002), xi–xiv.

98 For a discussion of these developments, see Komaruddin Hidayat, "Contemporary Liberal Islam in Indonesia, Pluralism, and the Secular State," in *A Portrait of Contemporary Indonesian Islam*, ed. Chaider S. Bamualim (Jakarta: Pusat Bahasa dan Budaya UIN, 2005), 53–65.

Mahfudh and Masdar Masʿudi were being published in the P3M journal, *Pesantren*. In 1985 Abdalla was invited to join a P3M project for the critical study of *kitab kuning*, and by then he had moved to Jakarta to be more closely involved with developments in the NGO sector there.

In 1993, he began studying at LIPIA, a Saudi-funded school in Jakarta that offered full scholarships for its students. Abdalla says that he found the studies there shallow, and sought intellectual stimulation elsewhere, particularly in the *halqah* that served as the embryo for the later development of the *Partai Keadilan*, as well as in discussion groups forming around the campus of the IAIN Syarif Hidayatullah in Ciputat. He also joined a group of other disaffected LIPIA students in the formation of their own study club called the Kajian 164. This group occasionally invited speakers such as Masdar Masʿudi, who inspired them with his radical reconceptualizations of *qaṭʿī* and *ẓannī*, as well as his vision of social justice elaborated in terms of *maṣlaḥa*.[99]

Abdalla himself argues for a dynamic vision of Islamic interpretations in relation to reconceptualizations of the exegetical categories of *qaṭʿī* and *ẓannī* as well as a revived appreciation of the agency of human reason in the practice of Qurʾān interpretation. Such approaches, however, are anathema to Indonesia's Islamists who have launched a barrage of attacks against Abdalla and JIL in various media. One particularly vivid example of this was published as the fantastic description of a dystopic Indonesian future culminating in the tragic presidency of one 'Uzil Bashar Afdhalla.'[100] It depicts a scenario nothing short of nightmarish for the country's *daʿwa*-minded Muslims. "Through the generous funding of the Asia Foundation," the agendas of the "anti-Sharīʿa, sin-loving" JIL make great headway in the first decade of the twenty-first century. Women and transvestites lead public prayers, and homosexuals are allowed to marry. More and more Indonesian Muslims come to abandon their faith, and in 2017 Indonesia becomes a "secular" nation through a referendum sponsored by Australia, Turkey, Israel, and the United States, whereupon there follows an aggressive rise of Christian separatist movements in the eastern archipelago and civil war in the streets of Jakarta.[101]

Despite such *ad hominem* diatribes, however, JIL is more than simply a brand-name for Abdalla's high-profile positions. Though he may be the

99 Personal communication, June 2004 at Jakarta.

100 The play on Abdalla's name here is obvious. What is striking, however, is the way in which this diatribe echoes some of the rhetoric promulgated in conservative Christian media in the United States during the run-up to the 2004 presidential elections.

101 This 2002 article published in *Suara Hidayatullah* has been summarized and commented upon in Madinier, "Du temps des chameaux," 160–61.

current celebrity face of the movement, JIL is composed of a large and diverse group of Indonesian Muslims, a number of whom are emerging as important thinkers in their own right. At the forefront is Luthfi Assyaukanie. He was born and raised in *pesantren* circles and then pursued advanced studies in the Middle East. However, unlike most Indonesian students studying in the Arab world, he went not to Egypt, or Saudi Arabia, but to Jordan. There Assyaukanie acquired a different perspective on 'totalizing' visions of Islam promoted by the *Ikhwān al-Muslimīn*, and grew increasingly critical of what he viewed as the unrealistic and misguided nature of their formal agendas as he observed their parliamentary failures in Amman during the late 1980s. He also used his time there to travel to other Muslim majority countries in the region, through which he developed an appreciation for the great diversity of "Islams" and a vision of Islam as a continually unfolding process at work in human history, rather than as an eternally unchanging system of law and doctrine.[102]

In a number of ways then, JIL can be seen as carrying forward some of these conversations as well as aspects of Islam and modernity by some of the *Pembaharuan* thinkers discussed in chapter 5. A major theme in JIL discussions has accordingly been the importance of respecting the diversity of cultures and interpretations within Islam, both in its historical tradition and in contemporary conversations. Assyaukanie and others promoted this idea through a JIL public relations campaign entitled '*Islam warna-warni*' ('an Islam of many colors').[103] Abdalla has continued conversations on this theme by revisiting the much-quoted Qur'ānic verse about the 'rope of God' that has been a common trope in conversations of many Muslim communities in Indonesia and elsewhere, interpreting this image not in terms of monolithic unity, but rather as a visual symbol of the spectrum of possible positions within the *umma*:

> Do people forget that ropes have two ends, and a stretch in the middle? There are those who grab the rope of God on one end, others who are fortunate enough to find a space in the middle, but there are still others who find their place on the other end. All are grabbing the rope of God, and with the great differences of opinion within the *umma*, they are all holding fast.[104]

102 Luthfi Assyaukanie, ed., *Wajah Liberal Islam di Indonesia* (Jakarta: Jaringan Islam Liberal, 2002), xxiii.

103 Luthfi Assyaukanie, "Islam Warna-Warni" (2002): http://islamlib.com/id/index.php?page=article&id=150.

104 Ulil Abshar Abdulla, "Kata Pengantar," in Nasaruddin Umar, *Qur'an untuk Perempuan* (Jakarta: Jaringan Islam Liberal, 2002), x.

In this vein he reacts sharply to those Muslims making absolute truth claims for their interpretations of Islam, and characterizes scripturalist approaches to defining Islam as a political strategy, rather than a jurisprudential method.

For Assyaukanie, Abdalla, and their colleagues at JIL, beneath this diversity, Islam maintains its coherence in communication with its fundamental values of justice and equality. This general mission has a pronounced impact upon the way in which thinkers and activists associated with JIL address particular issues of Islamic law and its relevance to contemporary Indonesian society. In January 2003, JIL hosted a workshop on these very topics to which they invited not only a number of prominent Indonesian Muslim intellectuals, but also the Sudani-American legal scholar Abdullahi Ahmed an-Na'im.[105] These JIL discussions of various Islamic issues, including law, are disseminated throughout Indonesia and beyond in a number of ways, including not only print publications but also an extensive website (www.islamlib.com) and a weekly radio talk show hosted by Abdalla. In its use of modern media, however, JIL faces stiff competition from the tech-savvy communications operations of Indonesia's burgeoning Islamist movements.

## INDONESIAN AND INTERNATIONAL ISLAMISTS

Chapter 4 examined some of the impacts that the permutations of political Islamism into the *da 'wa* movement under the New Order had for discussions of Islamic law in Indonesia. Developments along these lines took new turns in the context of the dramatic social changes during the final years of Suharto's New Order and the opening up of the Indonesian public sphere in the *Reformasi* period of the late 1990s. During that time, some *da 'wa* activists then began sensing a change in the weather with the government's warming to certain forms of organized Islam and certain segments of the Muslim student population were re-energized and inspired by a new generation of activists, a number of whom had spent time studying in the Middle East, and especially in Saudi Arabia.[106] In this, they differed from earlier generations of leaders in organizations like the Dewan Dakwah Islamiyah Indonesia (DDII) who were educated largely in Western-style schools in the Netherlands Indies/Indonesia.

105 Several of the papers, and excerpts from the discussions there have been published in Burhanuddin, ed., *Syariat Islam: Pandangan Muslim Liberal* (Jakarta: Jaringan Islam Liberal, 2003).

106 Lukman Hakiem, *Perjalanan Mencari Keadilan dan Persatuan: Biografi Dr. Anwar Harjono, SH* (Jakarta: Media Da'wah, 1993), 419ff.

On campuses from the 1980s onward, Islamic activists of an internally diverse range of ideological orientations had been gaining confidence and cultural momentum on the campuses of some of Indonesia's leading 'secular' (i.e. non-confessional) universities, including the University of Indonesia in Jakarta, Gadjah Mada University in Yogyakarta, and the Bandung Institute of Technology. At these and other places across the archipelago at this time, students began organizing themselves into energized 'cadres' or 'cells' that characterized what has come to be known as the *usroh* (lit. 'family') movement. This model of organization was based upon that of the Muslim Brotherhood, which was also an increasingly important source of ideological inspiration for Indonesian Islamist groups at that time. These *Ikhwānī* influences were particularly pronounced in the *Gerakan Tarbiyah* that gained momentum in the 1980s.

Under the heavy strictures placed upon Islamic political parties by the New Order regime during that period, the *usroh* model of activist organization flourished. It was specifically designed to foster intense relationships of mutual support and participation in religious observances that were directed toward the acquiring of Islamic knowledge, and engaging social activism, but on a small scale that did not register with those on the lookout for manifestations of mass political mobilization. As Greg Fealy and Anthony Bubalo have succinctly characterized it:

> Throughout the 1980s and early 1990s, the *Tarbiyah* movement remained overtly apolitical and appeared to the regime and university administrators as primarily a religious movement that posed little threat to the established order. Accordingly it was able to access state resources for training and predication programs.[107]

Indonesian Islamist activists associated with the movement were thus also able to consolidate their organization and gain greater public prominence, and they grew increasingly visible in the turbulent atmosphere following the fall of Suharto in 1998.[108] Of particular importance was the Kesatuan Aksi Mahasiswa Muslim Indonesia (KAMMI), which played an active role in street protests that accompanied the collapse of the New Order.[109] In the new political atmosphere of the proliferation of parties following this, some of these same Islamist activists came together to form various new organizations, one of the most successful of which was the Partai Keadilan

[107] Fealy and Bubalo, *Joining the Caravan*, 69.

[108] Many of them, including the Partai Keadilan Sejahtera thus praised "Demokrasi" as making possible their ascent to the national political stage. See, for example, H. Nandang Burhanudin, in *Penegakan Syariat Islam Menurut Partai Keadilan* (Jakarta: Al-Jannah, 2003), 1–5.

[109] Richard Kraince, "The Role of Islamic Student Groups in the *Reformasi* Struggle: KAMMI (Kesatuan Aksi Mahasiswa Muslim Indonesia)," *SI* 7.1 (2000): 1–50.

(Sejahtera) which was first organized around a platform that echoed many ideas about Islam, law, and society that had been popularized earlier by Natsir.[110] In the 1999 elections it managed to secure a handful of seats in the National Assembly by positioning itself as 'the party of *da 'wa*,' although it has since made a conscious effort to de-emphasize the formalistically 'Islamic' elements of its agenda through a turn toward broader appeals for justice, prosperity, and 'clean government'.[111]

This is not so say, however, that appeals for the formal implementation of the Sharī'a have disappeared from the public discourses of Indonesian Islam in the twenty-first century. In August 2000, for example, motions to restore the 'Seven Words' of the 1945 Jakarta Charter formally obliging Muslims in the country to observe Islamic law were put before the MPR by factions associated with Partai Bulan Bintang, Partai Persatuan Pembangunan (PPP), and other Islamist groups.[112] After a series of sometimes heated debates in the national assembly, however, the measure was defeated by opposition from larger Muslim organizations including the NU and Muhammadiyah.[113] Since then, much of the debate over the formal implementation of Islamic law in contemporary Indonesia has shifted from the national to the regional levels. During the *Reformasi* period, local initiatives for the formal implementation of some form of the Sharī'a have been advanced (with various degrees of accomplishment) in a number of provinces including West Java, South Kalimantan, and South Sulawesi. The most extensive case of this can be found in Aceh under the 'special autonomy' granted to the region by Jakarta in 2003.

The most comprehensive ideological agenda for the formal institution of an Islamic state in Indonesia, however, has been that advocated by the Hizbut Tahrir Indonesia (HTI) – a group which is not only connected to, but which takes its entire ideological agenda directly from an

[110] For more on this, see H. Nandang Burhanudin. *Penegakan Syariat Islam Menurut Partai Keadilan* (Jakarta: Al-Jannah, 2003), 91–145.

[111] For an examination of the history of this party and its relation to Islamist activists in the late New Order period, as well as its development in the *Reformasi* period, see Mathias Diederich, "A Closer Look at *Dakwah* and Politics in Indonesia: The *Partai Keadilan*," *Archipel* 64 (2002): 101–15.

[112] Joni Sumarjan, *Laporan Program Pemantauan Parlemen: Tinjauan Kritis Respon Parlemen Terhadap Masalah Piagam Jakarta Debat Penerapan Syariat Islam* (Jakarta: INSIDE, 2002), 2–5. One of the major sponsors of these motions, Partai Bulan Bintang, was led by Yusril Ihza Mahendra, who imagines himself and his party as carrying forward the legacy of Masjumi in the post-Suharto era. See Sabar Sitanggang, Maulana Muladi, and Agus Salam, *Catatan Kritis dan Percikan Pemikiran Yusril Ihza Mahendra* (Jakarta: Bulan Bintang, 2001).

[113] A collection of articles from the public debates that surrounded these motions has been published as Kurniawan Zein and Sarifuddin HA, eds., *Syariat Islam Yes/ Syariat Islam No: Dilema Piagam Jakarta dalam Amandemen UUD 1945* (Jakarta: Paramadina, 2001).

organization founded in the modern Middle East. Originally established in Palestine and Jordan in 1953 by Taqī al-dīn al-Nabhānī, the international movement of Ḥizb al-Taḥrīr has been based in London since the 1980s.[114] It was introduced to Indonesia in 1987, at first on university campuses in Jakarta, Bogor, Bandung, Yogya, and Surabaya. Under the New Order HTI membership tended to be secretive, but the organization's politically quietist public face earned them some degree of tolerance from the government.[115] While the organization has generally endorsed non-violent action as its modus operandi, it is the professed aim of the Ḥizb al-Taḥrīr to bring about a complete social transformation through the re-establishment of the caliphate and the comprehensive implementation of the Sharīʿa.[116]

Remarking on the spread of this organization from the Middle East to Central Asia, Olivier Roy and Mariam Abou Zahab have noted that the Ḥizb al-Taḥrīr texts circulating in that region "appear to be word-for-word translations of documents published in Arabic in the Middle East."[117] The situation seems to be the same for the textual and ideological productions in Indonesian, although some further elaborations of these core ideas in relation to current events are produced locally by Indonesians associated with the movement in the HTI periodical entitled *al-Wa'ie*.[118] There are, as far as I have been able to ascertain, no significant original thinkers attached to this organization in Indonesia, and the senior leadership itself seems unable to even comment in depth on the modern Arabic texts that they hold to be at the heart of the movement's vision for the implementation of the Sharīʿa and the establishment of a new caliphate and an Islamist utopia. The plans for the legal system of such a state are particularly vague, but greater amounts of work have been put into outlining political and economic aspects of their aspirations for a radically remade world *umma*.[119]

[114] For more on the international development of Ḥizb al-Taḥrīr, see Suha Taji-Farouki, *A Fundamental Quest: Hizb al-Tahrir and the Search for the Islamic Caliphate* (London: Grey Seal, 1996).

[115] Darul Aqsha, Dick van der Meij, and Johan Hendrik Meuleman, *Islam in Indonesia: A Survey of Developments from 1988 to March 1993* (Jakarta: INIS, 1995), 455.

[116] Official statements of the Ḥizb al-Taḥrīr agenda in English can be found on the organization's official website: www.hizb-ut-tahrir.org/english/english.html. The HTI has its own site at www.al-islam.or.id/.

[117] Olivier Roy and Mariam Abou Zahab, *Islamist Networks: The Afghan–Pakistan Connection*, trans. John King (New York: Columbia University Press, 2004), 9.

[118] The monthly *Al-Wa'ie: Membangun Kesadaran Umat* has been in circulation since 2001 and is available through selected local agents in most of Indonesia's provinces. It is also available online at the HTI website: http://hizbut-tahrir.or.id/main.php?page=alwaie.

[119] One often discussed dimension of this is their call for a new world economy based on the gold standard and the minting of an "Islamic form of currency" (*dīnār, dirham*) in an attempt to counter the pervasive patterns of the current economic domination of Muslim societies by multinationals.

Although ideologically on the fringe, the HTI has been gaining a degree of popularity in recent years by capitalizing on the mounting anger that many Indonesian Muslims feel toward the 'the West' for its apparent antagonism toward Islam. In this the HTI can be seen as partaking in, and benefiting from, a significantly broader cultural trend that Robert Hefner has recently discussed in terms of 'the conservative turn' in Indonesian Islam.[120] To those who for various reasons feel such increasing frustration with the ways in which the dominant geopolitical order is perceived to be negatively impacting the lives of Muslims at home and abroad, the HTI and other radical Islamist groups present attractive alternative visions of social transformation and clear models for the establishment of justice under a comprehensive legal system.

## MORE NEW SCHOOLS, AND 'SCHOOLS OF THOUGHT'

Islamist movements have, however, thus far had little success in recruiting members on IAIN campuses, as their ideologies of essentialized Islamic identity tend to be more attractive on the campuses of 'secular' institutions of higher learning where students are not regularly exposed to the same range and depth of historically contextualized approaches to Islam. The National Islamic University (Universitas Islam Negeri/UIN – formerly IAIN Syarif Hidayatullah) at Jakarta in particular has emerged as a national center of Islamic intellectualism in contemporary Indonesia and a significant bulwark against the general rise of reactionary Islamist movements. Referring to the location of its campus to the west of the city, some have even come to speak of the existence of a distinctive 'Ciputat school' of contemporary Indonesian Islamic thought (*madzhab Ciputat*).[121] In particular, the Ciputat campus has become associated with research focusing on critical re-readings of classical texts coupled with empirical and historically contextualized approaches to, and comparative perspectives on, Muslim traditions in formulating a vision of religion and its potential role in contemporary Indonesian society.[122] Faculty and students engaged

[120] Robert W. Hefner, "The Conservative Turn in Indonesian Islam: Politics and Education," talk presented at the Institute for Defence and Strategic Studies, Nanyang Technical University, Singapore, July 24, 2006.

[121] See, for example, Edy A. Effendy, ed., *Dekonstruksi Islam Mazhab Ciputat* (Bandung: Zaman Wacana Mulia, 1999).

[122] Dadi Darmadi, "IAIN dalam Wacana Intelektual Islam Indonesia," 333–68. Komaruddin Hidayat and Hendro Prasetyo, eds., *Problem dan Prospek IAIN: Antologi Pendidikan Tinggi Islam* (Jakarta: Departemen Agama RI, 2000); Fuad Jabali and Jamhari, eds., *IAIN dan Modernisasi Islam di Indonesia* (Jakarta: UIN Jakarta Press, 2003), 139–63.

in such work have taken on a considerable prominence in discussions of Islam, law, and society, on both the local and national levels through their frequent contributions to popular print and electronic media, as well as their participation in seminars, workshops, and other events in a variety of settings.

The IAIN Jakarta campus has been the site of a number of important intellectual developments for over three decades, and particularly since Harun Nasution (d. 1998) headed the institution in 1973–84.[123] In the 1990s, however, a series of developments had further strengthened its reputation as a center for dynamic and creative Muslim thought. Much of this has taken place under the direction of Azyumardi Azra. Born in West Sumatra to a Muhammadiyah-affiliated family in 1955, Azra was educated there in 'modern-style' schools before moving to Jakarta to attend the IAIN. In 1982 he went to New York, where he earned M.A. and Ph.D. degrees in History and Middle Eastern Studies at Columbia University.[124] Since returning to Indonesia in 1992, he has produced a remarkable range of published work covering historical studies as well as contributions to contemporary Muslim thought,[125] while at the same time serving in a number of teaching and administrative positions at his Ciputat *alma mater*. Since 1998 he has held the highest position of leadership on campus (*rektor*), during which time the school has undergone a vigorous phase of expansion and development.

From his position as Rektor, as well as a researcher, Azra remains extraordinarily engaged with work in various fields currently being purused in international scholarly and educational circles, frequently attending conferences and seminars abroad and hosting considerable numbers of foreign scholars at his campus in Ciputat. Through such activities he maintains an extensive and in-depth familiarity with international trends in higher

[123] Nasution was an active scholar as well as an academic administrator. Much of his own published work focused on matters of theology rather than jurisprudence, and was directed toward fostering a renaissance of Neo-Mu'tazili rationalism in Indonesia. For a collection of Nasution's essays on the subject, see *Islam Rasional: Gagasan dan Pemikiran* (Bandung: Mizan, 1995). For secondary studies of this phenomenon, see Saiful Muzani, "Mu'tazilah Theology and the Modernization of the Indonesian Muslim Community," *SI* 1.1 (1994): 93–131; Richard C. Martin and Mark Woodward, with Dwi S. Atmaja, *Defenders of Reason in Islam: Mu'tazilism from Medieval School to Modern Symbol* (Oxford: One World, 1997).

[124] A revised edition of this work has since been published as Azyumardi Azra, *The Origins of Islamic Reformism in Southeast Asia: Networks of Malay-Indonesian and Middle Eastern 'Ulamā' in the Seventeenth and Eighteenth Centuries* (Honolulu: University of Hawaii Press, 2004).

[125] In addition to publishing at least a dozen books and countless articles, Azra also served as the founding editor of *Studia Islamika* (SI), a tri-lingual – Indonesian, English, and Arabic – academic journal focusing on studies of Islam in Indonesia by international, as well as local scholars.

education and an outstanding openness to international cooperation, hosting Fulbright scholars, regularly inviting speakers and teaching staff from around the world, and establishing a range of formal programs of cooperation.[126] This cosmopolitan character that Azra has cultivated on campus has been a considerable asset in furthering his project of expanding the IAIN's mandate and the transformation of the Ciputat campus into a full university (UIN) with additional faculties for studies beyond an Islamic religious curriculum, and a professionalized research agenda.

In the course of these developments, changes have also been made in the specific area of the teaching of Islamic law on campus. In 2003, for example, the name of the law faculty was reformulated as the Fakultas Syariah dan Qanun, with a revised mission statement that declares the aims of working toward the development not only of Islamic jurisprudence, but of positive law as well.[127] Its institutional structure reflects these orientations, with departments of Islamic Personal Law, Islamic Criminal Law and Legal-Political Science, Comparative Jurisprudence and Law, and *Mu'āmalāt*, within which are a number of popular majors ranging from "Religious Courts" to "Sharī'a Banking and Islamic Insurance." The potential for the social influence of graduates from UIN and other IAIN faculties of 'Sharī'a and *Qanun*' has, furthermore, recently been expanded with the promulgation of Presidential Instruction (*Inpres*) no. 18/2003 that made it possible for graduates of these faculties to practice as advocates. A sampling of the work of students and faculty in this college at the Ciputat campus can be found in the pages of its official journal, entitled *Ahkam*.

Another major center on the Ciputat campus for work on issues of religion, law, and society, is the university's postgraduate program (*Pascasarjana*), which has pioneered interdisciplinary approaches to interpreting aspects of the Islamic tradition in light of historical contexts and contemporary social realities. Students and faculty involved in this project are also active as editors and contributors to the on-campus publication of over a dozen academic journals in Indonesian, Arabic, and English.[128] The contents of these publications, moreover, indicate a substantial range of diverse orientations toward Islam on campus, and thus it appears as if there is any

126 The most substantial of which has been the formation of the college of *Dirāsāt Islāmiyya* in a collaborative effort with Al-Azhar University in Cairo in 1999.

127 *Prospectus Towards Research University* (Jakarta: UIN Jakarta Press, 2003), 25.

128 Abuddin Nata *et al.*, *Membangun Pusat Keunggulan Studi Islam: Sejarah dan Profil Pimpinan IAIN Syarif Hidayatullah Jakarta, 1957–2002* (Jakarta: IAIN Jakarta Press, 2002), 321. For statistics on the publishing activities of IAIN staff in other media, see Jabali and Jamhari, *IAIN dan Modernisasi*, 153–59.

one shared characteristic of a 'Ciputat school' it could be said that it is a general openness to difference of opinion. Azra's own vision of Islam is one that emphasizes the idea that difference of opinion remains a 'mercy' for the community, and this has contributed in an important way to the fostering of an overall sense of intellectual endeavor on campus that is directed not toward the 'unification' of Muslims around one particular set of interpretations, but rather toward cultivating a spirit of intracommunal tolerance and the mutual appreciation of divergent understandings of Islam among Muslims.

As noteworthy as such developments are, however, they have been by no means restricted to the sphere of one campus in the nation's capital. For example, the Central Javanese city of Yogyakarta's dynamic intellectual, artistic, and political life has also fostered its own creative atmosphere conducive to new thought about the nature and interpretation of Islamic law. A group of young Muslims working there to reinvigorate discussions of *uṣūl al-fiqh* have also been referred to in terms of a new 'school' of thought under the designation of the *Mazhab Jogja*.[129] Nevertheless, those associated with the movement have addressed the revitalization of jurisprudential discourses in Islam in different ways, ranging from general concerns on the level of methodology and textual hermeneutics to more concrete explorations of such topics as business and finance regulations and the re-evaluation of the penal code. Their 'Mazhab Jogja' is then, like the *madhhab* of Ciputat, not in itself a cohesive jurisprudential methodology, but rather a loose movement acknowledging the need for the development of 'a new paradigm of *uṣūl*'.

Neither the Ciputat nor the Jogja *madhhabs* then represent anything like unified 'schools of thought'. Instead they serve to signify more complex constellations of approaches brought into contact through the conscious creation of spaces for new conversations and engagement with an increasingly broad and diverse range of sources and interpretive techniques. The use of the term *madhhab* is thus a somewhat curious choice of words in the self-ascriptions of these diffuse movements. However, it might be best understood as not simply a 'popularization' or misreading of a technical term from classical jurisprudence, but rather as a reflection of a contemporary awareness of a need not just to revise rulings on particular points of law, but rather to reformulate new approaches and methodologies of Muslim jurisprudence to deal with the complex issues of the contemporary world.

[129] Amin Abdullah *et al.*, *Mazhab Jogja: Menggagas Paradigma Ushul Fiqh Kontemporer* (Yogyakarta: ar-Ruzz Press, 2002), 9.

In this sense the dynamic proliferation of new interpretations of Islamic law in modern Indonesia implies more than simply the emergence of a number of new, distinct, and identifiable groups. It also invokes a vision of multileveled internal pluralism as well as a broadening of conversations between diverse groups of participants in which even extreme polarities can, on occasion, address one another on the level of debate rather than diatribe.[130]

[130] This is evidenced, for example, in such things the regular participation of representatives from HTI at JIL seminars and conferences.

# *Conclusion*

> Every age yearns for a more beautiful world. The deeper the desperation and the depression about the confusing present, the more intense that yearning.
>
> Johan Huizinga, *Herfsttij der Middeleeuwen*

The preceding pages have introduced the work of a number of Indonesian Muslim thinkers on the conception, formulation, and interpretation of Islamic law, situated within their own complex social, cultural, and political contexts. The material covered has been diverse, involving original local productions that engaged creatively with a broad range of sources that had become available to Indonesian Muslim reformers within the context of epistemological reorientations that accompanied rapid processes of modernization in the Archipelago. The last chapter in particular highlighted aspects of both the extent and the intensity of contemporary conversations about Islamic law and society in Indonesia. These discourses have been shaped by the political and economic circumstances of the post-Suharto period, but they are also informed by a complex history of ideas and exchanges relating to evolving understandings of such issues as innovation, tradition, and justice over the past hundred years.

Around the turn of the twentieth century, a combination of social transformations in patterns of education, new social relationships forged in the context of modern-style voluntary associations, and the introduction of print technology opened up new epistemological horizons and spaces for conversations on Islam and society. In these contexts, new participants joined into discussions of such issues, and in doing so effectively broke the monopoly that traditionally trained *'ulamā'* had previously held over Islamic religious discourse in the Archipelago. Some of the loudest among these new voices were those of reformers inspired by Islamic modernist and *Salafi* ideas spreading from the Middle East via nodes in regional networks such as Singapore. A primary example of this can be found in the life and work of A. Hassan, a Singapore-born Tamil Muslim printer and tire-vulcanizer who moved to Java and became involved in a new Muslim voluntary association known as PERSIS. His message was a clarion call for a reformulation of Islam along scripturalist lines – a new model of *ijtihād* that would clear the decks of both the accretions of medieval scholasticism and local cultural innovations, thus rediscovering a purified Islam that could better help the community face the challenges of the modern world.

Similar calls were echoed in other reformist organizations established in Java during that time, including the Muhammadiyah and al-Irsyad. Even within PERSIS at that time, however, some prominent reformists offered visions that to varying degrees mitigated simple scripturalism. One of the most prominent of these was the Javanese *kyai* Moenawar Chalil, who is best known for his landmark book *Return to the Qur'ān and Sunna*. Despite the title of his signature work, however, Chalil maintained a qualified respect for traditional Muslim scholarship while also drawing inspiration from the work of Muḥammad Abduh. This mediation of the spirit of Islamic modernism with an abiding regard for the classical corpus of Shafi'ī *fiqh* maintained the possibility of communication across the traditionalist/reformist divide that has remained an important aspect of Indonesian Islam to this day.

Some of the most interesting reflections of this in the mid-twentieth century came in the form of movements for the creation of a new Indonesian school of *fiqh* (*madhhab*). Different agendas for the creation of this 'national school of law' were advanced at that time by the Islamic reformist Hasbi Ash Shiddieqy and the Dutch-educated scholar of customary law (*adatrecht*), Hazairin. Hasbi accepted the establishment of a scripturalist Islam free of *bid'a* as a first step toward the eventual creation of a body of interpretation of those eternal truths that could meet the needs of modern Indonesian society. Hazairin came to his positions through his familiarity with Dutch academic jurisprudence and ethnographic research, read in light of a strong and abiding sense of Indonesian nationalism. While rejecting what he perceived to be the anti-Islamic ideology of colonial scholarship on the relationship between Islam and indigenous legal norms in the archipelago, Hazairin also introduced aspects of Western-derived social-scientific approaches into scholarly and public discourses on Islam, thus paving the way for further elaborations of such work by later generations of Indonesian Muslims.

In the later decades of the twentieth century, the introduction of academic approaches developed in the West came to be fostered by a series of powerful social and political actors, including the prominent Indonesian Ministers of Religious Affairs, Mukti Ali (1971–78) and Munawir

Sjadzali (1983–93). In their policies, and particularly in their direction of the nation's rapidly expanding system of state Islamic Studies institutes (IAIN), they worked to bring about a greater integration of Western scholarly approaches into conversations about Islam through the provision of increased opportunities for young Indonesian Muslims to pursue graduate work in Islamic Studies in Europe and North America. Upon their return to Indonesia, these students introduced new elements into Muslim conversations there, including methodologies oriented toward analyses of current social situations and the historical legacies that inform them. Their work thus helped to solidify a foundation of social science approaches within Indonesian Islamic conversations that has continued to support further intellectual and cultural developments to this day. These discussions are, moreover, increasingly conducted in an idiom that elides sharp distinctions between what might once have been considered 'Islamic' and 'Western' discourses.

Some of these scholars and activists combined their new academic approaches with liberal social positions on issues such as democratization and religious pluralism, as in the work of Nurcholish Madjid and his colleagues affiliated with the *Pembaharuan* movement. Over the past three decades these Indonesian Neo-Modernists have reconstructed dialogues with the legacies of medieval and early-modern Islamic intellectualism in a search for new models of Islam emphasizing values of democracy and pluralism. This movement, however, has provoked significant opposition from other sectors of Indonesia's diverse Muslim community. In particular, Islamists working from a modern conception of religious identity have critiqued these new, hybrid forms of Muslim discourse as inauthentic and un-Islamic.

Those criticisms, however, were to some extent less salient when applied to other contemporary Indonesian scholars who shared certain affinities with the *Pembaharuan* thinkers on issues of social justice. They were a group of *'ulamā'* trained within the *pesantren* networks generally affiliated with the traditionalist organization *Nahdlatul Ulama*, who often had a far greater command of the Arabic language, and of classical Islamic scholarship, than did many of the ideological Islamists who had castigated advocates of *Pembaharuan*. Through their contact with social activists in the framework of NGO-sponsored development programs among rural Muslim communities, Sahal Mahfudh and other *pesantren* leaders began integrating analytic insights from the social sciences into their reinvigorated discussion of sources from within the rich traditions of the Islamic religious sciences.

This resulted in a transformation of certain circles within NU as some traditionalists increasingly came to regard the texts of the *pesantren* curriculum not as a static body of knowledge to be memorized and transmitted, but rather as a heritage that can be critically engaged with in the search for alternatives formulations of the law to address contemporary concerns. This appreciation of the dynamic potential of classical forms of Islamic learning helped to encourage more recent generations of scholars from the *pesantren* milieu to enter into debates on the local and national levels with writings that exhibit an innovative combination of traditional Muslim textual methodologies with a highly developed awareness of the needs of the contemporary Indonesian community and a strong commitment to ideals of social justice. Indonesian Muslim scholars of this type have been able to benefit from both their traditional Islamic learning, and also from the increased social prominence gained through participation in NGO programs and institutions of higher Islamic learning such as the National Islamic University of Indonesia (UIN) and its associated network of IAIN schools.

On these campuses, and elsewhere across the country, Indonesian Muslims have pursued the critical and creative assimilation of ideas and approaches from a wide range of medieval and modern sources. Indeed a whole range of contemporary Muslim authors who are relatively marginalized individuals in their home countries in the Middle East and elsewhere are widely known in Indonesia, and there more than perhaps anywhere else in the world these disparate dissident voices are being read side-by-side with one other. In the process, their ideas are being compared, contrasted, and critically synthesized through discussions in academic circles, as well as in the broader public sphere. All of these developments have contributed to the current state of affairs in which Indonesia has become arguably the world's most vibrant center for contemporary Islamic thought.

This, to a considerable extent, is a reflection of the remarkable degree to which Indonesian thinkers have developed capacities for mediating not merely between research methods and results from 'the West' and traditional Islamic sources, but especially for their creative integration of diverse strands of modern Muslim thought from around the world into communication with a broad range of ideas developed in Europe, North America, and elsewhere by non-Muslim thinkers. The thought world of many young Indonesian thinkers and activists has thus come to be characterized by a considerable degree of movement back and forth between classical texts and modern Muslim writings from the Middle East and elsewhere, as well as Euro-American literature in the fields of Law, the Humanities, and the Social Sciences. An understanding of such intellectual complexities, and their broader cultural and political contexts, thus demands sensitivity to diversity both within and beyond Muslim communities, as well as a recognition of the complex ways in which modern scholarship on these matters has become part of multiple conversations in myriad modes along a spectrum of discourses ranging from the critical to the confessional.

Late twentieth-century Dutch contributions to the academic study of religion attempted to develop an empirical method for Religious Studies employing a classification of discourses, the terms of which were borrowed from the technical vocabulary of linguistics via their transformations in the field of Cultural Anthropology.[1] In their work they sought to distinguish between two different types of conversation about religion: an *emic* discourse reflecting patterns of thought and symbolic associations expressed from a believer's perspective, and an *etic* scholarly discourse involving historically oriented analyses of the relationships between ideas and society while refraining from engaging truth claims about meta-empirical reality.[2] This approach has been of considerable benefit to recent work in the academic study of religion. However, significant complications could arise if these categories are too rigidly constructed, particularly in dealing with the modern period as lines between academic and confessional, as well as between 'Muslim' and 'Western,' conversations have often been obscured in the permutations of public discourses of identity and power politics. Given this historical reality, any rethinking of the field of modern Muslim intellectual history must start with a frank recognition of the fact that for well over a century now the blending of *emic* and *etic* discourses on Islam has been a complex and creative dynamic in Muslim thought.

In introducing a late twentieth-century collection of studies on the historiography of Western philosophy, Richard Rorty and his colleagues likened some aspects of the field to that of ethnography, the value of which they appraised from a philosopher's perspective in these terms: "What we want to be told is whether that tribe has anything of interest to tell us – interesting to

[1] In the works of J. A. M. Snoek and J. G. Platvoet these categories have been deployed in constructing conversations both about particular religious traditions as well as scholarly discourses on the phenomena of religion in general. Joannes Augustinus Maria Snoek, *Initiations: Method and Theory in Concept Formation in the Study of Religions* (New York: P. Lang, 2000); J. G. Platvoet, *Comparing Religions: A Limitative Approach* (The Hague: Mouton, 1982).

[2] Particularly through the work of Kenneth L. Pike, *Language in Relation to a Unified Theory of the Structure of Human Behavior* (The Hague: Mouton, 1967). Here it must be noted, however, that Pike himself describes the emic and etic viewpoints as a "convenient – though partially arbitrary" heuristic, and stresses that they "do not constitute a rigid dichotomy" (37–42).

*our* lights, answering to *our* concerns . . ."[3] Such a view toward approaching cross-cultural conversations, however, should seem exaggeratedly ethnocentric to anyone engaged in the serious study of Islamic intellectual history in the modern period. Over the past century, for different communities all across the planet, political and economic developments have created a situation in which to various degrees 'our' questions are increasingly implicated in the formulation of 'their' questions (and vice versa), regardless of how we delineate these two exclusivistic groupings.

The challenge thus becomes one of negotiating the areas of both similarity and difference in the intellectual legacies and historical experiences of multiple civilizations as well as their respective, internally diverse subtraditions. The texts from both the Islamic and Western traditions of legal and social thought quoted in the epigraphs to the chapters of this book have been carefully selected to stimulate further reflections on some of the ways in which thinkers from these different backgrounds have addressed analogous issues of religion, law, and society. Indonesian Islam is a distinctive and even unique field of inquiry in a number of ways. It can, however, also serve as an informative case study for comparative reflections on the interpretation of religious ideals in modern societies. As such, it can open up new perspectives on developments elsewhere, particularly in places where broad-based religious resurgence has impacted on understandings of the rule of law and democracy, as well as on the rights and responsibilities of citizens in relation to the beliefs of both majority and minority populations in a modern nation-state.

With the accelerating pace of change and increasing complexities of interaction both within and between traditions in the modern period, ever greater demands are placed on those seeking to understand their own relative positions within these globalized conversations. To some extent, at least, such work can be facilitated by developing an historical consciousness of the diverse developments informing the current situation. This study has attempted this by signaling some of the ways in which, for example, the writings of eighteenth-century reformers, Dutch academic jurisprudence, Japanese military administration policies, and post-modern deconstruction theory have significantly impacted the directions of contemporary debates on law and society in the world's most populous Muslim nation.

3 Richard Rorty *et al.*, "Introduction," in *Philosophy in History: Essays on the Historiography of Philosophy* (Cambridge: Cambridge University Press, 1984), 6–7.

# *Bibliography*

Abaza, Mona. *Indonesian Students in Cairo: Islamic Education, Perceptions and Exchanges*. Paris: Cahiers d'Archipel, 1994.

Abbas, Siradjuddin. *Sejarah dan Keagungan Madzhab Syafi'i*. Jakarta: Pustaka Tarbiyah, 1996.

Abd al-Hayy, Nu'man, and Shahafari Ash'ari. *Organisasi Nahdlatul Wathan dan Perjuangan*. Pancor (Lombok): Penerbit NW, 1989.

Abdillah, Masykuri. *Responses of Indonesian Muslim Intellectuals to the Concept of Democracy (1966–1993)*. Hamburg: Abera, 1997.

Abd. Rahman. "The Pesantren Architects and their Socio-Religious Teachings, 1850–1950." University of California at Los Angeles dissertation, 1997.

Abdullah, Amin, *et al. Mazhab Jogja: Menggagas Paradigma Ushul Fiqh Kontemporer*. Yogyakarta: ar-Ruzz Press, 2002.

Abdullah, Taufik. *Schools and Polititcs: The Kaum Muda Movement in West Sumatra 1927–1933*. Ithaca: Cornell University Southeast Asia Program, 1971.

"Masa Awal Muhammadiyah di Minangkabau: Cuplikan dari Arsip Belanda." In *Kenang-kenangan 70 Tahun Buya Hamka*, ed. Solichin Salam *et al.*, 210–16. Jakarta: Pustaka Panjimas, 1983.

"Cita dan Corak Reformasi Islam di Indonesia: Sebuah Tafsiran." *Islam dan Masyarakat* (1987): 88–109. Jakarta: LP3ES.

"Pola Kepemimpinan Islam di Indonesia." *Islam dan Masyarakat* (1987): 54–87. Jakarta: LP3ES.

"*Zakat* Collection and Distribution in Indonesia." In *The Islamic Voluntary Sector in Southeast Asia*, ed. Mohamed Ariff, 50–84. Singapore: Institute of Southeast Asian Studies, 1991.

"The Formation of a New Paradigm: A Sketch on Contemporary Islamic Discourse." In *Toward a New Paradigm: Recent Developments in Indonesian Islamic Thought*, ed. Mark Woodward, 47–88. Tempe: Arizona State University, 1996.

Abdul-Samad, M. A. "Modernism in Islam in Indonesia with Special Reference to Muhammadiyah." In *Islam in the Indonesian Social Context*, ed. M. C. Ricklefs, 57–68. Clayton: Monash University Centre of Southeast Asian Studies, 1991.

Abdurrahman, H. Asjmuni. *Manhaj Tarjih Muhammadiyah: Metodologi dan Aplikasi*. Yogyakarta: Pustaka Pelajar, 2002.

Abdurrahman, Moeslim. *Islam Transformatif.* Jakarta: Pustaka Firdaus, 1995.
*Islam sebagai Kritik Sosial.* Jakarta: Penerbit Erlangga, 2003.
Abdurrahman, Moeslim, ed. *Muhammadiyah sebagai Tenda Kultural.* Jakarta: Ideo Press, 2003.
Abdurrahman. "Jong Islamieten Bond, 1925–1942: Sejarah, Pemikiran, dan Gerakan." Yogyakarta: IAIN Ph.D. Dissertation, 1999.
Abidun, Muhammad. "Kritik Nalar Fiqh." *Nuansa: Jurnal Pemikiran Keagamaan* 12 (2003): 31–41.
Abou El Fadl, Khaled. "The Ugly Modern and Modern Ugly: Reclaiming the Beautiful in Islam." In *Progressive Muslims,* ed. Omid Safi, 33–77. Oxford: Oneworld, 2003.
Abshar-Abdalla, Ulil. "Kembalilah ke Barak: Tantangan NU Pasca Gus Dur." In *NU Pasca Gus Dur,* ed. A. S. Laksana, 11–24. Jakarta: Fatma Press, 1997.
"Dr. Siti Musdah Mulia, MA – Kompilasi Hukum Islam sangat Konservatif!" http://islamlib.com/id/page.php?page=article&mode=print&id=408
Abu-Rabi', Ibrahim M. "Toward an Islamic Liberation Theology: Muhammad Husayn Fadlallah and the Principles of Shi'i Resurgence." In *Intellectual Origins of Islamic Resurgence in the Modern Arab World.* Albany: SUNY Press, 1996.
Abū Shūk, Aḥmad Ibrahīm. *Ta'rīkh ḥarakat al-iṣlāḥ wā'l-irshād wa-shaykh al-irshādiyyin Aḥmad Muḥammad al-Sūrkatī fī Indūnīsiyā.* Kuala Lumpur: Dar al-Fajr Mālayziyā, 2000.
Adams, Charles, C. "Muhammad Abduh and the Transvaal Fatwa." In *The MacDonald Presentation Volume,* 11–29. Princeton: Princeton University Press, 1933.
Adnan, Zifirdaus. "Islamic Religion: Yes, Islamic (Political) Ideology: No! Islam and the State in Indonesia." In *State and Civil Society in Indonesia,* ed. Arief Budiman, 441–77. Clayton: Monash University Centre of Southeast Asian Studies, 1990.
Ahmad, Amrullah, ed. *Dimensi Hukum Islam dalam Sistem Hukum Nasional, Mengenang 65 Th. Prof. Dr. H. Busthanul Arifin, SH.* Jakarta: Gema Insani Press, 1996.
Ahmad, War'ie Karim. "Toleransi Antarumat: Usaha Mencari Titik Persamaan, mengenal Pemikiran Dr. Muhammad Imarah." In *Kontekstualisasi Islam dalam Peradaban,* ed. Mas Guntur Romli and Shofia Tidjani. Cairo: FOSGAMA, 2002.
Alfian. "Islamic Modernism in Indonesian Politics: The Muhammadiyah Movement during the Dutch Colonial Period, 1912–1942." Diss. University of Wisconsin, Madison, 1969.
Ali, Fachry, and Bahtiar Effendi. *Merambah Jalan Baru Islam: Rekonstruksi Pemikiran Islam Indonesia Masa Orde Baru.* Bandung: Mizan, 1986.
Ali-Karamali, Shaista P., and Fiona Dunne. "The *Ijtihād* Controversy." *Arab Law Quarterly* 9 (1994): 238–57.
Amal, Taufik Adnan. *Islam dan Tantangan Modernitas: Studi atas Pemikiran Hukum Fazlur Rahman.* Bandung: Mizan, 1989.

Amal, Taufik Adnan, and Syamsu Rizal Panggabean. *Tafsir Kontekstual Al-Qur'an: Sebuah Kerangka Konseptual*. Bandung: Mizan, 1989.

Amelz, H. O. S. *Tjokroaminoto, Hidup dan Perdjuangannja*. Jakarta: Bulan Bintang, n.d.

Anam, Chairul. *Pertumbuhan dan Perkembangan Nahdlatul Ulama*. Solo: Jatayu, 1985.

Ananda, Endang Basri, ed. *70 Tahun Prof. Dr. H. M. Rasjidi*. Jakarta: Harian Umum Pelita, 1985.

Anderson, J. N. D. "Recent Reforms in the Islamic Law of Inheritance." *International and Comparative Law Quarterly* 14 (1965): 349–65.

*Islamic Law in the Modern World*. New York: New York University Press, 1959.

*Anggaran Dasar dan Rentjana Perdjoeangan Masjoemi Partai Politik Indonesia*. Bukit Tinggi: Dewan Pemimpin Daerah Masjoemi Soematera Barat, April 1946.

*Anggaran Dasar dan Roemah Tangga: Program Perdjoeangan dan Program Oesaha-Tjepat 'Masjoemi' Partai Politik Islam*. Bogor: Penerbit Masjoemi, February 1946.

An-Na'im, Abdullahi Ahmed. *Dekonstruksi Syari'ah: Wacana Kebebasan Sipil, Hak Asasi Manusia, dan Hubungan Internasional dalam Islam*. Yogyakarta: LKiS, 1994.

Anshari, H. Endang Saifuddin. *Pak Natsir 80 Tahun: Buku Kedua Penghargaan dan Penghormatan Generasi Muda*. Jakarta: Media Da'wah, 1988.

*Piagam Jakarta, 22 Juni 1945: Sebuah Konsensus Nasional tentang Dasar Negara Republik Indonesia, 1945–1949*. Jakarta: Gema Insani Press, 1997.

Anshari, H. Endang Saifuddin, and Syafiq A. Mugni. *A. Hassan: Wajah dan Wijah Seorang Mujtahid*. Bandung: Firma Al-Muslimun, 1985.

Antoun, Richard T. *Muslim Preacher in the Modern World: A Jordanian Case Study in Comparative Perspective*. Princeton: Princeton University Press, 1989.

Anwar, M. Syafi'i. "Sosiologi Pembaruan Pemikiran Islam Nurcholish Madjid." *Ulumul Qur'an* 4.1 (1993): 49.

"Negara dan Cendekaiwan Muslim Indonesia Orde Baru." In *Pembangunan dan Kebangkitan Islam di Asia Tenggara*, ed. Saiful Muzani. Jakarta: LP3ES, 1993.

Anwar, Syamsul. "Fatwā, Purification and Dynamization: A Study of Tarjīḥ in Muhammadiyah." *ILS* 12.1 (2005): 27–44.

Aqsha, Darul, *et al. Islam in Indonesia: A Survey of Events and Developments from 1988 to March 1993*. Jakarta: INIS, 1995.

Arief, Eddi Rudiana, *et al. Hukum Islam di Indonesia: Pemikiran dan Praktek*. Bandung: PT Remaja Rosdakarya, 1991.

Arifin, Busthanul. *Pelembagaan Hukum Islam di Indonesia: Akar Sejarah, Hambatan dan Prospeknya*. Jakarta: Gema Insani Press, 1996.

Arifin, Syamsul, *et al. Spiritualisasi Islam dan Peradaban Masa Depan*. Yogyakarta: SIPress, 1996.

Arkoun, Mohammed. *Nalar Islami dan Nalar Modern: Berbagai Tantangan dan Jalan Baru*. Jakarta: INIS, 1994.

*Rethinking Islam: Common Questions, Uncommon Answers*. Boulder: Westview Press, 1994.

Asa, Taryono. *Muhammadiyah dan Pemberdayaan Bangsa*. Jakarta: Ruhama Intergraf, 1995.

Ash Shiddieqy, *Hasbi: Sebab-sebab Perbedaan Faham para Ulama dalam Menetapkan Hukum Islam*. Yogyakarta: n.d.

*Al-Ahkaam (Hukum-hukum Fiqih Islam)*. Bandung: Al-Ma'arif, 1951.

*Pedoman Hukum Syar'y*. Jakarta: Pustaka Islam, 1952.

*Kuliah Ibadah: Ibadah ditinjau dari segi Hukum dan Hikmah*. Jakarta: Bulan Bintang, 1954.

*Kitab Hukum-hukum Islam*. Jakarta: Bulan Bintang, 1960.

*Problematika Hadits sebagai Dasar Pembinaan Hukum Islam*. Jakarta: Bulan Bintang, 1964.

*Tafsir Al-Quränul Madjied 'An-Nur'*. Jakarta: Bulan Bintang, 1965.

*Kriteria antara Sunnah dan Bid'ah*. Jakarta: Bulan Bintang, 1967.

*Asas Hukum Tata Negara Menurut Sjari'at Islam*. Yogyakarta: Matahari Masa, 1969.

*Ilmu-ilmu Al-Qurän: Media-media Pokok dalam Menafsirkan Al-Qurän*. Jakarta: Bulan Bintang, 1972.

*Pokok-pokok Pegangan Imam-imam Mazhab*. Jakarta: Bulan Bintang, 1973.

*Falsafah Hukum Islam*. Jakarta: Bulan Bintang, 1975.

*Pengantar Ilmu Perbandingan Mazhab*. Jakarta: Bulan Bintang, 1975.

*Koleksi Hadis-hadis Hukum*. Jakarta: Yayasan Teungku Muhammad Hasbi Ash-Shiddiqi, 1994.

*Hukum-hukum Fiqh Islam*. Semarang: Pustaka Rizki Putra, 1997.

*Pengantar Hukum Islam*. Semarang: Rizki Putra, 1997.

*Pengantar Ilmu Fiqh*. Semarang: Rizki Putra, 1997.

*Pokok-pokok Pegangan Imam-imam Mazhab*. Semarang: Rizki Putra, 1997.

*Sejarah dan Pengantar Ilmu Hadits*. Semarang: Pustaka Rizki Putra, 1997.

Al-Āshī, Ismā'īl b. 'Abd Al-Muṭallib. *Jami' al-jawāmi'al-muṣnafāt*. Cairo: Muṣṭafā al-Bābī al-Ḥalabī, 1925.

Asmuni, Abdul Rahman. *Majlis Tarjih Muhammadiyah*. Yogyakarta: IAIN Sunan Kalijaga, 1985.

Assyaukanie, Luthfi, ed. *Wajah Liberal Islam di Indonesia*. Jakarta: Jaringan Islam Liberal, 2002.

Atjeh, Aboebakar. *Sedjarah Hidup K. H. Wahid Hasjim dan Karangan Tersiar*. Jakarta: Panitia Buku Peringatan Alm. K. H. A. Wahid Hasjim, 1957.

*Islam – Sumber Djihad*. Jakarta: Universitas Islam Djakarta, 1967.

Al-Attas, Syed Muhammad Naguib. *Islam, Secularism and the Philosophy of the Future*. London: Mansell Publishing Limited, 1985.

Awad, Louis. *The Literature of Ideas in Egypt, Part I*. Atlanta: Scholars Press, 1986.

Ayer, A. J. *Philosophy in the Twentieth Century*. New York: Vintage Books, 1984.

Al-Azmeh, Aziz. "Modernist Muslim Reformism and the Text of the Past." In *Islam and the Proceedings of the Inaugural Symposium on Islam and the Challenge of Modernity: Historical and Contemporary Contexts, Kuala Lumpur, August 1–5, 1994*, 391–428, ed. Sharifah Shifa Al-Attas. Kuala Lumpur: ISTAC, 1996.

Azra, Azyumardi. "Guarding the Faith of the Ummah: The Religio-Intellectual Journey of Mohammad Rasjidi." *SI* 1.2 (1994): 87–120.

"Muhammadiyah: A Preliminary Study." *SI* 1.2 (1994): 187–200.

"Education, Law, Mysticism: Constructing Social Realities." In *Islamic Civilization in the Malay World*, ed. Mohd. Taib Osman. Istanbul: IRCICA, 1997.

*The Origins of Islamic Reformism in Southeast Asia: Networks of Malay-Indonesian Ulama and Middle Eastern 'Ulamā' in the Seventeenth and Eighteenth Centuries.* Honolulu: University of Hawaii Press, 2004.

Azra, Azyumardi, and Saiful Umam, *et al. Menteri-Menteri Agama RI: Biografi Sosial-Politik.* Jakarta: INIS, 1998.

Bagir, Haidar. "Dua Bentuk Respon Atas Pembaruan Islam." *Ulumul Qur'an* 4.1 (1993).

Bagir, Haidar, and Syafiq Basir, eds. *Ijtihad dalam Sorotan.* Bandung: Penerbit Mizan, 1988.

Bakar, Ibrahim bin Abu. *Islamic Modernism in Malaya: The Life and Thought of Sayid Syekh Al-Hadi, 1867–1934.* Kuala Lumpur: University of Malaya Press, 1994.

Bakri, Hasbullah, *et al.*, eds. *Prof. K. H. Ibrahim Hosen dan Pembaharuan Hukum Islam di Indonesia.* Jakarta: C.V. Putra Harapan, 1990.

Bakti, Andi. "Communication and Dakwah: Religious Learning Groups and their Role in the Protection of Islamic Human Security and Rights for Indonesian Civil Society." In *Comparative Education, Terrorism, and Human Security: From Critical Pedagogy to Peace Building?*, ed. Wayne Nelles, 109–25. New York: Palgrave Macmillan, 2003.

Baljon, J. M. S. *Modern Muslim Koran Interpretation (1880–1960).* Leiden: E. J. Brill, 1968.

*Religion and Thought of Shāh Walī Allāh Dihlawī, 1703–1762.* Leiden: E. J. Brill, 1986.

Balslev, Anindita Niyogi. *Cultural Otherness: Correspondence with Richard Rorty.* Altanta: Scholars Press, 1999.

Al-Banjārī, Muḥammad Arshad b. 'Abd Allāh. *Sabīl Al-Muhtadīn.* Singapore: Ḥaramayn, n.d.

Al-Banna, Hassan. *Five Tracts of Hassan Al-Banna, 1906–1949*, trans. C. Wendell. Berkeley: University of California Press, 1978.

Baried, Baroroh. "Une mouvement de femmes musulumanes: Aisyiyah." *Archipel* 13 (1977): 129–36.

Barnett Randy A. E. "A Law Professor's Guide to Natural Law and Natural Rights." *Harvard Journal of Law and Public Policy* 20 (1997): 655–81.

Barral, J. M., ed. *Orientalia Hispanica: Sive studia F. M. Pareja octogenario dictata.* Leiden: E. J. Brill, 1974.

Barton, Greg. "The International Context of the Emergence of Islamic Neo Modernism in Indonesia." In *Islam in the Indonesian Social Context*, ed. M. C.

Ricklefs, 69–82. Clayton: Monash University Centre of Southeast Asian Studies, 1991.

"Neo-Modernism: A Vital Synthesis of Traditionalist and Modernist Islamic Thought in Indonesia." *SI* 2.3 (1995): 1–75.

"Indonesia's Nurcholish Madjid and Abdurrahman Wahid as Intellectual Ulama: The Meeting of Islamic Traditionalism and Modernism in Neo-Modernist Thought." *SI* 4.1 (1997): 29–82.

*Abdurrahman Wahid: Muslim Democrat, Indonesian President.* Honolulu: University of Hawaii Press, 2002.

Barton, Greg, and Greg Fealy, eds. *Nahdatul Ulama, Traditional Islam and Modernity in Indonesia.* Clayton: Monash Asia Institute, 1996.

Basalim, Umar. *Pro-Kontra Piagam Jakarta di Era Reformasi.* Jakarta: Pustaka Indonesia Satu, 2002.

Baso, Ahmad. "Melawan Tekanan Agama: Wacana Baru Pemikiran Fiqih NU." In *Wacana Baru Fiqih Sosial,* ed. Jamal D. Rahman *et al.*, 131–43. Bandung: Mizan, 1997.

"Dari Kritik Wacana Agama Menuju Rasionalisme." In *Kultur Hibrida: Anak Muda NU di Jalur Kultural,* ed. Hairus Salim HS and Muhammad Riwan. Yogyakarta: LKiS, 1999.

"Problem Islam dan Politik: Perspektif *Kritik Nalar Politik* Mohammed Abed al-Jabiri." *TA* 4 (1999).

"Dari Tradisionalisme Menuju Post-Tradisionalisme Islam: Geliat Pemikiran Baru Islam Arab." *TA* 9 (2000): 47–61.

"Neo-Modernisme Islam versus Post-Tradisionalisme Islam." *TA* 9 (2000): 24–46.

"Posmodernisme sebagai Kritik Islam: Kontribusi Metodologis 'Kritik Nalar' Muhammad Abed al-Jabiri." In Muhammad Abed al-Jabiri, *Post-Tradisionalisme Islam.* Yogyakarta: LKiS, 2000.

Basyir, Ahmad Azhar. *Hukum Adat bagi Umat Islam.* Yogyakarta: Nur Cahaya, 1983.

Benda, Harry J. *The Crescent and the Rising Sun: Indonesian Islam under the Japanese Occupation 1942–1945.* The Hague: W. van Hoeve, 1958.

Benda, Harry J., James K. Irikura, and Koichi Kishi, eds. *Japanese Military Administration in Indonesia: Selected Documents.* New Haven: Yale University Southeast Asia Studies, 1965.

Benda-Beckmann, Franz von. *Property in Social Continuity: Continuity and Change in the Maintenance of Property Relationships through Time in Minangkabau, West Sumatra.* The Hague: Martinus Nijhoff, 1979.

Berg, L. W. C. van den. "Mohammedaansch recht en adat." *Het Regt in Nederlansch-Indië* 43 (1884): 137–55.

"Het Mohammedaansche Godsdienstonderwijs op Java en Madoera en de daarbij gebruikte Arabische boeken." *Tijdschrift voor Indische Taal-, Land- en Volkenkunde* 31 (1886): 518–55.

*Le Hadramaut et les colonies arabes dans l'archipel indien.* Batavia: Imprimerie du Gouvernment, 1886.

"De afwijkingen van het Mohammedaansche familie- en erfrecht op Java en Madoera." *BKI* 41(1892): 454–512.

"Nalezing – De afwijkingen van het Mohammedaansche familie- en erfrecht op Java en Madoera." *BKI* 45(1895): 291–314.

Binder, Leonard. *Islamic Liberalism: A Critique of Development Ideologies*. Chicago: University of Chicago Press, 1988.

Birch, R. W. "The Vernacular Press in the Straits." *JSBRAS* 4 (1879): 51–55.

Bisri, Cik Hasan. *Peradilan Islam dalam Tatanan Masyarakat Indonesia*. Bandung: PT Remaja Rosdakarya, 1997.

Bisri, A. Mustofa. "Gus Dur Pasca NU." In *NU Pasca Gus Dur*, ed. A. S. Laksana, 157–64. Jakarta: Fatma Press, 1997.

Bix, Brian, "Natural Law Theory: The Modern Tradition." In *Handbook of Jurisprudence and Legal Philosophy*, ed. Jules L. Coleman and Scott Shapiro. 62–103. Oxford University Press, 2000.

Bluhm, J. "A Preliminary Statement on the Dialogue Established between the Reform Magazine *al-Manār* and the Malayo-Indonesian World." *Indonesia Circle* (1983): 35–42.

Bluhm-Warn, J. "Al-Manar and Ahmad Soorkattie." In *Islam – Essays in Scripture, Thought and Society: A Festschrift in honour of Anthony H. Johns*, ed. Peter Riddell and Tony Street, 295–308. Leiden: E. J. Brill, 1997.

Bocquet-Siek, Margaret, and Robert Cribb. *Islam and the Panca Sila*. Townsville (Australia): Committee of South-East Asian Studies, James Cook University of North Queensland, 1991.

Boland, B. J. "Discussion on Islam in Indonesia Today." In *Studies on Islam: A Symposium on Islamic Studies Organized in Cooperation with the Accademia dei Lincei in Rome*, 37–50. Amsterdam: North-Holland Publishing Company, 1974.

*The Struggle of Islam in Modern Indonesia*. The Hague: Martinus Nijhoff, 1982.

Botiveau, Bernard. "Note sur les étudiants indonésians présents à l'Université Al-Azhar du Caire." *Archipel* 40 (1990): 41–44.

Boullata, Issa. *Trends and Issues in Contemporary Arab Thought*. Albany: SUNY Press, 1990.

Bowen, John R. *Muslims through Discourse*. Princeton: Princeton University Press, 1993.

"'You May Not Give it Away': How Social Norms Shape Islamic Law in Contemporary Indonesian Jurisprudence." *ILS* 5.3 (1998): 382–408.

*Islam, Law and Equality in Indonesia: An Anthropology of Public Reasoning*. New York: Cambridge University Press, 2003.

Brown, Daniel W. *Rethinking Tradition in Modern Islamic Thought*. Cambridge: University Press, 1996.

Bruinessen, Martin van. "Indonesia's Ulama and Politics: Caught between Legitimizing the Status Quo and Searching for Alternatives." *Prisma* 49 (June 1990): 52–69.

"Kitab Kuning: Books in Arabic Script Used in the Pesantren Milieu." *BKI* 146 (1990): 226–69.

"Kitab Kuning dan Perempuan, Perempuan dan Kitab Kuning." In *Wantia Islam Indonesia dalam Kajian Tekstual dan Kontekstual*, ed. Lies M. Marcoes-Natsir and Johan Hendrik Meuleman, 165–74. Jakarta: INIS, 1993.

*NU: Tradisi, Relasi-relasi Kuasa, dan Pencarian Wacana Baru*. Yogyakarta: LKiS, 1994.

"Pesantren and Kitab Kuning: Continuity and Change in a Tradition of Religious Learning." In *Texts from the Islands: Oral and Written Traditions of Indonesia and the Malay World*, ed. Wolfgang Marschall, 121–46. Berne: University of Berne Institute of Ethnology, 1994.

"Shari'a Court, Tarekat and Pesantren: Religious Institutions in the Banten Sultanate." *Archipel* 50 (1995): 165–200.

"Traditions for the Future: The Reconstruction of Traditionalist Discourse within NU." In *Nahdatul Ulama: Traditional Islam and Modernity in Indonesia*, ed. Greg Barton and Greg Fealy, 163–89. Clayton: Monash Asia Institute, 1996.

"Post-Suharto Muslim Engagements with Civil Society and Democratisation." Paper presented at the Third International Conference and Workshop *Indonesia in Transition* organized by KNAW and Labsosio, Universitas Indonesia – August 24–28, 2003/ www.let.uu.nl/m̃artin.vanbruinessen/personal/publications/Post_Suharto_Islam_and_civil_society.htm

Brunner, Rainer. *Islamic Ecumenism in the 20th Century: The Azhar and Shiism between Rapprochement and Restraint*. Leiden: E. J. Brill, 2004.

Bubalo, Anthony, and Greg Fealy. *Joining the Caravan: The Middle East, Islamism, and Indonesia*. Alexandria, NSW: Lowy Institute, 2005.

Budiman, Arief. "Indonesia: Transisi ke Arah Demokrasi?" *Indonesia dalam Transisi*, ed. Hanafi Sofyan. Jakarta: Halmahera Foundation, 1995.

Burhanuddin, ed. *Syariat Islam: Pandangan Muslim Liberal*. Jakarta: Jaringan Islam Liberal, 2003.

Burhanudin, H. Nandang. *Penegakan Syariat Islam Menurut Partai Keadilan*. Jakarta: Al-Jannah, 2003.

Burhanudin, Jajat. "Aspiring for Islamic Reform: Southeast Asian Requests for *Fatwās* from *Al-Manār*." *ILS* 12.1 (2005): 9–26.

Burhanudin, Jajat, and Ahmad Baedowi. *Transformasi Otoritas Keagamaan: Pengalaman Islam Indonesia*. Jakarta: Gramedia, 2003.

Burns, Peter. *Revelation and Revolution: Natsir and the Panca Sila*. Townsville (Australia): Committee of South-East Asian Studies, James Cook University of North Queensland, 1981.

*The Leiden Legacy: Concepts of Law in Indonesia*. Jakarta: PT Pradnya Paramita, 1999.

Burton, John. *The Sources of Islamic Law: Islamic Theories of Abrogation*. Edinburgh: Edinburgh University Press, 1990.

*The Collection of the Qur'an*. Cambridge: Cambridge University Press, 1997.

Bush, Robin. "Redefining 'Political Islam' in Indonesia: Nahdlatul Ulama and Khittah' 26." *SI* 7.2 (2000): 59–88.

Cabaton, A. "L'Enseignement supérieur aux Indes néerlandaises et le professeur Dr. C. Snouck Hurgronje." *RMM* 12 (1910): 544–49.

"La Presse indigène aux Indes néerlandaises." *RMM* 21 (1912): 330–48.
"La 'Sarékat Islam'." *RMM* 21 (1912): 348–56.
Cammack, Mark. "Indonesia's 1989 Religious Judicature Act: Islamization of Indonesia or Indonesianization of Islam?" *Indonesia* 63 (1997): 143–68.
Carré, Olivier. *Mysticism and Politics: A Critical Reading of Fī Ẓilāl Al-Qur'ān by Sayyid Quṭb, 1906–1966*, trans. Carol Artigues, ed. W. Sheppard. Boston: E. J. Brill, 2003.
Caspar, Robert. "Un aspect de la pensée musulmane moderne: Le renouveau do mo'tazilisme." *MIDEO* 4 (1957): 141–201.
Castles, Lance. "Notes on the Islamic School at Gontor." *Indonesia* 1 (June 1966): 30–45.
Chalil, Munawar. *Nilai Wanita*. Jakarta: Alma'arif, 1954.
*Biografi Empat Serangkai Imam Mazhab*. Jakarta: Bulan Bintang, 1955.
*Funksi Ulama dalam Masjarakat dan Negara*. Jakarta: Bulan Bintang, 1957.
*Kelengkapan Tarich Nabi Muhammad s.a.w*. Jakarta: Bulan Bintang, 1957.
*Tafsîr Qur'an Hidaajatul-Rahmaan*. Solo: Ab. Siti Sjamsijah, 1958.
*Kembali kepada Al Qur'an dan As-Sunnah*. Jakarta: Bulan Bintang, 1996.
Chartier, Roger. *Cultural History: Between Practices and Representations*, trans. L. G. Cochrane. Cambridge: Polity Press, 1988.
Cilardo, Agostino. *Dritto Ereditario Islamico delle Scuole Giuridiche Sunnite (Hanafita, Mâlikita, Sâfi'ita e Hanbalita) e delle Scuole Giuridiche Zaydita, Zâhirita e Ibâdita*. Rome: Instituto per l'Oriente, C. A. Nallino, 1994.
Commins, D. *The Salafi Islamic Reform Movement in Damascus*. Oxford: Oxford University Press, 1990.
*Compilation of Islamic Laws in Indonesia*. Jakarta: The Department of Religious Affairs, 1996.
Cook, Michael. "Ibn Qutayba and the Monkeys." *Studia Islamica* 89 (1999): 43–74.
*Commanding Right and Forbidding Wrong in Islamic Thought*. Cambridge: Cambridge University Press, 2001.
Coulson, Noel J. "The Concept of Progress and Islamic Law." In *Religion and Progress in Modern Asia*, ed. Robert Bellah, 74–92. New York: The Free Press, 1965.
"Al-Azhar in the Revolution." *Middle East Journal* 20 (1966): 31–49.
*Conflicts and Tensions in Islamic Jurisprudence*. Chicago: University of Chicago Press, 1969.
*Succession in the Muslim Family*. Cambridge: Cambridge University Press. 1971.
Crecelious, D. "Non-ideological Responses of the Egyptian Ulama to Modernization." In *Scholars, Saints and Sufis: Muslim Religious Institutions in the Middle East*, ed. Nikki R. Kiddie. Berkeley: University of California, 1972.
Crowe, Michael Bertram. *The Changing Profile of the Natural Law*. The Hague: Martinus Nijhoff, 1977.
Darmadi, Dadi. "IAIN dalam Wacana Intelektual Islam Indonesia." In *Problem dan Prospek IAIN: Antologi Pendidikan Tinggi Islam*, ed. Komaruddin Hidayat and Hendro Prasetyo, 333–68. Jakarta: Departemen Agama RI, 2000.

Daud, Ismail Che. *Tokoh-tokoh Ulama Semenanjung Malayu*. Kota Bharu: Majlis Ugama Islam dan Adat Istiadat Melayu Kelantan, 1992.

Davis, Winston. "Natural Law and Natural Right: The Role of Myth in the Discourses of Exchange and Community." In *Myth and Philosophy*. ed. Frank Reynolds and David Tracy, 349–79. Albany: SUNY Press, 1990.

*Dekrit Presiden Undang-Undang Dasar 1945 Piagam Djakarta*. Jakarta: P. N. Penerbit Pradnjaparamita, 1963.

Dewantara, Ki Hadjar. "Kultur Islam dan Kebudayaan Rakyat." *Panji Masjarakat* 4 (August 1959).

Dhofier, Zamakhsyari. *Tradisi Pesantren: Studi tentang Pandangan Hidup Kyai*. Yogyakarta: LP3 ES, 1982; reprint, 1990.

*Dictionnaire Biographique des Savants et Grandes Figures du Monde Musulman Periphérique, du XIXe siècle a nos jours*. Paris: CNRS/ EHESS, 1992–.

Didin, Syafruddin. "Maḥmūd Yūnus wa ittijāhātuhu fī tajdīd ta'līm al-lugha al-'arabiyya bi indūnīsiyā." *SI* 2.3 (1995): 173–98.

Diederich, Mathias. "A Closer Look at *Dakwah* and Politics in Indonesia: The *Partai Keadilan*." *Archipel* 64 (2002): 101–15.

Diehl, Katherine Smith. *Printers and Printing in the East Indies to 1850, vol. 1, Batavia*. New Rochelle: Aristide D. Caratzas, 1990.

Dijk, C. van. *Rebellion under the Banner of Islam: The Darul Islam in Indonesia*. The Hague: Martinus Nijhoff, 1981.

"'Communist Muslims' in the Dutch East Indies." In *State and Islam*, ed. C. van Dijk and A. H. de Groot, 77–95. Leiden: Research School CNWS, 1995.

Djaelani, Abdul Qadir. *Menelusuri Kekeliruan Pembaharuan Pemikiran Islam Nurcholish Madjid*. Bandung: Penerbit Yadia, 1994.

Djaja, Tamar. *Dr. Soekiman Wirjosandjojo, Ketua Oemoem 'Masjoemi'*. Boekit Tinggi: Penjiaran Ilmoe, n.d.

Djalil, Abdul, *et al. Fiqih Rakyat: Persatuan Fiqh dengan Kekuasaan*. Yogyakarta: LKiS, 2000.

*Djedjak Langkah Hadji A. Salim: Pilihan Karangan Utjapan dan Pendapat Beliau dari Dulu sampai Sekarang*. Jakarta: Tintamas, 1954.

Dobbin, Christine. *Islamic Revivalism in a Changing Peasant Economy: Central Sumatra, 1784–1847*. London: Curzon Press, 1983.

Douwes, Dick, and Nico Kaptein, eds. *Indonesia dan Haji: Empat Karangan*. Jakarta: INIS, 1997.

"Draf Kompilasi Hukum Islam Picu Kritik." *Republika On-line* www.republika.co.id/ASP/online_detail.asp?id=174636& kat_id=3

Drewes, G. W. J. "Snouck Hurgronje and the study of Islam." *BKI* 113 (1957): 1–15.

"Snouck Hurgronje: Pioneer in Islamic Studies." *Delta: A Review of Arts, Life, and Thought in the Netherlands* 1 (1958): 69–81.

*Directions for Travellers on the Mystic Path: Zakariyyā' Al-Anṣārī's* Kitāb Fatḥ Al-Raḥmān *and its Indonesian Adaptations – with an Appendix on Palembang Manuscripts and Authors*. The Hague: Martinus Nijhoff, 1977.

"Balai Pustaka and its Antecedents." In *Papers on Indonesian Languages and Literatures*, ed. Nigel Phillips and Khaidir Anwar, 97–104. London: Indonesian Etymological Project, 1981.

Dutton, Yasin. "The Introduction to Ibn Rushd's *Bidayat Al-Mujtahid*." *ILS* 1.2 (1994): 188–205.

Effendi, Ahmad Fuad, *et al. K. H. Imam Zarkasyi dari Gontor: Merintis Pesantren Modern*. Ponorogo: Gontor Press, 1996.

Effendi, Bahtiar. "Islam and the State in Indonesia: Munawir Sjadzali and the Development of a New Theological Underpinning of Political Islam." *SI* 2.2 (1995): 97–121.

Effendi, Djohan, and Ismed Natsir, eds. *Pergolakan Pemikiran Islam: Catatan-harian Ahmad Wahib*. Jakarta: LP3ES, 1981.

Effendy, Edy A., ed. *Dekonstruksi Islam Mazhab Ciputat*. Bandung: Zaman Wacana Mulia, 1999.

Eickelman, Dale F. "The Art of Memory: Islamic Education and its Social Reproduction." *Comparative Studies in Society and History* 20 (1978): 485–516.

"Traditional Islamic Learning and Ideas of the Person in the Twentieth Century." In *Middle Eastern Lives: The Practice of Biography and Self-Narrative*, ed. M. Kramer. Syracuse: Syracuse University Press, 1991.

"Mass Higher Education and the Religious Imagination in Contemporary Arab Societies." *American Ethnologist* 19.4 (1992): 643–55.

"The Coming Transformation in the Muslim World." 1999 Templeton Lecture on Religion and World Affairs delivered at the Foreign Policy Research Institute in Philadelphia on June 9, 1999/www.drsoroush.com/PDF/E-CMO-20000100-Eickelman.pdf

Eickelman, Dale F., and James Piscatori. *Muslim Politics*. Princeton: Princeton University Press, 1996.

Eldridge, Philip J. *Non-Government Organizations and Democratic Participation in Indonesia*. Kuala Lumpur: Oxford University Press, 1995.

El-Zine, M. A. Y. *Le Yemen et ses moyens d'information: Étude historique, politique, juridique sociale et critique – 1872–1974*. Algiers: Société Nationale d'Edition, 1978.

Esack, Farid. *Qur'an, Liberation, and Pluralism: An Islamic Perspective of Interreligious Solidarity Against Oppression*. Oxford: One World, 1997.

Esposito, John L., and John O. Voll. *Makers of Contemporary Islam*. Oxford: Oxford University Press, 2001.

Faiq, M. Hilmi, and Pradana Boy ZTF. *Kembali ke Al-Qur'an Menafsir Makna Zaman: Suara-suara Kaum Muda Muhammadiyah*. Malang: Universitas Muhammadiyah Malang, 2004.

Fanani, Ahmad Fuad. "Hermeneutika dan Alternatif Konstekstualisasi Al-Qur'an." *Tanwir: Jurnal Pemikiran Agama dan Peradaban* 1.2 (July 2003): 177–89.

Fauziyah AR, Ika Yunia. "Fiqh Sosial Perempuan." *Nuansa: Jurnal Pemikiran Keagamaan* 12 (2003): 55–64.

Federspiel, Howard M. *Persatuan Islam: Islamic Reform in Twentieth Century Indonesia*. Ithaca: Cornell University South East Asia Program, 1970.

*Muslim Intellectuals and National Development in Indonesia.* New York: Nova Science Publishers, 1992.

"The Endurance of Muslim Traditionalist Scholarship: An Analysis of the Writings of the Indonesian Scholar Siradjuddin Abbas." In *Toward a New Paradigm: Recent Developments in Indonesian Islamic Thought,* ed. Mark Woodward, 193–220. Tempe: Arizona State University Program for Southeast Asian Studies, 1996.

*Islam and Ideology in the Emerging Indonesian State: The Persatuan Islam (PERSIS), 1923–1957.* Leiden: E. J. Brill, 2001.

Feener, R. Michael. "Notes toward a History of Qur'anic Exegesis in Southeast Asia." *SI* 5.4 (1998): 47–76.

"A Re-examination of the Place of Al-Hallâj in the Development of Southeast Asian Islam." *BKI* 54.4 (1998): 571–92.

"Muharram Observances in the History of Bengkulu." *SI* 6.2 (1999): 87–130.

"Shaykh Yusuf and the Appreciation of Muslim 'Saints' in Modern Indonesia." *Journal for Islamic Studies* 18–19 (1999): 112–31.

"Indonesian Movements for the Creation of a 'National *Madhhab*'." *ILS* 9.1 (2002): 83–115.

"Contemporary Islam and Intellectual History." *ISIM Review* 17 (Spring 2006): 24–25.

"Islam, Technology and Modernity in the Nineteenth and Early Twentieth Centuries." In *The New Cambridge History of Islam,* vol VI. Cambridge: Cambridge University Press (forthcoming).

"Southeast Asian Localisations of Islam and Participation within a Global *Umma,* c. 1500–1800." In *The New Cambridge History of Islam,* vol. III. Cambridge: Cambridge University Press (forthcoming).

Feener, R. Michael, and Michael F. Laffan. "Sufi Scents across the Indian Ocean: Yemeni Hagiography and the Earliest History of Southeast Asian Islam." *Archipel* 70 (2005): 185–208.

Feener, R. Michael, and Mark E. Cammack, eds. *Islamic Law in Contemporary Indonesia: Ideas and Institutions.* Cambridge, MA: Harvard University Press, 2007.

Feillard, Andrée. "Les Oulémas indonésiens aujourd'hui: De l'opposition à une nouvelle légitimité." *Archipel* 46 (1993): 89–110.

*Islam et Armée dans l'Indonésie Contemporaine.* Paris: Editions l'Hartmann, 1995.

"Indonesia's Emerging Muslim Feminism: Women Leaders on Equality, Inheritance, and Other Gender Issues." *SI* 4.1 (1997): 83–112.

"Traditionalist Islam and the State in Indonesia: The Road to Legitimacy and Renewal." In *Islam in an Era of Nation States: Politics and Religious Renewal in Muslim Southeast Asia,* ed. Robert W. Hefner and Patricia Horvatich, 129–53. Honolulu: University of Hawaii Press, 1997.

"Indonesian Traditionalist Islam's Troubled Experience with Democracy (1999–2001)." *Archipel* 64 (2002): 117–44.

Feith, Herbert. *The Decline of Constitutional Democracy in Indonesia.* Ithaca: Cornell University Press, 1962.

"The Indonesian Student Movement of 1977–78." Unpublished typescript, 1978 (KITLV Bibliotheek 0219 8149).

Feith, Herbert, and Lance Castles, eds. *Indonesian Political Thinking, 1945–1965.* Ithaca: Cornell University Press, 1970.

Finnis, John M. *Aquinas: Moral, Political, and Legal Theory*. Oxford: Oxford University Press, 1998.

Frans Rudianto, HS. *Kebangkitan Islam di Indonesia dalam Percaturan Politik Nasional.* Jakarta: PT Golden Terayon Press, 1994.

Friedmann, Yohanan. *Prophecy Continuous: Aspects of Ahmadi Religious Thought and its Medieval Background.* Berkeley: University of California Press, 1989.

Foucault, Michel. "Nietzsche, Genealogy, History." In *The Focault Reader*, ed. Paul Rabinow, 76–100. New York: Pantheon Books, 1984.

Fuad Effendi, Ahmad, Amir Hamzah Wiryosukarto, *et al. K. H. Imam Zarkasyi dari Gontor: Merintis Pesantren Modern.* Ponorogo: Gontor Press, 1996.

Furnivall, J. S. *Netherlands India: A Study of Plural Economy.* Cambridge: Cambridge University Press, 1967.

Gallop, A. T. "Early Malay Printing: an Introduction to the British Library Collections." *JMBRAS* 63.1 (1990): 85–124.

Ghofur, Abdul. *Demokratisasi dan Prospek Hukum Islam di Indonesia: Studi atas Pemikiran Gus Dur.* Semarang: Pustaka Pelajar, 2002.

Gibb, H. A. R. *Whither Islam? A Survey of Modern Movements in the Moslem World.* London: V. Gollancz, 1932.

Gildin, Hilail, ed. *Political Philosophy: Six Essays by Leo Strauss.* Indianapolis: Pegasus, 1975.

Goldziher, I. *Die Richtungen der islamischen Koranauslegung.* Leiden: E. J. Brill, 1920.

Gonzalez-Quijano, Yves. "Le livre arabe dans les pays du subcontinent sud et sud-est asiatique." *Archipel* 40 (1990): 45–48.

Grotius, Hugo. *The Rights of War and Peace (De Jure Belli ac Pacis).* Washington: M. Walter Dunne, 1901.

H. A. Djalil Muhammad, and Haji Abdullah Syah, M. A., eds. *Sejarah Da'wah Islamiyah dan Perkembangannya di Sumatera Utara.* Medan: Majelis Ulama Daerah Tk. I Propinsi Sumatera Utara, 1983.

Haar, B. Ter. *Het adatproces der inlanders.* Leiden: E. J. Brill, 1915.

"Adaterfrecht op Java: Rechtsvorming en Rechtstoepassing." *Indisch Tijdschrift van het Recht* 148 (1938): 201–39.

*Adat Law in Indonesia*, trans. E. Adamson Hoebel and A. Arthur Schiller. New York: Institute of Pacific Relations, 1948.

Hadiwinata, Bob S. *The Politics of NGOs in Indonesia: Developing Democracy and Managing a Movement.* New York: Routledge Curzon, 2003.

Hahn, Ernest. "Sir Sayyid Ahmad Khan's 'The Controversy over Abrogation (in the Qur'an)': An Annotated Translation." *Muslim World*, 64.2 (1974): 124–33.

Haidar, M. Ali. *Nahdatul Ulama dan Islam di Indonesia: Pendekatan Fikih dalam Politik.* Jakarta: PT Gramedia Pustaka Utama, 1998.

Hairus, Salim HS and Muhammad Riwan, eds. *Kultur Hibrida: Anak Muda NU di Jalur Kultural.* Yogyakarta: LKiS, 1999.
Hakiem, Lukman. *Perjalanan Mencari Keadilan dan Persatuan: Biografi Dr. Anwar Harjono, SH.* Jakarta: Media Da'wah, 1993.
Hakiem, Lukman, and Tamsil Linrung. *Menunaikan Panggilan Risalah: Dokumentasi Perjalanan 30 Tahun Dewan Dakwah Islamiyah Indonesia.* Jakarta: DDII, 1997.
Hakiem, Lukman, ed. *Pemimpin Pulang: Rekaman Peristiwa Wafatnya M. Natsir.* Jakarta: Yayasan Piranti Ilmu, 1993.
Hakiem, Mohammad Luqman. "Mencegat Lompatan-Lompatan Gus Dur: Tinjauan Sufisme Al-Hikam." In *NU Pasca Gus Dur*, ed. A. S. Laksana, 107–22. Jakarta: Fatma Press, 1997.
Al-Halawi, Muhammad Abdul Aziz. *Fatwa dan Ijtihad Umar bin Khaththab: Ensiklopedi berbagai persoalan fiqih.* Surabaya: Risalah Gusti, 1999.
Hallaq, Wael B. "Was the Gate of *Ijtihād* Closed?" *IJMES* 16 (1984): 3–41.
"Introduction: Issues and Problems." *ILS* 3.2 (1996): 127–36.
*A History of Islamic Legal Theories: An Introduction to Sunnī Uṣūl Al-Fiqh.* Cambridge: Cambridge University Press, 1997.
*Authority, Continuity, and Change in Islamic Law.* New York: Cambridge University Press, 2001.
Halm, Heinz. *Die Ausbreitung der Šāfi'itischen Rechtschule von den Anfängen bis zum 8./14. Jahrhundert.* Wiesbaden: Ludwig Reichert, 1974.
Hamidy, U. U. *Riau Sebagai Pusat Bahasa dan Kebudayaan Melayu.* Pekan Baru: Bumi Pustaka, 1983.
Hamim, Thoha. "Moenawar Chalil's Reformist Thought: A Study of an Indonesian Religious Scholar, 1908–1961." Montreal, McGill University dissertation, 1996.
"Doktrin dan Tantangan Aswaja." *Aula: Majalah Nahdatul Ulama* 19.3 (March 1997): 58–62.
Hamka. *Ajahku: Riwajat hidup Dr. Abd. Karim Amrullah dan perdjuangan kaum agama.* Djakarta: Penerbit Widjaya, 1950.
*Tafsir Al-Azhar.* Jakarta: P. T. Pembimbing Masa, 1967–73.
*Tasauf Moderen.* Jakarta: Pustaka Panjimas, 1987.
Hamka, Rusjdi. "Mengiringi Safari Da'wah Warga Bulan Bintang." In *Pak Natsir 80 Tahun: Pandangan dan Penilaian Generasi Muda*, ed. H. Endang Saifuddin Anshari and M. Amien Rais, 15–24. Jakarta: Media Da'wah, 1988.
Hamzah, Abu Bakar. *Al-Imam: Its Role in Malay Society, 1905–1908.* Kuala Lumpur: Pustaka Antara, 1991.
Hamzah, Amir. *Pendidikan dan Pengajaran Muhammadiyah dalam Masa Pembaharuan Semesta.* Malang: Ken Mutia, 1965.
Hanafie, A. *Usul Fiqh.* Jakarta: Widjaja, 1959 (3rd printing 1963).
Handaroh, Siti. "Hubungan antara Adat dan Maslahat: Studi tentang Pemikiran Ahman Azhar Basyir." In *The Qur'an and Philosophical Reflections.* Yogyakarta: Titian Ilahi Press, 1998.

Hariri, Abdul-Hadi. "Afghani on the Decline of Islam: A Postscript." *WI* 14 (1973): 116–28.

Harjono, Anwar. *Hukum Islam: Keluasan dan Keadilannja*. Jakarta: Bulan Bintang, 1968.

"The Future of Islamic Law in Indonesia." *South East Asia Journal of Theology* 14.2 (1973): 56–60.

*Indonesia Kita: Pemikiran Berwawasan Iman-Islam*. Jakarta: Gema Insani Press, 1995.

*Perjalanan Politik Bangsa: Menoleh ke Belakang Menatap Masa Depan*. Jakarta: Gema Insani Press, 1997.

Harjono, Anwar, ed. *M. Natsir: Sumbangan dan Pemikirannya untuk Indonesia*. Jakarta: Media Da'wah, 1995.

Harlan, David. "Intellectual History and the Return of Literature." *American Historical Review* 94 (1989): 581–609.

Hasan, Ahmad Rifa'i, ed. *Warisan Intelektual Islam Indonesia*. Bandung: Mizan, 1987.

Hasan, M. Ali. *Perbandingan Mazhab Fiqh*. Jakarta: PT Raja Grafindo Persada, 1997.

Hasan, Noorhaidi. "Between Transnational Interest and Domestic Politics: Understanding Middle Eastern *Fatwās* on Jihad in the Moluccas." *ILS* 12.1 (2005): 73–92.

Hasbullah. *Sejarah Pendidikan Islam di Indonesia*. Jakarta: PT Raja Grafindo Persada, 1995.

Hassan, A. *Al-Boerhan*. Bandung: Persatuan Islam, 1928.

*Tafsîr Al-Furqän*. Bangil: Dewan Da'wah Islamiyah Indonesia, 1986.

*Tarjamah Bulughul Maraam (Ibnu Hajr al' Asqalani) Berikut Keterangan dan Penjelasannya*. Bangil: Pesantren Persatuan Islam, 1991.

*Pengajaran Shalat: Cara Shalat beserta Dalil-dalilnya*. Bangil: Pustaka Tamaam, 1996.

Hassan, A. *et al. Soal-Jawab tentang berbagai Masalah Agama*. Bandung: Diponegoro, 1985.

Hassan, Abdul Qadir. *Ushul Fiqih*. Bangil: Yayasan Al-Muslimun, 1992.

Hassan, Muhammad Kamal. *Mulsim Intellectual Responses to 'New Order' Modernization in Indonesia*. Kuala Lumpur: Dewan Bahasa dan Pustaka, 1980.

Haykel, B. "Al-Shawkani and the Jurisprudential Unity of Yemen." *Le Yémen, Passé et Présent de l'Unité*, ed. M. Tuchscherer. Aix-en-Provence: Édisud, 1988.

*Revival and Reform in Islam: The Legacy of Muhammad Al-Shawkani*. New York: Cambridge University Press, 2003.

Hazairin. *Ilmu Pengetahuan Islam dan Masjarakat*. Jakarta: Yayasan Perguruan Tinggi/Tintamas, 1951.

*Pergolakan Penjesuaian Adat kepada Hukum Islam*. Jakarta: Bulan Bintang, 1951.

*Indonesia Satu Masdjid*. Jakarta: Bintang Bulan, 1952.

*Hukum Kewarisan Bilateral Menurut Qur'ân dan Hadîth*. Jakarta: Tintamas, 1958.

*Hukum Kekeluargaan Nasional*. Jakarta: Tintamas, 1968.
*Demokrasi Pancasila*. Jakarta: Tintamas, 1970.
*Tujuh Serangkai tentang Hukum*. Jakarta: Tintamas, 1974.
*Hukum Kekeluargaan Nasional, ditambah dengan Lembaran Kerja untuk Rancangan Undang-undang Hukum Kewarisan Nasional Republik Indonesia*. Jakarta: Tintamas, 1982.
Hefner, Robert W. "Islam, State, and Civil Society: ICMI and the Struggle for the Indonesian Middle Class." *Indonesia* 36 (1993): 1–36.
"Modernity and the Challenge of Pluralism: Some Indonesian Lessons." *SI* 2.4 (1995): 21–45.
"Islamization and Democratization in Indonesia." In *Islam in an Era of Nation States*, ed. Robert Hefner and Patricia Horvatich, 75–128. Honolulu: University of Hawaii Press, 1997.
"Print Islam: Mass Media and Ideological Rivalries among Indonesian Muslims." *Indonesia* 64 (1997): 77–104.
*Civil Islam: Muslims and Democratization in Indonesia*. Princeton: Princeton University Press, 2000.
Hegel, Georg Wilhelm Friedrich. *Lectures on the Philosophy of Religion: One-volume Edition of the Lectures of 1827*, ed. Peter C. Hodgson. Berkeley: University of California Press, 1988.
Herring, B. B. "The Sarekat Islam: A Historical Perspective." In *Studies on Islam*, 1–14. James Cook University of North Queensland: Centre for Southeast Asian Studies, 1987.
Hidayat, Komaruddin. "Prolog: Budaya Lokal dalam Perspektif Baru." In *Sinergi Agama dan Budaya Lokal: Dialektika Muhammadiyah dan Seni Lokal*, ed. M. Thoyibi *et al.* Surakarta: Muhammadiyah University Press, 2003.
"Contemporary Liberal Islam in Indonesia, Pluralism, and the Secular State." In *A Portrait of Contemporary Indonesian Islam*, ed. Chaider S. Bamualim, 53–65. Jakarta: Pusat Bahasa dan Budaya UIN, 2005.
Hidayat, Komaruddin, and Hendro Prasetyo, eds. *Problem dan Prospek IAIN: Antologi Pendidikan Tinggi Islam*. Jakarta: Departemen Agama RI, 2000.
Hikam, Muhammad AS. "Gus Dur, Pembaharu, dan Cendekiawan Kelana: Sebuah Pengantar." In *NU Pasca Gus Dur*, ed. A. S. Laksana, 1–10. Jakarta: Fatma Press, 1997.
Himawan S., Anang Haris. *Epistemologi Syara': Mencari Format Baru Fiqih Indonesia*. Yogyakarta: Pustaka Pelajar, 2000.
Hisyam, Muhamad. *Caught Between Three Fires: The Javanese Penghulu under the Dutch Colonial Administration, 1882–1942*. Jakarta: INIS, 2001.
Hodgson, Marshall G. S. "Modernity and the Islamic Tradition." *Islamic Studies* 1.2 (1962).
*The Venture of Islam: Conscience and History in a World Civilization*. Chicago: Chicago University Press, 1974.
*Rethinking World History: Essays on Europe, Islam and World History*. Cambridge: Cambridge University Press, 1993.

Holleman, J. F. and H. W. J. Sonius, eds. *Van Vollenhoven on Indonesian Adat Law* The Hague: Martinus Nijhoff, 1981.
Hollenbach, David. *Claims in Conflict: Retrieving and Renewing the Catholic Human Rights Tradition.* New York: Paulist Press, 1979.
*The Global Face of Public Faith: Politics, Human Rights, and Christian Ethics.* Washington, DC: Georgetown University Press, 2003.
Hoogerwerf, E. J. *Persgeschiedenis van Indonesië tot 1942: Geannoteerde bibliographie.* Dordrecht: Foris Publications, 1990.
Hooker, M. B. *A Concise Legal History of Southeast Asia.* Oxford: Clarendon Press, 1978.
*Islamic Law in Southeast Asia.* Singapore: Oxford University Press, 1984.
*Indonesian Islam: Social Change through Contemporary Fatâwâ.* Honolulu: University of Hawaii Press, 2003.
Hosen, Ibrahim. *Fiqh Perbandingan dalam Masalah Nikah-Thalaq-Rudjuk dan Hukum Kewarisan.* Jakarta: Yayasan Ihja Ulumuddin Indonesia, 1971.
*Analyse: Ma huwa al-maysir/ Apakah Judi Itu?* Jakarta: Lembaga Kajian Ilmiah Institut Ilmu Al-Qur'an, 1987.
*Persoalan Taqlid dan Ijtihad.* Jakarta: Yayasan Wakaf Paramadina, 1987.
Howell, J. D. "Sufism and the Indonesian Islamic Revival." *Journal of Asian Studies* 60.3 (2001): 701–29.
Hugo, Graeme J., Terence H. Hull, Valerie J. Hull, and Gavin W. Jones. *The Demographic Dimension in Indonesian Development.* Singapore: Oxford University Press, 1987.
Huizinga, Johan. *The Autumn of the Middle Ages*, trans. Rodney J. Payton and Ulrich Mammitzch. Chicago: University of Chicago Press, 1996.
*Hukum Keluarga Mesir: Laporan Pelatihan Hakim Indonesia Gelombang II: Cairo 6–14 Desember 2003.* Jakarta: Yayasan Al-Hikmah, 2004.
Hull, Terence H. and Gavin W. Jones. "Demographic Perspectives." In *Indonesia's New Order: The Dynamics of Socio-Economic Transformation*, ed. Hal Hill, 123–78. Honolulu: University of Hawaii Press, 1994.
Husaini, Adian, and Nuim Hidayat. *Islam Liberal: Sejarah, Konsepsi, Penyimpangan, dan Jawabannya.* Jakarta: Gema Insani, 2002.
Husin, Asna. "Philosophical and Sociological Aspects of Da'wah: A Study of Dewan Dakwah Islamiyah Indonesia." Columbia University dissertation, 1998.
Ibn Al-Jawzī. *Kitāb Al-mawdū'āt.* Madina: Maktaba Al-Salafiyya, 1386–88 H./1966–68.
Ibn Khaldun. *The Muqaddimah: An Introduction to History*, trans. Franz Rosenthal. Princeton: Princeton University Press, 1958.
Ibn Sumayr, Sālim [Al-Ḥaḍramī]. *Matn Safinat Al-najā fī uṣūl al-dīn wa'l-fiqh.* Jakarta: n.d.
Ibrahimy, Moh. Nur El. *Teungku Muhammad Daud Beureueh: Peranannya dalam pergolakan di Aceh.* Jakarta: Gunung Agung, 1982.
Ichwan, Moch. Nur. "*'Ulamā'*, State and Politics: Majelis Ulama Indonesia after Suharto." *ILS* 12.1 (2005): 45–72.

Ihza, Yusril. "Combining Activism and Intellectualism: The Biography of Muhammad Natsir." *SI* 2.1 (1995): 111–48.

llyas, Yunahar, *et al.*, eds. *Muhammadiyah dan NU: Reorientasi Wawasan Keislaman.* Yogyakarta: Kerjasama LPPI/UMY, 1993.

*Indonesia: Muslims on Trial.* London: Tapol, 1987.

*Information on State Institute for Islamic Studies (IAIN).* Jakarta: Direktorat Pembinaan Perguruan Tinggi Agama Islam, Departemen Agama RI, 1988–89.

Iqbal, Muhammad. *The Reconstruction of Religious Thought in Islam.* Oxford: Oxford University Press, 1934.

Ismail, Faisal. "Pancasila as the Sole Basis for All Political Parties and for All Mass Organizations: An Account of Muslim Responses." *SI* 3.4 (1996): 1–92.

Jabali, Fuad and Jamhari, eds. *IAIN dan Modernisasi Islam di Indonesia.* Jakarta: UIN Jakarta Press, 2003.

Jabbar, Fakhrunnas M. A. *Buya H. Zaini Kunin: Sebutir Mutiara dari Lubuk Bendahara.* Pekanbaru: Universitas Islam Riau Press, 1990.

Al-Jabiri, Muhammad Abed. *Post-Tradisionalisme Islam.* Yogyakarta: LKiS, 2000.

Jackson, Sherman. "Fiction and Formalism: Toward a Functional Analysis of *Uṣūl Al-fiqh.*" In *Studies in Islamic Legal Theory,*" ed. Bernard G. Weiss, 177–201. Leiden: E. J. Brill, 2002.

Jahja, Muchtar. "Pidato Promosi Doctor Honoris Causa oleh IAIN Jogyakarta kepada Prof. Dr. Sjaich Mahmoud Shaltout." *Buku Tahunan Institut Agama Islam Negeri Al-Djami'ah Al-Islamijah Al-Hukumijah 1960–1962,* 109–72. Jogjakarta: IAIN Al-Djami'ah Al-islamijah Al-Hukumijah, 1962.

Jamil, M. Fathurrahman *Metode Ijtihad Majelis Tarjih Muhammadiyah.* Jakarta: Logos, 1995.

"The Muhammadiyah and the Theory of Maqasid Al-Shari'ah." *SI* 2.1 (1995): 53–68.

Jansen, J. J. G. *The Interpretation of the Koran in Modern Egypt.* Leiden: E. J. Brill, 1980.

"Polemics on Mustafa Mahmud's Koran Exegesis." *Proceedings of the Ninth Congress of the Union Européenne des Arabisants et Islamisants: Amsterdam, 1st to 7th September 1978,* ed. Rudolph Peters, 110–22. Leiden: E. J. Brill, 1981.

Johansen, Baber. *Contingency in a Sacred Law: Legal and Ethical Norms in the Muslim Fiqh.* Leiden: E. J. Brill, 1999.

Johns, A. H. "An Islamic System of Islamic Values? Nucleus of a Debate in Contemorary Indonesia." In *Islam and the Political Economy of Meaning,* ed. William R. Roff, 254–80. London: Croom Helm, 1987.

"Qur'anic Exegesis in the Malay World: In Search of a Profile." *Approaches to the History of the Interpretation of the Qur'an,* ed. Andrew Rippin, 257–87. Oxford: Clarendon Press, 1988.

"On Qur'anic Exegetes and Exegesis." *Islam - Essays in Scripture, Thought and Society: A Festschrift in honour of Anthony H. Johns,* ed. Peter Riddell and Tony Street, 3–49. Leiden: E. J. Brill, 1998.

Jomier, J. *Le commentaire Coranique du Manar: tendances modernes de l'exégèse coranique en Égypte.* Paris: Éditions G.-P. Maisonneuve & Cie, 1954.

"Quelques positions actuelles de l'exegésè coranique en Egypte relevées par une polémique récente." *MIDEO* 1 (1954).

"Programme et orientation des études à la faculté de théologie d'Al-Azhar." *Revue des Etudes Islamiques* 44 (1976): 253–72.

Jones, Gavin W. *Marriage and Divorce in Islamic Southeast Asia.* Kuala Lumpur: Oxford University Press, 1994.

Junus, Mahmud. *Sedjarah Pendidikan Islam di Indonesia.* Jakarta: 1960.

Juynboll, G. H. A. *The Authenticity of the Tradition Literature: Discussions in Modern Egypt.* Leiden: E. J. Brill, 1969.

Juynboll, Th. W. *Handleiding tot de Kennis van de Mohammedaansche Wet volgens de Leer der Sjâfi'itishe School.* Leiden: E. J. Brill, 1930.

Ka'bah, Rifyal. *Penegakan Syariat Islam di Indonesia.* Jakarta: Penerbit Khairul Bayan, 2004.

Kahin, George McTurnan. *Nationalism and Revolution in Indonesia.* Ithaca: Cornell University Press, 1952.

Kahin, George McTurnan, and Audrey R. Kahin. *Subversion as Foreign Policy: The Secret Eisenhower and Dulles Debacle in Indonesia.* New York: The New Press, 1995.

Kamali, Mohammad Hashim. *Principles of Islamic Jurisprudence.* Cambridge: Islamic Texts Society, 1991.

*Kami Memanggil.* Jakarta: Dewan Pemimpin Partai Masjumi Bahagian Penerangan, 1955.

Kaptein, Nico. *Muhammad's Birthday Festival.* Leiden: E. J. Brill, 1993.

"An Arab Printer in Surabaya in 1853." *BKI* 149.2 (1993): 356–52.

"The Berdiri Mawlid Issue among Indonesian Muslims in the Period from circa 1875 to 1930." *BKI* 149.1 (1993): 124–53.

*The Muhimmāt Al-Nafā'is: A Bilingual Meccan Fatwa Collection for Indonesian Muslims from the End of the Nineteenth Century.* Jakarta: INIS, 1997.

Karim, M. Rusli. *HMI, MPO dalam Kemelut Modernisasi Politik di Indonesia.* Bandung: Mizan, 1997.

Khalid, Deltev. "Some Aspects of Neo-Mu'tazilism." *Islamic Studies* 8 (1969): 319–47.

"Ahmad Amin and the Legacy of Muhammad Abduh." *Islamic Studies* 9.1 (1970).

Al-Khallāf, 'Abd Al-Wahhāb. *Maṣādir Al-tashrī' Al-islāmī fī mā lā naṣṣ fīhi.* Cairo: Dār Al-Kitāb Al-'Arabī, 1955.

*'Ilm uṣūl Al-fiqh.* Cairo: Matba'a Al-Naṣr, 1956.

Khoiruddin Nasution. *Status Wanita di Asia Tenggara: Studi Terhadap Perundang-undangan Perkawinan Muslim Kontemporer di Indonesia dan Malaysia.* Jakarta: INIS, 2002.

Khuluq, Latiful. "K. H. Asy'ari's Contribution to Indonesian Independence." *SI* 5.1 (1998): 41–67.

Kimber, Richard. "The Qur'anic Law of Inheritance." *ILS* 5.3 (1998): 291–325.

Kimman, Eduard. *Indonesian Publishing.* Baarn: Hollandia, 1981.

Koesnoe, Moh. *Kapita Selecta Hukum Adat: Suatu Pemikiran Baru*. Jakarta: Ikatan Hakim Indonesia, 2002.

*Kompilasi Hukum Islam di Indonesia*. Jakarta: Departemen Agama RI, 1995–96.

Kraemer, Hendrik. "La Presse arabe aux Indes néerlandaises." *RMM* 46 (1921): 214–19.

Kraus, Werner. *Zwischen Reform und Rebellion, über die Entwicklung des Islams in Minangkabau (Westsumatra) zwischen den beiden Reformbewegungen der Padri (1837) und der Modernisten (1908)*. Weisbaden: Franz Steiner Verlag, 1984.

Krawietz, Birgit. "Cut and Paste in Legal Rules: Designing Islamic Norms with *Talfiq*." *WI* 42.1 (2002): 2–40.

Kurzman, Charles, ed. *Liberal Islam: A Sourcebook*. New York: Oxford University Press, 1998.

LaCapra, Dominick. "Rethinking Intellectual History and Reading Texts." In *Modern European Intellectual History: Reappraisals and New Perspectives*, ed. Dominick LaCapra and Steven L. Kaplan, 47–85. Ithaca: Cornell University Press, 1982.

*Soundings in Critical Theory*. Ithaca: Cornell University Press, 1989.

Laffan, Michael. *Islamic Nationhood and Colonial Indonesia: The Umma Below the Winds*. London: Routledge, 2003.

"An Indonesian Community in Cairo: Continuity and Change in a Cosmopolitan Islamic Milieu." *Indonesia* 77 (April 2004): 1–26.

"The *Fatwā* Debated? *Shūrā* in one Indonesian Context." *ILS* 12.1 (2005): 93–121.

Laoust, Henri. "Le Réformisme Orthodoxe des Salafiya' et les caractères généraux de son orientation actuelle." *Revue des Études Islamiques* (1934): 175–224.

*Essai sur les doctrines sociales et politiques de Takî-d-dîn Ahmad b. Taimîya, canoniste Hanbalite né à Harrân en 661/1262, mort à Damas en 728/1328*. Cairo: Imprimerie de l'Institut Français d'Archéologie Orientale, 1939.

Layish, Aharon. "The Transformation of the Shariʿ from Jurists' Law to Statutory Law in the Contemporary Muslim World." *WI* 44.1 (2004): 85–113.

Lee, Robert D. *Overcoming Tradition and Modernity: The Search for Islamic Authenticity*. Boulder: Westview Press, 1997.

Leiden, C. *The Conflict of Traditionalism and Modernism in the Muslim Middle East*. Austin: University of Texas Press, 1966.

"Lembaga Penggugat *Pesantren*." *Aula: Majalah Nahdlatul Ulama* 19.8 (1997): 43–46.

Lemke, Wolf-Dieter. *Mahmud Saltut (1893–1963) und die Reform der Azhar: Untersuchungen zu Erneuerungsbestrebungen im agyptisch-islamischen Erziehungssystem*. Frankfurt am Main: P. D. Lang, 1980.

Lev, Daniel. *The Transition to Guided Democracy: Indonesian Politics, 1957–1959*. Ithaca: Cornell University Modern Indonesia Project, 1966.

*Islamic Courts in Indonesia: A Study in the Political Bases of Legal Institutions*. Berkeley: University of California Press, 1972.

Libson, Gideon. *Jewish and Islamic Law: A Comparative Study of Custom During the Geonic Period*. Cambridge, MA: Harvard University Press, 2003.

Liddle, R. William. "*Media Dakwah* Scripturalism: One Form of Islamic Political Thought and Action in New Order Indonesia." In *Toward a New Paradigm: Recent Developments in Indonesian Islamic Thought*, ed. Mark Woodward, 323–56. Tempe: Arizona State University Program for Southeast Asian Studies, 1996.

Lubis, Nur Ahmad Fadhil. "Institutionalization and the Unification of Islamic Courts under the New Order." *SI* 2.1 (1995): 1–52.

Lucas, Anton. *Local Opposition and Underground Resistance to the Japanese in Java, 1942–1945.* Melbourne: Monash University Centre of Southeast Asian Studies, 1986.

Lukens-Bull, Ronald A. "Metaphorical Aspects of Indonesian Islamic Discourse about Development." In *Toward a New Paradigm: Recent Developments in Indonesian Islamic Thought*, ed. Mark R. Woodward, 265–90. Tempe: Arizona State University Program for Southeast Asian Studies, 1996.

Lukito, Ratno. "Islamic Law and the Colonial Encounter: The Experience of India and Indonesia." In *The Dynamics of Islamic Civilization (Satu Dasawarsa Program Pembibitan, 1988–1998)*, ed. Wahyudi, 209–30. Yogyakarta: Titian Ilahi Press, 1998.

Lukman, Ali. "Persoalan Adat sebagai thema." *Sastra* 6. 2–4 (1960).

Luth, Thohir. *M. Natsir: Dakwah dan Pemikirannya.* Jakarta: Gema Insani, 1999.

Maʿarif, Zainul, ed. *Dekonstruksi Islam: Elaborasi Pemikiran Hassan Hanafi dan Nasr Hamid Abu Zayd.* Cairo: Lakpesdam Press, 2003.

Madaniy Malik. "Cara Pengambilan Hukum Islam dalam Bachtsul Masail Nahdlatul Ulama (Sebuah Alternatif Pengembangan)." *Aula: Majalah Nahdlatul Ulama* (Des. 1991): 53–63.

"Ijtihâd dalam Kemantapan Hidup Bermadzhab (Dari Halqah-halqah di *Pesantren* sampai dengan Munas Alim Ulama NU di Bandar Lampung)." *Al-Jamiah* 51 (1993): 21–33.

Madinier, Rémy. "Du temps des chameaux à celui du béton radioactive les nouveaux usages islamistes du passé." *Archipel* 64 (2002): 145–61.

Madinier, Remy, and Andrée Feillard. "At the Sources of Indonesian Political Islam's Failure: The Split between the Nahdlatul Ulama and the Masyumi in Retrospect." *SI* 6.2 (1999): 1–38.

Madjid, Nurcholish, ed. *Khazanah Intelektual Muslim.* Jakarta: Bulan Bintang, 1984.

"Tasauf sebagai Inti Keberagamaan." *Pesantren* 2. 3 (1985): 3–9.

*Islam, Kemoderenan, dan Keindonesiaan.* Bandung: Mizan, 1987.

*Islam Doktrin dan Peradaban: Sebuah Telaah Kritis tentang Maslalah Keimanan, Kemanusiaan, dan Kemoderenan.* Jakarta: Paramadina, 1992.

"Beberapa Renungan Tentang Kehidupan Keagamaan untuk Generasi Mendatang." *Ulumul Qur'an* 4.1 (1993): 4–25.

"Islamic Roots of Modern Pluralism, Indonesian Experience." *SI* 1.1 (1994): 55–78.

*Islam Agama Kemanusiaan: Membangun Tradisi dan Visi Baru Islam Indonesia.* Jakarta: Paramadina, 1995.

*Masyarakat Religius*. Jakarta: Paramadina 1997: 139–46.

"Profil Ulama Berpengertian, Istiqâmah, dan Tasâmuh." *Wacana Baru Fiqih Sosial*, ed. Jamal D. Rahman, 344–48. Bandung: Mizan, 1997.

*Tradisi Islam: Peran dan Fungsinya dalam Pembangunan di Indonesia*. Jakarta: Paramadina 1997.

*Indonesia Kita*. Jakarta: Universitas Paramadina, 2003.

*The True Face of Islam: Essays on Islam and Modernity in Indonesia*. Jakarta: Voice Center Indonesia, 2003.

Mahadi. *Beberapa Tjatetan Tentang Peradilan Agama*. Medan: Fakultas Hukum USU, 1969.

Mahasin, Aswab, *et al.*, eds. *Ruh Islam dalam Budaya Bangsa*. Jakarta: Yayasan Festival Istiqlal, 1996.

Mahayana, Maman S., Oyon Sofyan, and Achmad Dian. *Ringkasan dan Ulasan Novel Indonesia Modern*. Jakarta: Grasindo, 1992.

Mahdi, S. M. "Islamic Philosophy in Contemporary Islamic Thought." In *God and Man in Contemporary Islamic Thought*, ed. C. Malik. Beirut: American University Press, 1972.

Mahfudh, Sahal. *Kitab Kuning di Pesantren–Makalah untuk munazfarah pengembangan ulumud diniyah melalui telaah kitab kuning secara siyaqiyah (kontekstual) di Pondok Pesantren Darussalam Watucongol*. Magelang: n.p., 1988.

*Nuansa Fiqih Sosial*. Yogyakarta: Lembaga Kajian Islam dan Sosial (LKiS), 1994.

*Dialog dengan KH MA Sahal Mahfudh: Telaah Fikih Sosial*. Semarang: Yayasan Karyawan Suara Merdeka, 1997.

*Dialog Dengan Kiai Sahal Mahfudh: Solusi Problematika Umat*. Surabaya: Ampel Suci, 2003.

*Pesantren Mencari Makna*. Jakarta: Pustaka Ciganjur, 1999.

Mahfudh, Sahal, and Mustofa Bisri. *Ensiklopedi Ijmak: Persepakatan Ulama dalam Hukum Islam (Berdasarkan Karya Sa'di Abu Habieb)*. Jakarta: Pustaka Firdaus, 1987/2nd printing 2003.

Mahmud, Said, ed. *15 Tahun Institut Agama Islam Negeri Jami'ah Ar-Raniry Darussalam Banda Aceh*. Banda Aceh: Panitia Harijadi ke-XV IAIN Jami'ah Ar-Raniry, 1978.

Makdisi, George. "Muslim Institutions of Learning in Eleventh-Century Baghdad." *BSOAS* 24 (1961): 1–56.

"Law and Traditionalism in the Institutions of Learning of Medieval Islam." In *Theology and Law in Islam*, ed. G. E. von Grunebaum, 75–88. Wiesbaden: Otto Harrassowitz, 1971.

Mallat, C. *The Renewal of Islamic Law: Muhammad Baqer As-Sadr, Najaf and the Shi'i International*. Cambridge: Cambridge University Press, 1993.

Manan, Bagir. "Peranan Peradilan Agama dalam Pembinaan Hukum Nasional." In *Hukum Islam di Indonesia: Pemikiran dan Praktek*, ed. Juhaya S. Praja, 143–54. Bandung: Rosdakarya, 1991.

Mandal, Sumit. "Forging a Modern Arab Identity in Java in the Early Twentieth Century." In *Transcending Borders: Arabs, Politics, Trade, and Islam in Southeast*

*Asia*, ed. Huub de Jonge and Nico Kaptein, 163–84. Leiden: KITLV Press, 2002.

Al-Maragi, A. M. *Terjemah Tafsîr Al-Maragi*. Semarang: Toha Putra, 1992.

Al-Marāghī, Muṣṭafā. *Tafsīr Al-Marāghī*. Cairo: Muṣṭafā al-Bābī al-Ḥalabī, 1946.

*Al-ijtihād fī al-Islām*. Cairo: Al-Maktab Al-Fann, 1959.

Al-Marbawī, Muḥammad Idrīs. *Qamūs 'Arab-Malāyū*. Cairo: Muṣṭafā al-Bābī al-Ḥalabī, 1931.

*Baḥr Al-Māzī sharḥ bāgī mukhtaṣar ṣaḥīḥ Al-Tirmidhī*, 22 vols. Cairo: Muṣṭafā Al-Bābī Al-Ḥalabī, 1933–41.

Marcoes, Lies M. "The Female Preacher as a Mediator in Religion: A Case Study in Jakarta and West Java." In *Women and Mediation in Indonesia*, ed. Sita van Bemmelen *et al.*, 203–28. Leiden: KITLV Press, 1992.

Marcoes-Natsir, Lies M. "Profil Organisasi Wanita Islam Indonesia: Studi Kasus Peristri." In *Wantia Islam Indonesia dalam Kajian Tekstual dan Kontekstual*, ed. Lies M. Marcoes-Natsir and Johan Hendrik Meuleman, 95–110. Jakarta: INIS, 1993.

Mardin, S. "Some Explanatory Notes on the Origins of the *Mecelle*." *Muslim World* 51 (1961): 185–210.

Maritain, Jacques. *Natural Law: Reflections on Theory and Practice*, ed. and introduced by William Sweet. South Bend, IN: St. Augustine's Press, 2001.

Martin, Richard C., and Mark Woodward, with Dwi S. Atmaja. *Defenders of Reason in Islam: Mu'tazilism from Medieval School to Modern Symbol*. Oxford: One World, 1997.

Mas'adi, Ghufron A. *Pemikiran Fazlur Rahman tentang Metodologi Pembaharuan Hukum Islam*. Jakarta: Rajawali Pers, 1997.

Massier, A. W. H. "Van Recht naar Hukum: Indonesische juristen en hun taal, 1915–2000." Leiden University dissertation, 2003.

Mastuhu. "Kiai Tanpa Pesantren: K. H. Ali Yafie dalam Peta Kekuatan Sosial Islam Indonesia." In *Wacana Baru Fiqih Sosial*, ed. Jamal D. Rahman *et al.*, 259–72. Bandung: Mizan, 1997.

Mas'udi, Masdar F., ed. *Islam Indonesia Menatap Masa Depan*. Jakarta: P3M, 1990.

ed. *Fiqh Permusyawaratan: Perwakilan Rakyat* (Seri Halqah). Ciapsung: P3M, 1992.

"Menuju Keberagamaan yang Pluralistik: Reorientasi Pemikiran Keagamaan Nahdhatul Ulama-Muhammadiyah." In *Muhammadiyah dan NU: Reorientasi Wawasan Keislaman*, ed. Yunahar Ilyas, 183–91. Yogyakarta: Kerjasama LPPI UMY, LPKSM NU and PP Al-Muhsin, 1993.

"Pembaruan Nurcholish di Mata Orang *Pesantren*." *Ulumul Qur'an* 4.1 (1993): 28–33.

"Perempuan di antara Lembaran Kitab Kuning." In *Wanita Islam dalam Kajian Tekstual dan Kontekstual*, ed. Lies M. Marcoes-Natsir and J. H. Mueleman, 155–64. Jakarta: INIS, 1993.

*Islam and Women's Reproductive Rights*. Kuala Lumpur: Sisters in Islam, 2002.

Mas'udi, Masdar F., Mohamad Ichwan Syam, and Slamet Effendy Yusuf. *Dinamika Kaum Santri: Menelusuri Jejak dan Pergolakan Internal NU*. Jakarta: CV. Rajawali, 1983.

Mas'udi, Masdar F., with Lies Marcoes and Rosalia Sciortino. "Learning from Islam: Advocacy of Reproductive Rights in Indonesian *Pesantren*." *SI* 4. 2 (1997): 83–103.

Masud, Muhammad Khalid, Brinkley Messick, and David S. Powers, eds. "Muftis, *Fatwas*, and Islamic Legal Interpretation." In *Islamic Legal Interpretation: Muftis and their Fatwas*. Cambridge, MA: Harvard University Press, 1996.

Masyhur, M. *Saham H. O. S. Tjokroaminoto dalam kebangunan Islam dan nasionalsme di Indonesia*. Yogyakarta: Nur Chahaya, 1980.

Masyhuri, A. Aziz. *Masalah Keagamaan: Hasil Muktamar dan Munas Ulama NU kesatu 1926 s/d kedua puluh sembilan 1994*. Surabaya: PP RMI and Dinamika Press, 1997.

Matheson, Virginia. "Pulau Penyengat: Nineteenth Century Islamic Centre of Riau." *Archipel* 37 (1989): 153–72.

Matsura, Datu Michael O. "The Impact of Modern Development on Islam in Southeast Asia." In *International Seminar on Islam in Southeast Asia, Organized by the State Institute of Islamic Studies 'Syarif Hidayatullah' Jakarta in Cooperation with the Asia Foundation Jakarta*, 44–53. Jakarta: Lembaga Penelitian Syarif Hidayatullah, 1986.

Maududi, Abul A'la. *First Principles of the Islamic State*. Lahore: Islamic Publications Ltd., 1997 (7th edn).

McVey, Ruth. "Faith as the Outsider: Islam in Indonesian Politics." In *Islam in the Political Process*, ed. James P. Piscatori, 199–225. Cambridge: Cambridge University Press, 1983.

Metcalf, Barbara D. *Islamic Revival in British India: Deoband, 1860–1900*. Princeton: Princeton University Press, 1982.

Meuleman, Johan Hendrik, ed. *Tradisi, Kemoderenan dan Metamodernisme: Memperbincangkan Pemikiran Mohammed Arkoun*. Yogyakarta: LKiS, 1996.

Meuleman, Johan Hendrik, and Henri Chambert-Loir. "Les instituts islamiques publics indonésiens." In *Madrasa: La Transmission du Savoir dans le Monde Musulman*, ed. Nicole Grandin and Marc Gaborieau, 199–216. Paris: Éditions Arguments, 1997.

Miert, Hans van. "Een Koel Hoofd en een Warm Hart: Nationalisme, Javanisme, en Jeugdbeweging in Nederlands-Indië, 1918–1930." Leiden University dissertation, 1995.

Miichi, Ken. "Kiri Islam, Jaringan Intelektual dan Partai Politik: Sebuah Catatan Awal." *TA* 9 (2000): 155–69.

"Indonesia okeru isuramu saha to chisikijin netowaku." *Tōnan Ajia Kenkyu* 40.1 (2002): 42–73.

"Islamic Youth Movements in Indonesia." *IIAS Newsletter* 32 (2003): 22.

Minhaji, Akh. "Ahmad Hassan and Islamic Legal Reform in Indonesia, 1887–1958." McGill University dissertation, 1997.

"Kontribusi Dr. Wael B. Hallaq dalam Kajian Hukum Islam." In *Pengalaman Belajar Islam di Kanada*, ed. Yudian W. Asmin, 115–42. Yogyakarta: Permika and Titian Ilahi, 1997.

Minhaji, Akh, and Iskandar Arnel. *Petunjuk Praktis Belajar di Institute of Islamic Studies, McGill University, Montreal, Kanada*. Yogyakarta: Permika, 1997.

Mintaredja, Moh. Sjafa'at. *Renungan Pembaruan Pemikiran: Masyarakat Islam dan Politik di Indonesia*. Jakarta: Permata, 1971.

*Rekonstruksi Pemikiran Agama: Rationalisme versus Iman*. Jakarta: Tunas Jaya, 1975.

Misrawi, Zuhairi. "Dari Tradisionalisme Menuju Post-Tradisionalisme Islam: Geliat Pemikiran Baru Islam Arab." *TA* 9 (2000): 47–61.

Misrawi, Zuhairi, *et al. Dari Syariat menuju Maqashid Syariat: Fundamentalisme, Seksualitas, dan Kesehatan Reproduksi*. Jakarta: KIKJ/ Ford Foundation, 2003.

Mitchell, Richard P. *The Society of the Muslim Brothers*. New York: Oxford University Press, 1969.

Mobini-Kesheh, Natalie. "The Arab Periodicals of the Netherlands East Indies, 1914–1942." *BKI* 152.2 (1996): 236–56

*The Hadrami Awakening: Community and Identity in the Netherlands Indies*. Ithaca: Cornell University Southeast Asian Studies Program, 1996.

Morsink, Johannes. *The Universal Declaration of Human Rights: Origins, Drafting, and Intent*. Philadelphia: University of Pennsylvania Press, 1999.

Mudzhar, Mohamad Atho. *Fatwa-Fatwa Majelis Ulama Indonesia: Sebuah Studi tentang Pemikiran Hukum Islam di Indonesia, 1975–1988*. Jakarta: INIS, 1993.

Mugni, Syafiq A. *Hassan Bandung: Pemikir Islam Radikal*. Surabaya: Bina Ilmu, 1980.

Muhajir, Afifudin, and Imam Nahe'i. "Fungsionalisasi Ushul Fiqih dalam *Bahtsul Masa'il NU*." In *Kritik Nalar Fiqih NU: Transformasi Paradigma Bahtsul Masa'il*, ed. M. Imdadun Rahmat, 243–63. Jakarta: Lakpesdam, 2002.

Muhammad, Husein. *Fiqh Perempuan: Refleksi Kiai atas Wacana Agama dan Gender*. Yogyakarta: LKiS, 2001.

Muhammad, Munib Huda. *Mutiara Nahdlatul Ulama*. Jakarta: Fatma Press, 1998.

*Muktamar Masjumi ke VIII – 22–29 Des. 1956 di Bandung*. Jakarta: N. V. Pertjetakan Gunung Sahari, 1956.

Mulia, Musdah. *Pandangan Islam tentang Poligami*. Jakarta: Lembaga Kajian Agama dan Jender, 1999.

Mulkhan, Abdul Munir. *Masalah-Masalah Teologi dan Fiqh dalam Tarjih Muhammadiyah*. Yogyakarta: SI Press, 1994.

Mulyati, Sri, *et al. Islam and Development: A Politico-Religious Response*. Montreal: Permika, 1997.

Munadi, Kusmana and Yudhi, eds. *Proses Perubahan IAIN menjadi UIN Syarif Hidayatullah Jakarta: Rekaman Media Massa*. Jakarta: UIN Jakarta Press, 2002.

Munawar-Rachman, Budhy, ed. *Kontekstualisasi Doktrin Islam dalam Sejarah*. Jakarta: Paramadina, 1994.

Munhanif, Ali. "Islam and the Struggle for Religious Pluralism in Indonesia: A Political Reading of the Religious Thought of Mukti Ali." *SI* 3.1 (1996): 79–126.

Mursjid, Hasbullah. *Approach Da'wah Islamijah terhadap Komunisme/ Marxisme-Leninisme: Pidato Hari Lahir ke-II, Institute Agama Islam Negeri Djami'ah*

*Antasari*. Bandjarmasin: (unpublished MS/ KITLV Bibliotheek 01774452), Nov 20, 1966.

Mussalam, A. "Sayyid Qutb's Literary and Spiritual Orientation (1932–1938)." *Muslim World* 80.3 (1990).

"Sayyid Qutb and Social Justice, 1945–1948." *Journal of Islamic Studies* 4.1 (1993).

Mutholib, Abdul. *Prospek Hukum Islam Terhadap Hukum Nasional*. Surabaya: Bina Ilmu, 1987.

Muzadi, A. Muchith. *NU dan Fiqh Kontesktual*. Yogyakarta: LPKSM NU DIY, 1994.

Muzani, Saiful. "Mu'tazilah and the Modernization of the Indonesian Muslim Community: Intellectual Portrait of Harun Nasution." *SI* 1.1 (1994): 93–131.

Nafis, Abd. Wadud, and Darmanto, trans. *Sebab-sebab Munculnya Madzhab Fiqih*. Jakarta: Arista Brahmatyasa, 1996.

Nafis, Muhammad Wahyuni, ed. *Kontekstualisasi Ajaran Islam: 70 Tahun Prof. Dr. H. Munawir Sjadzali*. Jakarta: Yayasan Wakaf Paramadina, 1995.

Nagata, Judith. *The Reflowering of Malaysian Islam: Modern Religious Radicals and their Roots*. Vancouver: University of British Columbia Press, 1984.

Nahe'i. "Madzhab Maslahah: Studi Analysis Komparatif Konsep Maslahah Asy-saytibi dan Najmuddin Ath-Thufi sebagai Upaya Membangun Madhzhab Kemaslahatan." Malang: Universitas Islam Malang M.A. thesis, 2002.

Nakamura, Mitsuo. *The Crescent Arises over the Banyan Tree: A Study of the Muhammadiyah Movement in a Central Javanese Town*. Yogyakarta: Gadjah Madah University Press, 1983.

Nasir, Tamara, *et al.*, eds. *Hamka di Mata Hati Umat*. Jakarta: Sinar Harapan, 1983.

Nasr, Seyyed Vali Reza. *The Vanguard of the Islamic Revolution: The Jama 'at-i Islami of Pakistan*. Berkeley: University of California Press, 1994.

Nasserie, A. W. *Al-Islam wan-naçranijjah, atau Islam dan Christen*. Batavia: n.p., 1926.

Nasution, Adnan Buyung. *The Aspiration for Constitutional Government in Indonesia: A Socio-legal Study of the Indonesian Konstituante, 1956–1959*. Jakarta: Pustaka Sinar Harapan, 1992.

Nasution, Harun. *Pembaharuan dalam Islam*. Jakarta: Bulan Bintang, 1982.

*Pembaharuan dalam Islam*. Jakarta: Bulan Bintang, 1985.

*Muhammad Abduh dan Teologi Rasional Mu 'tazilah*. Jakarta: UI Press, 1987.

*Islam Rasional: Gagasan dan Pemikiran*. Bandung: Mizan, 1995.

Nasution, Khoiruddin. "*Maslahah* and its Application in Indonesian *Fatwa*." *SI* 3.4 (1996): 103–36.

Nasution, Lahmuddin. *Pembaruan Hukum Islam dalam Mazhab Syafi 'i*. Bandung: Rosda, 2001.

Nasution, Yunan Yusuf. *Corak Pemikiran Kalam Tafsir Al-Azhar: Sebuah Telaah tentang pemikiran Hamka dalam teologi Islam*. Jakarta: Pustaka Panjimans, 1990.

Nata, Abuddin, *et al. Membangun Pusat Keunggulan Studi Islam: Sejarah dan Profil Pimpinan IAIN Syarif Hidayatullah Jakarta, 1957–2002.* Jakarta: IAIN Jakarta Press, 2002.

Natsir, Mohammad. *Islam dan Akal Merdeka.* Tasikmalaja: Persatoean Islam, 1947. (Originally appeared in *Panji Islam* – Medan, 1941.)

*Islam Sebagai Ideologie.* Jakarta: Penjiaran Ilmu (post 1950) – tjetakan kedua.

*Capita Selecta* I. Bandung: W. van Hoeve, 1954.

*Capita Selecta* II. Jakarta: Pustaka Pendis, 1957.

*Tindjauan Hidup.* Jakarta: Penerbit Widjaya, 1957.

*Fiqhud-Da 'wah: Djedjak Risalah – Dasar2 Da 'wah.* Jakarta: Penerbit Madjalah Islam "Kiblat," 1969.

*Islam dan Kristen di Indonesia.* Jakarta: Peladjar/Bulan Sabit, 1969.

*Masalah Palestina.* Jakarta: Penerbit Hudaya, 1971.

*Mencari Modus Vivendi antar Ummat Beragama di Indonesia.* Jakarta: Media Da'wah, 1980.

*Pendidikan, Pengorbanan, Kepemimpinan, Primordialisme, dan Nostalgia.* Jakarta: Media Da'wah, 1987.

*Demokrasi di Bawah Hukum.* Jakarta: Penerbit Media Da'wah, 1988 (based upon lectures given in 1966).

*Islam sebagai Dasar Negara.* Jakarta: DDII, 2000.

*Agama dan Negara dalam Perspektif Islam.* Jakarta: Penerbit Media Dakwah, 2001.

*Demokrasi di bawah Hukum.* Jakarta: Penerbit Media Da'wah, 2002.

*Di Bawah Naungan Risalah.* Jakarta: Media Da'wah, 2002 (1st printed 1971).

Natsir, Mohammad, and A. S. Nasroen. *Hidup Bahagia.* Bandung: Penerbitan Vorkink – van Hoeve, 1954.

Al-Nawawī, Muḥammad b. 'Umar. *Sharḥ 'Uqūd Al-lujjayn fī bayān ḥuqūq Al-zawjayn.* Singapore: Al-Ḥaramayn, n.d.

Nayed, A. A. "The Radical Qur'anic Hermeneutics of Sayyid Qutb." *Islamic Studies* 31.3 (1992).

Nazwar, Akhria. *Syekh Ahmad Khatib: Ilmuwan Islam di Permulaan Abad ini.* Jakarta: Pustaka Panjimas, 1983.

Niel, Robert van. *The Emergence of the Modern Indonesian State.* The Hague: W. van Hoeve, 1970.

Noer, Deliar. *The Modernist Muslim Movement in Indonesia: 1900–1942.* New York: Oxford University Press, 1973.

*The Administration of Islam in Indonesia.* Ithaca: Cornell Modern Indonesia Project, 1978.

*Membincangkan Tokoh-tokoh Bangsa.* Bandung: Mizan, 2001.

Noor, Mas'uddin. *Piagam Djakarta Mendjiwai Undang-undang Dasar.* Jakarta: Departemen Agama, 1963.

Norton, Richard A. "Musa Al-Sadr." In *Pioneers of Islamic Revival,* ed. Ali Rahnema, 184–207. London: Zed Books, 1994.

Notosusanto. *Peradilan Agama Islam di Djawa dan Madura.* Yogyakarta: 1953.

*Organisasi dan Jurisprudensi Peradilan Agama di Indonesia.*Yogyakarta: Gadjah Mada, 1963.

Numani, Shibli. *Umar.* London: I. B. Tauris, 2004.

Nurlaelawati, Euis. "Modernization, Tradition, and Identity: The Compilation of Islamic Law and Legal Practices in the Indonesian Islamic Courts." Leiden University Thesis, 2006.

Nuruddin, Amiur. *Ijtihâd 'Umar Ibn Al-Khattâb: Studi tentang Perubahan Hukum dalam Islam.* Jakarta: Rajawali Pers, 1987.

Nurujulianti and Arief Subhan. "Lembaga-lembaga Syi'ah di Indonesia." *Ulumul Qur'an* 6.4 (1995): 20–26.

Ockeloen, G. *Catalogus dari Boekoe-boekoe dan Madjallah-madjallah jang diterbitkan di Hindia Belanda dari tahoen 1870–1937.* Amsterdam: Swets and Zeitlinger N. V., 1966.

Oepen, Manfred, and Wolfgang Karcher, eds. *The Impact of Pesantren in Education and Community Development in Indonesia.* Berlin: Fredrich-Naumann Stiftung, 1988.

Payzs, T. "Human Rights," and "Natural Law." In *New Catholic Encyclopedia*, VII: 209–14 and X: 251–71. New York: McGrawHill, 1967.

Peacock, James L. *Muslim Puritans: Reforming Psychology in Southeast Asian Islam.* Berkeley: University of California Press, 1978.

"Dahlan and Rasul: Indonesian Muslim Reformers." In *The Imagination of Reality: Essays in Southeast Asian Coherence Systems*, ed. A. L. Becker and Aram A. Yengoyan, 245–68. Norwood, NJ: ABLEX Publishing, 1979.

*Pedoman Pendjabat Kantor2 Agama* (2 vols.). Jakarta: Penerbitan Kementerian Agama, 1955.

Pelras, Ch. "Religion, Tradition, and the Dynamics of Islamization in South Sulawesi." *Archipel* 29 (1985): 107–36.

Perwataatmadja, Karnaen H. "Pembangunan dan Upaya Perbaikan Taraf Hidup: Sekilas Pandangan K. H. Ali Yafie." *Wacana Baru Fiqih Sosial*, ed. Jamal D. Rahman, 273–85. Bandung: Mizan, 1997.

Peters, Rudolph. "Idjtihad and Taqlid in 18th and 19th Century Islam." *WI* 30.3–4 (1980): 131–45.

"Reinhard Schulze's Quest for an Islamic Enlightenment." *WI* 30. 3–4 (1990): 160–62.

Pijper, G. F. "Mi'radj." *Fragmenta Islamica: Studien over het Islamisime in Nederlandsch-Indië.* Leiden: E. J. Brill, 1934: 125–58.

"Nieuwe godsdienstige denkbeelden in Benkoelen." In *Fragmenta Islamica: Studien over het Islamisime in Nederlandsch-Indië.* Leiden: E. J. Brill, 1934.

"De Ahmadijah in Indonesia." In *Bingkisan Budi: een bundel opstellen aan Dr. Phillipus Samuel van Ronkel door vrienden en leeringen aangeboden op zijn tachtigste verjaardag 1 Augustus 1950.* Leiden: A. W. Sijtoff, 1950: 247–54.

"Het Reformisme in de Indonesische Islam." *Studien over de Geschiedenis van de Islam in Indonesia 1900–1950.* Leiden: Brill, 1977.

Pike, Kenneth L. *Language in Relation to a Unified Theory of the Structure of Human Behavior*. The Hague: Mouton, 1967.

Piscatori, James P. *Islam in a World of Nation-States*. Cambridge: Cambridge University Press, 1986.

Platvoet, J. G. *Comparing Religions: A Limitative Approach*. The Hague: Mouton, 1982.

Pocock, J. G. A. *Politics, Language, and Time: Essays on Political Thought and History*. Chicago: University of Chicago Press, 1960.

Poonawala, Ismail K. "Muhammad Izzat Darwaza's Principles of Modern Exegesis: A Contribution Toward Quranic Hermeneutics." In *Approaches to the Qur'an*, ed. G. R. Hawting and Abdul-Kader A. Shareef, 225–46. London: Routledge, 1993.

Powers, David S. *Studies in Qur'an and Hadith: The Formation of the Islamic Law of Inheritance*. Berkeley: University of California Press, 1986.

Prabowo, Taufiq, and Claude Guillot. "Les *Pesantrèn* ou centres d'enseignement de l'Islam à Java." In *Madrasa: La transmission du savoir dans le monde Musulman*, ed. Nicole Grandin and Marc Gaborieau, 185–98. Paris: Éditions Arguments, 1997.

Prasetyo, Hendro. "Pancasila as an Islamic Ideology for Indonesian Muslims: An Interview with Munawir Sjadzali." *SI* 1.1 (1985): 185–205.

Prince, Gé. "Dutch Economic Policy in Indonesia." In *Economic Growth in Indonesia, 1820–1940*, ed. Angus Maddison and Gé Prince. Dordrecht: Foris Publications, 1989: 203–26.

*Profil Ma'had Aly li Al-Ulum Al-Islamiyah Qismi Al-Fiqh*. Situbondo, Jawa Timur: Pondok Pesantren Salafiyah Syafi'iyah Sukorejo, 2003.

*Prospectus Toward a Research University*. Jakarta: UIN Jakarta Press, 2003.

*Prospek Hukum Islam dalam Kerangka Pembangunan Hukum Nasional di Indonesia: Sebuah Kenangan 65 Tahun Prof. Dr. H. Busthanul Arifin*, SH. Jakarta, 1994.

Proudfoot, I. "A Formative Period in Malay Book Publishing." *JMBRAS* 59 (1986): 101–32.

"A Nineteenth-Century Malay Bookseller's Catalogue." *Kekal Abadi* 6.4 (1987): 1–11.

*Early Malay Printed Books: A Provisional Account of Materials Published in the Singapore-Malaysia Area up to 1920, Noting Holdings in Major Public Collections*. Kuala Lumpur: Academy of Malay Studies, 1993.

*The Print Threshold in Malaysia*. Clayton: Monash University Center of Southeast Asian Studies, 1994.

"Mass Producing Houri's Moles, or Aesthetics and Choice of Technology in Early Muslim Book Printing." In *Islam - Essays in Scripture, Thought, and Society: A Festschrift in Honour of Anthony H. Johns*, ed. Peter G. Riddell and Tony Street, 161–84. Leiden: E. J. Brill, 1997.

"From Recital to Sight-Reading: The Silencing of Texts in Malaysia." *Indonesia and the Malay World* 30.87 (2002): 117–44.

Puar, Yusuf Abdullah, ed. *Muhammad Natsir 70 Tahun: Kenang-kenangan kehidupan dan perjuangan*. Jakarta: Pustaka Antara, 1978.

*Perjuangan Ayatullah Khomeini*. Jakarta: Pustaka Antara, 1980.

Pulungan, J. Suyuthi. *Prinsip-Prinsip Pemerintahan dalam Piagam Madinah Ditinjau dari Pandangan Al-Quran*. Jakarta: Rajawali, 1994.

Putro, Suadi. *Mohammed Arkoun tentang Islam dan Modernitas*. Jakarta: Yayasan Wakaf Paramadina, 1998.

Putten, Jan van der. "Printing in Riau: Two Steps toward Modernity." *BKI* 153.4 (1997): 717–36.

Qardhawi, Yusuf. *Fiqhul Ikhtilaf: Gerakan Perbedaan yang Dibolehkan dan Perpecahan yang Dilarang*, trans. Aunur Rafiq Shaleh Tamhid. Jakarta: Robbani Press, 1995.

Qomar, Mujamil. *NU "Liberal": Dari Tradisionalisme Ahlussunnah ke Universalisme Islam*. Bandung: Mizan, 2002.

Al-Qurtuby, Sumanto. *KH MA Sahal Mahfudh: Era Baru Fiqih Indonesia*. Yogyakarta: Cermin, 1999.

Radtke, B. "Ijtihad and Neo-Sufism." *Asiatische Studien/ Études Asiatiques* 48.3 (1994): 909–21.

Rahardjo, Dawam. *Intelektual Inteligensia dan Perilaku Politik Bangsa: Risalah Cendekiawan Muslim*. Bandung: Mizan, 1993.

Rahardjo, Dawam, ed. *Pesantren dan Pembaharuan*. Jakarta: LP3ES, 1974.

ed. *Pergulatan Dunia Pesantren: Membangun dari Bawah*. Jakarta: P3M, 1985.

Rahardjo, Dawam, Sudjoko Prasodjo, M. Zamroni, M. Mastuhu, Sardjono Goenari, and Nurcholish Madjid. *Profil Pesantren: Laporan Hasil Penelitian Pesantren Al-Falak dan Delapan Pesantren Lain di Bogor*. Jakarta: LP3ES, 1974.

Rahman, Fazlur. *Islamic Methodology in History*. Karachi: Central Institute of Islamic Research, 1965.

*Islam and Modernity: Transformation of an Intellectual Tradition*. Chicago: University of Chicago Press, 1982.

*Tema Pokok Al-Qur'an*. Bandung: Penerbit Pustaka, 1983.

*Revival and Reform in Islam*, ed. Ebrahim Moosa. Oxford: OneWorld, 2000.

Rahman, Jamal D., ed. "Biografi dan Visi Seorang Ulama." In *Wacana Baru Fiqih Sosial: 70 Tahun K. H. Ali Yafie*. Bandung, Mizan, 1997: 3–48.

Rahmat, M. Imdadun, ed. *Kritik Nalar Fiqih NU: Transformasi Paradigma Bahtsul Masa'il*. Jakarta: Lakpesdam, 2002.

Rais, M. Amien. *Cakrawala Islam: Antara Cita dan Fakta*. Bandung: Mizan, 1987.

*Tauhid Sosial*. Bandung: Mizan, 1998.

Raillon, François. "The New Order and Islam, or the Imbroglio of Faith and Politics." *Indonesia* 57 (1994): 198–217.

Rakhmat, Jalaluddin. *Islam Alternatif: Ceramah-Ceramah di Kampus*. Bandung: Mizan, 1986.

"Sistem Pengambilan Hukum oleh Aimmatu Al-Madzahib (Tanggapan atas Ceramah K. H. Ali Yafie)." In *Kontroversi Pemikiran Islam di Indonesia*, ed. Muhtar Gandaatmadja *et al.*, 21–24. Bandung: PT Remaja Rosdakarya, 1990.

*Islam Aktual: Refleksi-Sosial Seorang Cendekiawan Muslim*. Bandung: Mizan, 1991

*Tafsir Bil Ma'tsur: Pesan Moral Alquran*. Bandung: PT Remaja Rosdakarya, 1993.

*Catatan Kang Jalal: Visi Media, Politik, dan Pendidikan*. Bandung: PT Remaja Rosdakarya, 1997.

*Menjawab Soal-soal Islam Kontemporer*. Bandung: Mizan 1998.

*Reformasi Sufistik: 'Halaman Akhir' Fikri Yathir*. Bandung: Pustaka Hidayah, 1998.

*Dahulukan Akhlak di atas Fikih*. Bandung: Muthahhari Press, 2002.

Ramage, Douglas E. *Politics in Indonesia: Democracy, Islam, and the Ideology of Tolerance*. London: Routledge, 1995.

*Rancang Fikih Pembebasan: Hasil olah pemikiran crew 'Tanwirul Afkar' Lembaga Kader Ahli Fikih Ma'had Aly*. Sukorejo: Ma'had Aly, 2003.

Rasjidi, H. M. *Islam dan Indonesia di Zaman Modern*. Jakarta: Bulan Bintang, 1968.

*Koreksi terhadap Drs. Nurcholish Madjid tentang Sekularisasi*. Jakarta: Bulan Bintang, 1977.

"Pergolakan Pemikiran Islam." *Kiblat* 29.16 (January 1982).

Rasyad, Aminuddin. "Raḥma al-Yūnusiyya: Mu'assisa al-ma'had al-dīnī li'l-banāt Padang Panjang, sūmaṭra al-gharbiyya." *SI* 4.2 (1997): 109–55.

Rasyid, M. Ryaas. "Kiai Haji Ali Yafie: Portret Perdamaian Ulama-Umara." In *Wacana Baru Fiqih Sosial*, ed. Jamal D. Rahman, 233–40. Bandung: Mizan, 1997.

Rejab, Ishak Mohammad. "Haji Husain Mohd. Nasir Al-Mas'udi: Tok Guru dan Pengarang." In *Ulama Silam dalam Kenangan*, ed. Ismail Mat. Bangi: Penerbit Universiti Kebangsaan Malaysia, 1992.

Ricklefs, M. C. *A History of Modern Indonesia c. 1300 to the Present*. Bloomington: Indiana University Press, 1993.

Riddell, Peter. *Islam and the Malay-Indonesian World: Transmission and Responses*. Honolulu: University of Hawaii Press, 2001.

Ridwan, Nur Khalik. *Santri Baru: Pemetaan, Wacana Ideologi dan Kritik*. Jogyakarta: Gerigi Pustaka, 2004.

Ritonga, Iskandar. "Pemikiran Hazairin tentang Pembaharuan Hukum Islam di Indonesia." MA Thesis. IAIN Syarif Hidayatullah (Jakarta), 1995.

Robinson, Francis. "Technology and Religious Change: Islam and the Impact of Print." *Modern Asian Studies* 27.1 (1993): 229–51.

"Other-worldly and This-worldly Islam and the Islamic Revival." *JRAS* 14.1 (2004): 47–58.

Roff, W. R. "The Malayo-Muslim World of Singapore at the Close of the Nineteenth Century." *Journal of Asian Studies* 24.1 (1964): 75–90.

*The Origins of Malay Nationalism*. New Haven: Yale University Press, 1967.

*Sejarah Surat2 Khabar Melayu*. Pulau Pinang: Saudara Sinaran Berhad, 1967.

"Indonesian and Malay Students in Cairo in the 1920s." *Indonesia* 9 (1970): 73–87.

"South-East Asian Islam in the Nineteenth Century." In *The Cambridge History of Islam*, ed. P. M. Holt *et al.*, II: 155–81. Cambridge: Cambridge University Press, 1970.

*Autobiography and Biography in Malay Historical Studies*. Singapore: Institute of Southeast Asian Studies, 1972.

*Bibliography of Malay and Arabic Periodicals Published in the Straits Settlements and the Peninsular Malay States, 1876–1941*. Oxford: Oxford University Press, 1972.

Rofiq, Ahmad. *Pembaharuan Hukum Islam di Indonesia*. Yogyakarta: Gama Media, 2001.

Romli, Mas Guntur, and Shofia Tidjani, eds. *Kontekstualisasi Islam dalam Peradaban*. Cairo: FOSGAMA, 2002.

Ronkel, Ph. S. van. *Supplement to the Catalogue of the Arabic Manuscripts Preserved in the Museum of the Batavia Society of Arts and Science*. Batavia: Albrecht & Co., 1913.

Rorty, Richard, *et al.*, *Philosophy in History: Essays on the Historiography of Philosophy*. Cambridge: Cambridge University Press, 1984.

Rosenthal, Franz. "The Technique and Approach of Muslim Scholarship." *Acta Orientalia* 24 (1947).

*Gambling in Islam*. Leiden: E. J. Brill, 1975.

Rosidi, Ajip. *Beberapa Mas'alah Umat Islam di Indonesia*. Bandung: Bulan Sabit, 1970.

*M. Natsir: Sebuah Biografi I*. Jakarta: Girimukti Pasaka, 1990.

Roy, Olivier. *The Failure of Political Islam*, trans. Carol Volk. Cambridge, MA: Harvard University Press, 1994.

Roy, Olivier and Mariam Abou Zahab. *Islamist Networks: The Afghan-Pakistan Connection*, trans. John King. New York: Columbia University Press, 2004.

Rumadi. "Kritik Nalar: Arah Baru Studi Islam." *TA* 9 (2000): 62–77.

Rusjdi. "Generasi Terachir Keluarga Paderi." *Gema Islam* 1.4 (1962): 24–27.

"Generasi Terachir Keluarga Paderi (sambungan)." *Gema Islam* 1.5 (1962): 6, 28–30.

"Sedjarah Penerbitan Madjalah Al-Munir: Pelopor Pers Islam dengan Aliran Moderen jang dibawanja." *Gema Islam* 1.1 (1962): 22–25.

Rusydi, Ibnu. *Bidayatul Mujtahid wa Nihayatul Muqtashid*. Jakarta: Trigenda Karya, 1997.

Sabiq, Sayyid. *Tarjamah dan Koreksi Fiqhus Sunnah*, trans. M. Thalib. Bandung: Gema Risalah Press, 1996.

Said, H. A. Fuad. *Syekh Abdul Wahab, Tuan Guru Babussalam*. Medan: Pustaka Babussalam, 1983.

Saimima, Iqbal Abdurrauf, ed. *Polemik Reaktualisasi Ajaran Islam*. Jakarta: Panjimas, 1988.

Salam, Solichin. *K. H. Ahmad Dahlan, Reformer Islam Indonesia*. Jakarta, 1963.

*Bung Karno dan Kehidupan Berpikir Dalam Islam*. Jakarta, 1964.

Saleh, Abdul Mun'im. *Madhhab Syafi'i: Kajian Konsep Al-Maslahah*. Yogyakarta: Ittaqa Press, 2001.

Salim, H. Agus. *Philosophical Explanation of Tauhid, Taqdir, and Tawakkal*, trans. J. T. Salim. Jakarta: PT Intermasa, 1987.

Salleh, Abdullah Al-Qari b. Haji. "To 'Kenali: His Life and Influence." In *Kelantan: Religion, Society, and Politics in a Malay State*, ed. William R. Roff, 87–100. Kuala Lumpur: Oxford University Press, 1974.

Santoso, Agus Edi, ed. *Tidak Ada Negara Islam: Surat-surat Politik Nurcholish Madjid – Mohamad Roem*. Jakarta: Penerbit Djambatan, 1997.

Schacht, J. "Sarî'a und Qânûn im modernen Ägypten." *Der Islam* 20 (1932): 209–36.

"Classicisme, traditionalisme et ankylose dans le loi religieuse de l'Islam." In *Classicisme et déclin culturel dans l'histoire de l'Islam*. Paris: G.-P. Maisonneuve, 1957: 141–66.

"Islamic Law in Contemporary States." *American Journal of Comparative Law* 7 (1959): 133–47.

"Problems of Modern Islamic Legislation." *Studia Islamica* 12 (1960): 99–129.

Schimmel, Annemarie. *Muhammad Iqbal, Prophetischer Poet und Philosopher*. Munich: E. Diederichs, 1989.

Schrieke, B. J. O. "Bijdrage tot de Bibliographie van de Huidige Godsdienstige te Sumatra's Westkust." *Tijdschift voor het Bataviaasch Genootschap* 59 (1921): 298–300.

Schulze, R. "Der Einfluss Islamischer Organizationen auf die Länder Südostasiens." In *Mitteilungen des Instituts für Asienkunde*, ed. W. Draghun. Hamburg, 1983.

"Das Islamische Achtzehnte Jahrhundert: versuch einer historiographischen Kritik." *WI* 30 (1990): 140–59.

Schussman, Aviva. "The Legitimacy and Nature of Mawlid Al-Nabi (Analysis of a *Fatwa*)." *ILS* 5.2 (1998): 214–34.

Schwarz, Adam. *A Nation in Waiting: Indonesia in the 1990s*. Boulder: Westview Press, 1994.

Shaham, Ron. *Family and the Courts in Modern Egypt: A Study Based on Decisions by the Sharî'a Courts, 1900–1955*. Leiden: E. J. Brill, 1997.

Shaltūt, Maḥmūd. *Tafsīr al-Qur'ān al-karīm, al-ajzā' al-'ashra al-ūlā*. Cairo: Dār Al-Qalam, 1960.

*Al-islām: 'Aqīda wa sharī'a*. Beirut: Dār Al-Sharq, 1988.

Shaltūt, Maḥmūd, and Muḥammad 'Alī Al-Sāyis. *Muqāranat Al-madhāhib fi'l-fiqh*. Cairo: Maṭba'at Muḥammad 'Alī Subayh, 1953.

Al-Shana'ani, Muhammad b. Ismail Al-Khalani. *Subulus Salam: Hadits-hadits Hukum*. Surabaya: al-Ikhlas, n.d.

Al-Shawkānī, Muḥammad b. 'Alī b. Muḥammad. *Irshād al-fuḥūl ilā taḥqīq 'ilm Al-uṣūl*. Beirut: Al-Thaqāfiyyah, 1993.

*Al-Badr al-ṭāli' bi-maḥāsin man ba'd al-qarn al-Sābi'* (Beirut: Dār al-Ma'rifa, n.d.).

*Nayl al-awṭār sharū muntaqā li-akhbār min aḥādīth sayyad Al-akhyār* (8 vols.). Beirut: Dār Al-fikr, 1414 H./ 1994.

Shepard, William. "The Development of the Thought of Sayyid Qutb as Reflected in Earlier and Later Editions of *Social Justice in Islam*. *WI* 32.2 (1992): 196–236.

*Sayyid Qutb and Islamic Activism: A Translation and Critical Analysis of 'Social Justice in Islam'*. Leiden: E. J. Brill, 1996.

Shiddiqi, Nourouzzaman. "Muhammad Hasbi Ash Shiddieqy: Pembaruan Pemikiran Islam." In *Jeram-Jeram Peradaban Muslim*, 217–53. Yogyakarta: Pustaka Pelajar, 1996.

*Fiqh Indonesia: Penggagas dan Gagasannya*. Yogyakarta: Pustaka Pelajar, 1995.

Shihab, Quraish. *"Membumikan" Al-Qur'an: Fungsi dan Peran Wahyu dalam Kehidupan Masyarakat*. Bandung: Mizan, 1992.

Shimogaki, Kazuo. *Between Modernity and Post-Modernity: The Islamic Left and Dr. Hasan Hanafi's Thought, a Critical Reading*. Japan: IUJ Insitute for Middle Eastern Studies, 1988.

Shiraishi, Takashi. *An Age in Motion: Popular Radicalism in Java, 1912–1926*. Ithaca: Cornell University Press, 1990.

Shouk, Ahmed Ibrahim Abu. "An Arabic Manuscript on the life and career of Ahmad Muhammad Sûrkatî and his Irshâdî Disciples in Java." In *Transcending Borders: Arabs, Politics, Trade, and Islam in Southeast Asia*, ed. Huub de Jonge and Nico Kaptein, 203–18. Leiden: KITLV Press, 2002.

*Tārīkh ḥarakat al-iṣlāḥ wā'l-'irshād wa-shaykh Al-'irshādiyyin Aḥmad Muḥammad al-Sūrkatī fī Indūnīsiyā*. Kuala Lumpur: Dār Al-Fajr – Mālayziyā, 2000.

*Silaturrahmi Nasional dan Peluncuran Home Page Keluarga Besar Dewan Dakwah*, Jakarta: DDII, 1998.

Siradj, H. Said Agiel. *Ahlussunnah wal Jama'ah dalam Lintas Sejarah*. Yogyakarta: LKPSM, 1997.

Siregar, Bismar. "Prof. Mr. Dr. Hazairin Seorang Mujahid Penegak Hukum Berdasar Ke-Tuhanan Yang Maha Esa." In *Renungan Hukum dan Iman*, 87–104. Jakarta: Grafikatama Jaya, 1988.

"Hukum Islam Sebagai Institusi Keagamaan." *Hukum Islam di Indonesia: Pemikiran dan Praktek*, ed. Juhaya S. Praja, 19–40. Bandung: Rosdakarya, 1991.

Sirry, Mun'im A. *Hukum Barat pun Islam: Membongkar Argumen Kejumudan Syariat*. Jakarta: Pusat Bahasa dan Budaya UIN Syarif Hidayatullah Jakarta, 2003.

Sirry, Mun'im A., ed. *Fiqih Lintas Agama: Membangun Masyarakat Inklusif-Pluralis*. Jakarta: Yayasan Wakaf Paramadina, 2004.

Sitanggang, Sabar, Maulana Muladi, and Agus Salam, eds. *Catatan Kritis dan Percikan Pemikiran Yusril Ihza Mahendra*. Jakarta: PT Bulan Bintang, 2001.

Sitanggang, Sabar, ed. *2,5 Jam bersama Yusril*. Jakarta: 2002.

Sjadzali, Munawir. "Dinamika dan Vitalitas Hukum Islam." *Panji Masyarakat* 459 (1985): 25–28.

*Islam dan Tata Negara: Ajaran, Sejarah, dan Pemikiran*. Jakarta: Universitas Indonesia Press, 1990.

"Landasan Pemikiran Politik Hukum Islam dalam Rangka Menentukan Peradilan Agama di Indonesia." In *Hukum Islam di Indonesia: Pemikiran dan Praktek*, ed. Juhaya S. Praja, 41–68. Bandung: Rosdakarya, 1991.

*Islam: Realitas Baru dan Orientasi Masa Depan Bangsa*. Jakarta: Universitas Indonesia Press, 1993.

"Relevansi Hukum Keluarga Islam dengan Kebutuhan Masa Kini." In *Dimensi Hukum Islam dalam Sistem Hukum Nasional*, ed. Amrullah Ahmad *et al.*, 223–26. Jakarta: Gema Insani Press, 1996.

*Ijtihâd Kemanusiaan*. Jakarta: Yayasan Paramadina, 1997.

Skovgaard-Petersen, Jakob. *Defining Islam for the Egyptian State: Muftis and Fatwas of the Dar al-Ifta*. Leiden: E. J. Brill, 1997.

Smith, Wilfred Cantwell. *The Meaning and End of Religion*. New York: Macmillan, 1963.

Snoek, Joannes Augustinus Maria. *Initiations: Method and Theory in Concept Formation in the Study of Religions*. New York: P. Lang, 2000.

Snouck Hurgronje, C. *Verspreide Geschriften (Gesammelte Schriften)*. Bonn: Kurt Schroeder Verlag, 1921–27.

*Mekka in the Latter Part of the 19th Century*. Leiden: E. J. Brill, 1931.

*Ambtelijke Adviezen, 1889–1936*, ed. E. Adriaanse.'s-Gravenhage, Martinus Nijhoff/ Rijks Geschiedkundige Publicatiën, 1957.

Soebagijo, I. N. *K. H. Mansur: Pembaharu Islam di Indonesia*. Jakarta: Gunung Agung, 1982.

Sofiah, M. S. "Sketsa Gerakan Pembaharuan Islam di Indonesia Abad 20." *Jauhar: Jurnal Pemikiran Islam Kontekstual* 3.1 (2002): 129–52.

Soloviev, V. S. *Politics. Law, and Morality*, ed. and trans. Vladimir Wozniuk. New Haven: Yale University Press, 2000.

Steenbrink, Karel. *Pesantren, Madrasah, Sekolah: Pendidikan Islam dalam Kurun Moderen*. Jakarta: LP3ES, 1986.

*Dutch Colonialism and Indonesian Islam, 1596–1950.*

Strauss, Leo. *Natural Right and History: A Cogent Examination of One of the Most Significant Issues in Modern Political and Social Philosophy*. Chicago: University of Chicago Press, 1950.

Suaedy, Ahmad, ed. *Pergulatan Pesantren dan Demokratisasi*. Yogyakarta: LKiS, 2000.

Sukma, Rizal. *Islam in Indonesian Foreign Policy*. London: RoutledgeCurzon, 2003.

Sulaiman, Irchamni. "Pesantren Mengembangkan Teknologi Tepat Guna." *Pergulatan Dunia Pesantren: Membangun dari Bawah*, ed. M. Dawam Rahardjo. Jakarta: P3M, 1985, 245–63.

Sumarjan, Joni. *Laporan Program Pemantauan Parlemen – Tinjauan Kritis Respon Parlemen Terhadap Masalah Piagam Jakarta Debat Penerapan Syariat Islam*. Jakarta: INSIDE, 2002.

Surjadi, A. *Da'wah Islam dengan Pembangunan Masjarakat Desa*. Bandung: Rivanty, 1971.

Sutrisno, Sulasatin. "Classical Malay Literature and its Heirs." In *Variation, Transformation, and Meaning: Studies on Indonesian Literatures in Honor of A. Teeuw*, ed. J. J. Ras and S. O. Robson, 37–52. Leiden: KITLV Press, 1991.

Suwito and Muhbib Abdul Wahab. "Majlis al-'ulamā' al-indūnīsī fī munādalat al-barnāmij al-siyāsī." *SI* 2.4 (1995): 113–39.

Swartz, Merlin L. *Ibn Al-Jawzī's Kitāb Al-Quṣaṣ wa'l-Mudhakkirīn*. Beirut: Dar El-Machreq Éditeurs, 1969.

*A Medieval Critique of Anthropomorphism: Ibn Al-Jawzī's* Kitāb akhbār aṣ-ṣifāt. Leiden: E. J. Brill, 2002.

Sweet, William, "Jacques Maritain." *The Stanford Encyclopedia of Philosophy* ed. Edward N. Zalta (2004), /http://plato.stanford.edu/archives/spr2004/ entries/ maritain/

Syaltout, M. *Tafsir Al-Quranul Karim (Pendekatan Syaltut dalam Menggali Esensi Al-Quran)*. Bandung: Diponegoro, 1989.

Syamsul, A. H. *Kharisma Kiai As'ad di Mata Umat*. Yogyakarta: LKiS, 2003.

Syariah, Pusat Konsultasi. *Penerapan Syariat Islam di Indonesia antara Peluang dan Tantangan*. Jakarta: Globalmedia Cipta Publishing, 2004.

Syari'ati, Ali. *Islam Agama Protes*, trans. Satrio Pinandito. Jakarta: Pustaka Hidayah, 1993.

Tabataba'i, Allamah, and S. M. Waris Hasan. "The Shi'i Interpretation of *Hadith* Literature." In *Shi'ism: Doctrines, Thought, and Spirituality*, ed. Hamid Dabashi *et al.*, 34–43. Albany: SUNY Press, 1988.

Tahir, Tarmizi. *Aspiring for the Middle Path: Religious Harmony in Indonesia*. Jakarta: CENSIS, 1997.

Taji-Farouki, Suha. *A Fundamental Quest: Hizb Al-Tahrir and the Search for the Islamic Caliphate*. London: Grey Seal, 1996.

Tanthowi, Pramono U. "Islam dan Reformasi: Oposisi Islam Terhadap Orde Baru Dasawarsa 1990-an." *Jauhar: Jurnal Pemikiran Islam Kontekstual* 3.1 (2002): 1–23.

Taufiqurrahman, M. "Scholars Prefer Religious Dialog to Islamic Proselytization." *The Jakarta Post* online http://www.thejakartapost.com/detailheadlines.asp?fileid=20041130.A01&irec=4)

Thahir, Mursyidah and Musthafa Helmy, eds. *Aku dan IIQ: Peran dan Kiprah Wanita IIQ antara Ide dan Fakta Kelangkaan Ulama Wanita*. Jakarta: Institut Ilmu Al-Qur'an, 2002.

Thalib, Sajuthi. *Hukum Kekeluargaan Nasional Berlaku bagi Imat Islam*. Jakarta: Penerbit Universitas Indonesia, 1974.

*Receptio a Contrario (Hubungan Hukum Adat dengan Hukum Islam)*. Jakarta: Penerbit Academica, 1980.

*Hukum Kewarisan Indonesia*. Jakarta: Bina Aksara, 1982.

*Lima Serangkai tentang Hukum*. Jakarta: Bina Aksara, 1983.

Thalib, Sajuthi, ed. *Pembaharuan Hukum Islam di Indonesia, in memoriam Prof. Mr. Dr. Hazairin*. Jakarta: Penerbit Universitas Indonesia, 1981.

Thoyibi, M., *et al.*, ed. *Sinergi Agama dan Budaya Lokal: Dialektika Muhammadiyah dan Seni Lokal*. Surakarta: Muhammadiyah University Press, 2003.

Tirtosudiro, Achmad. *Bang 'Imad: pemikiran dan gerakan dakwahnya*. Jakarta: Gema Insani Press, 2002.

Tjokroaminoto, H. O. S. *Islam and Sosialisme*. Jakarta: Penerbit Tride, 2003 (4th printing, Bulan Bintang).

Tuschiya, Kenji. *Democracy and Leadership: The Rise of the Taman Siswa Movement in Indonesia*, trans. Peter Hawkes. Honolulu: University of Hawaii Press, 1987.

Umar, Nasaruddin. "Upaya Membakukan Buku dan Membukukan Baku Aswaja." *Aula: Majalah Nahdatul Ulama* 19.3 (1997): 12–22.

*Qur'an untuk Perempuan*. Jakarta: Jaringan Islam Liberal, 2002

Voll, J. "Muhammad Hayya Al-Sindi and Muhammad ibn 'Abd Al-Wahhab: An Analysis of an Intellectual Group in 18th Century Madina." *BSOAS* 37 (1975).

"*Hadith* Scholars and Tariqahs: An Ulama Group in the 18th Century Haramayn and their Impact in the Islamic World." *Journal of Asian and African Studies* 15 (1980).

Vollenhoven, Cornelius van. *Miskenningen van het Adatrecht: Vier Voordrachten aan de Nederlandsche-Indische Bestuursacademie*. Leiden: E. J. Brill, 1909.

*Het Adatrecht van Nederlansch-Indië*. Leiden: E. J. Brill, 1918 –31.

*De Ontdekking van het Adatrecht*. Leiden: E. J. Brill, 1928.

*Opstellen over Adatrecht: 1901–31*. Leiden: E. J. Brill, 1933.

*Verspreide Geschriften* (3 vols.). Haarlem: H. D. Tjeenk Willink & Zoon, 1935.

Waardenburg, J. *L'Islam dans le Miroir de l'Occident*. Paris: Mouton, 1962.

"Some Thoughts on Modernity and Modern Muslim Thinking about Islam." In *Islam and the Challenge of Modernity – Proceedings of the Inaugural Symposium on Islam and the Challenge of Modernity: Historical and Contemporary Contexts, Kuala Lumpur, August 1–5, 1994*, ed. Sharifah Shifa Al-Attas, 317–50. Kuala Lumpur: ISTAC, 1996.

Wahid, Abdurrahman. *Muslim di Tengah Pergumulan*. Jakarta: Lappenas, 1981.

"Pengaruh Perubahan Sosial Pada Perkembangan Hukum Islam." *Aula: Majalah Nahdatul Ulama* 17.3 (Maret 1995): 34–46.

Wahid, Marzuki. "Post-Tradisionalisme Islam: Gairah Baru Pemikiran Islam di Indonesia." *TA* 9 (2000): 7–23.

Wahid, Marzuki, and Rumadi. *Fiqih Madzhab Negara: Kritik Atas Politik Hukum Islam di Indonesia* (revised edn). Yogyakarta: LKiS, 2001.

Wahyono, Padmo. *Negara Republik Indonesia*. Jakatra: Rajawali, 1982.

*Sistem Hukum Nasional dalam Negara Hukum Pancasila*. Jakarta: Rajawali, 1983.

Wahyudi, Yudian. "Hasbi's Theory of Ijtihād in the Context of Indonesian Fiqh." McGill University dissertation, 1993.

Wall, H. von de. "Eene Inlandsche Drukkerij te Palembang." *Tijdschrift voor Indische Taal-, Land- en Volkenkunde* 6 (1857): 193–98.

Ward, K. E. *The Foundation of the Partai Muslimin Indonesia*. Ithaca: Cornell Modern Indonesia Project, 1970.

Weismann, Itzchak. *Taste of Modernity: Sufism, Salafiyya, and Arabism in Late Ottoman Damascus*. Leiden: E. J. Brill, 2001.

Weiss, Bernard. "Interpretation in Islamic Law: The Theory of Ijtihad." *American Journal of Comparative Law* 26.2 (1978): 199–212.

*The Search for God's Law: Islamic Jurisprudence in the Writings of Sayf Al-Din Al-Amidi*. Salt Lake City: University of Utah Press, 1992.
Weiss, Bernard, ed. *Studies in Islamic Legal Theory*. Leiden: E. J. Brill, 2002.
*De Wetboeken, Wetten en Verordeningen, Benevens de Grondwet van de Republiek Indonesië*. Jakarta: P. T. Ichtiar Baru – van Hoeve, 1992.
White, Hayden. "Method and Ideology in Intellectual History." In *Modern European Intellectual History: Reappraisals and New Perspectives*, eds. Dominick LaCapra and Steven L. Kaplan, 280–310. Ithaca: Cornell University Press, 1982.
Widjaya, Roebaie. "Biografia – A. Hassan: Pengarang, Kritikus dan Debat Islam." *Hudjdjatul Islam* 1: 1 (1956): 35–41.
Widodo, M. Saleh. "Pesantren Darul Fallah: Exsperimen Pesantren Pertanian." In *Pesantren dan Pembaharuan*, ed. Dawam Rahardjo. Jakarta: LP3ES, 1974. 122–23.
Wieringa, E. P. *Catalogue of Malay and Minangkabau Manuscripts in the Library of Leiden University and other Collections in the Netherlands*. Leiden: Legatum Warnerianum, 1998.
Wildan, Dadan. *Yang Da'i Yang Politikus: Hayat dan Perjuangan Lima Tokoh Persis*. Bandung: Rosdakarya, 1997.
Willis, Avery T. Jr. *Indonesian Revival: Why Two Million Came to Christ*. South Pasadena, CA: William Carey Library, 1977.
Wilopo, ed. *Tentang Dasar Negara Republik Indonesia dalam Konstituante*. Bandung: n.p., 1958.
Wiryosukarto, Amir Hamzah, *et al.*, eds. *K. H. Imam Zarkasyi dari Gontor: Merintis Pesantren Modern*. Ponorogo: Gontor Press, 1996.
Wiwoho, B., *et al.*, eds. *Zakat dan Pajak*. Jakarta: PT Bina Rena Pariwara, 1991.
Yafie, K. H. Ali. "Sistem Pengambilan Hukum oleh Aimmatu Al-Madzahib." In *Kontroversi Pemikiran Islam di Indonesia*, ed. Muhtar Gandaatmadja *et al.*, 18–19. Bandung: PT Remaja Rosdakarya, 1990.
*Menggagas Fiqih Sosial: Dari Soal Lingkungan Hidup, Asuransi hingga Ukhuwah*. Bandung: Mizan, 1994.
*Teologi Sosial: Telaah Kritis Persoalan Agama dan Kemanusiaan*. Yogyakarta: LKPSM, 1997.
Yafie, K. H. Ali, *et al. Fiqih Perdagangan Bebas*. Jakarta: Teraju, 2003.
Yamin, Muhammad. *Naskah Persiapan Undang-undang Dasar 1945* (3 vols.). Jakarta, 1959–60.
Yunahar Ilyas, *et al.*, eds. *Muhammadiyah dan NU: Reorientasi Wasasan Keislaman*. Yogyakarta: Al-Muhsin, 1993.
Yunus, Mahmud. *Hukum Perkawinan dalam Islam menurut Mazhab Syafi'i, Hanafi, Maliki, Hanbali*. Jakarta: PT Hidakarya Agung, 1956.
*Haji ke Mekkah: Seri ibadat untuk kanak-kanak dan dewasa*. Jakarta: Hidakarya Agung, 1979 (13th printing).
Al-Zabîdi. *Ringkasan Shahîh Al-Bukhârî (Muhktasar Sahih Al-Bukhari)*. Bandung: Mizan, 1997.
Zada, Khamami. "Mencari Wajah Post-Tradisionalisme Islam." *TA* 9 (2000): 2–5.

Zaman, Muhammad Qasim. *The Ulama in Contemporary Islam: Custodians of Change*. Princeton: Princeton University Press, 2002.
Zebiri, K. *Mahmud Shaltut and Islamic Modernism*. Oxford: Clarendon Press, 1993.
Zein, Kurniawan and Sarifuddin HA. *Syariat Islam Yes/ Syariat Islam No: Dilema Piagam Jakarta dalam Amandemen UUD 1945*. Jakarta: Paramadina, 2001.
Zulkifli, "Seeking Knowledge unto Qum: The Education of Indonesian Shi'i Ustadhs." *IIAS Newsletter* 38 (September 2005): 30.
Zulkifly Syarif, S. Ag. *Biografi Tuan Haji Yahya Ansharuddin: Dari Kepenuhan Merintis Maktab Modern*. Pekanbaru: UNRI Press, 2003.

# *Index*

11334812R0017

Made in the USA
Lexington, KY
26 September 2011